1 MONTH OF
FREE
READING

at
www.ForgottenBooks.com

By purchasing this book you are eligible for one month membership to ForgottenBooks.com, giving you unlimited access to our entire collection of over 1,000,000 titles via our web site and mobile apps.

To claim your free month visit:
www.forgottenbooks.com/free914622

ISBN 978-0-265-95189-7
PIBN 10914622

THE
CONNECTICUT REGISTER

AND

MANUAL:

A

STATE CALENDAR

OF

PUBLIC OFFICERS AND INSTITUTIONS

FOR

1882.

[Compiled by CHARLES F. BROWN.]

High water is calculated for New London and Saybrook, or one hour later than New York. For Fairfield add 2h. 30m.: Bridgeport, add 2h. 15m.; New Haven, add 2h. 20m.; Hartford, sub. 5h.; Norwich, add 40m.

HARTFORD:
BROWN AND GROSS.

PREFACE.

In issuing the REGISTER and MANUAL for 1882, the publishers present their thanks to all persons who have furnished information for its pages. From the records in the Office of the Secretary of State, we have taken such statistics as could be found there. In other cases we have referred to Secretaries, Clerks, and other Officers whose authority was most to be relied upon. We have carefully endeavored to avoid errors, and to make the present issue accurate as possible.

. The Legislative matter, Jan., 1882, has been made as complete as could be, to the time of the work being put in press.

In the list of Attorneys, no names have been inserted but those who are duly authorized by the Courts to practice in the State.

Those who furnish matter for the Register, or desire any changes to be made, are reminded that the printing of the work begins about the 1st of December.

Commissioners for other States should give notice of any additions or changes directly to us, as there is no other means of reference.

INDEX.

	MOON'S PHASES.			SUN SOUTH.		
☺	Full Moon, 4d, 6h, 10m, M.		1d,	12h.	4m.	0s.
🌑	Last qr. 12d, 10h, 59m, M.		7d,	12h.	6m.	41s.
🌑	New Moon, 19d, 11h, 47m, M.		13d,	12h.	9m.	5s.
◐	First qr. 26d, 2h, 57m, M.		19d,	12h.	11m.	6s.
			25d,	12h.	12m.	40s.

M W	☉R. ☾S.	☾R.	H.W.	CALENDAR DAYS.
1 Su	7 23 4 37	4 52	7 05	
2 M	7 22 4 38	5 47	7 58	COURTS.
3 Tu	7 22 4 38	6 37	8 47	SUPREME.
4 W	7 22 4 38	rises.	9 29	2d Tuesday, at Hartford.
5 Th	7 21 4 39	6 15	10 12	SUPERIOR.
6 Fr	7 21 4 39	7 13	10 52	1st Tuesday, at New Haven.
7 Sa	7 20 4 40	8 12	11 29	1st Tuesday, at N. Haven (Crimi-
8 Su	7 19 4 41	9 09	eve 05	nal Term).
9 M	7 18 4 42	10 08	0 41	
10 Tu	7 18 4 42	11 07	1 22	1st Tuesday, at New London
11 W	7 17 4 43	morn.	2 05	(Criminal Term).
12 Th	7 17 4 43	0 06	2 53	4th Tuesday, at Hartford.
13 Fr	7 16 4 44	1 03	3 46	COMMON PLEAS.
14 Sa	7 15 4 45	2 11	4 43	1st M·, at H'tf'd, N.H. and Danb'y.
15 Su	7 14 4 46	3 15	5 47	3d M., at Norwalk (adj. Term).
16 M	7 14 4 46	4 18	6 52	
17 Tu	7 13 4 47	5 17	7 55	DISTRICT COURT OF LITCHFIELD CO.
18 W	7 12 4 48	6 12	8 48	1st Monday, at Winchester.
19 Th	7 11 4 49	sets.	9 41	DISTRICT COURT OF WATERBURY.
20 Fr	7 10 4 50	6 39	10 35	1st Monday, at Waterbury.
21 Sa	7 9 4 51	7 56	11 22	
22 Su	7 9 4 51	9 10	morn.	CHURCH DAYS.
23 M	7 8 4 52	10 24	0 05	1st, Circumcision.
24 Tu	7 6 4 54	11 33	0 55	6th, Epiphany.
25 W	7 5 4 55	morn.	1 47	8th, 1st Sunday after Epiphany.
26 Th	7 4 4 56	0 39	2 41	15th, 2d Sunday after Epiphany.
27 Fr	7 3 4 57	1 46	3 40	22d, 3d Sunday after Epiphany.
28 Sa	7 2 4 58	2 47	4 42	25th, Conversion of St. Paul.
29 Su	7 1 4 59	3 43	5 44	29th, 4th Sunday after Epiphany.
30 M	7 00 5 0	4 35	6 45	
31 Tu	6 59 5 1	5 19	7 37	

MOON'S PHASES.	SUN SOUTH.
☺ Full Moon, 3d, 1h, 10m, M.	1d, 12h. 13m. 53s.
🌑 Last qr. 11d, 3h, 46m, M.	7d, 12h. 14m. 23s.
🌑 New Moon, 17d, 10h, 2m, E.	13d, 12h. 14m. 25s.
🌑 First qr. 24d, 4h, 43m, E.	19d, 12h. 14m. 1s.
	25d, 12h. 13m. 13s.

M	W	☉R.	☾S.	☽R.	H. W.	CALENDAR DAYS.
1	W	6 58	5 2	5 58	8 26	
2	Th	6 57	5 3	rises.	9 04	
3	Fr	6 56	5 4	6 03	9 42	
4	Sa	6 55	5 5	7 03	10 21	**COURTS.**
5	Su	6 53	5 7	8 01	10 58	U. S. DISTRICT.
6	M	6 52	5 8	8 58	11 32	4th Tuesday, at New Haven.
7	Tu	6 51	5 9	9 58	aft. 06	SUPERIOR.
8	W	6 50	5 10	10 56	0 45	1st Tuesday, at Brooklyn.
9	Th	6 48	5 12	11 58	1 29	2d Tuesday, at Bridgeport.
10	Fr	6 47	5 13	morn.	2 18	2d Tuesday, at Middletown.
11	Sa	6 46	5 14	0 59	3 12	3d Tuesday, at Bridgeport (Crimi-
12	Su	6 45	5 15	2 02	4 16	nal Term).
13	M	6 44	5 16	3 01	5 23	
14	Tu	6 42	5 18	3 57	6 30	COMMON PLEAS.
15	W	6 41	5 19	4 45	7 35	1st Monday, at Bridgeport.
16	Th	6 39	5 21	5 31	8 33	1st Tuesday, at Norwich.
17	Fr	6 38	5 22	sets.	9 21	
18	Sa	6 37	5 23	6 43	10 11	**CHURCH DAYS.**
19	Su	6 36	5 24	7 59	10 58	2d, Purification Virgin Mary.
20	M	6 34	5 26	9 13	11 42	5th, Septuagesima.
21	Tu	6 33	5 27	10 25	morn.	12th, Sexagesima.
22	W	6 32	5 28	11 33	0 29	19th, Quinquagesima.
23	Th	6 30	5 30	morn.	1 21	22d, Ash Wednesday.
24	Fr	6 29	5 31	0 37	2 17	24th, St. Matthias.
25	Sa	6 27	5 33	1 36	3 15	26th, 1st Sunday in Lent
26	Su	6 26	5 34	2 30	4 19	
27	M	6 25	5 35	3 16	5 20	
28	Tu	6 23	5 37	3 59	6 16	

MOON'S PHASES.	SUN SOUTH.
☻ Full Moon, 4d, 7h, 51m, E.	1d, 12h. 12m. 28s.
☽ Last qr. 12d, 4h, 40m, E.	7d, 12h. 11m. 7s.
☾ New Moon, 19d, 7h, 29m, M.	13d, 12h. 9m. 32s.
☽ First qr. 26d, 8h, 45m, M.	19d, 12h. 7m. 48s.
	25d, 12h. 5m. 59s.

M	W	☉R.	☉S.	◯R.		H.W.		CALENDAR DAYS.
1	W	6 22	5 38	4	33	7	09	
2	Th	6 21	5 39	5	01	7	56	
3	Fr	6 19	5 41	5	40	8	37	
4	Sa	6 18	5 42	rises.		9	12	
5	Su	6 17	5 43	6	52	9	47	**COURTS.**
6	M	6 15	5 45	7	50	10	25	SUPREME.
7	Tu	6 14	5 46	8	51	11	11	3d Tuesday, at Bridgeport.
8	W	6 12	5 48	9	51	11	38	
9	Th	6 11	5 49	10	52	eve.	16	SUPERIOR.
10	Fr	6 10	5 50	11	42	1	02	1st Tuesday, at Hartford (Criminal Term).
11	Sa	6 8	5 52	morn.		1	53	
12	Su	6 7	5 53	0	50	2	51	3d Tuesday, at Waterbury (Criminal Term).
13	M	6 5	5 55	1	45	3	56	
14	Tu	6 4	5 56	2	37	5	02	3d Tuesday, at New London.
15	W	6 3	5 57	3	22	6	11	COMMON PLEAS.
16	Th	6 1	5 59	4	02	7	14	1st Monday, at Hartford, **New** Haven, and Bridgeport.
17	Fr	6 0	6 0	4	40	8	10	
18	Sa	5 59	6 1	sets.		8	59	DISTRICT COURT OF LITCHFIELD CO.
19	Su	5 57	6 3	6	45	9	44	1st Monday, at Canaan.
20	M	5 56	6 4	8	00	10	36	
21	Tu	5 54	6 6	9	12	11	21	**CHURCH DAYS.**
22	W	5 53	6 7	10	19	morn.		5th, 2d Sunday in Lent.
23	Th	5 52	6 8	11	18	0	06	12th, 3d Sunday in Lent.
24	Fr	5 50	6 10	morn.		0	57	19th, 4th Sunday in Lent.
25	Sa	5 49	6 11	0	19	1	52	25th, Annun. Virgin Mary.
26	Su	5 47	6 13	1	09	2	50	26th, 5th Sunday in Lent
27	M	5 46	6 14	1	54	3	49	
28	Tu	5 45	6 15	2	32	4	45	
29	W	5 43	6 17	3	05	5	41	
30	Th	5 42	6 18	3	35	6	31	
31	Fr	5 40	6 20	3	56	7	19	

MOON'S PHASES.	SUN SOUTH.

MOON'S PHASES.			
◐ Full Moon, 3d, 0h, 59m, E.	1d,	12h.	3m	50s.
◑ Last qr. 11d, 1h, 42m, M.	7d,	12h.	2m.	4s.
◒ New Moon, 17d, 4h, 50m, E.	13d,	12h.	0m.	26s.
◓ First qr. 25d, 2h, 8m, M.	19d,	11h.	59m.	0s.
	25d,	11h.	58m.	0s.

M	W	☉R.	☉S.	☽R.	H. W.		CALENDAR DAYS.
1	Sa	5 39	6 21	4 30	8	00	
2	Su	5 38	6 22	4 55	8	39	
3	M	5 36	6 24	rises.	9	15	**COURTS.**
4	Tu	5 35	6 25	7 43	9	53	U. S. CIRCUIT.
5	W	5 34	6 26	8 45	10	33	4th Tuesday, at New Haven.
6	Th	5 33	6 27	9 46	11	14	
7	Fr	5 31	6 29	10 45	11	56	SUPERIOR.
8	Sa	5 30	6 30	11 40	eve.	43	1st Tuesday, at New Haven (Crim-
9	Su	5 28	6 32	morn.	1	37	inal Term).
10	M	5 27	6 33	0 31	2	37	1st Tuesday, at Litchfield (Crim-
11	Tu	5 26	6 34	1 17	3	38	inal Term).
12	W	5 24	6 36	1 59	4	44	2d Tuesday, at Tolland.
13	Th	5 23	6 37	2 36	5	49	3d Tuesday, at Haddam.
14	Fr	5 22	6 38	3 10	6	50	
15	Sa	5 20	6 40	3 42	7	45	COMMON PLEAS.
16	Su	5 19	6 41	4 15	8	37	1st Monday, at Danbury.
17	M	5 18	6 42	sets.	9	20	1st Tuesday, at New London.
18	Tu	5 16	6 44	7 56	10	10	DISTRICT COURT OF LITCHFIELD CO.
19	W	5 15	6 45	9 03	11	00	1st Tuesday, at New Milford.
20	Th	5 14	6 46	10 05	11	46	
21	Fr	5 12	6 48	10 59	morn.		**CHURCH DAYS.**
22	Sa	5 11	6 49	11 47	0	33	7th, Good Friday.
23	Su	5 10	6 50	morn.	1	26	9th, Easter Sunday.
24	M	5 8	6 52	0 29	2	19	16th, 1st Sunday after Easter.
25	Tu	5 7	6 53	1 04	3	01	23d, 2d Sunday after Easter.
26	W	5 6	6 54	1 37	4	06	25th, St. Mark.
27	Th	5 5	6 55	2 06	4	56	30th, 3d Sunday after Easter.
28	Fr	5 3	6 57	2 32	5	48	
29	Sa	5 2	6 58	2 56	6	33	
30	Su	5 1	6 59	3 22	7	20	

MOON'S PHASES.	SUN SOUTH.
☺ Full Moon, 3d, 3h, 43m, M.	1d, 11h. 56m. 56s.
🌑 Last qr. 10d, 7h, 47m, M.	7d, 11h 56m. 21s.
🌑 New Moon, 17d, 2h, 45m, M	13d, 11h. 56m. 7s.
🌓 First qr. 24d, 7h, 53m, E.	19d, 11h. 56m. 15s.
	25d, 11h. 56m. 42s.

M	W	☉R.	☾S.	☽R.	H. W.	CALENDAR DAYS.
1	M	0 7	0	3 49	8 03	
2	Tu	59 7	1	rises.	8 45	COURTS.
3	W	58 7	2	7 37	9 24	SUPREME.
4	Th	56 7	4	8 38	10 10	1st Tuesday, at Hartford.
5	Fr	55 7	5	9 35	10 55	Last Tuesday, at Norwich.
6	Sa	54 7	6	10 30	11 40	U. S. DISTRICT.
7	Su	54 7	6	11 16	eve. 29	4th Tuesday, at Hartford.
8	M	4 52 7	8	11 58	1 24	SUPERIOR.
9	Tu	4 51 7	9	morn.	2 2	2d Tuesday, at Brooklyn.
10	W	4 50 7	10	0 35	3 19	2d Tuesday, at Danbury (Criminal Term).
11	Th	4 49 7	11	1 10	4 23	1st Tuesday, at Norwich (Criminal Term).
12	Fr	4 48 7	12	1 43	5 24	1st Tuesday, at Waterbury.
13	Sa	4 47 7	13	2 15	6 23	COMMON PLEAS.
14	Su	4 46 7	14	2 48	7 21	1st Monday, at Hartford, New Haven, and Bridgeport
15	M	4 45 7	15	3 25	8 14	3d Monday, at Stamfo d (adjourned Term). t r
16	Tu	4 44 7	16	sets.	9 02	DISTRICT COURT OF LITCHFIELD CO.
17	W	4 43 7	17	7 48	9 50	1st Monday, at Winchester.
18	Th	4 42 7	18	8 47	10 39	ECCLESIASTICAL.
19	Fr	4 41 7	19	9 39	11 27	2d Thursday, American Bible and other Societies in New York.
20	Sa	4 40 7	20	10 22	morn.	3d Thursday, Presbyterian General Assembly.
21	Su	4 39 7	21	11 01	0 09	
22	M	4 38 7	22	11 36	0 56	4th Tues., Baptist Mission Union.
23	Tu	4 37 7	23	morn.	1 43	4th Wednesday, American Sunday School Union.
24	W	4 37 7	23	0 06	2 30	
25	Th	4 36 7	24	0 33	3 17	CHURCH DAYS.
26	Fr	4 35 7	25	0 58	4 08	1st, St. Philip and St. James.
27	Sa	4 34 7	26	1 23	4 55	7th, 4th Sunday after Easter.
28	Su	4 34 7	26	1 49	5 48	14th, 5th Sunday after Easter.
29	M	4 33 7	27	2 19	6 39	18th, Ascension Day.
30	Tu	4 32 7	28	2 51	7 28	21st, Sunday after Ascension
31	W	4 31 7	29	3 28	8 17	28th, Whit-Sunday.

MOON'S PHASES.	SUN SOUTH.
☺ Full Moon, 1d, 3h, 45m, E.	1d, 11h. 57m. 34s.
◖ Last qr. 8d, 0h, 21m, E.	7d, 11h. 58m. 35s.
◖ New Moon, 15d, 1h, 45m, E.	13d, 11h. 59m. 47s.
◖ First qr. 23d, 1h, 13m, E.	19d, 12h. 0m. 51s.
	25d, 12h. 2m. 22s.

M	W	☾R.	☾S.	○R.	H. W.	CALENDAR DAYS.
1	Th	4 31	7 29	rises.	9 03	
2	Fr	4 30	7 30	8 22	9 50	**COURTS.**
3	Sa	4 30	7 30	9 03	10 40	
4	Su	4 29	7 31	9 59	11 21	SUPREME.
5	M	4 29	7 31	10 37	eve. 17	1st Tuesday, at New Haven.
6	Tu	4 28	7 32	11 13	1 08	SUPERIOR.
7	W	4 28	7 32	11 46	2 02	1st Tuesday, at Hartford (Crimi-
8	Th	4 27	7 33	morn.	2 59	nal Term).
9	Fr	4 27	7 33	0 17	3 56	1st Tuesday, Litchfield.
10	Sa	4 27	7 33	0 49	4 57	1st Tuesday, at Norwich.
11	Su	4 26	7 34	1 24	5 59	1st Tuesday, at Tolland.
12	M	4 26	7 34	2 02	7 00	COMMON PLEAS.
13	Tu	4 26	7 34	2 42	7 56	1st Monday, at Danbury.
14	W	4 25	7 35	3 30	8 47	
15	Th	4 25	7 35	sets.	9 30	**ECCLESIASTICAL.**
16	Fr	4 25	7 35	8 16	10 21	3d Tuesday, General Assoc., Conn.
17	Sa	4 25	7 35	8 57	11 03	
18	Su	4 25	7 35	9 34	11 44	**COMMENCEMENTS.**
19	M	4 25	7 35	10 06	morn.	Last Thursday, Trinity College.
20	Tu	4 25	7 35	10 35	0 24	Last Thursday, Yale College.
21	W	4 25	7 35	11 00	1 05	Last Thursday, Wesleyan Univ'y.
22	Th	4 25	7 35	11 26	1 47	
23	Fr	4 25	7 35	11 51	2 32	**CHURCH DAYS.**
24	Sa	4 25	7 35	morn.	3 17	4th, Trinity Sunday.
25	Su	4 25	7 35	0 19	4 09	11th, 1st Sunday after Trinity.
26	M	4 25	7 35	0 50	5 01	18th, 2d Sunday after Trinity.
27	Tu	4 25	7 35	1 25	5 58	25th, 3d Sunday after Trinity.
28	W	4 26	7 34	2 06	6 57	29th, St. Peter.
29	Th	4 26	7 34	2 55	7 54	
30	Fr	4 26	7 34	rises.	8 45	

MOON'S PHASES.	SUN SOUTH.
☺ Full Moon, 1d, 1h, 20m, M.	1d, 12h. 3m. 34s.
⦿ Last qr. 7d, 5h, 4m, E.	7d, 12h. 4m. 38s.
● New Moon, 15d, 2h, 13m, M.	13d, 12h. 5m. 28s.
⦿ First qr. 23d, 5h, 29m, M.	19d, 12h. 6m. 2s.
⦿ Full Moon, 30d, 9h, 13m, M.	25d, 12h. 6m. 15s.

M	W	☉R.	☉S.	☽R.	H. W.	CALENDAR DAYS.
1	Sa	4 26	7 34	7 53	9 33	
2	Su	4 27	7 33	8 35	10 27	
3	M	4 27	7 33	9 13	11 24	
4	Tu	4 28	7 32	9 48	aft. 0	
5	W	4 28	7 32	10 21	0 48	
6	Th	4 28	7 32	10 54	1 40	COURTS.
7	Fr	4 29	7 31	11 26	2 36	SUPERIOR.
8	Sa	4 29	7 31	morn.	3 32	1st Tuesday, at New Haven (Crim-
9	Su	4 30	7 30	0 02	4 35	inal Term).
10	M	4 30	7 30	0 41	5 39	
11	Tu	4 31	7 29	1 26	6 41	
12	W	4 32	7 28	2 15	7 38	
13	Th	4 32	7 28	3 09	8 30	
14	Fr	4 33	7 27	sets.	9 13	
15	Sa	4 34	7 26	7 33	9 56	
16	Su	4 34	7 26	8 07	10 37	
17	M	4 35	7 25	8 35	11 16	CHURCH DAYS.
18	Tu	4 36	7 24	9 02	11 51	
19	W	4 37	7 23	9 28	morn.	2d, 4th Sunday after Trinity.
20	Th	4 38	7 22	9 55	0 27	9th, 5th Sunday after Trinity
21	Fr	4 38	7 22	10 20	1 07	16th, 6th Sunday after Trinity.
22	Sa	4 39	7 21	10 49	1 48	23d, 7th Sunday after Trinity
23	Su	4 40	7 20	11 21	2 36	25th, St. James.
24	M	4 41	7 19	11 58	3 26	30th, 8th Sunday after Trinity.
25	Tu	4 42	7 18	morn.	4 24	
26	W	4 43	7 17	0 42	5 25	
27	Th	4 44	7 16	1 35	6 28	
28	Fr	4 45	7 15	2 35	7 30	
29	Sa	4 46	7 14	3 42	8 27	
30	Su	4 47	7 13	rises.	9 17	
31	M	4 48	7 12	7 46	10 08	

MOON'S PHASES.	SUN SOUTH.

MOON'S PHASES.			
◐ Last qr. 5d, 11h, 25m, E.	1d,	12h.	6m.	4s.
◑ New Moon, 13d, 4h, 22m, E.	7d,	12h.	5m.	31s.
◐ First qr. 21d, 8h, 7m, E.	13d,	12h.	4m.	37s.
☺ Full Moon, 28d, 4h, 31m, E.	19d,	12h.	3m.	24s.
	25d,	12h.	1m.	53s.

M	W	☉R.	☉S.	☾R.	H. W.	CALENDAR DAYS.
1	Tu	4 49	7 11	8 19	10 56	
2	W	4 50	7 10	8 53	11 41	
3	Th	4 51	7 9	9 27	eve. 26	
4	Fr	4 52	7 8	10 03	1 18	
5	Sa	4 53	7 7	10 42	2 12	**COURTS.**
6	Su	4 54	7 6	11 26	3 12	U. S. DISTRICT.
7	M	4 55	7 5	morn.	4 17	4th Tuesday, at New Haven.
8	Tu	4 56	7 4	0 14	5 21	
9	W	4 58	7 2	1 06	6 22	SUPERIOR.
10	Th	4 59	7 1	2 01	7 19	3d Tuesday, Litchfield.
11	Fr	5 0	7 0	2 58	8 08	4th Tuesday, at Hartford (Crim-
12	Sa	5 1	6 59	3 58	8 51	inal Term).
13	Su	5 2	6 58	sets.	9 27	4th Tuesday, at Bridgeport (Crim-
14	M	5 4	6 56	7 06	10 08	inal Term).
15	Tu	5 5	6 55	7 33	10 44	4th Tuesday, at Brooklyn.
16	W	5 6	6 54	8 01	11 19	
17	Th	5 7	6 53	8 24	11 53	COMMON PLEAS.
18	Fr	5 8	6 52	8 51	morn.	1st Tuesday, at New London.
19	Sa	5 10	6 50	9 22	0 30	DISTRICT COURT OF LITCHFIELD CO.
20	Su	5 11	6 49	9 57	1 13	1st Monday at Canaan.
21	M	5 12	6 48	10 38	1 59	
22	Tu	5 14	6 46	11 23	2 54	**CHURCH DAYS.**
23	W	5 15	6 45	morn.	3 52	
24	Th	5 16	6 44	0 17	4 56	6th, 9th Sunday after Trinity.
25	Fr	5 17	6 43	1 21	6 04	13th, 10th Sunday after Trinity.
26	Sa	5 19	6 41	2 30	7 08	20th, 11th Sunday after Trinity.
27	Su	5 20	6 40	3 42	8 06	24th, St. Bartholomew.
28	M	5 21	6 39	rises.	8 57	27th, 12th Sunday after Trinity.
29	Tu	5 23	6 37	6 49	9 44	
30	W	5 24	6 36	7 25	10 34	
31	Th	5 25	6 35	8 02	11 21	

MOON'S PHASES.	SUN SOUTH.

MOON'S PHASES.
◖ Last qr. 4d, 8h, 38m, M.
● New Moon, 12d, 8h, 11m, M.
◗ First qr.20d, 8h, 40m, M.
☺ Full Moon, 27d, 0h, 22m, M.

SUN SOUTH.			
1d,	11h.	59m.	48s.
7d,	11h.	57m.	50s.
13d,	11h.	55m.	7s.
19d,	11h.	53m.	39s.
25d,	11h	51m.	55s.

M W	☉R.	☉S.	☽R.	H. W.	CALENDAR DAYS.
1 Fr	5 26	6 34	8 40	eve. 06	
2 Sa	5 28	6 32	9 24	0 57	
3 Su	5 29	6 31	10 11	1 53	**COURTS.**
4 M	5 30	6 30	11 03	2 53	U. S. CIRCUIT.
5 Tu	5 32	6 28	11 58	3 56	3d Tuesday, at Hartford.
6 W	5 33	6 27	morn.	4 57	SUPERIOR.
7 Th	5 34	6 26	0 46	5 57	1st Tuesday, at Tolland.
8 Fr	5 36	6 24	1 52	6 51	2d Tuesday, at Hartford.
9 Sa	5 37	6 23	2 51	7 39	2d Tuesday, at New Haven.
10 Su	5 38	6 22	3 48	8 22	2d Tuesday, at New London
11 M	5 40	6 20	4 47	8 59	2d Tuesday, at Haddam.
12 Tu	5 41	6 19	sets.	9 32	3d Tuesday, at Danbury
13 W	5 43	6 17	6 29	10 11	3d Tuesday, at Waterbury (Criminal Term).
14 Th	5 44	6 16	6 57	10 47	
15 Fr	5 45	6 15	7 25	11 24	COMMON PLEAS.
16 Sa	5 47	6 13	7 58	morn.	1st Monday, at Hartford, New
17 Su	5 48	6 12	8 37	0 01	Haven, and Bridgeport.
18 M	5 50	6 10	9 20	0 44	DISTRICT COURT OF LITCHFIELD CO.
19 Tu	5 51	6 9	10 11	1 33	1st Monday, at New Milford.
20 W	5 52	6 8	11 08	2 27	DISTRICT COURT OF WATERBURY.
21 Th	5 54	6 6	morn.	3 28	1st Tuesday, at Waterbury.
22 Fr	5 55	6 5	0 12	4 34	
23 Sa	5 56	6 4	1 20	5 40	**CHURCH DAYS.**
24 Su	5 58	6 2	2 32	6 44	3d, 13th Sunday after Trinity.
25 M	5 59	6 1	3 46	7 41	10th, 14th Sunday after Trinity.
26 Tu	6 00	6 0	rises.	8 35	17th, 15th Sunday after Trinity.
27 W	6 01	5 59	5 55	9 19	21st, St. Matthew.
28 Th	6 03	5 57	6 33	10 10	24th, 16th Sunday after Trinity.
29 Fr	6 05	5 55	7 16	11 00	29th, St. Michael and All Angels.
30 Sa	6 06	5 54	8 04	11 48	

MOON'S PHASES.	SUN SOUTH.
◖ Last qr. 3d, 9h, 29m, E.	1d, 11h. 49m. 35s.
◖ New Moon, 12d, 1h, 13m, M.	7d, 11h. 47m. 47s.
◖ First qr. 19d, 7h, 6m, E.	13d, 11h. 46m. 14s.
☺ Full Moon, 26d, 9h, 46m, M.	19d, 11h. 45m. 00s.
	25d, 11h. 44m. 9s.

M	W	☻R.	☺S.	◯R.	H. W.	CALENDAR DAYS.
1	Su	6 07	5 53	8 55	eve. 37	
2	M	6 09	5 51	9 51	1 33	**COURTS.**
3	Tu	6 10	5 50	10 48	2 31	
4	W	6 12	5 48	11 46	3 28	SUPREME.
5	Th	6 13	5 47	morn.	4 27	3d Tuesday, at Norwich.
6	Fr	6 14	5 46	0 45	5 23	4th Tuesday, at Bridgeport.
7	Sa	6 16	5 44	1 43	6 14	SUPERIOR.
8	Su	6 17	5 43	2 41	7 02	1st Tuesday, at New Haven (Crim-
9	M	6 18	5 42	3 38	7 46	inal Term).
10	Tu	6 19	5 41	4 34	8 26	2d Tuesday, Litchfield (Criminal
11	W	6 21	5 39	sets.	9 01	Term).
12	Th	6 22	5 38	5 30	9 38	3d Tuesday, at Bridgeport (Crim-
13	Fr	6 24	5 36	6 02	10 20	inal Term).
14	Sa	6 25	5 35	6 38	10 59	COMMON PLEAS.
15	Su	6 26	5 34	7 19	11 40	1st Monday, Bridgeport.
16	M	6 28	5 32	8 07	morn.	3d Monday at Norwalk (adjourned
17	Tu	6 29	5 31	9 02	0 23	Term).
18	W	6 30	5 30	10 02	1 14	1st Tuesday, at Norwich.
19	Th	6 32	5 28	11 07	2 08	DISTRICT COURT OF LITCHFIELD CO.
20	Fr	6 33	5 27	morn.	3 08	1st Monday, at Winchester.
21	Sa	6 34	5 26	0 15	4 10	
22	Su	6 36	5 24	1 26	5 13	**CHURCH DAYS.**
23	M	6 37	5 23	2 38	6 15	1st, 17th Sunday after Trinity.
24	Tu	6 38	5 22	3 51	7 15	8th, 18th Sunday after Trinity.
25	W	6 40	5 20	5 05	8 10	15th, 19th Sunday after Trinity.
26	Th	6 41	5 19	rises.	8 59	18th, St. Luke.
27	Fr	6 42	5 18	5 50	9 48	22d, 20th Sunday after Trinity.
28	Sa	6 43	5 17	6 42	10 39	28th, St. Simon and St. Jude.
29	Su	6 45	5 15	7 37	11 28	29th, 21st Sunday after Trinity.
30	M	6 46	5 14	8 36	eve. 17	
31	Tu	6 47	5 13	9 35	1 10	

MOON'S PHASES.

◑ Last qr. 2d, 2h, 10m, E.
○ New Moon, 10d, 6h, 32m, E.
◑ First qr. 18d, 3h, 53m, M.
☺ Full Moon, 24d, 9h, 14m, E.

SUN SOUTH.

1d,	11h.	43m.	41s.
7d,	11h.	43m.	49s.
13d,	11h.	44m.	28s.
19d,	11h.	45m.	24s.
25d,	11h.	47m.	15s.

M	W	◑R.	☺S.	○R.		H. W.		CALENDAR DAYS.
1	W	6 48	5 12	10 34	2	02		
2	Th	6 50	5 10	11 35	2	55		
3	Fr	6 51	5 9	morn.	3	48		
4	Sa	6 52	5 8	0 33	4	39		
5	Su	6 53	5 7	1 30	5	30		
6	M	6 54	5 6	2 27	6	17		**COURTS.**
7	Tu	6 56	5 4	3 25	7	05		
8	W	6 57	5 3	4 31	7	58		SUPERIOR.
9	Th	6 58	5 2	5 21	8	32		1st Tuesday, at Norwich.
10	Fr	6 59	5 1	sets.	9	10		2d Tuesday, at Brooklyn.
11	Sa	7 0	5 0	5 17	9	53		2d Tuesday, at Middletown.
12	Su	7 1	4 59	6 05	10	37		COMMON PLEAS.
13	M	7 2	4 58	6 57	11	24		1st Monday, at Hartford, New
14	Tu	7 3	4 57	7 57	morn.			Haven, and Danbury.
15	W	7 4	4 56	8 59	0	07		DISTRICT COURT OF LITCHFIELD CO.
16	Th	7 5	4 55	10 06	0	57		1st Monday, at Canaan.
17	Fr	7 6	4 54	11 15	1	50		
18	Sa	7 7	4 53	morn.	2	46		
19	Su	7 8	4 52	0 23	3	46		**CHURCH DAYS.**
20	M	7 9	4 51	1 30	4	45		1st, All Saints.
21	Tu	7 10	4 50	2 44	5	48		5th, 22d Sunday after Trinity.
22	W	7 11	4 49	3 56	6	49		12th, 23d Sunday after Trinity.
23	Th	7 12	4 48	5 07	7	47		19th, 24th Sunday after Trinity.
24	Fr	7 13	4 47	rises.	8	40		26th, 25th Sunday after Trinity.
25	Sa	7 14	4 46	5 21	9	27		30th, St. Andrew, the Apostle.
26	Su	7 15	4 45	6 19	10	22		
27	M	7 15	4 45	7 19	11	11		
28	Tu	7 16	4 44	8 20	11	55		
29	W	7 17	4 43	9 20	eve.	40		
30	Th	7 17	4 43	10 21	1	28		

MOON'S PHASES.	SUN SOUTH.
◐ Last qr. 2d, 10h, 8m, M.	1d, 11h. 49m. 19s.
● New Moon, 10d, 10h, 50m, M.	7d, 11h. 51m. 47s.
◑ First qr. 17d, 11h, 51m, M.	13d, 11h. 54m. 49s.
☺ Full Moon, 24d, 10h, 53m, M.	19d, 11h. 57m. 28s.
	25d, 12h. 0m. 27s.

M	W	☉R.	☉S.	☾R.	H. W.	CALENDAR DAYS.
1	Fr	7 18	4 42	11 20	2 14	
2	Sa	7 18	4 42	morn.	3 02	COURTS.
3	Su	7 19	4 41	0 17	3 51	U. S DISTRICT.
4	M	7 20	4 40	1 14	4 40	1st Tuesday, at Hartford.
5	Tu	7 20	4 40	2 11	5 31	SUPREME.
6	W	7 21	4 39	3 10	6 21	1st Tuesday, at New Haven.
7	Th	7 21	4 39	4 09	7 13	SUPERIOR.
8	Fr	7 22	4 38	5 06	8 01	1st Tuesday, at Hartford (Crimi-
9	Sa	7 22	4 38	6 06	8 49	nal Term).
10	Su	7 23	4 37	sets.	9 31	1st Tuesday, Litchfield.
11	M	7 23	4 37	5 47	10 21	1st Tuesday, at Tolland.
12	Tu	7 23	4 37	6 50	11 08	2d Tuesday, at Waterbury.
13	W	7 24	4 36	7 57	11 53	
14	Th	7 24	4 36	9 07	morn.	COMMON PLEAS.
15	Fr	7 24	4 36	10 16	0 39	1st Monday, at Bridgeport.
16	Sa	7 24	4 36	11 25	1 31	3d Monday, at Stamford (ad-
17	Su	7 25	4 35	morn.	2 24	journed Term).
18	M	7 25	4 35	0 34	3 19	DISTRICT COURT OF LITCHFIELD CO.
19	Tu	7 25	4 35	1 44	4 23	1st Monday, at New Milford.
20	W	7 25	4 35	2 53	5 25	
21	Th	7 25	4 35	4 01	6 27	CHURCH DAYS.
22	Fr	7 25	4 35	5 06	7 28	3d, 1st Sunday in Advent.
23	Sa	7 25	4 35	6 07	8 25	10th, 2d Sunday in Advent.
24	Su	7 25	4 35	rises.	9 13	17th, 3d Sunday in Advent.
25	M	7 25	4 35	6 03	10 01	21st, St. Thomas.
26	Tu	7 25	4 35	7 04	10 47	24th, 4th Sunday in Advent.
27	W	7 24	4 36	8 06	11 29	25th, Christmas.
28	Th	7 24	4 36	9 06	eve. 08	26th, St. Stephen.
29	Fr	7 24	4 36	10 04	0 50	27th, St. John, Evangelist.
30	Sa	7 24	4 36	10 59	1 32	28th, Holy Innocents.
31	Su	7 23	4 37	11 58	-2 15	

GOVERNMENT OF CONNECTICUT,

FOR TWO YEARS FROM JAN. 5, 1881.

EXECUTIVE DEPARTMENT.

His Excellency
HOBART B. BIGELOW, New Haven,
GOVERNOR.

Morris F. Tyler, New Haven, Executive Secretary.
Frank D. Rood, Clerk.

His Honor
WILLIAM H. BULKELEY, Hartford,
LIEUTENANT-GOVERNOR.

CHARLES E. SEARLS, Thompson,
SECRETARY.

R. S. Hinman, Horace Heath, Clerks.

DAVID P. NICHOLS, Danbury,
TREASURER.

George Williams, E. B. L. Carter, Clerks.

WHEELOCK T. BATCHELLER, Winchester,
COMPTROLLER.

E. W. Moore, L. B. Hubbard, Clerks.

JEREMIAH OLNEY, Thompson,
SCHOOL FUND COMMISSIONER.

Carnot O. Spencer, Wm. H. Pond, Clerks.

STATE LIBRARY; COMMITTEE, the Governor, the Secretary, and Hon. Dwight W. Pardee. LIBRARIAN, Charles J. Hoadly.

2

LEGISLATIVE.

General Assembly, January, 1882.

SENATE.

[Senators from districts having even numbers hold office for one year, from districts having odd numbers for two years from the Wednesday after the first Monday of January, 1882.]

1st, John R. Hills, r, Hartford.
2d, John S. Cheney, r, Manchester.
3d, Rial Strickland, d, Enfield.
4th, Andrew S. Upson, r, Farmington.
5th, James S. Elton, r, Waterbury.
6th, Edward F. Jones, r, Branford.
7th, George M. Gunn, d, Milford.
8th, William J. Mills, d, New Haven.
9th, Robert Coit, r, New London.
10th, Charles P. White, r, North Stonington.
11th, Charles P. Sturtevant, r, East Lyme.
12th, Oliver Hoyt, r, Stamford.
13th, Tallmadge Baker, r, Norwalk.
14th, Morris W. Seymour, d, Bridgeport.
15th, William N. Northrop, d, Newtown.
16th, Henry Hammond, r, Killingly.
17th, Eugene S. Boss, r, Windham.
18th, Lorrin A. Cooke, r, Barkhamsted.
19th, Milo B. Richardson, d, Salisbury.
20th, Albert P. Bradstreet, r, Thomaston.
21st, Richard P. Spencer, r, Saybrook.
22d, Joseph W. Alsop, d, Middletown.
23d, Ralph P. Gilbert, r, Hebron.
24th, Ebenezer C. Dennis, r, Stafford.

HOUSE OF REPRESENTATIVES.

HARTFORD COUNTY.

HARTFORD, George G. Sill, d, Charles H. Cooley, r.
Avon, Frederick Ripley, r.
Berlin, Henry N. Galpin, r.
Bloomfield, Henry D. Barnard, d.
Bristol, Charles S. Treadway, r, Elijah Manross, r.
Burlington, Charles C. McAleer, d.

Canton, George Mills, 2d, d.
East Granby, Jefferson R. Holcomb, d.
East Hartford, Arthur G. Olmsted, r, Charles W. Roberts, d.
East Windsor, Orson S. Wood, r, Charles E. Woodward, d.
Enfield, Loren H. Pease, r, J. Warren Johnson, r.
Farmington, Thomas Cowles, r, Lucius C. Humphrey, r.
Glastonbury, Charles H. Talcott, r, Aaron W. Kinne, r.
Granby, Artemus G. Harger, r, George R. Case, r.
Hartland, Henry J. Gates, r, George H. Clark, r.
Manchester, Charles H. Owen, r, Clinton W. Cowles, d.
Marlborough, John A. Haling, d.
New Britain, Ambrose Beatty, d, James Thomson, d.
Newington, David L. Robbins, d.
Plainville, Edward S. Towne, r.
Rocky Hill, James H. Warner, d.
Simsbury, Ebenezer G. Curtis, d, Daniel O. Reed, d.
Southington, J. Frank Pratt, r, George F. Smith, r.
South Windsor, John P. Jones, d.
Suffield, Silas W. Clark, r, James Rising, r.
West Hartford, E. Buel Root, r.
Wethersfield, Edwin F. Griswold, r, Edward D. Robbins, r.
Windsor, Daniel W. Phelps, r, Lemuel R. Lord, r.
Windsor Locks, John W. Coogan, d.

NEW HAVEN COUNTY.

NEW HAVEN, A. Heaton Robertson, d, Timothy J. Fox, d.
Beacon Falls, Andrew W. Culver, r.
Bethany, Samuel R. Woodward, d.
Branford, William A. Wright, d.
Cheshire, Benjamin A. Jarvis, d, Charles B. Terrell, d.
Derby, William E. Downes, r, Charles H. Pine, r.
East Haven, Orlando B. Thompson, d.
Guilford, Elisha C. Bishop, r, Edward Griswold, r.
Hamden, Bela A. Mann, d.
Madison, Horace O. Hill, r.
Meriden, William W. Lyman, r, Grove H. Wilson, r.
Middlebury, George O. Ellis, r.
Milford, Charles A. Tomlinson, d, Thomas W. Stow, d.
Naugatuck, Franklin B. Tuttle, d.
North Branford, William B. Curtis, r.
North Haven, Andrew F. Austin, r.
Orange, Edward E. Bradley, d.
Oxford, James H. Bartlett, r.
Prospect, George F. Tyler, r.

Seymour, John W. Rogers, r.
Southbury, Asahel F. Mitchell, r.
Wallingford, Phineas T. Ives, d, John W. Blakeslee, d.
Waterbury, Charles W. Gillette, r, Henry C. Griggs, r.
Wolcott, Samuel M. Bailey, r.
Woodbridge, Charles T. Walker, r.

NEW LONDON COUNTY.

NEW LONDON, Henry B. Downer, d, Bryan F. Mahan, d.
Norwich, George C. Ripley, r, William S. Congdon, r.
Bozrah, Joshua C. Leffingwell, r.
Colchester, Uriah W. Carrier, d, John English, Jr., d.
East Lyme, John W. Luce, r.
Franklin, Oliver L. Johnson, r.
Griswold, Henry A. Lathrop, r.
Groton, Parmenas Avery, d, Sumner H. Gove, r.
Lebanon, Nathaniel B. Williams, r, Charles C. Loomis, r.
Ledyard, James A. Billings, r.
Lisbon, Augustus F. Read, d.
Lyme, Henry B. L. Reynolds, r, Benajah P. Bill, d.
Montville, Raymond N. Parish, r.
North Stonington, Orrin Chapman, r, Charles H. Brown, r.
Old Lyme, Erastus E. Clark, d.
Preston, Chester W. Barnes, d, Charles P. Hewitt, d.
Salem, Gurdon F. Allyn, r.
Sprague, Dennis McCarthy, g.
Stonington, Stiles T. Stanton, r, Alexander S. Palmer, Jr., d.
Voluntown, Timothy Parker, r.
Waterford, Nathaniel Chapman, d.

FAIRFIELD COUNTY.

BRIDGEPORT. Augustus H. Abernethy, d, Peter W. Wren, d.
Bethel, Harry S. Glover, r.
Brookfield, Samuel Thornhill, d.
Darien, Charles Brown, r.
Danbury, Howard W. Taylor, d, Charles J. Deming, d.
Easton, Stephen D. Wheeler, r.
Fairfield, Henry F. Sherwood, d, Francis M. Pike, d.
Greenwich, Cornelius Mead, d, Charles E. Wilson, d.
Huntington, Daniel S. Brinsmade, r.
Monroe, Andrew B. Curtis, r.
New Canaan, Selleck Y. St. John. r.
New Fairfield, Alexander Turner, d.
Newtown, William H. Glover, d, Edson W. Wilson, r.
Norwalk, George R. Cowles, r, Charles W. Bell, r.

Redding, Thomas Sanford, d, Ebenezer F. Foster, d.
Ridgefield, Edward J. Couch, r, Lewis E. Smith, r.
Sherman, Allan W. Paige, r.
Stamford, Edwin L. Scofield, r, William W. Gillespie, r.
Stratford, Anson H. Blakeman, r,
Trumbull, Elliott P. Nichols, d.
Weston, Gregory T. Osborne, d.
Westport, John W. Hurlbutt, d.
Wilton, James T. Hubbell, d.

WINDHAM COUNTY.
BROOKLYN, Henry M. Cleveland, r.
Ashford, Charles L. Dean, r, Danforth O. Lombard, r.
Canterbury, Marvin H. Sanger, d, Francis S. Bennett, d.
Chaplin, Erastus M. Loomis, r.
Eastford, Simeon A. Wheaton, d.
Hampton, Daniel M. Deming, r.
Killingly, Ashel J. Wright, r, James N. Tucker, r.
Plainfield, Henry F. Newton, r, Havilah M. Prior, r.
Pomfret, Frederick Hyde, d, Thomas O. Elliott, r.
Putnam, Lucius H. Fuller, r, Thomas J. Thurber, r.
Scotland, M. Luther Barstow, r.
Sterling, Silas A. Waite, r.
Thompson, Edwin T. White, r, William H. Arnold, r.
Windham, John M. Hall, r, Samuel Bingham, r.
Woodstock, Henry M. Bradford, r, Zenas Marcy, r.

LITCHFIELD COUNTY.
LITCHFIELD, Willis J. Beach, d, Garner B. Curtiss, d.
Barkhamsted, Hubert B. Case, d, William H. Ward, r.
Bethlehem, Nehemiah L. Bloss, d.
Bridgewater, Peter Wooster, d.
Canaan, Samuel W. Bradley, d.
Colebrook, Andrew J. Terrell, d, Solomon Sackett, r.
Cornwall, Charles H. Harrison, d, Luman C. Wickwire, d.
Goshen, Hubert Scovill, r, Franklin E. Wadhams, r.
Harwinton, Chester A. Hayes, r, Horace W. Barber, r.
Kent, Charles Lee, d.
Morris, William Griswold, d.
New Hartford, Thaddeus L. Root, r, Anson J. Allen, d.
New Milford, Frederick S. Richmond, d, Amos H. Bowers, d.
North Canaan, Henry G. Williams, d.
Norfolk, Plumb Brown, r, Alva S. Cowles, r.
Plymouth, Enos Blakeslee, r.
Roxbury, Myron W. Odell, d.

Salisbury, John H. Hurlburt, d, Lewis P. Ashman, d.
Sharon, Edgar J. Reed, d, William Dakin, d.
Thomaston, Joseph K. Judson, r.
Torrington, Frederick Devoe, r, George A. Allen, r.
Warren, Clark S. Swift, r.
Washington, Erastus J. Hurlbut, r, Gould C. Whittlesey, r.
Watertown, Augustus N. Woolson, r.
Winchester, Joseph H. Norton, r, John D. Yale, d.
Woodbury, William J. Clark, r, William Cothren, r.

MIDDLFSEX COUNTY.

MIDDLETOWN, D. Ward Northrop, d, James Lawton, d.
Haddam, Henry H. Brainerd, r, Orrin Shailor, d.
Chatham, Delos D. Brown, r, Nathaniel C. Johnson, r.
Chester, A. Hamilton Gilbert, r.
Clinton, George A. Olcott, r.
Cromwell, Henry W. Stocking, r.
Durham, Talcott P. Strong, r, Julius Davis, d.
East Haddam, Richard H. Gladwin, r, Joseph W. Hungerford, r.
Essex, William T. McCresry, d.
Killingworth, Augustus W. Stevens, d, Sidney T. Davis, d.
Middlefield, Alva B. Coe, r.
Old Saybrook, Osias H. Kirtland, r.
Portland, John M. Penfield, d.
Saybrook, John Child, r, Ezra J. B. Southworth, r.
Westbrook, John A. Post, r.

TOLLAND COUNTY.

TOLLAND, Henry E. Steele, d, Charles Young, d.
Andover, Erastus D. Post, r.
Bolton, Joseph C. Alvord, r.
Columbia, Samuel B. West, r.
Coventry, William F. Sweet, d. Edgar Bass, d.
Ellington, J. Abbott Thompson, r.
Hebron, Alfred W. Hutchinson, r, Joel Jones, r.
Mansfield, George W. Merrow, r, Olin S. Chaffee, r.
Somers, Lorenzo Wood, r, Randolph H. Fuller, r.
Stafford, M. R. Griswold, d, William A. King, r.
Union, Hartly Walker, d, Thomas J. Young, d.
Vernon, Alva N. Belden, r, Louis Philipp, r.
Willington, William D. Irons, r, Matthew Burdick, r.

POLITICAL RECAPITULATION.

JANUARY SESSION, 1881.

SENATE,	Rep.	Dem.	Gr.	Ind.
	17	7		

HOUSE OF REPRESENTATIVES.

COUNTIES.

	Rep.	Dem.	Gr.	Ind.
Hartford,	28	17		
New Haven,	19	14		
New London,	17	12	·	
Fairfield,	15	17		
Windham,	20	4		
Litchfield,	20	21		
Middlesex,	14	8		
Tolland,	15	7		
	165	107	1	

Republican majority, 1881—Senate 10, House 48; Joint Ballot 58.

VOTES FOR STATE OFFICERS.

NOVEMBER, 1880.

GOVERNOR.

| Hobart B. Bigelow, r, | 67,070 | James E. English, d, | 64,293 |
| Henry C. Baldwin, gr, | 897 | George P. Rogers, pro, | 488 |

LIEUT.-GOVERNOR.

| William H. Bulkeley, r, | 67,204 | Charles M. Pond, d, | 64,153 |
| Francis S. Sterling, gr, | 894 | Abel S. Beardsley, pro, | 474 |

SECRETARY.

| Charles E. Searls, r, | 67,066 | Stephen S. Blake, d, | 64,176 |
| Lucien V. Pinney, gr, | 886 | William S. Williams, pro, | 464 |

TREASURER.

| David P. Nichols, r, | 67,034 | Merrick A. Marcy, d, | 64,351 |
| Thomas E. Ryan, gr, | 882 | Edmund Tuttle, pro, | 460 |

COMPTROLLER.

| Wheelock T. Batcheller, r, | 67,185 | Charles R. Fagan, d, | 64,142 |
| Henry R. Wright, gr, | 884 | Edwin B. Lyon, pro, | 452 |

VOTES FOR SENATORS.

NOVEMBER, 1881.

1. John R. Hills, r,	3,087	Elisha Johnson, d,	2,739
3. Rial Strickland, d,	2,258	Arthur G. Pomeroy, r,	2,156
4. Andrew S. Upson, r,	2,351	Elisha N. Welch, d,	2,267
5. James S. Elton, r,	2,547	Chauncey B. Webster, d,	2,346

7.	George M. Gunn, *d*,	2,391	J. H. Bartholomew, *r*,		2,198
9.	Robert Coit, *r*,	1,812	Albert T. Burgess, *d*,		1,503
11.	C. P. Sturtevant, *r*,	1,820	Henry Lyon, *d*,		1,474
13.	Tallmadge Baker, *r*,	2,224	Jonathan E. Wheeler, *d*,		1,696
15.	Wm. N. Northrop, *d*,	2,269	Samuel Sherman, *r*,		2,149
17.	Eugene S. Boss, *r*,	1,650	Henry S. Marlor. Jr., *d*,		1,024
18.	Lorrin A. Cooke, *r*,	1,623	Jared B. Foster, *d*,		1,295
19.	Milo B. Richardson, *d*,	2,120	Ralph E. Canfield, *r*,		814
21.	Rich'd P. Spencer, *r*,	1,550	Clinton B. Davis, *d*,		1,453
23.	Ralph P. Gilbert, *r*,	983	Alfred R. Goodrich, *d*,		872

CONGRESSIONAL DISTRICTS.

WITH POPULATION IN 1880.

1st, Hartford and Tolland Counties—149,489.
2d, New Haven and Middlesex Counties—192,113.
3d, New London and Windham Counties—116,994.
4th, Fairfield and Litchfield Counties—164,087.

SENATORIAL DISTRICTS.

WITH POPULATION IN 1880.

1. Hartford—42,553.
2. Berlin, East Hartford, Glastonbury, Manchester, Marlborough, Newington, Rocky Hill, Southington, South Windsor, and Wethersfield—27,847.
3. Bloomfield, Canton, East Windsor, East Granby, Enfield, Granby, Hartland, Simsbury, Suffield, Windsor, Windsor Locks—26,598.
4. Avon, Bristol, Burlington, Farmington, New Britain, Plainville, West Hartford— 28,379.
5. Beacon Falls, Bethany, Middlebury, Naugatuck, Oxford, Prospect, Waterbury, Wolcott, Southbury—30,089.
6. Cheshire, Guilford, Madison, Meriden, North Branford, Wallingford—30,786.
7. Branford, Derby, East Haven, Hamden, Milford, North Haven, Orange, Seymour, Woodbridge—32,769.
8. New Haven—62,882.
9. Groton, New London, North Stonington, Stonington—24,778.
10. Ledyard, Norwich, Preston—25,033.
11. Bozrah, Colchester, East Lyme, Franklin, Griswold, Lebanon, Lisbon, Lyme, Montville, Old Lyme, Salem, Sprague, Voluntown, Waterford—24,512.

12. Darien, Greenwich, New Canaan, Ridgefield, Stamford, Wilton—27,703.
13. Fairfield, Norwalk, Stratford, Trumbull, Westport, Weston—27,673.
14. Bridgeport—29,148.
15. Bethel, Brookfield, Danbury, Easton, Huntington, Monroe, New Fairfield, Newtown, Redding, Sherman—27,520.
16. Ashford, Eastford. Killingly, Putnam, Thompson, Woodstock—22,334.
17. Brooklyn, Canterbury, Chaplin, Hampton, Plainfield, Pomfret, Scotland, Sterling. Windham—20,337.
18. Barkhamsted, Colebrook, Goshen, Harwinton, New Hartford, Norfolk, Torrington, Winchester—17,744.
19. Bridgewater, Canaan, Cornwall, Kent, New Milford, North Canaan, Salisbury, Sharon, Roxbury—17,759.
20. Bethlehem, Litchfield, Morris, Plymouth, Thomaston, Warren. Washington, Watertown, Woodbury—16,540.
21. Chatham, Chester, Clinton, Durham, East Haddam, Essex, Haddam. Killingworth, Old Saybrook, Saybrook, Westbrook—17,132.
22. Cromwell, Middlefield, Middletown, Portland—18,455.
23. Andover, Bolton, Columbia, Coventry, Hebron, Vernon—11,898.
24. Ellington, Mansfield, Somers, Stafford, Tolland, Union, Willington—12,214.

JUDICIARY.

U. S. Circuit and District Courts in Connecticut.

SUPREME COURT, CIRCUIT JUSTICE.—WARD HUNT, Utica, N. Y.

CIRCUIT COURT JUDGE.—SAMUEL BLATCHFORD, New York City.

DISTRICT JUDGE.—NATHANIEL SHIPMAN. Hartford.

CLERK OF THE CIRCUIT AND DISTRICT COURTS.—EDWIN E. MARVIN, Hartford.

JUDICIARY.

DISTRICT ATTORNEY.—Daniel Chadwick, Lyme.

MARSHAL.—Joseph D. Bates, Hartford.

DEPUTY MARSHALS.—Geo. R. Bill, New Haven, Wm. F. Disbrow, Bridgeport.

Masters in Chancery.

Johnson T. Platt, New Haven; Henry E. Taintor, Hartford.

Commissioners of the U. S. Circuit Court.

Hartford: William Hamersley, H. E. Burton, Edwin E. Marvin, Ratcliffe Hicks, Charles E. Fellowes, Sylvester C. Dunham.
Bridgeport: Morris W. Seymour.
Litchfield: George M. Woodruff.
Meriden: James P. Platt.
Middletown: A. W. Bacon.
New Haven: Samuel L. Bronson, Johnson T. Platt, Jonathan Ingersoll.
New London: John P. C. Mather.
Norwich: Allen Tenny.
Norwalk: A. B. Woodward.
Thompson: Abiel Converse.
Waterbury: George E. Terry.
Willimantic: John M. Hall.

Registers in Bankruptcy.

1st Dist., Henry E. Burton, Hartford.
2d　"　Johnson T. Platt, New Haven.
3d　"　Robert Coit, New London.
4th　"　Louis N. Middlebrook, Bridgeport.

Supreme Court of Errors.

CHIEF JUSTICE.—JOHN D. PARK, Norwich, elected Judge, 1864; Chief Justice, 1874.

ASSOCIATE JUDGES.—Elisha Carpenter, Hartford, 1865; Dwight W. Pardee, Hartford, 1873; Dwight Loomis, Rockville, 1875; Miles T. Granger, North Canaan, 1876.

REPORTER.—JohngHooker, Hartford.

Superior Court.

JUDGES.—Edward I. Sanford, New Haven, 1867; Roland Hitchcock, Winchester, 1874; Earl Martin, Killingly, 1874; Sidney B. Beardsley, Bridgeport, 1874; Moses Culver, Middletown, 1875; James A. Hovey, Norwich, 1876.

Court of Common Pleas.

HARTFORD COUNTY.—David S. Calhoun, Hartford, Judge, Charles E. Fellowes, Hartford, Clerk.
NEW HAVEN COUNTY.—David Torrance, Derby, Judge. John S. Fowler, New Haven, Clerk.
Wm. L. Foster, New Haven, Assistant Clerk.
NEW LONDON COUNTY.—John P. C. Mather, New London, Judge.

Charles W. Butler, New London, Clerk.
Frank T. Brown, Norwich, Assistant Clerk.
FAIRFIELD COUNTY.—Frederick B. Hall, Bridgeport, Judge.
Wilfred E. Norton, Bridgeport, Clerk.
B. A. Hough, Danbury, Assistant Clerk.
DISTRICT COURT OF LITCHFIELD COUNTY.—Barkhamsted, Bridgewater, Canaan, Colebrook, Cornwall, Kent, New Hartford, New Milford, Norfolk, North Canaan, Salisbury, Sharon, and Winchester.
Donald J. Warner, Salisbury, Judge.
Wm. F. Hurlbut, West Winsted, Clerk.
The Judges are elected for four years.

SUPERIOR COURT.

Allotment of Judges from July, 1881, to July, 1882.
HARTFORD COUNTY.
CIVIL TERMS.

Hovey, J.—2d Tuesday in September, until 1st Tuesday in November.
Culver, J,—1st Tuesday in November to end of term.
Martin, J.—4th Tuesday in January, '82, to 4th Tuesday in March.
Beardsley, J.—4th Tuesday in March, '82, to end of term.

CRIMINAL TERMS.

Pardee, J.—4th Tuesday in August.
Sanford, J.—1st Tuesday in December.
Culver, J.—1st Tuesday in March, '82.
Martin, J.—1st Tuesday in June, '82.

NEW HAVEN COUNTY.
CIVIL TERMS.

Sanford, J.—2d Tuesday in September, until 1st Tuesday in November.
Martin, J.—1st Tuesday in November to end of term.
Beardsley, J.—1st Tuesday in January, '82, to 2d Tuesday in March.
Hitchcock, J.—2d Tuesday in March, '82, to end of term.

CRIMINAL TERMS.

Granger, J.—1st Tuesday in July.
Culver, J.—1st Tuesday in October.
Hitchcock, J.—1st Tuesday in January, '82.
Loomis, J.—1st Tuesday in April, '82.

WATERBURY CIVIL TERMS.

Carpenter, J.—2d Tuesday in December.
Martin, J.—1st Tuesday in May, '82·

CRIMINAL TERMS.

Park, Ch. J.—3d Tuesday in September.
Beardsley, J.—3d Tuesday in March, '82·

NEW LONDON COUNTY.

CIVIL TERMS.

Martin, J.—2d Tuesday in September.
Hovey, J.—1st Tuesday in November.
Hovey, J.—3d Tuesday in March, '82·
Beardsley, J.—1st Tuesday in June, '82·

CRIMINAL TERMS.

Culver, J.—1st Tuesday in January, '82·
Hovey, J.—1st Tuesday in May, '82·

FAIRFIELD COUNTY.

CIVIL TERMS.

Hitchcock, J.—3d Tuesday in September, to 1st Tuesday in December.
Hovey, J.—1st Tuesday in December to end of term.
Sanford, J.—2d Tuesday in February, '82, to 3d Tuesday in April.
Culver, J.—3d Tuesday in April, '82, to end of term.

CRIMINAL TERMS.

Park, Ch. J.—4th Tuesday in August.
Beardsley, J.—3d Tuesday in October.
Hitchcock, J.—3d Tuesday in February, '82·
Sanford, J.—2d Tuesday in May, '82·

WINDHAM COUNTY.

Carpenter, J.—4th Tuesday in August.
Sanford, J.—2d Tuesday in November.
Culver, J.—1st Tuesday in February, '82·
Hovey, J.—2d Tuesday in May, '82·

LITCHFIELD COUNTY.

Loomis, J.—3d Tuesday in August.
Pardee, J.—2d Tuesday in October, Crim. Term.
Hitchcock, J.—1st Tuesday in December.
Granger, J.—1st Tuesday in April, '82, Crim. Term.
Sanford, J.—1st Tuesday in June, '82·

MIDDLESEX COUNTY.

Beardsley, J.—2d Tuesday in September.
Beardsley, J.—2d Tuesday in November.
Hovey, J.—2d Tuesday in February, '82.
Sanford, J.—3d Tuesday in April, '82.

TOLLAND COUNTY.

Culver, J.—1st Tuesday in September.
Beardsley, J.—1st Tuesday in December.
Martin, J.—2d Tuesday in April, '82.
Hitchcock, J.—1st Tuesday in June, '82.
The Judges are elected for eight years.
For Terms of Courts, see Calendar pages.

PROBATE COURTS.
HARTFORD COUNTY.

HARTFORD,
Bloomfield,
E. Hartford,
Glastonbury,
Newington,
Rocky Hill,
West Hartford,
Wethersfield,
Windsor Locks, } J. H. White.
Enfield, Frederick E. Ely.
Farmington,
Plainville, } C. L. Whitman.
Granby, Albert C. Latham.
*Hartland, ——— ———.
Manchester, Rufus R. Dimock.

Avon, Matthew C. Woodford.
Berlin, } Valentine B.
New Britain, } Chamberlain.
Bristol, Asahel Brockett.
Burlington, Romeo Elton.
Canton, Samuel N. Codding.
East Granby, Isaac P. Owen.
East Windsor, } Mahlon H.
South Windsor, } Bancroft.
Marlborough, James J. Bell.
Simsbury, John C. Roberts.
Southington, Walter S. Merrell.
Suffield, William L. Loomis.
Windsor, H. Sidney Hayden.

NEW HAVEN COUNTY.

NEW HAVEN,
Hamden,
North Haven,
Orange,
Seymour,
Woodbridge, } Samuel A. York.
Bethany, Nathan Clark.
Branford, Henry H. Stedman.

Derby, Charles Reed.
East Haven, Chas. A. Bray.
Guilford,
N. Branford p't, } E. R. Landon.
Madison, Henry B. Wilcox.
Meriden, E. A. Merriman.
Oxford, Lewis Barnes.
Southbury, see Litchfield Co.

---

*Tie vote. Orson C. Gates, 86; Ebenezer H. Miller, 86.

Cheshire, } Benj. A. Jarvis.
Prospect, }
Milford, Wm. G. Mitchell.
Naugatuck. } Geo. D. Bissell.
Beacon Falls, }

Wallingford, } Othniel I.
N. Branford p't, } Martin.
Waterbury, }
Middlebury, }
Thomaston, } Chas. W. Gillette.
Wolcott, }

NEW LONDON COUNTY.

NEW LONDON, } William
Waterford, } Belcher.
Norwich, }
Franklin, }
Griswold, } Supply T.
Lisbon, } Holbrook.
Preston, }
Sprague, }
Bozrah, Samuel G. Johnson.
Colchester, { Rexford R.
{ Carrington.

East Lyme, M. W. Comstock.
Groton, William H. Potter.
Lebanon, George D. Spencer.
Ledyard, George Fanning.
Lyme, Frederick Fosdick.
Montville, Henry A. Baker.
N. Stonington, Chas. P. White.
Old Lyme, David Morley.
Salem, Austin O. Gallup.
Stonington, Rich'd A. Wheeler.

FAIRFIELD COUNTY.

BRIDGEPORT, }
Easton, }
Hunting'on, } Morris B.
Monroe, } Beardsley.
Trumbull, }
Danbury, } Norman
New Fairfield, } Hodge.
Bethel, George S. Crofut.
Brookfield, Benj. Griffen.
Stamford, } John Clason.
Darien, }
Stratford, Robert H. Russell.

Fairfield, Samuel Glover.
Greenwich, Daniel S. Mead, Jr.
Newtown, Monroe Judson.
Norwalk, }
New Canaan, } Asa B.
Wilton, } Woodward.
Redding, Lemuel Sanford.
Ridgefield, Hiram K. Scott
Sherman, John N. Woodruff.
Westport, } Silas B. Sherwood.
Weston, }

WINDHAM COUNTY.

BROOKLYN, Wm. Woodbridge.
Ashford, Davis A. Baker.
Canterbury, Marvin H. Sanger.
Chaplin, Ephraim W. Day.
Eastford, H. H. Burnham.
Hampton, Patrick H. Pearl.
Killingly, Thomas J. Evans.
Plainfield, Waldo Tillinghast.

Pomfret, Edward P. Hayward.
Putnam, John A. Carpenter.
Sterling, Luther Gallup.
Thompson, George Flint.
Voluntown, Orrin S. Rix.
Windham, } Huber Clark.
Scotland, }
Woodstock, Oliver H. Perry.

LITCHFIELD COUNTY.

LITCHFIELD, } George M. Woodruff.
Goshen,
Morris,
Warren,

Barkhamsted, Daniel Youngs.
No. Canaan, } J.B.Hardenbergh.
Canaan,
Cornwall, Silas C. Beers.
Harwinton, Martin L. Goodwin.
Kent, Jerome F. Gibbs.
New Hartford, Henry R. Jones.
New Milford, } J. H. McMahon.
Bridgewater,
Norfolk, Robbins Battell.

Plymouth, Byron Tuttle.
Roxbury, Lyman P. Eastman.
Salisbury, Lorenzo Tupper.
Sharon, J. Wade Hughes.
Thomaston, see New Haven Co.
Torrington, Jos. F. Calhoun.
Washington, H. H. Morehouse.
Watertown, Wm. B. Hotchkiss.
Winchester, } Augustus H. Fenn.
Colebrook,
Woodbury,
Bethlehem, } Jas. Huntington.
Southbury,

MIDDLESEX COUNTY.

MIDDLETOWN, } Silas A. Robinson.
Cromwell,
Durham,
Middlefield,

East Haddam, Julius Attwood.
Essex, Edward W. Redfield.
Killingworth,Lyman E. Stevens.
Old Saybrook, Henry Hart.

Haddam, George W. Arnold.
Chatham, } William A. Chapman.
Portland,
Clinton, Henry C. Hull.
Saybrook, } Joseph B. Banning.
Chester,
Westbrook, George C. Moore.

TOLLAND COUNTY.

TOLLAND, } John B. Carpenter.
Willington,
Andover, } Wm. A. Collins.
Bolton,
Columbia,
Somers, Solomon Fuller.

Coventry, Dwight Webler.
Ellington, } Gelon W. West.
Vernon,
Hebron, Marshall Porter.
Mansfield, Isaac P. Fenton.
Stafford, } John O. Booth.
Union,

The Judges are elected for two years.

STATE COMMISSIONERS.

ON TURNPIKE ROADS.

Bridgeport and Newtown—Ebenezer Wheeler, Trumbull; Wm. J. Dick, Newtown.
Essex—Jared E. Redfield, Essex; Calvin L. Ely, Lyme.

Huntington—F. G. Perry, Huntington; Isaac E. Booth, Trumbull.

New Haven and Derby—George H. Peck, Royal M. Bassett, Derby, George Augur, New Haven.

Oxford—Alfred Birch, Woodbury; John Candee, Benjamin Nichols, Oxford.

Wells Hollow—Frederick G. Perry, Huntington; Isaac E. Booth, Trumbull.

Weston—E. B. Goodsell, Bridgeport; Edson W. Hall, Easton.

ON FERRIES.

Chapman's—William S. Tyler, Haddam; Jacob R. Greenfield, East Haddam.

Enfield—Orville S. Douglas, Suffield; William Steele, Enfield.

Essex—Charles E. Hough, Essex; R. L. Griffin, Lyme.

East Windsor—Isaac Schwab, East Windsor; John R. Montgomery, Windsor Locks.

Middle Haddam—Horace Johnson, Chatham; John J. Cone, Middletown.

Middletown and Portland—Evelyn B. Strong, Middletown; Henry M. Smith, Portland.

New London and Groton—Leander F. Gardner, Groton; Oliver Perkins, Groton.

South Windsor—Henry E. Phelps, Windsor; Erastus W. Ellsworth, South Windsor.

Warner's—Jonathan Warner, Chester; Jabez Comstock, Lyme.

ON BRIDGES.

Bennett's—Frederick Sanford.

Connecticut River Company—George G. Sill, Wm. M. Hudson, Hartford; John B. Moseley, Glastonbury.

Enfield—Amos Chappell, Suffield; Wm. Abbe, Enfield.

Hartford—Heman A. Tyler, Hartford; Maro S. Chapman, Manchester; Geo. D. Bartlett, Glastonbury.

Tomlinson's—Jonathan Ingersoll, W. J. Atwater, New Haven; Stephen Hemingway, Henry Smith, Alexander W. Forbes, Alfred Hughes, East Haven; Henry W. Averill, Branford.

Washington—George T. Smith, Milford; Albert Wilcox, Jasper K. Whiting, Stratford.

Zoar Bridge—John G. Stevens, Monroe; Benjamin Nichols, Oxford.

ON FISHERIES.

William M. Hudson, Hartford; Robert G. Pike, Middletown; George N. Woodruff, Sherman.

INSPECTORS OF STEAM BOILERS.

First Cong. Dist.—Frank S. Allen, Hartford. .
Second Cong. Dist.—Frederick H. Laforge, Waterbury.
Third Cong. Dist.—Joseph Allen, Norwich.
Fourth Cong. Dist.—John Cotter, Norwalk.

INSPECTOR-GENERAL OF GAS-METERS AND ILLUMI-
NATING GAS.

William G. Mixter, New Haven.

STATE CHEMISTS.

William T. Cutter, East Lyme; Joseph Hall, Hartford.

AUDITORS OF PUBLIC ACCOUNTS.

R. Walton Farmer, Hartford; Thomas J. Raymond, Norwalk.

Commissioners for other States.

BRIDGEPORT.   William K. Seeley, New York.
   George W. Warner, New York, New Jersey, Pa., Ohio, Ind.,
     Ill., Mich., Wis., Iowa, Mo , Mass.
   N. S. Wordin, Minnesota.
DANBURY.   Roger Averill, New York.
   David B. Booth, New York.
GUILFORD.   E. R. Landon, New York.
HARTFORD.   Sylvester Barbour, New York.
   Charles E. Fellowes, New York, Ohio.
   Goodman and Parker, for all the States except Delaware.
   David G. Gordon, for all the States except Maine, Vermont,
     Delaware, Nevada, Oregon.
   William Hamersley, New York, Illinois, Indiana, Wiscon-
     sin, Michigan, Ohio, Mass., Penn., Tenn.
   Charles J. Hoadly, Maine, R. I., Ark., New Mexico.
   William L. Matson, New York.
   Zalmon A. Storrs, New York.
   W. E. Simonds, Maine, R. I., Ver., Missouri, Mich., Wash.
     Territory, Oregon, Ind., N. C., S. C., Ala., Ga., Fla., Cal.,
     Iowa, Kan., Texas.
   Henry E. Taintor, Maine, N. H., Ver., Mass., R. I., N. Y.,
     Penn., N. C., Ga., Miss., La., Ohio, Indiana, Mich., Wis ,
     Iowa, Tenn., Ark., Kan., Minn., Neb.
LITCHFIELD.   George M. Woodruff, New York.
  3

MIDDLETOWN. Arthur B. Calef, Penn. and New York.
　Frank F. Starr, N. Y., Dist. of Columbia, Texas.
NEW HAVEN. Adolph Asher, Massachusetts.
　Frederick W. Babcock, New York, Mass., Wis., Missouri.
　C. H. Fowler, Mass. and New York.
　John C. Hollister, Michigan, Georgia, New York, New Jer-
　　sey, Penn., Mass., Cal., Missouri.
　S. Arthur Marsden, New York, Mass., Mich., Penn., Ill.,
　　Ga., Fla., N. C., S. C., Cal., Kansas, R. I., Iowa, N. J.,
　　Minn., Ohio.
　Arthur D. Osborne, Michigan, Wis., Minn.
　Charles Robinson, New York, Maine, Mich.
　Henry Rogers, Pennsylvania.
　Wm. K. Townsend, New York.
　M. Frank Tyler, Mass.
NEW LONDON. John Danforth, Mass., South Carolina, New
　York, New Jersey, Penn., Ohio, Illinois, Mich., Maryland,
　Texas.
NORWALK. A. B. Woodward, New York.
NORWICH. Ebenezer Learned, New York, Ohio, Indiana.
　George Perkins, New York.
　John T. Wait, Maine, N. H., Ver., R. I., New York, Penn.,
　　Mich., Ill., Tenn., Ark., Del., Mo., La., Cal., Fla., Texas.
SAYBROOK. *Deep River*, John W. Marvin, New York, Mich.,
　Minnesota.
STAMFORD. Samuel Fessenden, New York.
WATERBURY. Stephen W. Kellogg, New York.
WOODBURY. William Cothren, New York, Ohio, Mich., Ind.,
　Ill., Wisconsin.

NOTARIES PUBLIC.

Appointed by the Governor. They hold office from the date
of their commission, and for two years from the first day of
February of the year in which they are commissioned, unless
their commissions are sooner revoked by the Governor.

ASHFORD. Danforth O. Lombard, John H. Simmons.
AVON. Henry Clark.
BERLIN. Albert A. Barnes, Charles M. Brown, John Norton,
Alfred North.
BETHEL. Granville B. Andrews, Eli W. Gilbert, David T.

Hubbell, Henry C. Judd, Horace R. Northrop, Frederick Shepard, Nathan Seeley, Amos Woodman.

BETHLEHEM. Henry W. Peck, Samuel L. Bloss.

BLOOMFIELD. John E. Cox, Henry W. Rowley.

BOLTON. Nathan S. Maine.

BOZRAH. Augustus D. Herrick, Charles S. Pendleton, Albert Waterman.

BRANFORD. J. H. Bartholomew, Edward H. Rogers.

BRIDGEPORT. Charles S. Adams, Richard C. Ambler, Chas. K. Averill, F. J. Banks, Thomas L. Bartholomew, Nelson M. Beach, Morris B. Beardsley, Alfred B. Beers, F. N. Benham, Henry E. Bowser, Orlando H. Brothwell, Andrew Burke, William A. Burroughs, Charles S. Canfield, Lyman S. Catlin, Luzon W. Clark, Michael Eberhard, Thomas R. Cruttenden, William E. Disbrow, Henry B. Drew, Alfred B. Fairchild, Thomas B. Fairchild, John F. Fayerweather, Herman Ganz, Amos Fuller, Granville W. Goodsell, Walter Goddard, Philip L. Holzer, R. E. Hough, John S. Griffith, Edwin F. Hall, Julius S. Hanover, W. R. Higby, William B. Hinks, D. F. Hollister, Frank L. Holt, Howard G. Hubbell, F. W. Hurd, John A. Hurley, James King, Rudolph Kost, R. B. Lacey, David B. Lockwood, Frederick J. Lockwood, Francis W. Marsh, James R. Middlebrook, Willis F. Morehouse, Stephen Nichols, Horace Nichols, John F. Noble, William H. Noble, Wilfred E. Norton, Eugene B. Peck, John E. Pond, Charles P. Porter, Isaac B. Prindle, Charles B. Read, Egbert Rockwell, Howard A. Scribner, Richard Sewell, William E. Seeley, Michael S. Sheridan, Charles Sherwood, L. M. Slade, George A. Staples, William M. Staples, Goodwin Stoddard, Edward S. Sumner, Samuel B. Sumner, Herrick A. Sutton, Albert M. Tallmadge, Frank B. Taylor, Dwight H. Terry, Curtis Thompson, George W. Warner, Thomas L. Watson, George F. Wildman, William C. Wildman, Rudolphus E. Whittlesey, Charles E. Wilmot.

BRIDGEWATER. Alexander Hawley, Charles Treat.

BRISTOL. Morgan W. Beach, D. A. Miller, Samuel P. Newell, Geo. H. Mitchell, Miles L. Peck, John H. Sessions, Charles S. Treadway.

BROOKFIELD. Sidney E. Hawley, Andrew Northrop, Henry S. Peck.

BROOKLYN. L. B. Cleveland, Edward L. Cundall, John Palmer, John P. Wood.

CANAAN. Dwight W. Clark, Dwight E. Dean, Edmund D. Lawrence, Charles B. Maltbie, Uriel H. Miner, A. C. Randall. *Falls Village*, Lee P. Dean.

CANTERBURY. Alfred H. Bennett, Joseph P. Lester, Marvin H. Sanger.

CANTON. Jasper H. Bidwell, W. W. Bidwell, Levi Case, Samuel N. Codding, Moses S. Dyer. *Collinsville*, Oliver F. Perry.

CHAPLIN. Jared W. Lincoln.

CHATHAM Josiah Ackley, John Carrier, L. H. Markham, Nathaniel C. Smith.

CHESHIRE. Edward A. Cornwall, Milton C. Doolittle, Howard C. Ives.

CHESTER. J. T. Clark, E. C. Hungerford.

CLINTON. Ezra E. Post, John B. Wright.

COLEBROOK. Rollin D. Baldwin, Reuben Rockwell.

COLCHESTER. Joseph N. Adams, Charles H. Babcock, Francis L. Carrier, Nathaniel Foote, Salmon C. Gillette, Daniel H. Hammond, Alfred J. Loomis, Israel L. Loomis.

COLUMBIA. Robert Brown, Joseph Hotchkiss, Joseph Hutchins, William H. Yeomans.

CORNWALL. Silas C. Beers, Virgil F. McNeil, Wilson P. Sturgis.

COVENTRY. Henry A. Brewster, Luther P. Gager, Chauncey Howard. *South Coventry*, Loring Winchester.

CROMWELL. Silas C. Beers, Stephen P. Polley, Ralph B. Savage, William H. Stickney, Samuel B. Wilcox.

DANBURY. Jabez Amsbury, Roger Averill, John W. Bacon, George W. Barnum, 2d, Albert G. Benedict, George B. Benjamin, Ezra P. Bennett, William C. Bennett, David B. Booth, Lucius H. Boughton, Benjamin E. Cowperwaite, Harris L. Crofutt, U. B. Dunaway, William A. Ely, Samuel Gregory, Martin H. Griffin, Jr., Norman Hodge, Luman L. Hubbell, Benezet A. Hough, Lucius P. Hoyt, William A. Leonard, David P. Nichols, David Pearce, William S. Peck, Horace Purdy, Dwight E. Rogers, Henry C. Ryder, Aaron C. Seeley, L. P. Treadwell, Edgar Tweedy, Harry Williams.

DARIEN. George W. Clock, Charles F. Hull, Melville E. Mead, Ira Scofield, James B. Selleck, James M. Tooker.

DERBY. William C. Atwater, John D. Ballou, Egbert Bartlett, George L. Beardsley, William S. Browne, Franklin Burton, Thomas F. Birdsey, Thos. L. J. Bulluss, William J. Clark, E. V. Clemens, S. A. Cotter, Benjamin F. Culver, Alton Farrell, Frederick L. Gaylord, A. K. Hatheway, Geo. H. Peck, Robert Peck, David Torrance. *Ansonia*, Charles H. Pine, Wm. Powe. *Birmingham*, Wm. S. Downs.

DURHAM. Leverett M. Leach, Henry G. Newton, Rufus W. Mathewson.

EASTFORD. Hiram H. Burnham.

EAST HADDAM. Cyrus W. Chapman, Almon Day, Thomas Gross, Jr., S. R. Holmes, David S. Purple.

EAST HARTFORD. Percy S. Bryant, Arthur P. Moore, Ephraim Rood.

EAST HAVEN. S. W. F. Andrews, George M. Baldwin, L. P. Deming, Jonathan Dudley, Wm. E. Goodyear, Charles W. Hemingway, Hiram Jacobs, John R Lute, Wm. P. Niles.

EAST LYME. Daniel Caulkins, Moses W. Comstock, Charles P. Sturtevant.

EASTON. George J. Banks, Ebenezer S. Gillette, Joseph W. Johnson.

EAST WINDSOR. Homer D. Allen, Caleb Leavitt, Eugene T. Spooner.

ELLINGTON. Michael H. Mandell.

ENFIELD. David Brainard, Amos D. Bridge, Willis Gowdy, F. A. King, Loren H. Pease, William Stimson.

ESSEX. Charles S. Hough, James Phelps, Jared E. Redfield, C. O. Spencer, Alfred M. Wright.

FAIRFIELD. Henry Bradley, William H. Johnson, Wm. B. Glover, Daniel Meloney, John H. Perry, Albert W. Sanford. *Southport*, Charles M. Gilman, O. H. Perry, E. C. Sherwood.

FARMINGTON. Thomas Cowles, Julius Gay, Richard H. Gay, Carlos L. Mason, Walter S. Porter, Wm. W. Woodford.

FRANKLIN. Thomas G. Kingsley, H. L. M. Ladd, Ashbel Woodward.

GLASTONBURY. Wm. S. Goslee, Thomas H. L. Talcott.

GOSHEN. Eugene E. Allyn, Frederick E. Hurlburt.

GRANBY. Theo. M. Maltbie.

GREENWICH. H. W. R. Hoyt, Joseph H. Marshall, Myron L. Mason, Daniel S. Mead, Jr., George G. McNall, Robert J. Walsh, Edward J. Wright.

GRISWOLD. Henry T. Crosby, L. M. Green, Barton C Kegwin, E. C. Kegwin, Alexander H. Lester.

GROTON. Lemuel Clift, E. R. Coe, John J. Copp, David A. Daboll, John O. Fish, John Fitch, C. H. Gaylord, Robert N. Gray, Samuel B. Latham, Philo Little, Orrin E. Miner, Wm. F. Mitchell, Thomas E. Packer, Asa Perkins, 2d, William H. Potter, Jabez Watrous, Jr., James L. Weaver.

GUILFORD. George S. Davis, Edward R. Landon, S. T. Morgan, F. W. Seward.

HADDAM. George W. Arnold, Walter N. Gay, Edward D. Gilbert.

HAMDEN. Charles P. Augur, Silas Benham, Ellsworth B. Cooper, Elias Dickerman, Edwin P. Edwards, Walter W. Woodruff.

HAMPTON.   David Greenslit.
HARTFORD.   John C. Abbott, David L. Aberdien, Sherman
W. Adams, B. R. Allen, Myron A. Andrews, Isaiah Baker, Jr.,
William E. Baker, Stephen Ball, Henry S. Barbour, Joseph L.
Barbour, Sylvester Barbour, George D. Bates, Joseph D. Bates,
Morgan W. Beach, Edward B. Bennett, Samuel J. Bestor,
Lorenzo M. Blake, Lewis H. Brainard, Joseph Breed, James H.
Brewster, Frederick P. Brehm, John H. Brocklesby, John P.
Bronk, Alfred B. Bull, Henry L. Bunce, Charles L. Burdett,
George H. Burdick, Albert L. Burke, John F. Burt, Silas Chap-
man, Jr., Richard S. Burt, Patrick F. Butler, James R. Chap-
man, Edward H. Clark, James W. Clark, Mahlon N. Clark,
Charles J. Cole, Silas H. Cornwell, Horace Cornwall, E. P.
Cowles, Walter G. Cowles, G. F. Davis, Asa W. Day, George
H. Day, John C. Day, Charles S. Davidson, Leonard A. Dick-
inson, E. B. Dillingham, Sylvester C. Dunham, Charles E. Dus-
tin, Frederick Eberle, Frederick G. Eberle, Theodore G. Ellis,
Samuel E. Elmore, William H. Ellsworth, Henry W. Erving,
Wm. A. Erving, Charles E. Fellowes, H. B. Freeman, Henry H.
Fitch, William H. Fitch, H. E. Fitts, Edward L. Gaylord, Sim-
eon J. Fox, Robert F. Gaylord, T. J. Gill, Charles S. Gillette,
A. J. Glazier, Edward Goodman, Alfred W. Green, Robert A.
Griffing, David G. Gordon, Miles W. Graves, Charles E. Gross,
Louis Gundlach, Isaac W. Hakes, William Hamersley, A. E.
Hart, H. E. Harrington, Albert N. Hatheway, Horace Heath,
W. F. Henney, Ratcliffe Hicks, John E. Higgins, Appleton R.
Hillyer, Charles J. Hoadly, Francis A. Hoadly, George W.
Hubbard, Charles C. Hurlbut, Frank E. Hyde, W. W. Hyde,
Ward W. Jacobs, Charles M. Joslyn, William H. King, Henry
A. Kippen, James H. Knight, William Knox, Herbert B. Lang-
don, Charles H. Lawrence, A. G. Loomis, Cooke Lounsbury,
Robert Lunny, 2d, Frederick S. Lyman, Theodore Lyman, E.
E. Marvin, William L. Matson, W. J. McConville, W. B. Mc-
Cray, Charles L. McIntosh, Richard McCloud, John T. McMa-
nus, Thomas McManus, Lent B. Merriam, James H. Miller,
Hiram R. Mills, F. O. Mosebach, Leonard Morse, George B.
Newton, Henry Osborn, Francis H. Parker, Wm. H. Parry,
Edward W. Parsons, John C. Parsons, Edward B. Peck, Nathan
F. Peck, Wilbert W. Perry, James B. Powell, S. O. Prentice,
Henry C. Robinson, Edward F. Rogers, David A. Rood, Warren
Rowley, Charles H. Russell, George E. Sanborne, C. F. Sedg-
wick, Joseph Schwab, George G. Sill, Clinton Spencer, Lewis
Sperry, Lewis E. Stanton, George G. Sumner, J. H. Tallman,
Henry E. Taintor, James P. Taylor, Stephen Terry, John H.

Thacher, W. H. Townsend, Heman A. Tyler, Geo. Ulrich, Wm. Very, George H. Warner, George A. Washburne, John C. Wasserbach, John Watson, John H. Welch, John W. Welch, Mahlon R. West, Charles T. Welles, M. H. Whaples, John P. Wheeler, Edward S. White, William A. Willard, Hiram Willey, Abram E. Williams, John R. Wittig, Oliver Woodhouse, William S. Wooster, Wm. H. Woodward.

HEBRON. F. C. Bissell, George S. Bestor, John G. Page.

HUNTINGTON. Charles Beard, E. P. Curtis, Jr., Henry Glover, Charles Judson, F. G. Ferry, Horace Wheeler.

KENT. Marshall C. Gibbs.

KILLINGLY. Mowry Amsbury, Arthur G. Bill, Henry N. Clemens, Wm. E. Hyde, Oliver P. Jacobs, Wm. P. Kelley, Wm. H. Oatley, George W. Pike, Edwin L. Palmer, James H. Potter, L. H. Rickard, Milton A. Shumway, George H. Wheaton, Chauncey C. Young. *West Killingly*, Edward L. Cundall, Henry Hammond, Henry L. Hammond, James H. Potter.

KILLINGWORTH. Orlando E. Redfield.

LEBANON. Anson Fowler, Wm. A. Fuller, Henry M. Kelley, James M. Peckham.

LEDYARD. Elisha S. Allyn, Nathaniel B. Geer.

LISBON. Hezekiah L. Read.

LITCHFIELD. J. H. Catlin, George E. Jones, William F. Jones, George C. Woodruff, George M. Woodruff.

LYME. John W. Bill, Benjamin Rathbone, Henry B. Sisson,

MADISON. J. Myron Hull, Ezra S. Smith, Sereno H. Scranton.

MANCHESTER. Sanford O Benton, John S. Cheney, Richard O. Cheney, Clinton W. Cowles.

MANSFIELD. Charles H. Babcock, James P. Burrows, Joseph D. Chaffee, John Fitch, Henry Huntington, John G. C. McFarlane, Ralph W. Storrs, Geo. T. Swift.

MERIDEN. Owen B. Arnold, John Barrett, Thomas A. Benham, Jr., Eli C. Birdsey, Linus Birdsey, John F. Butler, Bela Carter, Geo. M. Clark, Wm. H. Catlin, A. Chamberlin, Jr., Asa H. Churchill, Geo. R. Curtiss, Lewis K. Curtis, Wilbur F. Davis, John E. Durand, Clarence E. Ellsbree, C. Robert Fasy, Frank S. Fay, Geo. A. Fay, Edwin D. Hall, Lewis Hall, Selah A. Hull, Isaac B. Hyatt, Charles P. Ives, George W. Ives, Charles W. Mann, E. A. Merriman, George N. Morse, Junius S. Norton, Jr., A. L. Otis, A. B. Paddock, Benjamin Page, Jr., Ralph A. Palmer, Wm. H. Perkins, Franklin Platt, James P. Platt, Frank D. Proudman, Gustave Rebstock, Charles L. Rockwell, Charles

H. Shaw, Frank J. Seidensticker, Geo. W. Smith, Wilbur H.
Squire, A. L. Stevens, Julius A. Talmadge, S. H. W. Yale.
MIDDLEBURY.   L. Abbott, Charles L. Nichols.
MIDDLEFIELD.   Lyman A. Mills, Moses W. Terrill.
MIDDLETOWN.   Conrad G. Bacon, James E. Bidwell, Eldon
B. Bird·ey, James Bishop, Walter L. Blake, Wm. H. Burrows,
Geo. W. Burr, Abbott G. Butler, Arthur B Calef, Jr., J. N.
Camp, Frederick B. Chaffee. M. B. Copeland, Edward Douglass,
Augustus Eastman, James K. Guy, Frederick L. Gleason, Geo.
H. Harris, George W. Harris, Elijah S. Hubbard, Jonathan B.
Kilbourne, D. Ward Northrop, Robert G. Pike, Augustus Put-
nam, George Rand, Henry H. Smith, Frank F. Starr. Elihu W.
N. Starr, Orrin E. Stoddard, Charles G. R. Vinal, Wm. Wood-
ward.
MILFORD.   William A. Bull, Anon Clark, John W. Fowler,
Jonas G. French, Henry C. Platt, Alexander T. Peck, Wm. H.
Pond.
MONROE.   Charles M. Beardsley, Lacey Higgins, Martin J.
Mallett, Daniel A. Nichols, Charles B. Wheeler, Frederick W.
Wheeler.
MONTVILLE.   Henry A. Baker, Orrin H. Whiting.
MORRIS.   Garry H. Miner.
NAUGATUCK.   Henry C. Baldwin, L. S. Beardsley, George D.
Bissell, Edward B. Goodyear, William Kennedy, George A.
Lewis, Jeremiah B. Luddy, Benton A. Peck, Luther S. Platt,
Robert M. Smith, Adelbert C. Tuttle.
NEW BRITAIN.   James H. Beach, A. N. Bennett, Lyman
S. Burr, V. B. Chamberlain, F. H. Churchill, Nelson A. Cowles,
Augustus P. Collins, Frederick H. Hubbard, John D. Humphrey,
Edward C. Jones, Charles S. Landers, Albert Morton, Howard
C. Noble, Charles A. Northend, Charles B. Oldershaw, Julius
H. Pease, Charles Peck, J. A. Pickett, James W. Ringrose,
James Shepard, Andrew J. Sloper, Levi O. Smith, Wm. W.
Smith, Edward N. Stanley, W. F. Walker, John Walsh, M. S.
Wiard.
NEW CANAAN.   Francis L. Aiken, Russell L. Hall, Noah W.
Hoyt, S. Y. St. John.
NEW FAIRFIELD.   Charles D. H. Kellogg.
NEW HARTFORD.   Howell W. Brown, O. T. Hungerford,
Nathan Morse, Orrin S. Thompson.
NEW HAVEN.   Edward A. Anketell, E. P. Arvine, Adolph
Asher, Prentiss O. Avery, F. W. Babcock, Louis A. Babcock,
Charles L. Baldwin, Edward W. Baldwin, Wm. T. Bartlett, Ed-
ward L. Bassett, Edson S. Beach, John K. Beach, Eugene A.

Beecher, Leopold Besser, Frederick A. Betts, George Blakeman,
Charles C. Blatchley, Charles F. Bollman, Herbert L. Bradley,
John C. Bradley, Maurice F. Brennan, Charles S. Bunnell, H. H.
Bunnell, Curtis S. Bushnell, George A. Butler, Sylvanus Butler,
John G. Chapman, Frederick A. Chase, James G. Clark, J. P.
Cleaveland, L. W. Cleaveland, Anton Coe, James F. Colby,
Elbridge C. Cook, Geo. R. Cooley, Lafayette Comstock, Robert
J. Couch, R. P. Cowles, Hugh Daily, Sylvester R. Davis, Eu-
gene DeForest, Lucius P. Deming, George L. Dickerman, T. P.
Dickerman, Edwin C. Dow, Virgil M. Dow, Cornelius T. Dris-
coll, Alfred Edwards, John E. Earle, Joseph C. Earle, Lewis
Elliott, Wm. W. Farnham, Wm. T. Fields, George L. Finney,
Truman S. Foote, Charles E. Fowler, Charles H. Fowler, Austin
B. Fuller, Simeon J. Fox, Charles I. French, Samuel A. Galpin,
Philip Goodhart, Frank H. Gaylord, David B. Gerrett, Charles
K. Gorham, John W. Geary, Enos A. Hale, Thomas C. Hollis,
Samuel Halliwell, Charles S. Hamilton, George W. Hamilton,
Francis E. Harrison, Edward R. Hayes, Charles W. Hemingway,
Benjamin Higbie, Edwin A. Hill, Eugene C. Hill, Burton J.
Hine, Isaac W. Hine, George E. Hoadley, John C. Hollister,
Sanford H. Holmes, Hobart L. Hotchkiss, Benjamin P. Hub-
bard, H. P. Hubbard, Savillian R. Hull, Jonathan Ingersoll,
Francis G. Ingersoll, Thomas C. Ingersoll, Hoadley B. Ives,
Abel B. Jacocks, W. G. Judson, A. H. Kellam, Charles Kim-
berly, E. Elliot Kimberly, George H. Larned, Thomas J. Law-
ton, Augustus Lines, Wm. R. Lloyd, Samuel Lloyd, H. C. Long,
Benjamin C. Lum, Franklin M. Lum, Richard F. Lyon, S. A.
Marsden, James M Mason, C. B. Matthewman, Edward Mc-
Carthy, Alexander McAlister, William J. Mills, Eli Mix, Ben-
jamin F. Mansfield, Edwin F. Mansfield, Frederick Morris,
Luzon B. Morris, Chas. T. Morse, Elliott H. Morse, Wm. Moul-
throp, Lyman E. Munson, Charles H. R. Nott, John G. North,
Andrew O'Neil, Arthur D. Osborne. G. Edward Osborne, James
Olmsted, Henry C. Pardee, Henry E. Pardee, Eugene B. Peck,
Edmund R. Pendleton, L. L Phelps, Daniel G. Phipps, Rufus S.
Pickett, Henry Pierpont, James P. Pigott, Johnson T. Platt,
Joseph D. Plunkett, Philip Pond, Frank Prescott, Edward Pur-
rington, John B. Reddan, Horatio G. Redfield, George A. Rey-
nolds, James Reynolds, John A. Richardson, A. Heaton Robert-
son, Wm. C. Robinson, George A. Root, William E. Rowland,
Edward S. Rowland, E. S. Rogers, Henry Rogers, Henry D.
Russel', Talcott H. Russell, Wm. H. Sanborn, Alvin P. Sanford,
David C. Sanford, Whiting S. Sanford, Charles S. Scott, Chas.
W. Scranton, Seth T. Seeley, Joseph Sheldon, T. J. Sloan, Chas.

W. Shelton, George Sherman, John H. Shumway, John Shuster, Andrew T. Smith, H. E. Smith, J. Gibbs Smith, Siegwart Spier, Wm. H. Stevenson, Ezra L. Stiles, J. Preston Strong, David Strouse, George H. Sutton, Chas. L. Swan, Jr., Joseph J. Sweeney, Norman A. Tanner, Nelson Taylor, George Terry, Wm. E. Thompson, Edward A. Thompson, Sherwood S. Thompson, Wm. K. Townsend, Edwin A. Tracy, Charles H. Trowbridge, John H. Tuttle, Julius Twiss, George A Tyler, Morris F. Tyler, Charles L. Ullman, Daniel H. Veader, S. H. Wagner, Fred. H. Waldron, Israel K. Ward, John B. Ward, Elihu Watrous, Herbert C. Warren, Charles H. Webb, I. D. Weed, Wm J. Weld, Charles R. Whedon, Alfred N. Wheeler, Oliver S. White, Wm. R. White, John H. Whiting, C. B. Willis, Charles Wilson, Dexter R. Wright, William A. Wright, James A. Wood, Henry C. Young.

NEW LONDON. Charles Allyn, Chas. W. Barnes, William Belcher, Chas. W. Butler, Richard N. Belden, Augustus Brandegee, Jr, Charles Capouilliez, J. L. Chew, Alfred Coit, Robert Coit, George Colfax, W. H. H. Comstock, B. A. Copp, John C. Crump, Timothy S. Daboll, A. S. Darrow, John E. Darrow, John Danforth, Ferris W. Douglass, James H. Hill, Walter Learned, Daniel Lee, Reuben Lord, Jr., F. W. Miner, Wm. H. H. Morgan, Lester H. Phillips, Lester S. Phillips, Gideon F. Raymond, Wm. H. Rowe, Charles G. Sistare, Wm. M. Stark, Justus A. Southard, John A. Tibbitts, Thomas M. Waller, Henry C. Weaver, Ralph Wheeler, Calvin G. Williams, Thomas M. Williams, Geo. D. Whittlesey.

NEW MILFORD. Richard B. Cogswell, L. Dunning. Henry Ives, Carlos P. Merwin, T. Dwight Merwin, Henry S. Mygatt, Charles H. Noble, Charles Randall, H. Leroy Randall, John S. Turrill.

NEWTOWN Charles Fairman, Asa N. Hawley, Monroe Judson, Henry T. Nichols, Charles C. Warner, Henry L. Wheeler.

NORFOLK. Joseph N. Cowles, Joseph B. Eldridge.

NORTH BRANFORD. Edward Smith.

NORTH HAVEN. Stephen C. Gilbert, J. Boardman Smith, Zenas J. Ward.

NORTH STONINGTON. Charles H. Brown, Elijah Bailey, Wm. B. Hull.

NORWALK. Alfred E. Austin, Heman H. Barbour, Legrand C. Betts, Wm. S. Bouton, Alfred H. Camp, Everett W. Church, Robert B. Craufurd, R. S. Craufurd, Wm. A. Curtis, Charles T. Craw, Lester S. Cole, Jeremiah Donovan, John H. Ferris, Winfield S. Hanford, John R. P. Hoyt, Joseph D. Huntington, J.

Belden Hurlbut, James W. Hyatt, George O. Keeler, Edward O. Keeler, Jacob M. Layton, Wm. K. Lewis, Chas. E. Lockwood, S. B. Meech, Jonas J. Millard, Geo. E. Miller, Wm. E. Montgomery, John A. Osborn, J. S. Randall, Franklin H. Sage, David K. Selleck, Henry K. Selleck, John S. Seymour, Burr Smith, Charles H. Street, Benj. J. Sturges, Nelson Taylor, Edward P. Weed, Patrick J. Leonard, Leander G. Wilcox, Charles P. Woodbury. *South Norwalk*, M. B. Pardee.

NORWICH. James Allan, John C. Averill, Frank H. Brown, Lucius Brown, Amos A. Browning, Willis A. Briscoe, Henry H. Burnham, Chauncey K. Bushnell, Charles E. Chandler, Charles B. Chapman, George D. Coit, Wm. S. Congdon, E. C. Cooke, A. S. Childs, Ashbel S. Crandall, John N. Crandall, John Cross, John L. Dennison, Walter Fuller, Charles W. Gale, Ulysses S. Gardner, Gardiner Greene. Jr., Samuel Harrison, Burrill W. Hyde, Lewis A. Hyde, Wm. H. Jennings, Jr., Edward H. Learned, Bela P. Learned, Daniel Lee, Clinton Lucas, Stephen B. Meach, Edwin Palmer, Henry L. Parker, Ira L. Peck, Chas. H. Phelps, George C. Ripley, William Roath, A. Irving Royce, J. Hunt Smith, John L. Spalding, Nicholas Tarrant, Allen Tenny. Seneca H. Thresher, Edwin A. Tracy, Wm. C. Tucker, John M. Thayer, Seneca S. Thresher, John T. Wait, Oliver P. Wattles, Charles Webb, Samuel A. Whitney, Horace B. Winship, Frank L. Woodward, Alfred E. Wyman, David Young.

OLD LYME. Daniel Chadwick, James Griswold.

OLD SAYBROOK. Edwin Ayer, Henry Hart, Ozias H. Kirtland, James Rankin.

ORANGE. Charles H. Amesbury, Charles K. Bush, Walter A. Main. *West Haven*, Asa H. Churchill.

OXFORD. Robinson R. Hinman, Samuel L. Tuttle, W. H. Williams.

PLAINFIELD. Horace E. Balcom, Joseph A. Dean, Robert Gray, Samuel P. Robinson, Jeremiah Starkweather, Edgar M. Warner.

PLAINVILLE. Robert C. Usher.

PLYMOUTH. Jason C. Fenn.

POMFRET. Pardon B. Johnson.

PORTLAND. Leroy Brainard, Wm. W. Coe, Ferdinand Gildersleeve, Henry Kilby, Dennis A. McQuillin, Charles H. Sage, John H. Sage.

PRESTON. Charles E. Chandler, Aaron Lucas, Chester S. Prentice.

PROSPECT. B. B. Brown.

PUTNAM. John A. Carpenter, Harrison Johnson, Joseph Lippitt, S. H. Seward, Perry P. Wilson, Jerome Tourtelotte.

REDDING. Wm. E. Dunscomb, Wm. B. Hill, David H. Miller, David S. Nash, W. H. Osborne, George A. Sanford, Thomas Sanford.

RIDGEFIELD. Lewis H. Bailey, David S. Nash, John D. Nash, Hiram K. Scott, D. Smith Gage.

ROCKY HILL. Samuel Dimock, Edward L. Gaylord, Rufus W. Griswold.

ROXBURY. Aaron W. Fenn.

SALEM. Frederick E. Chadwick.

SALISBURY. Sidney P. Ensign, Thomas L. Norton, Wm. E. Pettee, John S. Perkins, Hubert Williams.

SAYBROOK. E. H. Peckham. *Deep River*, John W. Marvin, Gideon Parker, Henry R. Wooster.

SCOTLAND. James Burnett, Abner Robinson.

SEYMOUR. Henry Bradley, Burton W. Smith.

SHARON. Alonzo A. Bates, Herman C. Rowley, Gilbert L. Smith.

SHERMAN. Lafayette Joyce, Charles A. Mallory.

SIMSBURY. E. G. Woodford, Jeffrey O. Phelps.

SOMERS. John A. Garland.

SOUTHBURY. G. T. Pierce, George F. Shelton, Egbert L. Warner.

SOUTHINGTON. Charles D. Barnes, Randolph W. Cowles, R. M. Douglass, Marcus H. Holcomb, John S. Phinney, Francis D. Whittlesey.

SOUTH WINDSOR. Sandford Buckland, John S. Clapp, Lyman Grant, Frederick A. King, Lewis Sperry.

STAFFORD. Joseph W. Chandler, J. F. Chamberlin, Charles F. Harwood, Alverado Howard, Wm. H. Spedding. *Stafford Springs*, J. W. Chandler, R. S. Hicks.

STAMFORD. Harry Bell, Samuel H. Cohen, George B. Christian, Julius B. Curtis, Marcus L. Dunn, Samuel Fessenden, H. Stanley Finch, George W. Glendining, Charles E. Holley, Nathaniel R. Hart, John E. Keeler, Francis R. Leeds, Schuyler Merritt, E. W. Riker, Edwin L. Scofield, Geo. E. Scofield, Samuel C. Silliman, Jr., Wm. C. Strowbridge, Jr., A. R. Turkington, Franklin Underhill, Wm. W. Waterbury, Wm. Ferris Waterbury, John W. Webster.

STERLING. Silas J. Matteson.

STONINGTON. Jerome S. Anderson, Peleg S. Barber, Samuel H. Chesebro, Oliver B. Grant, M. S. Greene, Nathaniel B. Hancox, George Hubbard, John A. Morgan, Henry B. Noyes, Peleg Noyes, Wm. J. H. Pollard, Moses A. Pendleton, Charles Perrin, Elias P. Randall, Francis Sheffield, Thomas D. Sheffield, Richard A. Wheeler.

STRATFORD. Anson H. Blackman, Edwin L. Britten, Claudius B. Curtis, Thomas B. Fairchild, V. R. C. Giddings, Samuel F. Houghton, A. B. Judd, Robert H. Russell, Henry P. Stagg, Herrick A. Sutton, Lucius B. Vail, LeGrand Wells.

SUFFIELD. Alonzo Allen, Wm. L. Loomis, Hezekiah S. Sheldon, Alfred Spencer, Jr.

THOMASTON. Albert P. Bradstreet, F. Willette Etheridge, Arthur J. Hine, George H. Stoughton.

THOMPSON. Hiram Arnold, Floyd Cranska.

TOLLAND. Edwin O. Dimock, Lucius S. Fuller, Charles A. Hawkins, Arthur J. Morton.

TORRINGTON. Allen G. Brady, Charles F. Brooker, William Brooks, John W. Brooks, Joseph F. Calhoun, Edward T. Coe, George W. Cole, John W. Gamwell, Chas. L. McNeil, Elisha Turner. *Wolcottville*, Isaac W. Brooks.

VERNON. Wm. W. Andross, Benezet H. Bill, E. C. Chapman, Dwight Marcy, Emerson W. Moore, Charles D. Talcott, Gelon W. West. *Rockville*, John H. Kite.

VOLUNTOWN. Caleb B. Potter, George Rouse.

WALLINGFORD. Jonathan M. Andrus, Clarence H. Brown, Wm. B. Hall, George A. Hopson, Leverett M. Hubbard, Edwin B. Ives, Henry Martin.

WASHINGTON. Gould C. Whittlesey.

WATERBURY. Anson F. Abbott, Charles S. Abbott, George W. Beach, Homer F. Bassett, Albert J. Blakeslee, Augustus M. Blakeslee, Wm. W. Bonnett, Ed. L. Bronson, Lucien F. Bennett, Burton G. Bryan, A. P. P. Camp, Herbert P. Camp, Charles C. Comerford, C. A. Colley, E. A. Curtis, Franklin L. Curtis, George H. Cowell, Edward F. Cole, Francis B. Field, Edward A. Frisbie, Jr., Edward L. Frisbie, Charles W. Gillette, Benjamin Hallas, Gilman C. Hill, Edwin S. Hoyt, J. Edward Johnson, Francis J. Kane, Stephen W. Kellogg, F. J. Kingsbury, Charles E. Lamb, Robert A. Low, G. S. Parsons, Charles G. Root, Arthur O. Shepardson, F. A. Spencer, Mark L. Sperry, Henry M. Stocking, Geo. E. Terry, Silas B. Terry, Frederick C. Webster, Daniel F. Webster, John W. Webster, F. L. Welton, Mitchell S. Wheeler.

WATERFORD. Frederick P. Morgan.

WATERTOWN. Bennett C. Atwood, Leman W. Cutler.

WEST HARTFORD. Samuel J. Bestor, Merton S. Buckland, Myron A. Andrews.

WESTON. M. V. B. Rowland.

WESTPORT. Joseph G. Hyatt, William E. Nash, Henry E. Sherwood, B. L. Woodworth, Moses W. Wilson.

WETHERSFIELD. Henry A. Deming.

WILLINGTON. Marcus B. Fisk, Adolph Korper.

WILTON. George A. Davenport, Lockwood K. Ferris, Wm. D. Gregory, James T. Hubbell, J. B. Hurlbutt, Samuel H. Ruscoe, Samuel H. Scott.

WINCHESTER. George A. Alfred, Albert M. Beach, Henry A. Bills, George M. Carrington, Rollin H. Cooke, Mortimer E. Dutton, F. D. Fyler, Henry Gay, Elias E. Gilman, Irving P. Griswold, Charles B. Holmes, Samuel A. Herman, Frederick L. Loomis, Harry L. Roberts, George S. Rowe, Albert F. Spencer, Henry C. Young. *Winsted*, George M. Carrington, Rufus E. Holmes. *West Winsted*, Henry Gay.

WINDHAM. Samuel Bingham, Lloyd E. Baldwin, Edwin A. Buck, Huber Clark, Cranston C. Crandall, A. Judson Glazier, George W. Hanover, John M. Hall, Charles P. Hempstead, Elisha H. Holcomb, Jr., John L. Hunter, Ferdinand N. King, Allen Lincoln, John A. Perkins, O. H. K. Risley, Henry F. Royce, Elliott B. Sumner, Chester Tilden, Marcus L. Tryon, James Walden. *Willimantic*, Christopher Hempsted, Geo. W. Meloney.

WINDSOR. Richard D. Case, John B. Woodford.

WINDSOR LOCKS. Elijah Ashley, John W. Coogan, John B. Douglass, J. W. Johnson.

WOLCOTT. Henry Minor.

WOODBRIDGE. Daniel C. Augur.

WOODBURY. David S. Bull, Wm. Cothren, Scoville Nettleton, George F. Shelton.

WOODSTOCK. *North Woodstock*. Ezra C. May.

COUNTIES.

HARTFORD COUNTY.

Commissioners—Westell Russell, Hartford, 1882; Lucius G. Goodrich, Simsbury, 1883; Thaddeus H. Spencer, Suffield, 1884.

Clerk of Courts—Charles W. Johnson, Hartford.

Assistant Clerk—Francis Chambers, Hartford.

State Attorney—William Hamersley, Hartford.

Sheriff—Alva W. Spaulding, Hartford, to June 1, 1884.

Deputy Jailor—Apollos Fenn, Hartford.

Deputy Sheriffs.

Hartford, Charles A. Lord, Thomas B. Chapman; Bristol, Henry C. Butler; Collinsville, John E. Wheelock; East Hart-

ford, Arthur P. Moore; Granby, Albert Gillette; Hartland,
Albert N. Stillman; Manchester, George A. Bidwell, New Britain,
Henry C. Williams: So. Glastonbury, Sanford E. Sheffield;
Simsbury, John W. Phelps; Southington, John C. Lewis; Suf-
field, Webb E. Burbank; Warehouse Point, James Price, Jr.

Attorneys at Law.

[Those marked * are Commissioners of the Superior Court.]

HARTFORD. Sherman W. Adams, *David L. Aberdein,
Leverett N. Austin, *Henry S. Barbour, *Joseph L. Barbour,
Sylvester Barbour, E .B. Bennett, *John B. Betts, Charles H.
Briscoe, John H. Brocklesby,*John P. Bronk, Percy S. Bryant,
John R. Buck, Heury E. Burton, Wharton Butler, David S.
Calhoun, *Joseph G. Calhoun, Geo. Case, Uriah Case, Franklin
Chamberlin, *Francis Chambers, Charles R. Chapman,*Charles
H. Clark, Sidney E. Clark, F. E. Cleveland, Charles J. Cole,
*Goodwin Collier, William R. Cone, John W. Coogan, *Horace
Cornwall, John C. Day, Robert E. Day, *Samuel J. Day, S. C.
Dunham, Wm. L. Eaton, Wm. W. Eaton, Frederick Eberle,
Frederick G. Eberle, *Willard Eddy, Lucien Edwards, Arthur
F. Eggleston, Charles E. Fellowes, Francis Fellowes, H. B.
Freeman, F. G. Fuller, *George S. Gilman, *Edward Goodman,
David G. Gordon, *Daniel J. Griffin, *Charles E. Gross, Wm.
Hamersley, A. N. Hatheway, Joseph R. Hawley, John J. H.
Holcomb, *John Hooker, Chauncey Howard, R. D. Hubbard,
Alvan P. Hyde, *E. H. Hyde, Jr., Frank E. Hyde, *Wm.
Waldo Hyde, Chas. W. Johnson, Elisha Johnson, Samuel F.
Jones, *Charles M. Joslyn, *Cooke Lounsbury, Theodore
Lyman, T. M. Maltbie, Edwin E. Marvin, William L.
Matsou, George P. McLean, Richard McCloud, *W. J.
McConville, *Thomas McManus, *Hiram R. Mills, *Leonard
Morse, F. O. Mosebach, Hugh O'Flaherty, Charles H. Owen,
Jona E. Palmer, Francis H. Parker, John C. Parsons, Chas. E.
Perkins, Wilbert W. Perry, John T. Peters, *S. O. Prentice,
*Henry C. Robinson, Charles T. Russ, *Charles A. Safford,
George G. Sill, W. E. Simonds, *Authur D. Smith, *Lewis E.
Sperry, *Lewis E. Stanton, T E. Steele, Z. A. Storrs, *Geo.
G. Sumner, H. E. Taintor, J. Tallman, Stephen Terry, Albert
H. Walker, Roger Welles, Thomas G. Welles. *Edgar T. Welles,
Mahlon R. West, *E. S. Westcott. John H. White, *Edward S.
White, *Hiram Willey, John R. Wittig.
BERLIN. Frank A. Browne:
BLOOMFIELD. Jonathan E. Palmer, *Hiram R. Mills.
BRISTOL. *James P. Andrews, *Morgan W. Beach, Henry

A. Mitchell, Samuel P. Newell, George A. Goudy, *N. E. Pierce.

CANTON. *Collinsville*, Wm. W. Bidwell.

EAST HARTFORD. Percy S. Bryant.

ENFIELD. J. W. Johnson. *Thompsonville*, Charles H. Briscoe, *John H. Halliday, *John Hamlin.

FARMINGTON. *Thomas Cowles, J. J. Dempsey.

GLASTONBURY. William S. Goslee.

GRANBY. T. M. Maltbie, William C. Case.

MANCHESTER. *North Manchester*, Olin R. Wood, C. R. Hatheway. *Buckland*, Charles H. Owen.

NEW BRITAIN. Milton H. Bassett, Lyman S. Burr, V. B. Chamberlain, Austin Hart, Frank L. Hungerford, Philip J. Markley, Charles F. Mitchell, Henry Nash, Henry O. Nash, Julius H. Pease, John Walsh, Charles E. Woodruff.

NEWINGTON. Roger Welles.

PLAINVILLE. ·M. A. Nickerson.

ROCKY HILL. *Arthur D. Smith.

SOUTHINGTON. Marcus H. Holcomb, *Walter S. Merrell. *Plantsville*, *R. M. Douglass.

SUFFIELD. Leverett N. Austin.

WINDSOR LOCKS. J. W. Johnson, *J. B. Douglass.

Commissioners of Superior Court.

Lawyers marked with a * above, and the following:

HARTFORD. Charles H. Russell.

BRISTOL. Benjamin F. Hawley.

EAST HARTFORD. Samuel O. Goodwin.

ENFIELD. Franklin Smith.

FARMINGTON. Carlos L. Mason.

GLASTONBURY. R. E. Merrick.

MARLBOROUGH. Mary Hall.

NEW BRITAIN. Damel J. Savin, John W. Stoughton.

ROCKY HILL. G. O. Chambers.

SIMSBURY. N. Webster Holcomb.

WINDSOR. Ellsworth N. Phelps.

JUSTICES OF THE PEACE.

With the number of Jurors and Justices of the Peace to which each town is entitled.

HARTFORD, 47. David L. Aberdein, Sherman W. Adams, Sylvester Barbour, Edward B. Bennett, John H. Brocklesby,

John R. Buck, Henry E. Burton, George Case, Uriah Case, Charles R. Chapman, Charles J. Cole, Horace Cornwall, John C. Day, Sylvester C. Dunham, Wm. L. Eaton, Fred. Eberle, Willard Eddy, Arthur F. Eggleston, Charles E. Fellowes, H. B. Freeman, Daniel J. Griffin, Charles E. Gross, Wm. Hamersley, A. N. Hathaway, Wm. F. Henney, Elisha Johnson, Samuel F. Jones, Cooke Lounsbury, Theodore Lyman, Edwin E. Marvin, Leonard Morse, Richard McCloud, Hugh O'Flaherty, John C. Parsons, Charles E. Perkins, John T. Peters, Samuel O. Prentice, George G. Sill, Lewis E. Stanton, Timothy E. Steele, Henry E. Taintor, James H. Tallman, Stephen Terry, Mahlon R. West, J. Hurlburt White.

AVON, 6. James E. Lusk, Philemon R. Day, Chester R. Woodford, Ludwig M. N. Wolf, James N. Bishop, Leverett F. Webster.

BERLIN, 10. Albert A. Barnes, W. W. Norton, John O. Carroll, George Taylor, Henry Hollister, Andrew J. Warner, John R. Hooker, Franklin Strong, George H. Gray, John Maloy.

BLOOMFIELD, 8. Samuel B. Newberry, Martin H. Field, Francis G. Barber, Curtis H. Case, Nathan F. Miller, Henry C. Hoskins, John E. Cox, Norris Holcomb.

BRISTOL, 15. S. P. Newell, George A. Gowdy, Laporte Hubbell, Hiram H. Hurlburt, Asahel Brockett, Henry Beckwith, Gad Norton, S. M. Sutliff, Asaph C. Fuller, Morgan W. Beach, M. M. Woodford, Timothy E. Hawley, Noble E. Pierce, Augustus H. Warner.

BURLINGTON, 6. Norris W. Bunnell, Romeo Elton, Geo. W. Pratt, Anthony Moore, Jr., George R. Hegeman, Seth Keeney.

CANTON, 10. Wm. W. Bidwell, Wm. E. Simonds, Chas. Blair, Chas. S. Osborn, Wm. G. Hallock, Oliver C. Adams, Julius E. Case, Wells A. Lawton, Anson W. Bristol, Watson Case.

EAST GRANBY, 9. Isaac P. Owen, Cicero H. Merwin, Richard H. Phelps, Charles A. Tudor, Joel B. Holcomb, James H. Viets.

EAST HARTFORD, 13. Henry Albro, Wm. M. Stanley, Seth Bisley, Edward O. Goodwin, W. C. Cummings, Ralph Risley, David A. Tuttle, John Foley, J. K. Hall, George A. Williams, E. J. Carroll, Geo. H. Goodwin.

EAST WINDSOR, 14. Jabez S. Allen, Henry L. Barnes, Nelson S. Osborn, Geo. E. Wadsworth, Benjamin L. Bissell, Chas. A. Bissell, Joseph T. Hull, Francis Gowdy.

ENFIELD, 20. Charles H. Briscoe, J. Warren Johnson, Roswell D. Parsons, A. D. Bridge, Horace Patten, R. D. Parsons,

4

F. E. Ely, S. Hathaway, Theo. I. Pease, Joseph N. Allen, Chas. E. Price, C. F. Morrison, Chas. M. Abbe.

FARMINGTON, 14. Thomas Cowles, Jr., Chas. L. Whitman, Martin L. Parsons, Ezra C. Ayres, John P. Lewis, George Dunham, Thomas L. Porter. Alpheus Porter, Lucius D. Pond.

GLASTONBURY, 17. George C. Andrews, Albert A. Bogue, Henry B. Doane, William S. Goslee, Nathaniel W. French, Chas. J. Loomer, Norman W. Strickland, Thos. H. L. Talcott, John W. Hubbard, Justus R. Morgan, Geo. A. Treat, Henry E. Loomis, Edgar Hale, Thomas S. Curtis, Samuel Hollister.

GRANBY, 13. Watson Dewey, Theodore M. Maltbie, Wallace Kendall, Asel H. Rice, Denison Case, Lucian Reed, John Burwell, John W. Ruick, William C. Case, R. J. Hayes, A. G. Harger, M. A. Colton.

HARTLAND, 6. J. Gates Miller, Flavel C. Newton.

MANCHESTER, 13. Walter W. Cowles, Daniel Wadsworth, George W. Cheney, Chas. S. Cheney, Robert N. Strong, Wm. B. Lincoln, Rufus R. Dimock, Olin R. Wood, James F. Bunce, Mason Agard.

MARLBOROUGH, 5. Amos B. Latham, Henry D. Barrows, Alfred Haling.

NEW BRITAIN, 30. James H. Beach, Austin Hart, Julius H. Pease, Michael Gray, Arthur W. Rice, Thomas Begley, Henry O. Nash, Chas. E. Mitchell, Frank L. Hungerford, James W. Ringrose, L. S. Burr, David G. Gordon, Wm. Seiring, John Walsh, Chas. E. Woodruff, Wm. E. Latham, V. B. Chamberlain, Milton H. Bassett.

NEWINGTON, 8. John S. Kirkham, Geo. E. Chidley, Samuel A. Steele, Elias M. Steele.

PLAINVILLE, 5. Major A. Nickerson, T. G. Wright, D. W. Fox.

ROCKY HILL, 6. Eugene R. Silliman, Henry R. Taylor.

SIMSBURY, 14. Dudley B. McLean, Jeffery O. Phelps, Chas. L. Roberts, Alonzo G. Case, Gilbert A. Taylor, Michael A. Flynn, Asa Haskins, Thos. R. Case.

SOUTHINGTON, 11. John J. Barnes, Marcus H. Holcomb, Walter S. Merrell, A. M. Lewis, Seth E. Frost, Charles S. Woodruff.

SOUTH WINDSOR, 9. Seth Vinton, Bradford A. Grant, Lewis Sperry, Edmund Watson.

SUFFIELD, 15. Samuel White, Simeon B. Kendall, H. K. Ford, E. J. Copley, H. G. Leonard, James B. Rose.

WEST HARTFORD, 8. Samuel J. Bestor, Benj. S. Bishop, Jas. S. Flagg, Henry Talcott, Chas. H. Flagg, Adolph C. Sternberg, Timothy Sedgwick, 2d.

WETHERSFIELD, 13. Albert N. Galpin, Ebenezer G. Havens, Wm. W. Adams, John Welles.

WINDSOR, 10. John L. Clark, Oliver S. Mills, Eli S. Hough.

WINDSOR LOCKS, 6. John P. Healey, Elijah Ashley, John B. Douglass, John W. Coogan, S. B. Douglass.

NEW HAVEN COUNTY.

Commissioners—Lewis B. Perkins, Oxford, 1882; Hiram Jacobs, East Haven, 1883; Marcus E. Baldwin, Woodbridge, 1884.

Clerk of Courts—Arthur D. Osborne, New Haven.

Assistant Clerks—Jonathan Ingersoll, Edward A. Anketell, New Haven; Edward F. Cole, Waterbury.

State Attorney—Tilton E. Doolittle, New Haven.

Sheriff—John C. Byxbee, New Haven; to June 1, 1884.

Deputy Jailor—George A. Stevens, New Haven.

Deputy Sheriffs.

New Haven, William B. Catlin, Jonathan W. Pond, Wm. E. Higgins; Meriden, Linus Birdsey; Derby, Henry Whipple; Guilford, Elisha Hart; Madison, Wm. S. Hull; Milford, Samuel A. Miles; Naugatuck, Wm. Brophy; Seymour, David Tucker; Wallingford, George W. Morse; Waterbury, John H. Hayes; Branford, Henry D. Linsley; Southbury, Theodore F. Wheeler; Orange, James H. Peck; Cheshire, Robert Cook; Ansonia, J. H. Whiting.

County Treasurer—Harmanus M. Welch, New Haven.

Attorneys at Law.

NEW HAVEN. *John W. Alling, *S. W. F. Andrews, *Edward A. Anketell, *E. P. Arvine, *Adolph Asher, William W. Bailey, *Simeon E. Baldwin, *Fred'k W. Babcock, John S. Beach, *Wm. L. Bennett, *Stuart Bidwell, *James Bishop, *Henry T. Blake, *C. C. Blatchley, *Levi N. Blydenburg, Charles F. Bollman, Edward A. Bowers, John W. Bristol, *Louis H. Bristol, *Samuel L. Bronson, *Charles K. Bush, John K. Beach, *Julius C. Cable, *Wm. C. Case, *Wilson H. Clark, *James G. Clark, L. W. Cleaveland, *James F. Colby, *Geo. R. Cooley, *Hugh Dailey, *Lucius P. Deming, *George L. Dickerman, *T. E. Doolittle, *Edwin C. Dow, *Cornelius T. Driscoll, D. Cady Eaton, *William W. Farnam, Emerson Y. Foote, *Charles H. Fowler, *John S. Fowler, *Timothy J. Fox, John C. Gallagher, *Chas. K. Gorham, *George M. Gunn, *E. Edwin Hall, *H. F. Hall, Jr., *S. D. Hall, *Chas. S. Hamilton,

*Henry B. Harrison, Lynde Harrison, James I. Hayes, *John
C. Hollister, *Hobart L. Hotchkiss, *L. M. Hubbard, *Savillian
R. Hull, *Chas. R. Ingersoll, *Francis G. Ingersoll, *Jonathan
Ingersoll, *Thomas C. Ingersoll, Charles Ives, *Abel B. Jacocks,
*William DeW. Kellogg, *Wm. H. Kenyon, *Patrick F.
Kiernan, Henry W. Lamb, *William H. Law, Jr., *Edward L.
Linsley, *Burton Mansfield, *Samuel A. Marsden, *Charles
B. Matthewman, *John B. Mills, Wm. J. Mills, *Eli Mix, *Luzon
B. Morris, Charles T. Morse, *Joseph B. Morse, *Lyman E.
Munson, *Henry G. Newton, *Arthur D. Osborne, *George W.
Osborn, Robert H. Osborn, *Henry E. Pardee, Albert D.
Penney, *L. L. Phelps, *John P. Phillips, *Rufus S. Pickett,
*Henry C. Platt, *Johnson T. Platt, *Joseph D. Plunkett,
*Edwin Purrington, *Abraham H. Robertson, *Wm. C. Robin-
son, *John A. Robinson, *Edward H. Rogers, *Henry Rogers,
*Henry D. Russell, *Talcott H. Russell, Walter J. Scott,
*Joseph Sheldon, Edwin A. Smith, *Siegwart Spier. *David
Strouse, *Henry Stoddard, *Wm. B. Stoddard, *Wm. W.
Stone, *John P. Studley, *Charles L. Swan, *James S.
Thompson, *Wm. K. Townsend, W. J. Trowbridge, Dwight
W. Tuttle, *Grove J. Tuttle, *Julius Twiss, *Morris F. Tyler,
*George A. Tyler, *Charles L. Ullman, *Simeon H. Wagner,
*John B. Ward, *Geo. H. Watrous, *Francis Wayland, *James
H. Webb, *Chas. R. Whedon, *Alfred N. Wheeler, *Charles A.
White, *Henry D. White, *Roger S. White, *Oliver S. White,
*John H. Whiting, *James A. Wood, *Dexter R. Wright,
*William A. Wright, *Samuel A. York, *Edmund Zacher.
Fair Haven, *Curtis S. Bushnell.

    BRANFORD. *Wm. A. Wright.
    CHESHIRE. *William Kelsey, *George Hine, *Robert W.
Wright.
    DERBY. *Birmingham*, *William S. Downs, Wm. E. Downs,
*Edwin B. Gager, *Seabury B. Platt, David Torrance, *Wm.
B. Wooster, *Wm. H. Williams. *Ansonia*, *John D. Ballou,
*Charles Reed, *Verenice Munger, *Daniel E. McMahon.
    GUILFORD. Edward R. Landon, *Hollis T. Walker, Edwin
C. Woodruff.
    HAMDEN. *Charles S. Everest.
    MERIDEN. *John Barrett, *Wilbur F. Davis, Geo. A. Fay,
Frank S. Fay, Willis I. Fenn, *Chas. P. Ives, *Chas. W. Mann,
*E. A. Merriman, *Franklin Platt, James P. Platt, *Orville H.
Platt, *William Slattery, George W. Smith, *Chas. H. Shaw,
John Q. Thayer.
    NAUGATUCK. *Henry C. Baldwin, *Burton A. Peck, *Wm.
Kennedy, *J. M. Sweeney.

NORTH HAVEN. Edward L. Linsley.
SOUTHBURY. Granville T. Pierce.
SEYMOUR. *Harris B. Munson, *W. H. Williams.
WALLINGFORD. *Leverett M. Hubbard, *O. H. D. Fowler,
*Seymour D. Hall, *Henry F. Hall, Jr., *Eli S. Ives.
WATERBURY. Henry I. Boughton, *Lucien F. Burpee,
*Charles A. Colley, *George H. Cowell, *Edward F. Cole,
Thomas Donahue, 2d, C. W. Gillette, *Franklin C. Holmes,
Stephen W. Kellogg, Greene Kendrick, Robert A. Lowe, *Henry
R. Morrill, *H. B. Munson, *Martin Myers, John O'Neil, Jr.,
*Chas. G. Root, *Elliott J. Stoddard, *Geo. E. Terry, *Daniel
F. Webster, John W. Webster.
WOODBRIDGE. * Wilson H. Clark.

Commissioners of Superior Court.

Lawyers marked with a * above and the following:

NEW HAVEN. John F. Bishop, Elisha Blackman, Henry A.
Blakeman, Frederick Botsford, William D. Brinley, Edwin M.
Clark, Horace Day, John E. Earle, Jacob E. Emery, Harvey S.
Nettleton, William P. Niles, Seth T. Seeley, John Tuttle, Wil-
liam H. Wheeler, Samuel A. Galpin, Frederick Morris, Allen
Mix, Jr., Lucius W. Fitch, Edward Y. Foote, Phillip Goodhart,
Samuel Halliwell, Robert L. Hazard, Horace P. Hoadley, Henry
C. Kingsley, B. L. Lambert, Birdsey C. Lake, William H.
Leishman, Frank Maley, Peter McQuaid, Robert T. Merwin,
Caleb Mix, Gardner Morse, Lewis E. Osborn, Sidney B. Oviatt,
Joseph B. Sargent, Charles R. Spiegel, Edward F. Stevens,
George Terry, Charles H. Webb.
BEACON FALLS. John A. Coe, Julius A. Hart.
BETHANY. Edwin N. Clark.
BRANFORD. Henry Rogers, Elizur Rogers, Eli F. Rogers,
Charles F. Hotchkiss.
DERBY. Egbert Bartlett, William B. Bristol, Charles E.
Clark, Robert C. Narramore, Robert Peck, C. N. Rogers, Albert
F. Sherwood, Nathan C. Treat.
MERIDEN. John E. Durand, Charles H. Sawyer.
MIDDLEBURY. George S. Pope.
MILFORD. Harvey Beach, C. Sleeman Coan, George H. Fur-
man, Samuel B. Gunn, Samuel A. Mills, Thomas W. Stow.
NAUGATUCK. George D. Bissell, James T. Breen.
NORTH HAVEN. Whitney Elliott.
OXFORD. Nathan J. Wilcoxson.
SEYMOUR. S. Hart Culver.

WALLINGFORD. James T. Redmond.
WATERBURY. Benjamin Hallas, Edward G. Kilduff, Edwin
A. Lum, John B. Scott, Bryan J. Smith, Evelyn L. Smith,
Noah B. Tuttle.
WOODBRIDGE. William H. Warner.

JUSTICES OF THE PEACE.

NEW HAVEN, 56. Earliss P. Arvine, Adolph Asher, James
Bishop, C. F. Bollman, Sylvanus Butler, George R. Cooley, Jos-
lyn P. Cleveland, Hugh Dailey, John S. Fowler, Timothy J.
Fox, Hobart L. Hotchkiss, Jonathan Ingersoll, Charles T.
Morse, Eli Mix, S. Arthur Marsden, A. Heaton Robertson.
Charles L. Swan, Jr., John P. Studley, Julius Twiss, Charles
R. Whedon, E. Zacher, Samuel A. York, M. F. Brennan, T. C.
Ingersoll, Frank F. Kiernan, Alfred N. Wheeler, John C. Gal-
lagher, Herman Thrall, Siegwart Spier, Samuel L. Bronson,
Cornelius T. Driscoll, E. Gilbert Austin, Frederick W. Babcock,
S. Harrison Wagner, Levi N. Blydenburgh, Royal T. Smith,
Luzon B. Morris, William J. Mills, Willis G. Judson, Joseph D.
Plunkett, Michael Herrity, John Tuttle, James I. Hayes, Ezra
B. Dibble, David Strouse, Michael E. Tracy, James H. Good-
sell, George A. Tyler, Wallace N. Robbins, Burton Mansfield,
John B. Mills, William H. Law, Jr., John W. Geary, James A.
Wood, Daniel Healey, Leopold Besser.
BEACON FALLS, 8. Herbert C. Baldwin, Buel Buckingham.
BETHANY, 7. Samuel R. Woodward, E. S. Hotchkiss, Na-
than Clark.
BRANFORD, 8. William E. Hatch, Marcus O. Babcock, Ed-
ward H. Rogers, Wm. A. Wright.
CHESHIRE, 12. Theo. A. Cook, Jesse Humiston, William
Kelsey.
DERBY, 18. John W. Storrs, David Torrance, Luzon Rowell,
Verenice Munger, John B. Quilinan, A. Leninger, Charles Reed,
John Lindley, Daniel E. McMahon, John C. Reilly, Seabury B.
Platt, Mark Buckingham, John B. Gardner, W. S. Downs, Ed-
win B. Gager, William J. Clark, John D. Ballou.
EAST HAVEN, 9. Hiram Jacobs, Henry Smith, Dwight W.
Tuttle, Grove J. Tuttle, S. W. F. Andrews.
GUILFORD, 14. Edward R. Landon, John R. Rossiter, John
Beattie, Henry E. Norton, J. Seymour Benton, Hollis T. Walker,
Harvey Elliott, Richard M. Leete, A. G. Hull, Lynde Harrison,
Leverett C. Stone, Edwin C. Woodruff.
HAMDEN, 11. Horace Tuttle, Bela A. Mann, Andrew J.
Doolittle, James H. Webb.

MADISON, 11. Henry B. Wilcox, John H. Meigs, John P. Hopson, Horace G. Hill, Henry E. Stone, M. A.Wilcox, Samuel D. Cruttenden, C. Henry Whedon, Washington Bristol.

MERIDEN, 17. George A. Fay, E. A. Merriman, Charles H. Shaw, J. P. Platt, F. S. Fay, Selah A. Hull, J. C. Hinsdale, Levi E. Coe, C. J. Heineman. J. Q. Thayer, G. W. Smith, C. W. Mann, M. J. Slattery, W. F. Davis.

MIDDLEBURY, 5. Moses W. Terrill, Alva B. Coe, P. M. Augur, T. H. Coles, H. W. Hurlbut, J. T. Inglis.

MILFORD, 14. John T. Minor, James W. Beach, Elias Clark, P. S. Bristol, H. J. Bristol, David Miles, Harvey S. Clark.

NAUGATUCK, 9. Hial S. Stevens, H. G. Denniston, Homer Twitchell, Edward B. Mallette, George A. Fenton, Miner S. Baldwin, Herbert A. Hard, Luther S. Platt.

NORTH BRANFORD, 6. Charles Page, F. C. Bartholomew, Edward Smith.

NORTH HAVEN, 8. Andrew F. Austin, Cyrus Cheeney, Jesse O. Eaton, J. Boardman Smith.

ORANGE, 8. Benj. T. Clark, Wm. H. Talmadge, George W. Metcalf, Elias T. Main, Donaldson S. Thompson, James R. Ayres, Stephen E. Booth, Sheldon J. Alling.

OXFORD, 10. David Hawley, Lewis B. Perkins, Nathan C. Riggs, Clark E. Lum, Benjamin Nichols, Harpin A. Lum, Samuel L. Tuttle, William H. Williams.

PROSPECT, 5. Benjamin B. Brown.

SEYMOUR, 10. John W. Rogers, F. M. Clemens, H. S. Chamberlain, George Leavenworth, A. Storrs.

SOUTHBURY, 10. Henry S. Wheeler, William S. Hooper, Isaac Watson, Granville T. Pierce, Charles Hotchkiss.

WALLINGFORD, 14. Franklin Johnson, O. I. Martin, Hezekiah Hall, Patrick McKenna, Charles D. Yale, George Cook, Turhand Cook, Edward F. Cook, Jared P. Kimberly, Homer R. Johnson, Charles E. Smith, Patrick Mooney, Matthew Haviland, Robert B. Wallace.

WATERBURY, 22. Michael Carroll, George H. Cowell, Elliott J. Fenn, Charles G. Root, Frederick A. Spencer, Daniel F. Webster, Franklin L. Welton, Nelson J. Welton, Henry I. Boughton, Charles W. Gillette, Stephen W. Kellogg, John O'Neill, Jr., John W. Webster, George E. Terry, Thomas Donahue, 2d, George L. Fields, Edward F. Cole, Henry R. Morrill, Greene Kendrick.

WOLCOTT, 5. Frederick L. Nichols, Amos M. Johnson, Benjamin F. Finch.

WOODBRIDGE, 7. Theo. R. Baldwin, Wilson H. Clark, Samuel F. Perkins, Marcus E. Baldwin, William H. Warner.

NEW LONDON COUNTY.

Commissioners—David R. Stevens, New London, 1882; Paul B. Greene, Norwich, 1883; Erastus Geer, Lebanon, 1884.

Clerk of Courts—John C. Averill, Norwich.

Assistant Clerk—John C. Kellogg, Norwich.

State Attorney—Thomas M. Waller, New London.

Sheriff—Frank Hawkins, Griswold, to June 1, 1884.

Deputy Sheriffs.

Norwich, Joab B. Rogers, Silas H. Dewey; New London, George P. Hinckley; North Stonington, Gilbert Billings; Colchester, Addison M. Taintor; Mystic Bridge, John H. Hoxie; Lebanon, Asa C. Peckham; Montville, George N. Wood; Stonington, George R. Green.

Deputy Jailors—E. H. Beckwith, Norwich; George G. Fitch, New London.

County Treasurer—Leonard Hempstead, New London.

Attorneys at Law.

NEW LONDON. William Belcher, Augustus Brandagee, Chas. W. Butler, N. A. Chapman, Robert Coit, Wm. C. Crump, John G. Crump, A. S. Darrow, Andrew C. Lippitt, A. C. Lippitt, Jr., Bryan F. Mahan, John P. C. Mather, Samuel Park, G. F. Raymond, William M. Stark, John A. Tibbits, Thomas M. Waller, Ralph Wheeler.

NORWICH. *John C. Averill, Wm. L. Brewer, Willis A. Briscoe, *Lucius Brown, *Frank T. Brown, *Franklin H. Brown, Amos A. Browning, Henry H. Burnham, *Richard E. Cash, *J. B. Coit, Charles W. Comstock, *Wm. S. Congdon, J. J. Desmond, George W. Foote, Gardiner Greene, Jr., Jeremiah Halsey, Edward Harland, S. T. Holbrook, William H. Jennings, John C. Kellogg, Henry Latham, Solomon Lucas, Ebenezer Learned, Albert F. Park, Webster Park, Donald G. Perkins, Calvin L. Rawson, Frank A. Robinson, George C. Ripley, *Wm. H. Shields, Charles F. Thayer, *S. H. Thresher, *Seneca S. Thresher, *Edward H. Thomas, Allen Tenny, J. M. Thayer, John T. Wait, O. P. Wattles, David Young.

COLCHESTER. Erastus S. Day, Joel H. Reed.

GROTON. John J. Copp. *Mystic River*, Lemuel Clift, *A. P. Tanner.

OLD LYME. *P. O. Lyme*, Daniel Chadwick, James Griswold, J. G. Perkins.

STONINGTON. George Sharswood, Jr., H. A. Hull. *Mystic*, *John B. Grinnell, Albert Denison.
Westerly, R. I., *Francis Sheffield, A. B. Crafts.
WATERFORD. A. S. Darrow, N. A. Chapman.

Commissioners of Superior Court.

Lawyers marked with a * above, and the following:

NEW LONDON. Anson Brown.
NORWICH. H. A. Baker, William W. Barnes, G. H. Bottom, J. K. Brewer, John T. Brown, A. A. Browning, Elbridge C. Cook, Gardiner Greene, Jr., Wm. H. Jennings, Jr., Gilbert D. Lamb, George S. Lovelace, James Ritchie, F. A. Robinson, H. B. Winship.
EAST LYME. Francis W. Bolles.
FRANKLIN. T. H. C. Kingsbury.
GROTON. Philo Little, Orrin E. Miner.
GRISWOLD. Wm. A. Weeks.
MONTVILLE. Henry A. Baker.
PRESTON. Asahel Tanner.
SPRAGUE. J. B. C. Du Plessis, Charles H. Ladd, A. D. Wilcox.
STONINGTON. Solomon L. Edwards, Peleg Noyes, Charles Perrin, Thomas D. Sheffield, George D. Stanton.

JUSTICES OF THE PEACE.

NEW LONDON, 30. Augustus Brandagee, John P. C. Mather, John H. Crocker, John C. Crump, John G. Crump, Ferris W. Douglass, Oscar F. Hewitt, Walter Learned, Bryan F. Mahan, Wm. N. Stark, John A. Tibbitts, Ralph Wheeler, G. F. Raymond, Wm. Belcher, Reuben Lord, Jr., T. M. Waller, Chas. W. Butler, A. C. Lippitt, Jr., A. C. Lippitt, Isaac W. Thompson.
NORWICH. John C. Averill, Frank T. Brown, Franklin H. Brown, John T. Brown, Lucius Brown, Amos A. Browning, Henry H. Burnham, Walter H. Burr, Charles H. Carpenter, Elbridge C. Cook, Jeremiah J. Desmond, Increase W. Carpenter, William S. Congdon, Paul B. Greene, Gardner Greene, Jr., Jeremiah Halsey, Edward Harland, Supply T. Holbrook, Wm. H. Jennings, Jr., John C. Kellogg, Ebenezer Learned, Solomon Lucas, Albert F. Park, Webster Park, Donald G. Perkins, George C. Ripley, Wm. H. Shields, Allen Tenny, John M. Thayer, Seneca S. Thresher, Wm. C. Tucker, Oliver P. Wattles, avid Young.

BOZRAH, 5. Neremiah C. Cook, Joshua C. Leffingwell, Chas.
A. Johnson, M. S. Gardner, Wm. Hall.

COLCHESTER, 13. Erastus S. Day, Joel H. Reed, Fràncis L.
Carrier, Benjamin Adams, Asa Brainard, C. C. Palmer, Leander
Chapman, Demas Carrier, R. R. Carrington.

EAST LYME, 7. Nelson L. Stewart, G. P. Rose, A. E. S.
Bush, Daniel Calkins, F. B. Way, Lyman Bacon.

FRANKLIN, 5. Henry W. Kingsley, Amos F. Royce, E. Eugene Ayer, B. F. Huntington.

GRISWOLD, 11. Barton C. Kegwin, J. G. Bill, A. Edmond,
Wm. Soule, Joseph Rood, O. Hinkley, E. C. Kegwin, Daniel L.
Phillips, Samuel Barber, George Tyler, Wm. P. Young.

GROTON, 21. William H. Potter, Chas. P. Chipman, Seth N.
Williams, Nelson Morgan, Nathan S. Fish, Roswell Brown,
Elias H. Potter, Amos Clift, Simeon A. Chapman.

LEBANON, 13. George D. Spencer, Walter G. Kingsley, N. C.
Barker, Wm. A. Fuller, H. A. Spafard.

LEDYARD, 10. Charles A. Satterlee, Palmer Allyn, Russell
Gallup, James A. Stoddard, John Hurlbutt, Dwight A. Gallup,
George H. O'Brien, Israel Allyn, T. A. Avery, Isaac W. Geer.

LISBON, 5. Henry Lyon, Russell W. Fitch, Patrick Connell.

LYME, 7. Fred. Fosdick, B. P. Bill, J. G. Ely.

MONTVILLE, 10. M. V. B. Brainard, Geo. O. Gadbois, Wm.
Fitch, Elisha M. Rogers, Jedediah R. Gay, 2d, John L. Comstock, Wm. F. Thacher.

NORTH STONINGTON, 11. Charles P. White, Francis H.
Brown, George N. Edwards.

OLD LYME, 7. James Griswold, J. G. Perkins, E. Sheffield,
E. C. Smith, C. L. Morley, John Smith, T. S. Swan.

PRESTON, 10. James F. Forsyth, John W. Gallup, Hugh
King, Samuel Johnson, James H. Fitch.

SALEM, 5. John R. Treadway, Charles A. Williams.

SPRAGUE, 7. Richard J. Brophy, Nathan Bennett, W. P.
Kelley, Nathan Geer, John Witter, Chas. T. Hazen, George J.
Lawton.

STONINGTON, 22. Albert Dennison, M. S. Greene, Albigence Hyde, J. A. Lamb, Geo. E. Tripp, Elias Williams.

WATERFORD, 12. James Daigan, Nathaniel A. Chapman,
Richard Tinker, Martin G. Rogers, W. F. Scott, B. A. Crocker,
Gilbert Rogers, G. G. Hammond, L. N. Williams, James B.
Cattell, Joseph Peabody, G. W. Chamberlain.

FAIRFIELD COUNTY.

Commissioners—Charles B. Wheeler, Monroe, 1882; John O· Paige, Sherman, 1883; Nathan M. Belden, Wilton, 1884.

Clerk of Courts—Henry T. Blake, Bridgeport.

Assistant Clerks—E. Stewart Sumner, Bridgeport; David B. Booth, Danbury.

State Attorney—Samuel Fessenden, Stamford.

Sheriff—Charles H. Crosby, Bridgeport, to June 1, 1884.

Deputy Sheriffs.

Bridgeport, Wm. Scofield, Wm. E. Desbrow; Bethel, Henry C. Judd; Danbury, Harris L. Crofut; Fairfield, Edward Henshaw; Greenwich, William S. Reynolds; Huntington, Selah B. Blakeman; Monroe, Chas. S. French; Newtown, Beach Nichols, New Canaan, Russell L. Hall; Norwalk, John F. Raymond; So. Norwalk; David Dayton; Stamford, Samuel McCoun; Stratford, James H. Blakeman; Westport, Frederick Kemper.

Deputy Jailor—Chas. H. Hoyt, Danbury.

County Treasurer—W. C. Quintard, Norwalk.

Attorneys at Law.

BRIDGEPORT. *R. C. Ambler, *Wm. J. Beecher, Henry T. Blake, Stephen S. Blake, *Morris B. Beardsley, *A. B. Beers, John A. Boughton, *Ebenezer Burr, Jr., *Chas. S. Canfield, *J. C. Chamberlin, Joseph Collins, Wm. A. Dalton, *Dan'l Davenport, *R. E. DeForest, *Charles A. Doten, *Theo. W. Downs, *V. R. C. Giddings, Edwin F. Hall, *F. B. Hall, *David F. Hollister, *F. L. Holt, *Francis Ives, *J. A. Joyce, *Bernard Keating, *William H. Kelsey, F. G. Lewis, D. B. Lockwood, Michael McGuinness, L. N. Middelbrook, *Dwight Morris, Wm. H. Noble, Frank P. Norman, *W. E. Norton, *Eugene B. Peck, John J. Phelan, *J. W. Parrott, Frank L. Rodgers, *Henry S. Sanford, *William K. Seeley, Morris W. Seymour, *William R. Shelton, *Charles Sherwood, *Lucius M. Slade, Wm. H. Stevenson, E. S. Sumner, *E. Stewart Sumner, *Goodwin Stoddard, *Sam'l B. Sumner, A. M. Tallmadge, Amos S. Treat, Curtis Thompson, *Morris Tuttle, Geo. W. Warner, *Levi Warner, Mark D. Wilber, *Wm. C. Wildman.

DANBURY. *Roger Averill, *A. T. Bates, *David B. Booth, *Lyman D. Brewster, *Wm. Burke, *J. R. Farnham, *Benezet A. Hough, William A. Leonard, *Theodore McDonald, Howard B. Scott, *Howard W. Taylor, *Wm. F. Taylor, O. A. G. Todd, *Samuel Tweedy, *John J. Walsh, *Granville M. White.

BROOKFIELD. Samuel Sherman.

EASTON. Charles R. Dudley.

FAIRFIELD. Wm. B. Glover. *Southport*, Chas. M. Gilman, John H. Perry.

GREENWICH. *H. W. R. Hoyt, Myron L. Mason, *Frederick A. Hubbard, R. Jay Walsh.

NEWTOWN. *William J. Beecher. *Sandy Hook*, *William O'Hara, *James A. Wilson.

NORWALK. Alfred E. Austin, *Benjamin F. Birdsall, *Joseph F. Foote, J. B. Hurlbutt, John E. Keeler, *John H. Perry, F. W. Perry, *Albert Relyea, John S. Seymour, *William R. Smith, *Levi Warner, *Asa B. Woodward, *Joseph W. Wilson. *South Norwalk*, *Nelson Taylor, *Nelson Taylor, Jr., *Franklin H. Sage, *E. B. Goodell, *Allan W. Paige.

STAMFORD. Galen A. Carter, Jr., *Samuel H. Cohen, *Julius B. Curtis, *Joshua B. Ferris, *H. Stanley Finch, *Samuel Fessenden, Nathaniel R. Hart, *John E. Keeler, *Michael Kenealy, *James H. Olmsted, *Clarence L. Reid, *Edwin L. Scofield, Wm. C. Strowbridge, Jr., Charles P. Woodbury.

STRATFORD. *V. R. C. Giddings, Henry E. Smith.

TRUMBULL. *R. C. Ambler.

WESTPORT. Edward M. Lees, Edward J. Taylor. *Green's Farms*, *Albert Relyea.

WILTON. George A. Davenport. *Cannon's Station*, J. Belden Hurlbutt.

Commissioners of Superior Court.

Lawyers marked with a * above, and the following.

BRIDGEPORT. J. E. Dunham, F. J. Hughes, Bradley H. Hull, John F. Noble, John Stevenson, Wm. M. Staples, J. S. Wessels, A. B. Clute, Walter Goddard, R. B. Lacey.

DANBURY. William A. Ely, Timothy Jones, Joseph A. Joyce, Wm. A. Leonard, George Wakeman.

BETHEL. George S. Crofut, Frederick Shepard.

BROOKFIELD. E. H. Northrop.

FAIRFIELD. Henry Bradley, David Wheeler.

GREENWICH. Daniel S. Mead, Jr., Charles E. Merritt, C. A. Newman.

HUNTINGTON. Horace Wheeler.

MONROE. Lacey Higgins.

NEW CANAAN. R. L. Hall, B. D. Purdy, F. M. Bliss.

NORWALK. Charles Olmstead, Silas P. Tuttle, E. L. Stevenson, O. E. Wilson.

RIDGEFIELD. George H. Boughton.

REDDING. Lemuel Sanford, Stebbins Baxter.

SHERMAN. Daniel B. Mallory.

STAMFORD. David H. Clark, B. F. Hatheway, E. W. Riker, Francis R. Leeds.

STRATFORD. Albert Wilcoxson, Eugene Morehouse.

WESTPORT. Joseph G. Hyatt, S. B. Sherwood, Henry W. Lyon, Jonathan C. Wheeler, Rufus Wakeman.

JUSTICES OF THE PEACE.

BRIDGEPORT, 27. Samuel B. Sumner, John B. Pinkerman, Robert E. DeForest, Charles S. Canfield, Eugene B. Peck, Fred. H. Stratton, Morris W. Seymour, Goodwin Stoddard, Edwin G. Sanford, Simon R. Libby, John C. Hall, David B. Lockwood, Walter C. Nevers, Daniel M. Ford, Rodney S. Barrett, Elias Tibballs, Morris B. Beardsley, Francis P. Norman, Amos Fuller, Julius J. Gorham, Henry Dikeman, Marshall E. Morris, Charles Sherwood, William R. Shelton, Bradley H. Hull, Edward T. Rew.

DANBURY, 17. Thomas B. Fanton, Arthur H. Averill, Benjamin O. N. Rockwell, Benezet A. Hough, David B. Booth, Lyman D. Brewster, Howard B. Scott, Samuel Tweedy, Samuel A. Barnum, Barnum P. Jackson, Russel W. Hoyt, George McArthur, James Ryder, Edwin B. Harris, Theodore Lyon, Howard W. Taylor.

BETHEL, 12. E. R. Barnum, A. H. Dimond, Samuel A. Couch, A. J. Whitney.

BROOKFIELD. Harvey Roe, Henry S. Stevens, Benjamin Griffen, David H. Mecker, Edwin G. Terrill, John H. Barlow, Ezra A. Somers.

DARIEN, 8. Nathan Dauchy, James B. Selleck, C. W. Lounsbury, Thaddeus Bell, Edward R. Farnham.

EASTON, 8. Geo. S. Platt, Joseph W. Johnson, George Freeborn.

FAIRFIELD, 18. Wm. Lyon, David Wheeler, John H. Perry, Wm. B. Glover, Wm. Coleman, Wm. Bradley, Francis L. Sherwood, Alva Jennings, John M. Brothnell, Matthew V. Woodward.

GREENWICH, 21. Amasa A. Marks, Philip W. Holmes, Alfred A. Rundle, George A. Lockwood, Charles E. Studwell, Edward Greenwood, Joseph H. Marshall, Joseph E. Russell.

HUNTINGTON, 7. Joseph Tomlinson, Wells Allis, Daniel S. Clarke.

MONROE, 8. Ernest L. Staples, F. D. Hollister, John G. Stevens.

NEW CANAAN, 14. Joseph F. Silliman, Frank M. Bliss, Levi S. Weed.

NEW FAIRFIELD, 5. B. B. Kellogg, John J. Treadwell, Geo. W. Wheeler, Edward Treadwell, H. H. Wildman.

NEWTOWN, 17. John M. Beardsley, Silas B. Wheeler, Geo. W. Bradley, Samuel Barnum, Charles W. Dayton, Norman Northrop, Michael Cavanagh, John Stilson, Eli J. Morris, Geo. Botsford.

NORWALK, 20. Asa B. Woodward, Joseph W. Wilson, Wm. R. Smith, Henry K. Selleck, Dudley P. Ely, Alfred E. Austin, Wm. S. Bouton, Andrew Selleck, Frederick Mead, Joseph F. Foote, Samuel E. Olmsted, Frederick S. Lyon, N. Taylor, Jr., Franklin H. Sage.

REDDING, 9. Lemuel Sanford, Frederick Cole, Edward P. Shaw, Wm. E. Dunscomb.

RIDGEFIELD, 12. Wm. W. Seymour, Hiram K. Scott, John F. Gilbert, Ferdinand W. Burt.

SHERMAN, 5. Allan W. Paige, Austin Giddings, George N. Woodruff, John O. Paige.

STRATFORD, 11. Eugene Morehouse, V. R. C. Giddings, H. B. Cuzner, Wm. B. Wood.

STAMFORD, 21. Julius B. Curtis, David H. Clark, H. H. Goidy, John B. Knapp, Hiram Deming, George W. Birch, Marcus Waterbury, E. T. Nicoll.

TRUMBULL, 7. LeGrand G. Beers, Samuel G. Beardsley, Joseph A. Treadwell, Ormel Hall.

WESTON, 6. M. V. B. Rowland, D. S. Parsons.

WESTPORT, 14. Eliphalet T. Gray, Thomas D. Elwood, Albert Relyea, Silas B. Sherwood, Edward J. Taylor, Moses W. Wilson, J. C. Taylor, George S. Adams, Charles H. Taylor.

WILTON, 11. Aaron M. Reed, Samuel B. Fancher, Nathan M. Belden, Henry E. Chichester, Samuel Bennett.

WINDHAM COUNTY.

Commissioners—Edwin H. Hall, Windham, 1882; John D. Converse, Thompson, 1883; Richard H. Ward, Plainfield, 1884.

Clerk of Courts—Edward L. Cundall, Danielsonville.

Assistant Clerk—Huber Clark, Willimantic.

State Attorney—John B. Penrose, Plainfield, (P. O. Central Village.)

Sheriff—Charles H. Osgood, Putnam, to June 1, 1884.

Deputy Sheriffs.

Brooklyn, Frank E. Baker; Central Village, Nathaniel P. Thompson; Thompson, Wm. W. Cummings; West Killingly, Oliver W. Bowen; Willimantic, Charles B. Pomeroy; Woodstock Valley, James B. Tatem.

Deputy Jailor—P. B. Sibley, Brooklyn.

County Treasurer—Alva Wylie, Brooklyn.

Atttorneys at Law.

WINDHAM. *Willimantic*, Joel R. Arnold, Huber Clark, John M. Hall, *John L. Hunter, George W. Meloney, Elliot B. Sumner, George A. Conant, A. J. Bowen.

BROOKLYN. Edward L. Cundall, *Louis B. Cleveland.

ASHFORD, *Jared D. Richmond.

EASTFORD. C. M. Brooks.

HAMPTON. Chauncy F. Cleveland.

KILLINGLY. *Danielsonville*, Edward L. Cundall, Milton A. Shumway, L. H. Rickard, *T. E. Graves, *A. G. Bill, J. H. Potter.

PLAINFIELD. *Central Village*, John J. Penrose, *Edgar M. Warner.

POMFRET. *Pomfret Landing*, Joseph Mathewson.

PUTNAM. *Harrison Johnson, *J. M. Lyon, Gilbert W. Phillips, Chas. E. Searls, *Samuel H. Seward.

THOMPSON. Abiel Converse, Charles E. Searls.

WOODSTOCK. *South*, George S. F. Stoddard.

Commissioners of Superior Court.

Lawyers marked with a * above and the following:

WINDHAM. William Swift.

EASTFORD. Jairus Chapman, Calvin M. Brooks.

HAMPTON. David Greenslit.

PUTNAM. Ralph J. Savin.

THOMPSON. Isaac Ross, Marcus Child.

WEST KILLINGLY. Charles C. Cundall, Edwin L. Palmer.

JUSTICES OF THE PEACE.

WINDHAM, 20. Lucius C. Kinne, William B. Avery. James E. Hayden, Jonathan Hatch, John D. Wheeler, Silas J. Loomer, Lewis Buckingham, Joel R. Arnold, John M. Hall, Geo. W. Meloney, John L. Hunter, Frederick Rogers, Wm. Swift, E. B.

Sumner, Frank M. Lincoln, Huber Clark, George A. Conant, E. P. Kenyon, Allen Lincoln.

BROOKLYN, 10. Edward L. Cundall, Willard Day, Albert Day, Wm. H. Putnam.

ASHFORD, 8. George Platt, Sherman E. Paine, John F. Brooks, Wm. G. Shippy.

CANTERBURY, 10. Amos Witter, B. J. Huling, James D. Ransom, Marvin H. Sanger, Elderkin Waldo.

CHAPLIN 6. Ephraim W. Day, Jesse S. Turner, John W. Griggs, Porter B. Peck.

EASTFORD, 7. E. G. Harris, James M. Keith, Andrew J. Bowen.

HAMPTON, 6. Israel E. Harvey, Henry G. Taintor, Patrick H. Pearl, George M. Holt, David Greenslit, Geo. R. Hammond.

KILLINGLY, 20. Wm. E. Hyde, Lucius H. Rickard, James N. Lewis, Geo. H. Wheaton, Wm. H. Oatley, Joseph W. Stone, M. A. Shumway, Arthur G. Bill, T. E. Graves, Lysander Warren, John Kilby, R. D. Foster, Samuel Hutchins.

PLAINFIELD, 15. Wm. S. Babcock, Wm. I. Hyde, John S. French, George Torrey, Richard H. Ward, John L. Chapman, John D. Rood, Joseph A. Dean, Edgar M. Warner.

POMFRET, 10. Wm. I. Bartholomew, John W. Clapp, Jas. J. Slade, Calvin D. Williams, N. W. Chapman, R. L. Bullard, Charles P. Grosvenor, Thomas W. Williams.

PUTNAM, 8. Thomas J. Thurber, Gilbert W. Phillips, Warren W. White, S. H. Seward, George F. Willis, Harrison Johnson.

SCOTLAND, 5. Samuel B. Sprague, Wm. G. Anthony.

STERLING, 6. Amos J. Gallup, Andrew J. Bitgood, Henry D. Dixon, Josiah Slade.

THOMPSON, 20. Samuel H. Davis, Nathan Rawson, James N. Kingsbury, Oscar Tourtelotte, Lawson Aldrich, Alonzo O. Woodart, Barton Jacobs, John M. Cunningham, Charles E. Searls, Joshua P. Knight, Henry H. Dike, Dyer A. Upham, Randolph H. Chandler, Frank H. Converse, George T. Bixby, L. H. Holbrook, Winsor Bates, John Perrin, Ira D. Bates.

WOODSTOCK, 17. O. Fisher, D. E. May, Geo. S. F. Stoddard, J. M. Paine, A. A. Paine, W. B. Lester, H. T. Child, O. H. Perry, E. Bishop, W. D. Carroll, N. E. Morse, Wm. B. Lester, S. D. Skinner.

LITCHFIELD COUNTY.

Commissioners—Joseph F. Calhoun, Torrington, 1882; George Pierpont, Plymouth, 1883; Lyman Dunning, North Canaan, 1884.

Clerk of Courts—William L. Ransom, Litchfield.

Assistant Clerk—Dwight C. Kilbourn, Litchfield.

State Attorney—James Huntington, Woodbury.

Sheriff—Charles J. Porter, Goshen, to June 1, 1884.

Deputy Sheriffs.

Litchfield, Truman Catlin; New Hartford, Wm. E. Thompson; New Milford, Charles D. Blinn, North Canaan, Robert Van Deusen; Thomaston, Edwin A. Bradley; West Winsted, Wm. B. Phillips; Woodbury, George R. Crane; Washington, Alfred H. Wyant; Falls Village, Henry Brinton; West Cornwall, Chauncey E. Baldwin.

Attorneys at Law.

LITCHFIELD. Charles B. Andrews, Henry B. Graves, *Geo. A. Hickox, *Dwight C. Kilbourn, *Charles C. Moore, *Henry H. Prescott, *Wm. L. Ransom, Edw. W. Seymour, *George C. Woodruff, *George M. Woodruff.

BARKHAMSTED. *Riverton,* *Hiram Goodwin.

CANAAN. *Falls Village,* *Lee P. Dean, *Dwight W. Clarke.

CORNWALL. *Leonard J. Nickerson.

GOSHEN. Albert Wadhams.

HARWINTON. *Abijah Catlin.

NEW HARTFORD. *Jared B. Foster, *Nathan Morse, *John B. Betts.

NEW MILFORD. James H. McMahon, *T. Dwight Merwin, *F. R. Tiffany, John S. Turrill. *Gaylordsville,* Edward S. Merwin.

NORTH CANAAN. *P. O. Canaan,* Jacob B. Hardenbergh, A. T. Roraback.

PLYMOUTH. *Terryville,* *Henry B. Plumb.

SALISBURY. Donald J. Warner, Donald T. Warner. *Lakeville,* Hubert Williams.

SHARON. *Willard Baker, *Charles F. Sedgwick, *James Wade Hughes.

THOMASTON. Albert P. Bradstreet, *Frank W. Etheridge.

TORRINGTON. *Wolcottville,* George W. Cole, *Gideon H. Welch.

5

WATERTOWN. *C. B. Atwood.

WEST CORNWALL. *Leonard J. Nickerson.

WINCHESTER. *West Winsted*, *Frank E. Cleveland, Wm. H. Ely, A. H. Fenn. Florimond D. Fyler, *Samuel A. Herman, *S. B. Horne, *Hiram P. Lawrence, *Wellington B. Smith, John F. Wynne.

₩ WOODBURY. Wm. Cothren, *James Huntington, *George F. Shelton.

Commissioners of Superior Court.

Lawyers marked with a * above and the following:

LITCHFIELD. Charles Adams.

BARKHAMSTED. Samuel H. Case.

BETHLEHEM. Joshua Bird, Samuel L. Bloss, George C. Stone.

CORNWALL. Wm. P. Sturgiss, George C. Harrison.

GOSHEN. J. H. Wadhams, John M. Wadhams.

HARWINTON. George W. Dains.

KENT. Wellington Watson.

NEW MILFORD. Perry Hufcut.

PYLMOUTH. N. T. Baldwin, Aaron P. Fenn.

ROXBURY. Minot L. Beardsley.

SALISBURY. A. J. Spurr, D. D. Warner.

TORRINGTON. Allen G. Brady.

WASHINGTON. George C. Hitchcock, William J. Ford, David C. Whittlesey.

WINCHESTER. Charles H. Hayden.

WOODBURY. Charles D. Minor, James T. Breen, Willis A. Strong.

JUSTICES OF THE PEACE.

LITCHFIELD, 21. George M. Woodruff, Charles B. Andrews, Eli D. Weeks, T. L. Jennings, F. S. Porter, A. J. Pierpont, D. C. Kilbourn, Frank W. Wessels, George W. Bement, H. O. Morse, D. P. Griswold, S. G. Beach, D. G. Turney, Willis G. Barton, William Deming, H. B. Graves.

BARKHAMSTED, 8. Sheldon Merrell, J. W. Colt, James Mills, Warren Alford, S. F. Roberts, Nelson J. Church, Abel C. Everet.

BETHLEHEM, 5. James Allen, H. S. Jackson, Amos C. Lake, Marvin S. Todd.

BRIDGEWATER, 5. Frederick A. Peck, Austin H. Gillett, Joseph T. Beers.

CANAAN, 14. Lee P. Dean, W. G. Kellogg, D. R. Spaulding, H. C. Crandall, J. W. Gibbs.

COLEBROOK, 7. Timothy Persons, Wesley C. Root, Andrew J. Terrell.

CORNWALL, 11. Arthur D. Warner, Leonard J. Nickerson, Solon B. Johnson, Silas G. Patterson, James F. Reed, Niles Scoville, Theodore Kellogg, Daniel L. Beach, Joseph L. Whitney.

GOSHEN, 8. John H. Wadhams, Ira B. Babcock, George Hammond, George W. Humphrey, Elisha Baldwin. Horace L. Seelye, Sherman Kimberly.

HARWINTON, 7. Willis Catlin, N. A. Wilson, James Mather. George W. Dains.

KENT, 10. Marshall C. Gibbs, Luther Eaton.

MORRIS, 5. Homer Stoddard, James M. Benton, Rollin H. Harrison.

NEW HARTFORD, 14. Orrin Fitch, John F. Smith, Nathan Morse, Samuel Allen, Orvis Griggs, Henry R. Jones, James Forbes.

NEW MILFORD, 20. Henry W. Evans, James H. McMahon, Perry N. Hall, Arthur E. Knowles, Francis E. Baldwin, Henry N. Lyon, Liverius Dunning, John S. Turrill, Israel B. Smith, Alexander Levy, Edward Hunt, I. F. Northrop.

NORFOLK, 9. R. I. Crissey, Horace B. Knapp, Myron C. Johnson, Alvin S. Cowles, John K. Shepard.

NORTH CANAAN, 7. Ira S. Bunnell, Wesley Trescott, J. B. Hardenbergh, A. T. Roraback, Wallace A. Roberts, Edward S. Roberts, Samuel A. Bennett.

PLYMOUTH, 13. Byron Tuttle, Jason C. Fenn, Edwin M. Talmadge, William W. Clemence.

ROXBURY, 6. Lyman P. Eastman, Cyrus E. Prindle.

SALISBURY, 16. Porter S. Burrall, John A. McArthur, Wilson E. Hicks, Daniel Pratt, James Ensign, Frederick Everts, Donald J. Warner, Donald T. Warner, Lorenzo Tupper, Hubert Williams.

SHARON, 13. Charles L. Prindle, Ezra H. Bartram, J. N. Bartram, Willard Baker, Z. E. Hunt.

THOMASTON, 12. Albert P. Bradstreet, Israel B. Woodward, Frank W. Etheridge, Henry F. Bradford, Miles Morse, Joseph K. Judson, Byron W. Pease, Frederick A. Canfield, James E. Bishop, Thomas H. Newton, George A. Stoughton, F. B. Taylor.

TORRINGTON, 10. Gideon H. Welch, Joseph F. Calhoun,

O. R. Fyler, Henry I. Jackson, George A. Allen, George W.
Cole, Isaac W. Brooks, Luther Bronson, John M. Burr, Stanley
Griswold.

WARREN, 5. Franklin B. Curtis, Benjamin E. Carter, John
B. Derrickson, N. B. Strong, H. E. Shove.

WASHINGTON, 10. Guy C. Ford, John G. Fenn, George S.
Cogswell, Charles D. Camp.

WATERTOWN, 8. Caleb T. Hickox, George F. Hungerford,
C. B. Atwood, Geo. B. French.

WINCHESTER, 12. Wm. F. Hurlbut, A. M. Perkins, N. D.
Ford, R. H. Moore, W. H. Ely, J. McCarthy, 2d, S. B. Horne,
A. H. Fenn.

WOODBURY, 11. William Cothren, Reuben B. Martin, David
S. Bull, H. H. Morris, M. F. Skelley, Scoville Nettleton, Eli M.
Towne.

MIDDLESEX COUNTY.

Commissioners—Willis E. Terrill, Middlefield, 1882; Rufus
C. Shepard, Old Saybrook, 1883; Miner C. Hazen, Haddam,
1884.

Clerk of Courts—Charles G. R. Vinal, Middletown.

Assistant Clerk—Frederic Vinal, Middletown.

State Attorney—W. F. Willcox, Chester (P. O. Deep River).

Sheriff—John I. Hutchinson, Essex; to June 1, 1884.

Deputy Sheriffs.

Middletown, Gardner B. Smith; Portland, George O. Mosher;
Clinton, John P. Johnson; East Hampton, Thomas S. Brown;
East Haddam, Ralph B. Swan; Higganum, Robert B. Clock;
Deep River, Henry S. Ward.

Deputy Jailors—William E. Odber, Haddam; John Wilcox,
Middletown.

County Treasurer—George W. Harris, Middletown.

Attorneys at Law.

MIDDLETOWN. Arthur W. Bacon, *Conrad G. Bacon, *Eldon
B. Birdsey, *Arthur B. Calef, M. Eugene Culver, Daniel J.
Donahue, *Wm. T. Elmer, *Lovell Hall, *John M. Murdock,
*D. Ward Northrop, *Wesley U. Pearne, *Robert G. Pike,
*S. A. Robinson, Charles C. Tyler, *Charles G. R. Vinal, Sam-
uel L. Warner, Frederic Vinal.

CHATHAM. *East Hampton*, *Lovell Hall.
CHESTER. *Nathan C. Peters, *Jonathan T. Clark, *Washington F. Willcox.
DURHAM. Henry G. Newton.
EAST HADDAM. *Julius Attwood, *Francis H. Parker.
Hadlyme, *Hiram Willey. *Johnsonville*, E. Emery Johnson.
ESSEX. *James Phelps, *James L. Phelps, Henry L. Pratt.
PORTLAND. *Dennis A. McQuillin, John M. Murdoch.
SAYBROOK. *Deep River*, *Washington F. Willcox.
WESTBROOK. *David A. Wright.

Commissioners of Superior Court.

Lawyers marked with a * above and the following:

MIDDLETOWN. George W. Burke, Clarence F. Bacon, Arthur B. Calef, Jr.
HADDAM. Henry M. Selden, Cornelius Brainerd, John H. Russell.
CHATHAM. Josiah Ackley, Emmet B. Smith, Daniel A. Markham.
EAST HADDAM. Eugene W. Chaffee.
SAYBROOK. Gilbert W. Denison.

JUSTICES OF THE PEACE.

MIDDLETOWN, 32. Thomas J. Atkins, Arthur W. Bacon, Arthur B. Calef, Michael W. Lawton, M. Eugene Culver, Daniel J. Donahoe, Wm. T. Elmer, Wesley U. Pearne, Silas A. Robinson, Charles G. R. Vinal, Samuel L. Warner, Frederic Vinal, Conrad G. Bacon, Eldon B. Birdsey, George W. Guy, Elihu W. N. Starr, Robert G. Pike.
HADDAM, 14. Jonathan W. Clark, Abiel J. Sherman, Stephen H. Burr, Giles Thayer, Charles D. Merwin, Truman A. Spencer, Noah Burr, Ephraim P. Arnold, Jared S. Clark.
CHATHAM, 9. E. B. Rich, J. C. Shepard, H. D. Chapman.
CHESTER, 6. Walter S. Clark, Joseph E. Silliman, Jonathan Warner, J. Tyler Smith, Noah C. Perry, Julius Smith.
CLINTON, 8. Elias W. Wellman.
CROMWELL, 8. Elisha Stevens, M. R. Warner.
DURHAM, 7. Samuel W. Loper, Wm. H. Walkley, N. H. Parsons.
EAST HADDAM, 16. Silas R. Holmes, E. E. Johnson, J. Attwood, Alden Smith, W. H. Sisson, John B. Hungerford, A. E. Purple, Geo. A. Rogers.

ESSEX, 8. Giles Potter, Henry L. Pratt, Samuel Griswold, Benjamin A. Gladding, Edward W. Redfield, Noah Starkey, Henry Hayden, Francis H. Tiffany.

KILLINGWORTH, 7. Andrew W. Burr, Lyman E. Stevens.

MIDDLEFIELD, 6. Valerius H. Coles, Henry W. Hurlbut, James T. Inglis, P. M. Augur, M. W. Terrill, Alvah B. Coe.

OLD SAYBROOK, 6. Henry Hart, Edwin Ayer, John N. Clarke.

PORTLAND, 18. Rodney B. Freeman, Lucius P. Stewart, Wm. H. Bartlett, D. A. McQuillin, Enoch Sage.

SAYBROOK, 7. John W. Marvin, John S. Lane, George F. Spencer, Joseph B. Banning.

WESTBROOK, 8. Oliver H. Norris, Carlos H. Chapman, Wm. N. Kirtland, Benjamin F. Bushnell, Alpheus Wright, David A. Wright, George C. Spencer.

TOLLAND COUNTY.

Commissioners—John R. Champlin, Willington, 1882; David W. Huntington, Coventry, 1883; Edward D. Alvord, Bolton, 1884.

Clerk of Courts—Erwin O. Dimock, Tolland.

Assistant Clerk—G. W. West, Rockville.

State Attorney—Benezet H. Bill, Rockville.

Sheriff—William M. Corbin, Rockville, to June 1, 1884.

Deputy Sheriffs.

Tolland, Austin L. Edgerton; Hebron, Harvey Crane; Columbia, Arthur H. Little; Rockville, George Woodward; Coventry, Sumner Payne; Somersville, T. M. Gowdy; Stafford Springs, Ezra T. Converse; Union, Wm. A. Corbin; Willington, Charles F. McFarland.

County Treasurer—Charles A. Hawkins, Tolland.

Attorneys at Law.

TOLLAND. Erwin O. Dimock, *Edwin S. Agard.

ANDOVER. Myron P. Yeomans.

SOMERS. Solomon Fuller.

STAFFORD. Stafford Springs,* S. E. Fairfield,* Roswell D. Davison, *Wm. A. King, *C. M. Brooks.

VERNON. Rockville, Benezet H. Bill, Dwight Marcy, Sam'l F. McFarland, Charles Phelps, Gelon W. West.

WILLINGTON. Seth C. Eaton.

Commissioners of Superior Court.

Lawyers marked with a * above, and the following:

COVENTRY. S. Taylor.
HEBRON. Charles H. Brown, John S. Wells, J. G. Page.
MANSFIELD. John N. Barrows.
STAFFORD. F. L. Batchelder, Isaiah Hiscock, E. Y. Fisk.
UNION. C. Paul.
WILLINGTON. L. Holt, L. W. Holt, A. J. Turner.

JUSTICES OF THE PEACE.

TOLLAND, 12. Smith H. Brown, Gilbert H. Preston, William C. Ladd, Geo. W. Brown, Samuel B. Slater, Erwin O. Dimock, Geo. P. Field, A. B. Clough, L. W. Martin, Elisha Arnold, Gilbert P. Babcock.

ANDOVER, 6. Myron P. Yeomans, Roger E. Phelps, William Babcock, Walter Abbey, Andrew Phelps.

BOLTON, 6. Jabez L. White, John W. Sumner, Edwin D. Alvord, Chauncy T. Hunt.

COLUMBIA, 6. Carlos Collins, N. H. Clark, J. E. H. Gates, Norman P. Little.

COVENTRY, 16. Charles A. Kingsbury, Nathaniel Root, Jr., Henry A. Brewster.

ELLINGTON, 9. M. H. Mandell, Wm. D. Slater, Benjamin Pinney, Darius Crane, Horatio Kibbe, Joseph Hopkins, Sylvester Morris, R. A. Taft, Ira H. Lewis.

HEBRON, 11. Horace F. Porter, David M. Buell, Andrew Prentice, Sylvester Root, Wm. T. Warner.

MANSFIELD, 16. Isaac P. Fenton, E. C. Pike, E. G. Sumner.

SOMERS, 10. Solomon Fuller, James C. Pease, Loren Griswold, Charles Hibbard, Alvan D. Noble, Arnold Converse.

STAFFORD, 19. F. A. Harwood, Jacob Glover, Henry Gerould, J. C. Cross, Augustus Alden, Miner Kinney, George Washburn, M. P. Hanly, John G. Slater, R. D. Davison, J. M. Chaffee, J. C. Fuller, M. P. Shahan, Anthony Adams, E. N. Lull, Charles O. Smith, G. S. Davis, L. G. Cummings, H. W. Davis.

UNION, 6. Royal Chapman, Thomas Rindge, A. J. Wales.

VERNON, 18. John S. Dobson, George Talcott, C. Dennison Talcott, Gelon W. West, Benezet H. Bill, E. S. Henry, Cyrus Winchell, Charles Phelps, Ryal G. Holt, William W. Andress, Arthur T. Bissell, Charles P. Thompson, Dwight Marcy, Henry F. Parker.

WILLINGTON, 10. Seth C. Eaton, Wm. Irons.

TOWN OFFICERS.

The Town Elections are held on the first Monday in October. The following lists give the names of the Town Clerk, Town Treasurer, Registrar, Selectmen, Constables, Collectors of Taxes, Grand Jurors. Assessors, Board of Relief, Board of Education, and Reg:strars of Voters. The Acting School Visitors are designated with a *. The School Visitors are chosen for three years, and the dates indicate the time when their terms expire.

ANDOVER. Town Clerk, Reg. and Treas., Charles F. Lincoln. Selectmen, Charles H. Loomis, William A. Brown, Charles Johnson. Const , Roscoe E. Bishop, Arthur C. Brown, Charles L. Backus, Henry F. Standish, S. Henry Daggett, Charles H. Baker, Flavel Lyman. Coll., Willard Fuller. G. Jurors, Charles L. Backus, Charles R. Kingsbury, Hiram A. Brown, Daniel M. Burnap, Flavel Lyman, Lafayette Kenyon, Assessors, George F. Blackman, Erastus D. Post, Roger E. Phelps. Board of R., John F. Bingham, S. Henry Daggett, Bissell E. Post. Board of Ed., Albert W. Lyman, Henry Dorrance, 1882; Walter Abbey, Charles H. Loomis, 1883; Charles L. Backus, *Edgar D. White, 1884. Reg. of Voters, Charles L. Backus, Edwin H. Cook.

ASHFORD. Clerk and Treas., Davis A. Baker. Reg. Henry H. Platt. Selectmen, Mason S. Kendall, Loomis E. Stowell, Stephen B. Tift. Const. and Col., Herbert F. Dawley. G. Jurors, Arnold Upton, John T. Greene, Asa H. Bruce. Assessors, Andrew H. Byles, Charles W. Brett. Board of R., Nelson Hammond, Dwight Lincoln. Board of Ed., John T. Greene, Henry R. Woodward, 1882; Gilbert E. S. Amidon, Harvey W. Morey, 1883, Sherman E. Paine, John A. Brown, 1884. Reg. of Voters, Peter Platt, Thomas J. Peck.

AVON. Clerk, Reg. and Treas., Oliver T. Bishop, Selectmen, Fitch L. Bishop, James M. Wilson, Jarvis W. Edgerton. Const., E. E. Hart, Prescott H. Woodford, Henry Tabei. Coll., James M. Wilson. G. Jurors, Frank S. Hart, Samuel Gibson, Dwight A. Avery. Assessors, Chester R. Woodford, Harrison Woodford, George V. Lusk. Board of R., Edmund Sanford, Seth F. Woodford. Board of Ed., Philemon R. Day, Joseph S. Woodford, 1882; Nicholas J. Seeley, Dan. D. Derrin,. 1883; Matthew C. Woodford, Charles H. Miller, 1884. Reg. of Voters, Harvey Woodford, 2d, Joseph B. North.

BARKHAMSTED. Clerk and Reg., Owen E. Case. Treas., Hubert B. Case. Selectmen, M. A. Hart, C. H. Tiffany, Henry B. Phelps. Const., Hiram B. Holcomb, William J. Case, Samuel Munson. Coll., William E. Howd. G. Jurors, Henry H. Payne, William H. Hubbard. Assessors, Albert Perry, Sheldon Johnson. Board of R., Luman Pease, Samuel H. Case, William J. Ripley. Board of Ed., Sheldon Merrill, Daniel Youngs, Edward J. Youngs, Hiram C. Brown. *Joseph B. Clark. Reg of Voters, 1st district, Shelden Merrill, William E. Howd; 2d Dist., George A. Baker, Wilfred D. Youngs: 3d Dist., Byron O. Hawley, Hiram C. Brown.

BEACON FALLS. Clerk and Treas.. Julius A. Hart. Reg., Oliver D. Buckingham. Selectmen, Herbert C. Baldwin, David M. French, Noyes Wheeler. Const., Charles B. Clark, Harvey E. Atwood, David J. Carrington. Coll., George A. Twitchell. G. Jurors, Andrew W. Culver, David T. Sanford. Assessors, Jerome B. Hubbell, Herbert C. Baldwin. Board of R., George A Twitchell, Charles B. Clark, David M. French. Board of Ed., David T. Sanford, Jerome B. Hubbell, Buel Buckingham. Reg. of Voters, Charles B. Clark, Harris F. Osborn.

BERLIN. Clerk and Treas., Alfred North. Reg., E. Brandegee. Selectmen, S. C. Wilcox, H. Sage, H. M. Cowles. Const., E. H. Warner, Richard Moon, Joseph J. Morse, William Webster, Charles Marvin, Huber Bushnell. Coll., William Bulkley. G. Jurors, Eben C. Woodruff, Edward S. Tubbs, Francis Deming, Charles M. Browne, Frederick North, Edwin L. Morse. Assessors, Andrew J. Warner, Edward C. Hall. Board of R., Charles N. Alling, Walter E. Penfield, Edward E. Stevens. Board of Ed., James Roche, Francis Deming, 1882; George L. Taylor, Eben C. Woodruff, 1883; Samuel F. Talmadge, Theron Upson, 1884. Reg. of Voters, William Bulkley, John Norton.

BETHANY. Clerk, Reg. and Treas., Edwin N. Clark. Selectmen, Samuel R. Woodward, S. Gilbert Davidson, Evlyn O. Pardee. Const., Henry H. Hotchkiss, Theron E. Allen, Frederick W. Sperry. Coll., George B. Hotchkiss. G. Jurors, Garry B. Johnson, Denzil B. Hoadley, Evlyn O. Pardee. Assessors, John J. Warner, Theron E. Allen. Board of R, Wales H. French, Dwight N. Clark, George W. Woodward. Board of Ed., S. R. Woodward, G. B. Hotchkiss, Lewis F. Morris. Reg. of Voters, Ernest Z. Hotchkiss, George B. Hotchkiss.

BETHEL. Clerk, George S. Crofut. Reg., William H. Judson. Treas., Samuel S. Ambler. Selectmen, Frederick Judd, George M. Cole, Benjamin F. Foster. Const., Edward Johnson, John S. Pearce, Thomas A. Evans. Coll. of Taxes, Samuel Gillett. G. Jurors, Joseph A. Banks, Charles E. Edmonds, Henry W. Timanus. Assessors, E. Starr Judd, Charles H. Shepard,-Francis B. Andrews. Board of R., William H. Judson, Byron R. Morgan, Silas H. Hickok. Board of Ed., George M. Lyon, *William Brown, 1882; Frederick Shepard, George F. Waters, 1883; Eli T. Andrews, Granville B. Andrews, 1884. Reg. of Voters, Gideon S. Peck, Henry H. Baird.

BETHLEHEM. Clerk, George C. Stone. Reg., William R. Harrison. Treas., Jonathan Wooten. Selectmen, Henry Catlin, Ralph Munson. Const, and Coll., Samuel Gunn, Frank Thompson, John D. Waldron. G. Jurors, Frederick Allen, Frank Stoughton, Frederick G. Stockman. Assessors, Nehemiah L. Bloss, Warren H. Taylor. Board of R., Marvin S. Todd, Alexander Hamilton, J. B. Ames. Board of Ed., George C. Stone, Samuel P. Hayes, 1882; Marvin S. Todd, Fred. S. Curtis, 1883; William R. Harrison, Marshall E. Beecher, 1884. Reg. of Voters, George W. Percy, Hiram G. Kilbourne.

BLOOMFIELD. Clerk and Reg., John E. Cox. Treas., Elihu B. Case. Selectmen, John Blackwell, Franklin B. Miller, Alfred N. Filley. Const., Henry C. Alderman, Henry T. Fagan, George F. Hubbard, George F. Capen, Byron D. Barnard, Franklin E. Burr. Coll., Frederick A. Pinney. G. Jurors, William G. Hubbard, John Wilcox, S. B. Pinney, William G. Case, Doddridge R. Cadwell, Chester F. Goodwin. Assessors, Francis G. Barber, John Wilcox, Timothy G. Jerome. Board of R., Henry C. Hoskins, William G. Hubbard, Eli Brown. Board of Ed., Francis G. Barber, William A. Hallock, Louis J. Filley, 1882; Nathan F. Miller, Frank E. Burr, William J. Gabb, 1883; *Henry Gray, John Wilcox, Franklin B. Miller, 1884; Reg. of Voters, William J. Gabb, Henry G. Isham.

BOLTON. Clerk and Reg., Sherman P. Sumner. Treas., Samuel W. Williams. Selectmen, Jabez L. White, Arnold H. Long, Joseph C. Alvord. Const., William Bartliff, and Coll., Marvin W. Howard, Charles P. Coleman, Selden W. Skinner, Wilber F. Strong, Albert W. Cowles, Benjamin Lyman, William N. Loomis. G. Jurors, John W. Sumner, Alphonso R. Barrows, George Curtis, Lorin S. Maine, Charles E. Carpenter. Assessors, William C. White, Ward B. Gleason., Board of R., Warren Risley, Elijah B. Bishop. Board of Ed., Charles E. Hammond, Ferdinand E. Williams, William C. White, Edwin D. Alvord. Reg. of Voters, John W. Sumner, Oliver C. Johnson.

BOZRAH. Clerk, Samuel G. Johnson, Reg., Augustus D. Herrick. Treas., N. C. Cook. Selectmen, A. J. Hough, Chas. A. Johnson, Henry J. Way. Const., Simeon Abel, 1st, Selden Wightman, Orimel A. Johnson, A. B. Pendleton, John N. Fargo. Coll., Elijah A. Tracy. G. Jurors, S. H. Allen, Frederick A. Parker, A. D. Winchester, Edward Johnson, Joshua C. Leffingell. Assessors, Edward Johnson, John H. Leffingell, John J. Gager. Board of R., N. C. Cook, Jehiel L. Johnson, John H. Miner. Board of Ed., *O. D. Herrick, Charles A. Gager. Reg. of Voters, Simeon Abel, 1st, Albert Waterman.

BRANFORD. Clerk and Treas., Henry H. Stedman. Reg., Walter H. Zink. Selectmen, John S. Blackstone, George H. Page, William Page. Const., Henry D. Linsley, Seria Palmer, J. J. Matthews, William Foote. Coll., Henry W. Averill. G. Jurors, Almon Beers, William H. Farrell, N. H. Bishop, James McDermott. Assessors, Richard Dibble, Henry H. Fowler. Board of R., Samuel O. Plant, Roger Hall, George W. Beach. Board of Ed., N. K. Northam, James W. Fay, James McNamara, Roger Hall, 1882; T. F. Hammer, Rodolphus Bartholomew, Thomas McDermott, William Regan, 1883; Daniel O'Brien, J. H. Hutchinson, W. H. Zink, Lester J. Nichols, 1884. Reg. of Voters, 1st Dist., Joseph C. Sharkey, James Halley; 2d Dist., Roger Hall, Henry S. Hall.

BRIDGEPORT. Clerk and Reg., Charles E. Wilmot. Treas., Isaac B. Prindle. Selectmen, Thomas Stirling, Eli Thompson. Const., Daniel W. Jones, Frank B. Taylor, James P. Lockwood, Wallace N. Ballou, George F. Wildman, Seymour Whiting. Coll., Benjamin K. Mills. G. Jurors, Joseph A. Joyce, David Wooster, William J. Gould, Assessors, Amos Fuller, Stephen M. Conger, Sr. Aaron Wallace. Board of R., William H. Greene, Peter J. Black, Walter C. Nevers. Board of Ed., David Ginand, George N. French, Julius S. Hanover, Nathaniel Wheeler, 1882; Frederick W. Zingsem, George C. Waldo, James Staples, Peter W. Wren, 1883; William B. Hincks, Augustus H. Abernethy, Edward W. Marsh, Thomas J. Synnott, 1884. Reg. of Voters, John Keppy, William Costello.

BRIDGEWATER. Clerk, Austin H. Gillette. Reg., Smith R.
Weeks. Treas., Arza C. Norris. Selectmen, Fred. A. Peck,
Amos Northrop, Horace N. Sanford. Const., James H. Keeler,
Jr., Daniel H. Canfield, Edwin R. Allen, Almon D. Smith, Gid-
eon W. Northrop. Coll., Reuben J. Keeler. G. Jurors, George
C. Bennett, Ransom B. Wheeler. Assessors, James G. Welton,
James H. Keeler, Jr. Board of R., Peter Wooster, Josiah L.
Minor. Board of Ed., Burr Mallett, Peter Wooster, 1882; *Eli
Sturtevant, Horace N. Sanford, 1883; Austin H. Gillette, Hor-
ace D. Gillette, 1884. Reg. of Voters, Daniel H. Canfield, Chris-
topher C. Shannon.

BRISTOL. Clerk, Reg. and Treas., Benjamin F. Hawley.
Selectmen, Charles L. Frisbie, Samuel D. Bull, Edward Ingra-
ham. Const., George R. Tuttle, and Coll., Michael B. Rohan,
Elijah Manross, Samuel M. Thomas. G. Jurors, Horatio C.
Clayton, Ambrose Tyler, Lawrence Fitzsimmons, Ralph G. Rig-
by, Sherman E. Woodford. Assessors, Hiram H. Hurlburt, Lu-
ther B. Norton, Elbert E. Thorpe. Board of R., Charles C. P.
Goodrich, Daniel S. Lardner, Nathan L. Birge. Board of Ed.,
Benjamin F. Hawley, George R. Barbour, 1882; Michael B.
Roddan, Anson Bingham, 1883; *Delavan DeWolf, Gad Norton,
1884. Reg. of Voters, 1st district, Edward B. Dunbar, Hobart
A. Warner; 2d district, Charles W. Brown, Albert P. Stark.

BROOKFIELD. Clerk and Treas., Henry S. Beers. Reg.,
Amos L. Williams. Selectmen, Harvey Roe, Ezra N. Somers,
Horace Beers. Const., John H. Barlow, James Lee, William
A. Perkins, Seth Stevens, Thomas P. Bristol, Barzillai T. Jack-
son. Coll., Barzillai T. Jackson. G. Jurors, Almon Odell,
Henry C. Gray, John H. Merwin, Samuel Thornhill, James W.
Morehouse, Philo C. Merwin. Assessors, Samuel Thornhill,
Benjamin Griffen, Frederick A. Bennett. Board of R., Henry
D. Lake, Charles Stewart, Almon H. Taylor. Board of Ed.,
A. C. Pierce, E. L. Whitcome, Charles Stuart. Reg. of Voters,
Thomas P. Bristoll, Sidney E. Hawley.

BROOKLYN. Clerk, Reg. and Treas., Alva Wylie. Select-
men, William H. Putnam, Wm. H. Cutler, Darius Day. Const.,
Theodore D. Pond, and Coll., George C. Keach. G. Jurors, W.
R. Thurber, W. R. Johnson, S. H. Tripp, H. F. Cox, Arba A.
Allen, P. B. Sibley. Assessors, Frank E. Baker, Elisha Evans.
Board of R., William Searls, Willard Day, Jonah Young.
Board of Ed., Joseph B. Stetson, Frank Day, 1882; E. S.

Beard, H. H. Green, 1883; Willard Day, A. H. Turner, 1884.
Reg. of Voters, William R. Thurber, Henry H. Green.

BURLINGTON. Clerk and Treas., Samuel G. Bradley. Reg.,
William Elton. Selectmen, Samuel Russell, Gilbert H. Hol-
comb, George J. Hinman. Const., Julius B. Smith, Frank
Butler, William Eaton, Adna N. Barnes, Vincent Veiring, Jr.,
Linneus F. Turner. Coll., Linneus F. Turner. G. Jurors,
Burdett A. Peck, Ebenezer Henry, John Aldrich, Edward P.
Spencer, Edwin Gillett, Seth Keney. Assessors, Sylvester
Curtis, Norris W. Bunnell. Board of R., Edward N. Gillard,
Willis S. Baldwin, John A. Reeve. Board of Ed., Seth A.
Keney, Romeo Elton, Lucius B. Pond, Duane N. Griffin, B.
O'R. Sheridan. Reg. of Voters, 1st Dist., George W. Wright;
2d Dist., Anthony Moore.

CANAAN. (P. O. Falls Village.) Clerk, Reg. and Treas.,
Henry C. Gaylord. Selectmen, Daniel Brewster, Lucius Wil-
cox, Daniel H. Dean. Const., O. N. Brinton, and Coll., Lee
D. Brewster, Frederick G. Dean, James H. Hakes, Charles E.
Hanchett, W. L. Millard, N. S. Spaulding. G. Jurors, Lewis
Cady, William H. Cook, C. E. Wolcott, Henry Sturges, Wells
Yale, H. P. Morse. Assessors, Myron H. Dean, Sidney Ensign.
Board of R., John N. Dean, Allen Chapman, O. M. Brinton.
Board of Ed., Dwight E. Dean, Daniel N. Moore, 1882; Elisha
B. Gillett, Myron H. Dean, 1883; J. D. Clemens, C. B. Maltbie,
1884. Reg. of Voters, A. P. Chapman, C. B. Maltbie.

CANTERBURY. Clerk and Reg., William S. Adams, Treas.,
Marvin H. Sanger. Const., Charles E. Waldo, and Coll., Nellen
W. Smith. G. Jurors, James D. Ransom, Alfred N. Bennett,
Henry N. Bushnell, James B. Palmer, Thomas C. Francis.
Assess., Comfort S. Burlingame, Walter Smith. Board of R.,
Jirah Hyde, Wm. H. Larkham, George F. Richmond, Nathan
Allen, George L. Cary. Board of Ed., Oscar Peek, Charles B.
Hicks, Nathan Allen, 1882; George Sanger, Henry Kendall,
John H. Peck, 1883; C. S. Burlingame, Wm. S. Adams, Luman
D. Bennett, 1884. Reg. of Voters, Marvin H. Sanger, John D.
Pellett.

CANTON. Clerk, Anson W. Bristol (P. O. Canton Center).
Reg., David B. Hale. Treas., Jasper H. Bidwell. Selectmen,
Julius E. Case, John Case, Everett Case. Const., Frederick A.
Bidwell, Henry C. Ruick, Henry C. Rogers, Giles C. Calhoun,

Wills A. Lawton. Coll., Perley A. Wheeler. G. Jurors, John
D. Andrews, Amos G. Hart, Wm. G. Hallock, George F. Lewis,
Clinton Ɖ. Woodford, Watson Case. Assess., Samuel N. Cod-
ding, Frederick A Bidwell, George W. Lamphier. Board of R.,
Chas. H. Blair, Oliver C. Adams, Henry Case. Board of Ed.,
James Case, David C. Holbrook, 1882; Wm. W. Bidwell, Bur-
ton O. Higley, 1883; D. B. Hubbard, Jasper H. Bidwell,
1884. Reg. of Voters, 1st Dist., John E. Wheelock, Rollin O.
Humphrey; 2d Dist., Sherman E. Brown, Edwin P. Lamphier.

CHAPLIN. Clerk and Treas., J. W. Lincoln. Reg., Orrin
Witter. ' Selectmen, Ephraim W. Day, Ɖason A. Bates, James
R. Utley. Const., Eliphalet Reed, E. W. Bingham, and Coll.
G. Jurors, Joseph A. Edmond, G. A. Ross, O. Bennett, Ɖ. A.
Bates, E. G. Corey, F. C. Lummis. Assess., James R. Utley,
Wm. Ɖartin. Board of R., Joseph Foster, C. E. Griggs, G. C.
Kingsbury. Board of Ed., *Francis Williams, W. N. Webster,
1882; C. Edwin Griggs, Wm. Ɖartin, 1883; Joseph Foster, Ɖ.
A. Bates, 1884. Reg. of Voters, F. C. Lummis.

CHATHAƉ. Clerk, Reg., and Treas., Wm. H. Bevin. Select-
men, Leonard Willey, Evelyn Roberts, Lyman O. Wells.
Const., Lyman B. Higgins, and Coll., A. H. Worthington, James
Dickson, John H. Selden, F. E. Taylor, F. H. Dunham.
G. Jurors, L. S. Carpenter, John P. Purple, J. D. Barton,
George H. White, R. D. Tibbals, Edwin A. Brainard. Assess.,
Henry S. Gates, Davis S. Strong. Board of R., E. G. Cone,
Charles L. Strong. B. B. Hall. Board of Ed., Daniel Denison,
A. H. Conklin, A. P. Chapman, 1882; *J. S. Ives, H. D.
Chapman, John C. Shepard, 1883; Henry B. Brown, Albert
O. West, L. F. Wood, 1884. Reg. of Voters, L. H. Ɖark-
ham, George A. Strong, A. H. Worthington, Davis S. Strong.

CHESHIRE. Clerk, Ɖilton C. Doolittle. Reg., Ɖyron N.
Chamberlin. Treas., Edwin R. Brown. Selectmen, Benjamin
A. Jarvis, Alonzo E. Smith, Julius Ɖoss. Const., Henry Bea-
dle, James Ɖ. Lanyon. Coll., Alfred Bristol. G. Jurors, Chas.
H. Hall, Edgar H. Beadle, Benjamin H. Peck, Sherman Welton,
Alexander Welton. Assess., Norman S. Platt, Charles S. Gil-
lette, Hugh Brennan. Board of R., Alexander Doolittle, George
Keeler, Wm. H. Ɖarshall. Board of Ed., George R. Johnson,
Frank N. Hall, 1882; Joseph P. Beach, John H. French, 1883;
Sanford J. Horton, Charles T. Hotchkiss, 1884. Reg. of Voters,
Henry Beadle, Henry H. Holcomb.

CHESTER. Clerk and Reg.. J. Kirtland Denison. Treas., Jos. E. Silliman. Selectmen, E. C. Hungerford, C. Geo. Ladd, Jos. H. Leet. Const., John Jagger, and Coll., R. Clifford Tyler. G. Jurors, A. H. Gilbert, Fisk Shailer, J. L. Lord. Assess., H. H. Clark, C. J. Bates, Wm. N. Clark. Board of R., J. Linus Clark, Walter S. Clark, Leonard Baker. Board of Ed., Ambrose Pratt, Sylvester W. Turner, W. F. Willcox. Reg. of Voters, Frank G. Clark, E. B. Pratt.

CLINTON. Clerk, Reg., and Treas., Heury C. Hull. Selectmen, Henry A. Elliot, Wm. C. Bushnell, Henry L. Wellman. Const., Wm. C. Bushnell, and Coll., Edwin H. Wright. G. Jurors, Alfred Davis, Asa L. Bushnell, Henry Stevens. Assess., John P. Johnson, Charles E. Merri'ls, David A. Stannard. Board of R., John A. Stanton, Wm. S. Grinnell, Warren A. Doolittle. Board of Ed., John B. Wright, James L. Davis, Elisha E. Wright, Wm. H. Kelsey, 1882; Frederick A. Sturges, Wilbur Brooks, Henry L. Wellman, Luke E. Wood, 1883, Alonzo H. Stevens, James A. Spencer, George E. Elliot, Jedediah H. Hurd, 1884. Reg. of Voters, John A. Stanton, George E. Elliot.

COLCHESTER. Clerk and Reg., George D. Bingham. Treas., Wm. B. Otis. Selectmen, H. P. Buel, R. R. Carrington, R. T. Carrier. Const., James Doyle, Charles Taylor, John N. Strong, Benjamin Adams, George Kramer, Jr., L. P. Skinner. Coll., C. C. Palmer, George H. Rogers. G. Jurors, John Kramer, George Chapman, Ralph T. Carrier, Joseph A. Gardner, C. H. Skinner, Joseph Crocker. Assess., Jonathan S. Clark, Asa Brainard, Asa R. Bigelow. Board of R., Hoxie Brown, Benjamin Adams, George Peck. Board of Ed., Demas Carrier, Alden Baker, 1882; S. G. Willard, Bernard Bray, 1883; R. R. Carrington, Dighton Moses, 1884. Reg. of Voters, Ira A. Dinsmore, Wm. H. Hayward.

COLEBROOK. Clerk and Treas., John S. Wheeler. Reg., Rollin D. Baldwin. Selectmen, Rollin D. Baldwin, William H. Vining, Solomon Sackett. Const., George J. Whipple, Lewis E. Dewey, Robert Hoffman. Coll., Horace North. G. Jurors, Patrick Burke, Edwin S. Preston, George F. Howe. Assess., Wesley C. Root, Hiram S. Hamilton, Board of R., Wolcott Deming, Andrew J. Terrell, Edwin L. Simons. Board of Ed., John A. Deming, Wm. G. Kinney, *John A. Moore, 1882; James McCaffrey, Leonard D. Benham, Samuel A. Cooper, 1883; Andrew

J. Terrell, Rollin D. Baldwin. Lucien O. Bass, 1884. Reg. of Voters, 1st Dist., Wesley C. Root, Edward Oles; 2d Dist., John A. Deming, Thomas B. Spencer.

COLUMBIA. Clerk and Reg., Norman P. Little. Selectmen, Willard B. Clark, John A. Hutchins, Earl M. Holbrook. Const, W. W. Battey, Denison Avery, Horace E. Brown, Charles R. Buell, William A. Lyman. Coll., Samuel F. West. G. Jurors, E. P. Spafford, S. B. West, Simon Hunt, J. H. Townsend, Joel Tucker, E. L. Hall. Assessors, S. S. Isham, A. A. Hunt, N. H. Clark. Board of R., E. M. Clark, Justin Holbrook, J. E. H. Gates. Board of Ed., F. D. Avery, N. H. Clark, William H. Yeomans, C. E. Little, J. P. Little, *N. K. Holbrook. Reg. of Voters, Arthur H. Little, Asahel O. Wright.

CORNWALL. Clerk, Silas C. Beers. Reg., Edward Sanford. Treas., Victory C. Beers. Selectmen, Samuel S. Reed, Michael Troy, Ralph I. Scoville. Const., James A. Ford, Almon L. Miner, Walter W. Wells. G. Jurors, Myron I. Millard, George Hughes, Archibald Bennett. Assessors, Ingersoll Reed, Chas. H. Harrison. Board of R., James Blake, William W. Baldwin, Philo M. Kellogg. Board of Ed., Leonard J. Nickerson, Chas. H. Preston, 1882; Wilbur F. Harrison, John F. Andrew, 1883; Arthur D. Warner, Samuel J. White, 1884. Reg. of Voters, John W. Beers, Frederick Kellogg.

COVENTRY. Clerk and Treas., Dwight Webler. Reg., Maurice B. Bennett. Selectmen, Francis Porter, Alexander S. Hawkins, H. E. H. Gilbert. Const., William A. Lathrop, William Craughwell, Orrin Turner, Alexander H. Pomroy, S. P. Swift, George B. Carpenter. Coll., S. L. French. G. Jurors, George W. Franklin, Orrin Turner, Charles Reynolds, Austin Boynton, Alfred J. Turner, John B. Brown. Assessors, William O. Gardiner, D. B. Russell. Board of R., William Trowbridge, George H. Clark, William P. Rose. Board of Ed., Frederick S. Sweet, Andrew B. Kingsbury, 1882; Maurice B. Bennett, John Brown, 1883; Alexander S. Hawkins, Andrew Kingsbury, 1884. Reg. of Voters, Silas W. Loomis, Andrew B. Kingsbury.

CROMWELL. Clerk, Reg. and Treas., R. B. Savage. Selectmen, George W. Stevens, William M. Noble, Bulkley Edwards. Const., R. B. Savage, and Coll., Timothy Ranney, A. J.

Briggs, H. W. Buckley, F. Winkle, Hiram Ralph, Lee Sizer.
G. Jurors, William E. Hulburt, William R. McDonald, Seth Paddock, George H. Butler, I. H. Warner, A. N. Pierson. Assessors, Albert Dowd, Seth J. Paddock. Board of R., H. W. Stocking, Frederick Wilcox, David Edwards. Board of Ed., William A. Stickney, Henry A. Ely, Albert Dowd, William E. Hurlbut, *Henry S. Stevens, Edward Como. Reg. of Voters, George P. Savage, John Nolan.

DANBURY. Clerk and Reg., David B. Booth. Treas. Levi P. Treadwell. Selectmen, David Pearce, Nathaniel B. Selleck, George W. Hamilton. Const., William E. Bailey, Michael J. Keating, William K. Cowan, James B. Bryan, Henry A. Hoyt. G. Jurors, Christian Quien, Chester G. Ambler, Edwin B. Harris, Theodore Lyon, Abner B. Holley. Assessors, Ezra A. Mallory, Samuel A. Barnum, Charles F. Starr. Board of R., Theodore Lyon, Jarvis P. Hull, Nathan B. Dibble. Board of Ed., James W. Hubbell, William F. Taylor, 1882; Abner B. Holley, Martin P. Lawlor. 1883; Andrew C. Hubbard, Byron J. Hall, 1884. Reg. of Voters, Harris L. Crofut, William T. St. John.

DARIEN. Clerk and Treas., John S. Waterbury. Reg., Samuel Sands. Selectmen, Ira Scofield, Thaddeus Bell, Chas. A. Bates, Jr. Const., George Fowler, C. G. Waterbury, S. O. Keeler, William H. Walmsley. Coll, George W. Clock. G. Jurors, C. A Hobbie, W. T. Barker, James A. Shaw, Samuel B. Belden. Assessors, N. Danehy, Charles Brown, Sands Selleck. Board of R., Samuel Sands, Lewis S. Reed, Ambrose Richards. Board of Ed., Louis S. French, Charles S. Whitney, Albert Scofield, James Curzon, James B. Selleck. Reg. of Voters, N. Dauchy, Wm. H. Wilmot, Jr.

DERBY. Clerk, Daniel E. McMahon. (P. O., Ansonia,) Reg., Thomas J. O'Sullivan. (P. O. Birmingham.) Treas, Theo. S. Bassett. Selectmen, E. W. Webster, P. McManus, Robert O. Gates. Const., John R. Kelley, John H. Lines, John W. Dyer, F. Dwight Woodruff, Joseph Colwell, Ferris A. Castle. Fred. J. Baldwin. Coll., N. C. Treat. G. Jurors, Hugh McGowan, Robert Gates, Ira B. Newcomb, Andrew Martinez, Charles French, Patrick Gilligan. Assessors, Henry Whipple, Eli H. Wakelee, Charles L. Hill. Board of R., George H. Peck, John Cowell, Robert Hoadley. Board of Ed., John Lindley, H. T. Brady, Clark W. Rogers, George H. Peck, J. N. Whitlock,

6

O. W. Witherspoon, P. Ν. Kennedy, Josiah H. Whiting. Reg. of Voters, 1st Dist., John C. Reilly, F. D. Jackson; 2d Dist., John L. Lindley, Νorris Drew.

DURHAΝ. (P. O., Durham Centre.) Clerk, N. H. Parsons. Reg., B. B. Beecher. Treas., William A. Parmelee. Selectmen, S. F. Leete, Bishop Atwell, Ashahel Nettleton. Const., John Atwell, E. D. Burke. Coll., John Talmadge. G. Jurors, H. S. Νerwin, Judson E. Francis. Assessors, William C. Ives, James E. Bailey. Board of R., Νiles T. Νerwin, Ransom Prout, John Asman, Timothy E. Hull, William T. D. Coe. Board of Ed., Judson E. Francis, Stephen A. Seward, 1882; A. P. Roberts, James E. Bailey, 1883; *N. H. Parsons, Samuel W. Soper, 1884. Reg. of Voters, Curtis E. Atwell, James K. Elliott.

EASTFORD. Clerk and Treas., J. D. Barrows. Reg., E. K. Robbins. Selectmen, James Ν. Keith, S. C. Simmons, Alfrèd D. Cady. Const., Henry A. Braman, Frederick Upham, Νonroe F. Latham. Coll., C. E. Barrows. G. Jurors, C. Ν. Brooks, James H. Wilbur, H. H. Burnham. Assessors, Henry Trowbridge, H. P. Bullard. Board of R., D. P. Carpenter, S. C. Simmons. Board of Ed., S. A. Wheaton, C. E. Barrows, 1882; S. O. Bowen, H. P. Bullard, 1883; C. Ν. Jones, E. W. Warren, 1884. Reg. of Voters, E. K. Robbins, E. P. Arnold.

EAST GRANBY. Clerk and Reg., Elmore Clark. Treas., Isaac P. Owen. Selectmen, Samuel A. Clark, Cicero H. Νerwin, Daniel C. Hayes. Const., Francis Granger, J. Duane Viets, Henry P. Goddard, Edward C. Tallmadge, Timothy W. Griswold. Coll., Νorton A. Holcomb. G. Jurors, Ebenezer Talbot, Henry P. Holcomb, William A. Viets, Homer Griffin, Jeremy H. Holcomb. Assessors, Jeremy H. Holcomb, Thomas H. Holmes. Board of R., Ebenezer Talbot, Levi C. Viets. Board of Ed., *Henry L. Clark, Wilber H. Gay, 1882; Richard H. Phelps, B. Ellsworth Smith, 1883; Timothy W. Griswold, Frederic F. Stevens, 1884. Reg. of Voters, Timothy W. Griswold, Νorton A. Holcomb.

EAST HADDAΝ. Clerk and Reg., Julius Attwood. Treas., Thomas Gross Jr. Selectmen, John G. Barber, William H. Νartin, Wilbur F. Wright. Const., Ralph B. Swan, Francis W. Brainard, Wm. E. Gates, John S. Griffin, Chas. S. Jewett. Coll., Arthur J. Silliman. G. Jurors, N. O. Harris, John C.

Boylston, E. Emory Johnson, Abiel Stock, Francis E. Gates, Erastus Rogers. Assessors, David S. Purple, Charles H. Rich, John S. Brainard. Board of R., James Alexander, Francis W. Swan, William E. Hungerford. Board of Ed., Wm. C. Greene, Silas R. Holmes, 1882; Salmon McCall, Norris W. Rathbun, 1883; George Rumney, Edward C. Brownell, 1884. Reg. of Voters, Richard E. Hungerford, Cyrus W. Chapman.

EAST HARTFORD. Clerk, Joseph O. Goodwin. Reg., George S. Phelps. Treas., Ezra E. Smith. Selectmen, Ashbel Gilman, Lawrence V. Lester, John H. Elmer. Const., Arthur P. Moore, Charles J. Stewart, Edward F. Risley, Omri P. Brewer, Wm. Foley, Wm. H. Olmsted. Coll., Ralph A. Olmsted. G. Jurors, Ephraim Rood, George W. Pratt, Ralph Risley, Norman L. Anderson, Frederick S. Putnam, Wm. Reed. Assess., Charles N. Bidwell, John Kennedy, Henry P. Brewer, Hosmer P. Stedman, Ira T. Roberts. Board of R., George W. Darlin, Norman L. Anderson, Aaron G. Olmsted. Board of Ed., Elijah Ackley, John T. McMahon, 1882; *Joseph O. Goodwin, Patrick Garvan, 1883; *Francis R. Childs, Arthur W. Eaton, 1884. Reg. of Voters, Thomas Dowd, Omri P. Brewer.

EAST HAVEN. Clerk, Charles T. Hemingway. Reg., Wm. H. Shannon. Treas., Orlando B. Thompson. Selectmen, Leonard R. Andrews, Ruel S. Thompson, Henry Smith. Const., Daniel M. Church, Gilbert Van Sickle, Reuben H. Coe, Martin Reynolds, Edwin Russell, Henry J. H. Thompson, William H. Chidsey. Coll., John Jackson. G. Jurors, John Ives Bradley, Jonathan Dudley, John J. Tyler, Grove S. Tuttle, F. W. Watrous, Harvey Chidsey. Assess., Albert Forbes, Lyman A. Granniss. Board of R., Samuel Chidsey, Merwin Bailey. Board of Ed., Charles H. Fowler, S. W. F. Andrews, 1882; Grove J. Tuttle, Wm. H. Bradley, 1883; Dwight W. Tuttle, Jonathan Dudley, 1884. Reg. of Voters, 1st Dist., Orlando B. Thompson, Wm. H. Chidsey; 2d Dist., Oliver Bailey, Cornelius Thompson.

EAST LYME. Clerk, Gilbert P. Coates. Reg., Elisha N. Comstock. Treas., John W. Luce. Selectmen, Peter A. Comstock, Edwin Howard, John Lee. Const., Dwight B. Pierce, and Coll., Robert B. Gorton, Turner C. Haynes, Nelson Rogers. G. Jurors, Francis W. Bolles, John T. Beckwith, Arthur L. Crocker. Assess., Nelson Rogers, Eugene Beckwith, James Miner. Board of R., James R. White, Nathan P. Newton,

George W. Congdon. Board of Ed., Enoch L. Beckwith, Geo. Huntley, 1882; Daniel Calkins, Elisha Munger, 1883; Josiah Benton, Calvin E. Davis, 1884. Reg. of Voters, 1st Dist., Irvin Watrous; 2d Dist, Lyman Bacon.

EASTON. Clerk, Ebenezer S. Gillette. Reg , Martin Dudley. Treas., Joseph W. Johnson. Selectmen, George S. Platt, Stephen D. Wheeler, Joseph E. Fields. Const., James J. Ward, Charles S. Powell, Charles S. Clark, Wm. A. Sherman, Daniel Edwards, Edward Seeley, Wm. J. Candee. Coll., Wm. W. Jennings. G. Jurors, Benjamin T. Beers, Edward K. Freeborn, Charles C. Sherman, Almon H. French, Daniel P. Parrack, Lewis Edwards. Assess., Wm. W. Jennings, Moses H. Thorp. Board of R., George S. Banks, Charles S. Everett, George J. Banks. Board of Ed., Charles H. Rowell, James A. Wheeler, 1882; Charles F. Silliman, Wm. H. Greenman, 1883; George S. Gillette, Chauncey McCarty, 1884. Reg. of Voters, George Freeborn, George J. Banks.

EAST WINDSOR. Clerk, Reg , and Treas., Mahlon H. Bancroft (P. O. Warehouse Point). Selectmen, S. D. Rockwell, George H. Sloan, John N. Clark. Const., Herbert C. Parsons, and Coll., Frederick B. Baker. G. Jurors, John C. Bartlett, Henry W. Bissell, Winthrop L. Allen, Joseph A. Pascoe, William M. Dunham, John Mason. Assess., Joseph A. Pascoe, Lewis T. Skinner. Board of R., Joseph T. Hull, James B. Colton, Josiah O. Ellsworth. Board of Ed., Jabez S. Allen, John F. Fitts, Mahlon H. Bancroft, 1882; Edward Goodridge, John B. Noble, George S. Phelps, 1883; Orson S. Wood, S. Terry Wells, Homer S. Allen, 1884. Reg. of Voters, Jabez S. Allen, Francis A. Hamilton.

ELLINGTON. Clerk, Reg., and Treas., Oliver M. Hyde. Seleetmen, John Beasley, Daniel N. Kimball, Henry C. Aborn. Const., Henry K. Warner, and Coll., Thomas Manock, William Crane, Alfred U. Chaster, Carlos Thrall, George Smith, Clark D. Mackey. G. Jurors, James H. Steele, Orrin D. Newell, Harlin Nash, Sylvester Morris, Stephen I. Johnson, Ephraim H. Dimock. Assess., Henry M. Niles, Orrin D. Newell, Ira H. Lewis. Board of R., George W. Kimball, Darius Crane, Charles B. Sikes. Board of Ed., Dwight F. Lull, *Sylvester Morris, Joel A. Warren, 1882; Robert Patton, Henry C. Aborn, Edwin Talcott, 1883; *Charles T. Norton, Myron H. Dimock, Carlos R. Sadd, 1884. Reg. of Voters, Michael H. Mandell, Julius A. Kibbe.

ENFIELD. Clerk, Reg., and Treas., Frederick E. Ely. Select-men, Benjamin F. Lord, Augustus Landschultz, Wm. Mulligan. Const., Timothy W. Pease, George B. Bradford, Dwight A. Abbe, Alexander Buhler, Charles H. Barton, Gabriel A. Armstrong, John C. Weising and Coll. G. Jurors, George Bridge, Charles W. Clark, Jesse Randall, Wilham Hilditch, Joseph Buck, James R. Sloanc. Assess., Loren H. Pease, Calvin O. King, Asa Lewis. Board of R., John N. Spencer, Daniel H. Abbe, Charles C. Bill, Wills Spencer, Robert B. Morrison. Board of Ed., E. F. Parsons, George W. Winch, Edward Prickett, Frederick A. King, Joseph N. Allen, David P. Sanford. Reg. of Voters, Loren H. Pease, James B. Benson.

ESSEX. Clerk, James L. Phelps. Reg., Edward W. Pratt. Treas., Edward W. Redfield. Selectmen, Wm. C. Hough, Alfred M. Wright, Jared C. Pratt. Const., Benjamin A. Gladding, and Coll., Edward W. Pratt, Wm. N. Robbins, John M. Culver. G. Jurors, Henry L. Pratt, Eben P. Lincoln, Richard H. Mather, Edwin Pratt. Assess , Chauncey Spencer, Francis H. Tiffany. Board of R., Edwin Pratt, Ansel Bushnell, Julius Andrews. Board of Ed., R. H. Mather, Giles Potter, C. H. Hubbard. Reg. of Voters, Henry L. Pratt.

FAIRFIELD. Clerk, Daniel Moloney. Reg. and Treas., Edmund Hobart. Selectmen, Andrew P. Wakeman, Samuel Pike, John B. Morehouse. Const., Daniel Moloney, and Coll., Thomas Jennings, David B. Bulkley, James M. Wilson, Daniel Ahern, J. Eli Wakeman, Jr   G. Jurors, Patrick Riley, George Bonney, Moses B. Banks, John M. Brothwell, James D. Jennings, Henry G. Wilson. Assess., Samuel Pike, William Bradley, Arthur Bennett. Board of R., Moses B. Banks, John M. Brothwell, Michael B. Lacey. Board of Ed., J. F. Jennings, James K. Lombard, 1882; J. Jay Jones, John Warren, 1883; D. J. Cremin, M. V. B. Dunham, 1884. Reg. of Voters, Samuel Pike, Francis B. Wakley.

FARMINGTON. Clerk and Reg., Thomas L. Porter. Treas., Erastus Gay. Selectmen, Winthrop M. Wadsworth, Phineas B. Goodwin, Martin L. Parsons. Const., Chauncey D. Ewing. and Coll., Samuel D. Hills, John H. Thompson, Adrian R. Wadsworth, Henry A. Cowles, Isaac Judd, Solon Balger. G. Jurors, Thomas Cowles, Robert B. Treadwell, Alpheus Porter, Timothy H. Root, Myron W. Thompson, Winslow A. Goodhue.

Assess., Thomas Scott, Sherman Sanford, John P. Lewis.
Board of R., Elijah L. Lewis, Charles H. Graham, Robert B.
Treadwell. Board of Ed., *Thomas E. Davies, Samuel Frisbie,
*Thomas Cowles, Jr., 1882; Julius Gay, James A. Smith, Geo.
W. Allen, 1883; Edward Norton, *Thomas K. Fessenden, Chas.
L. Whitman, 1884. Reg. of Voters, Thomas Cowles, Robert B.
Treadwell, Carlos L. Mason, George W. Frisbie.

FRANKLIN. Clerk and Treas., Samuel G. Hartshorn. Reg.,
Andrew B. Smith. Selectmen, Henry W. Kingsley, Joseph I.
Hyde, Henry Bellows. Const., Albert W. Hillard, and Coll.,
Charles A. Kingsley, Otis B. Hyde, James D. Simpson, Samuel
N. Hyde. G. Jurors, John M. N. Lathrop, William C. Smith,
Oliver L. Johnson, George E. Starkweather, Lavins A. Robin-
son. Assess., E. Eugene Ayer, John M. N. Lathrop, Ansel
Pendleton. Board of R., Joseph I. Hyde, John Q. Cross, Gil-
bert Lamb. Board of Ed., George Lewis Ladd, Henry Bellows,
1882; Albert W. Hillard, George H. Griffing, 1883; Henry W.
Kingsley, John Herrick, 1884. Reg. of Voters, Oliver L. John-
son, George H. Griffing.

GLASTONBURY. Clerk and Reg., Samuel C. Hardin. Treas.,
Albert A. Bogue. Selectmen, John B. Moseley, Eugene S.
Strickland, George S. Andrews. Const., Frederick W. Dean,
Daniel Gilligan, George A. Treat, Hartwell M. Brainard. Coll.,
Daniel L. Talcott. G. Jurors, Arthur M. Brainard, Charles W.
Jones, Nelson A. Hardin, Roswell E. Merrick, T. Dwight Goslee,
George S. House. Assess., Roswell E. Merrick, Lincoln E.
Crosby, George R. Hale, Charles J. Loomer. Board of R., Isaac
Broadhead, Aaron W. Kinne, Elijah Miller. Board of Ed.,
John W. Hubbard, Edwin Crosby, 1882; William S. Wright,
William H. Griswold, 1883; Austin Gardner, Alonzo A. Bab-
cock, 1884. Reg. of Voters, John C. Rockwell, Russell S.
Cowles.

GOSHEN. Clerk and Reg., Joseph Howard North. Treas.,
Willard E. Gaylord. Selectmen, Fessenden Ives, Samuel P.
Oviatt, Frederick E. Hurlbut. Const., Albert Sperry, Frank
W. Seaton, Edmund J. Apley. Coll., Hubert S. Scovill. G.
Jurors, S. W. Scovill, George G. Crandall, F. A. Lucas, Ira
Babcock, Edward Norton, Henry Barton. Assess., Theron H.
Page, Daniel N. Lucas, James Wadhams. Board of R., Wilbur
H. Wadhams, George W. Humphrey, Patrick McElhone. Board
of Ed., John H. Wadhams, Henry Norton, 1882; M. D. F.

Smith, John D. Barton, 1883; Frederick A. Lucas, S. A. Bartholomew, 1884. Reg. of Voters, Willard E. Gaylord, Lyman Hall.

GRANBY. Clerk, Chester P. Loomis. Reg., Buel B. Alling. Treas., Denison Case. Selectmen, John W. Ruic, Charles Weed, Wilson Griffin. Const., Nelson W. Phelps, and Coll., Albert H. Gillett, S. Fred. Holcomb, George R. Case, Duane C. Wilcox, Henry G. Viets, James H. Smith G. Jurors, Watson Dewey, Ansel H. Rice. Geo. Spring, Willis L. Hayes, Munson Holcomb. Assess., Condit Hayes, Fred'k J. Jewett, Henry G.. Viets. Board of R., Watson Dewey, Buel B. Alling, Luzerne C. Holcomb. Board of Ed., Lucian Reed. Buel B. Alling, A. L. Holcomb, 1882; Willis L. Hayes, F. J. Jewett, Lewis C. Spring, 1883; James B. Cleaveland, Lyman I. Holcomb, Geo. O. Beach, 1884. Reg. of Voters, Lucian Reed, Geo. Spring.

GREENWICH. Clerk and Reg, George G. McNall. Treas., Nehemiah H. Husted. Selectmen, Wm. H. Craft, J. Albert Lockwood, Whitman S. Mead. Const., John Dayton, Philip Finnegan, John Lotz, Charles Francis Adams, George Selleck, Edwin C. Brundage. Coll., Hiram June. G. Jurors, Wm. E. Ferris, Joseph G. Merritt, Philip Wiegand, George W. Brush, John A. Husted, Franklin N. Wilcox. Assess, Jabez Mead, Underhill Lyon, Wm. S. Finch, Seaman Mead, Sylvester D. Husted. Board of R., Benjamin K. Tompkins, Henry B. Marshall, Allen Howe. Board of Ed, James H. Brush, James L. Marshall, 1882; Thomas H Delano, Wm. S. Craft, 1883; Amasa A. Marks, Myron L. Mason, 1884. Reg. of Voters, John G. Reynolds, Zophar Mead.

GRISWOLD. Clerk, Henry Spalding. Reg., William Soule, Treas., James O. Sweet. Selectmen, Israel Mathewson, Andrew Edmond, Stephen Tiffany. Const., Josiah Brown, Joseph W. Dawley, George R. Lathrop, C'arence B. Kegwin, A. F. Burton, Hiram Miner. Coll., Jepthah G. Bill. G. Jurors, Wm. C. Bliven, Richard R. Buck, L. M. Green, Dwight R. Kegwin, William P. Young, Andrew H. Meech. Assess., Albert G. Brewster, Wm. Fogarty. Board of R., Jepthah G. Bill, Edward Cook, Patrick Leyden. Board of Ed., John D. Eccleston, E. C. Kegwin, Barton C. Kegwin, Samuel Barber, Jas. Finn. Reg. of Voters, Joseph E. Leonard, Benjamin F. Lewis, E. C. Kegwin, Ira F. Lewis.

GROTON. Clerk, James D. Avery, Reg., Walter R. Denison.
Treas., John O. Fish. Selectmen, Thomas W. Noyes, L. D.
Baker, J. S. Heath. Const., B. N. O'Brien, D. H. Johnson, T.
J. Sawyer, Jr., Geo. W. Packer, Jr., Seth N. Williams, George
C. Burch. Coll., Daniel Morgan. G. Jurors, James B. Saun-
ders, Roswell Brown, Reuben Heath, Philo Little, Levi Lamb.
Assess., Simon Huntington, John T. Batty, James N. Turner.
Board of R., Caleb P. Bailey, Gurdon Gates, Wm. E. Wheeler.
Board of Ed., Wm. H. Potter, Samuel S. Lamb, Joseph Hall,
Horace Clift. Reg. of Voters, 1st Dist., F. H. Brewer, J. T.
Beatty; 2d Dist., P. N. Alexander, S. H. Gove; 3d, S. B.
Latham, J. A. Fitch.

GUILFORD. Clerk, Edward R. Landon. Reg , Henry Ben-
ton, 2d. Treas., Harris Pendleton, Jr. Selectmen, Elisha C.
Bishop, David K. Parmelee, Theodore Fowler. Const., Richard
W. Starr, William H. Lee, Harvey W. Leete, John A. Phelps.
Asahel B. Morse, Baldwin C. Dudley, George E. Munson.
Colls., George N. Seward, Dudley Chittenden. G. Jurors,
Alvin B. Palmer, Henry E. Parmelee, John W. Norton, George
W. Carter, Charles N. Potter, D. Dwight Chittenden, Assess.,
John Dudley, James D. Goldsmith, Cyrus O. Bartlett. Board
of R , John W. Norton, David B. Rossiter. Board of Ed.,
George W. Banks, Charles Griswold, J. Seymour Benton, 1882;
Alvin B. Palmer, Erwin W. Rossiter, Richard N. Leete, 1883;
Frederick P. Griswold, John R. Rossiter, W. S. Marks, 1884.
Reg. of Voters, Calvin N. Leete, J. Seymour Benton.

HADDAM. Clerk and Reg., John H. Russell. Treas., Rus-
sell Shailer. Selectmen, Ephraim P. Arnold, Frank A. House,
Horace A. Bonfoey, Henry H. Brainerd, Warren S. Williams.
Const., Sam'l Arnold, Edward L. Johnson, Leonard D. Skinner,
Alvin B. Spencer, Frank H. Arnold. Coll., Nathan Keller, Sam-
uel Arnold. G. Jurors, Stephen H. Burr, Wm. P. Arnold, Chas.
S. Wilcox, David O. Dickinson, Oliver C. Neff, Washington K.
Smith. Assess., Orrin Shailer, Noah Burr, Wm. C. Selden.
Board of R., Samuel Arnold, Washington K. Smith, Chauncey
S. Tyler. Board of Ed., *Alpheus W. Tyler, Orrin Shailer,
Charles O. Gillett, 1882; Isaac Arnold, Ephraim P. Arnold,
Samuel B. Bailey, 1883; John H. Russell, Gilbert N. Clark,
Arnold H. Hayden, 1884. Reg. of Voters, 1st Dist., George W.
Arnold, Arnold H. Hayden; 2d Dist., Wilber F. Smith, Gilbert
N. Hubbard; 3d Dist., Ezra F. Brainerd, Chas. O. Gillett.

HANDEN. Clerk, Reg., and Treas., Ellsworth B. Cooper. Selectmen, Charles P. Augur, W. W. Woodruff, Edwin W. Potter. Const., Merrit L. Potter, Charles L. Morse, Lewis Joyce, John Mautte. Coll., Jesse Warner. G. Jurors, George H. Allen, George C. Rogers. Assess., George H. Allen, Gilbert S. Benham. Board of R., John Osborn, Leverett A. Dickerman, Ellsworth B. Cooper. Board of Ed., Norris B. Mix, John H. Dickerman, Charles I. Dickerman, 1882; Silas Benham, Andrew McKeon, Elias Dickerman, 1883; Ellsworth A. Bradley, *Leverett A. Dickerman, Jas. H. Webb, 1884. Reg. of Voters, Andrew McKeon, Charles L. Morse.

HAMPTON. Clerk, Reg., and Treas., William H. Burnham. Selectmen, David Greenslit, Israel E. Harvey, George H. Kimball. Const., George W. Fuller, George W. Bennett, Elisha S. Fuller. G. Jurors, John R. Tweedy, Nathan J. Holt, Giles H. Snow. Assess., Addison J. Greenslit, Horace Jackson. Board of R., Henry G. Taintor, Daniel M. Deming, Austin E. Pearl. Board of Ed., Addison J. Greenslit, Charles Gardiner, Henry G. Snow, 1882; David Greenslit, Edgar H. Newton, Elisha S. Fuller, 1883; *Joseph W. Congdon, Henry Clapp, Allen Jewett, 1884. Reg. of Voters, Patrick H. Pearl, Asa Kimball.

HARTFORD. Clerk and Reg., John E. Higgins. Treas., Charles C. Strong. Selectmen, Roswell W. Brown, Edward W. Parsons, Ralph Foster, Valentine Cooper, George W. Fowler. Const., Richard B. Hetherton, Benjamin F. Doty, Willis A. Pierce, William H. Vosburgh, Thomas Longdon, Lester W. Cowles, Everett S. Geer. Coll., Frederick S. Brown. G. Jurors, Stephen Terry, Henry E. Burton, Henry E. Taintor, James H. Tallman, William F. Henney, Leonard Morse. Assessors, John Allen, Henry R. Tryon, Michael F. Dooley. Board of R., Nelson G. Hinckley, John McGoodwin, George O. Preston, Board of Ed., *John H. Brocklesby, David Crary, John R. Buck. 1882; Mahlon R. West, Gurdon W. Russell, Melancthon Storrs, 1883; George G. Sill, Joseph H. Twichell, Charles C. Kimball, 1884. Reg. of Voters, Thomas Eustice, Henry W. Hutchinson. Town Auditors, Patrick McGovern, Patrick Moran.

HARTLAND. Clerk and Reg., Benjamin H. Selby. Treas., Flavel C. Newton. Selectmen, Orton B. French, Amos W. Dean, Phineas C. Stevens. Const., Almon C. Banning, William Davis, Albert N. Stillman, Norton M. Dickinson, Miron E. Miller, Henry S. Mattocks. Colls., Elbert J. Banning, Nelson

Hayes. G. Jurors, Elbert J. Banning, Uriah Nickerson, Nelson Emmons. George H. Clark, Seth Giddings, A. W. Coe. Assessors, Henry .I. Gates, Timothy E. Williams. Board of R., Ebenezer H. Miller, Amos N. Osborn, Almon C. Banning. Board of Ed., Timothy E. Williams, George N. Thompson, Homer S. Bell, *Merrick Knight, Alonzo B. Gaines, Orton B. French, George B. Cornish. Reg. of Voters, Oliver P. Cowdery, Herbert H. Griswold.

HARWINTON. Clerk, George E. Cook. Reg., Norman A. Wilson. Treas., Martin L. Goodwin. Selectmen, Henry E. Hinman, Sherman B. Barber, Orange A. Hubbell. Const., Benjamin F. Page, Henry N. Kinney. Coll., Sherman Barber. G. Jurors, Henry E. Hinman, George E. Cook, Abijah Catlin. Assessors, Virgil R. Barker, David Vaill. Board of R.. Martin L. Goodwin, Stephen B. Cook, Norman A. Wilson. Board of Ed., Emerson N. Hayes, *Martin Cook, Henry D. Reynolds, Martin L. Goodwin, Albert G. Wilson. Reg. of Voters, Virgil R. Barker, Henry D. Reynolds.

HEBRON. Clerk and Treas., Stephen B. Fuller. Reg., David N. Buell. Selectmen, James H. Jagger, John H. Buell, William E. Latham. Const., Jared B. Fillmore, and Coll., Alfred J. Holbrook, John H. Buell, John H. Wood, William H. Wilson, Justin Kellogg. G. Jurors, Anson Little, Eugene W. Latham, Arthur G. Turner, Frank W. Brown, Charles H. Brown, Sylvester Root. Assessors, Jared B. Fillmore, Charles D. Way, Julius Hills. Board of R., John S. Welles, John R. Gilbert, Henry Post. Board of Ed., Anson Little, Frank R. Post, Ralph L. Gilbert, F. Clarence Bissell, Josiah A. Mack, Jared W. Ellsworth, Cyrus H. Pendleton, George N. Porter, Loren A. Waldo. Reg. of Voters, Josiah N. Buell, James A. Way.

HUNTINGTON. Clerk and Treas., Edward W. Downs. Reg., Gould A. Shelton. Selectmen, Stephen T. Palmer, Henry I. Brownson, Smith Wheeler. Const., S. Byron Brownson, H. Stanley Brinsmade, Henry A. Warner, George H. Church, Ira C. Northrup, George Smith, Stiles B. Nichols. G. Jurors, David T. Beecher, Charles H. Nettleton, William Buckingham, E. L. Walker, Robert L. Tenney. Assessors, William C. Hine, Daniel A. Nichols, William T. Beard. Board of R., Almon B. Ruggles, Lewis J. Shelton, Lyman Lattin. Board of Ed., Gould A. Shelton, Horace Wheeler, 1882; *Edward S. Hawley,

Lewis B. Gray, 1883; Daniel S. Brinsmade, Gordon ♪. Wakelee, 1884. Reg. of Voters, 1st Dist., Daniel S. Brinsmade, William J. Norse; 2d Dist., Edward J. Buckingham, Frederick R. Clark.

KENT. Clerk, Jerome F. Gibbs. Reg., John W. King. Treas., Charles H. Gaylord. Selectmen, Luther Eaton, Clark Paige, John Straight. Const., Frederick A. Mallory. Coll., Chas. A. Eaton. G. Jurors, George L. Segar. Assessors, F. A. Mallory, S. S. Green, Charles L. Spooner. Board of R., Richard Lee, Frank Evetts, Gilbert A. Vincent. Board of Ed., Thomas D. Barclay, Isaac C. Sturgis, John Chase, G. A. Vincent. Reg. of Voters, Gilbert A. Vincent, Albert Roberts.

KILLINGLY. (P. O. Danielsonville.) Clerk, Reg., and Treas., Henry S. Young. Selectmen, Ezekiel R. Burlingame, Charles P. Card, Franklin Wood, George R. Davis, Edwin A Hill. Const., Edward A. Carpenter, Laurens Card, Augustus A. Vaughn, Stephen S. Hawkins, Thomas W. Stevenson, John Tennant. Coll., George W. Pike. G. Jurors, Charles H. Keach, Nathan A. Short, Irvin D. Hawkins, Francis F. Young, William W. White. Assessors, Caleb W. Knight, Alonzo B. Potter, William N. Lewis, Francis E. Baker, Edmund L. Warner. Board of R., Walter F. Day, Publius D. Foster, David B. Wheaton, Benjamin F. Chapman, Wheaton A. Bennett. Board of Ed., Anthony Ames, Marshal P. Dowe, Ashabel E. Darling, 1882: *Charles P. Blackman, Edward S. Hountress, Chauncey H. Wright, 1883; James Dingwell, Herbert C. Columbus, Edwin A. Hill, 1884. Reg. of Voters, 1st Dist., Emmons H. Brown, Edward Davis; 2d Dist., Daniel C. Frost, Wheaton A. Bennett; 3d Dist., William H. Oatley, Nelson ♪. Reynolds.

KILLINGWORTH. Clerk and Reg., Henry Hull. Treas., Randolph P. Stevens. Selectmen, Andrew W. Burr, J. Philander Lane, William Bristol. Const., Randolph S. Burr, Adelbert H. Stevens. Coll., J. Philander Lane. G. Jurors, Sidney T. Davis, Avington D. Parmelee, Sherman E. Griswold. Assessors, Isaac Kelsey, Lauren L. Nettleton. Board of R., David R. Stevens, Orson L. Dudley. Board of Ed., Edward P. Armstrong, Washington E. Griswold, Alfred A. Stevens. Reg. of Voters, David R. Stevens, Nathan H. Evarts.

LEBANON. Clerk and Treas., Walter G. Kingsley. Reg., Jonathan Lyman. Selectmen, Joseph C. Crandall, Charles J.

Abell, Darius H. Leonard, Jr., Charles B. Noyes, Joseph
C. Crandall. Const., Asa C. Peckham, Jacob McCall, Albert
G. Kneeland, Nathan Bass. Coll., William W. Peckham.
G. Jurors, Justin L. Babcock, Joshua B. Card, Silas P.
Abell, Wm. W. Gillett. Assessors, Frank K. Noyes, Erastus
S. Geer, Ansel Wilcox, Daniel T. Fuller. Board of R., Ho-
bart McCall, William F. Gates, Henry W. Abell, Wm. H.
Loomis. Board of Ed., George D. Spencer, Frederick A.
Abell, 1882; David H. McCall, Edward S. Hinckley, 1883;
Isaac Gillett, W. P. Barber, 1884. Reg. of Voters, Frank K.
Noyes, Frank P. Fowler.

LEDYARD. Clerk, Jacob Gallup. Reg., John A. Gray.
Treas., Jacob Gallup. Selectmen, Nathan S. Gallup, Stiles
Crandall, Isaac G. Geer. Const., L. H. Griswold, John A. Tur-
ner, Stephen H. Peckham, Daniel W. Lamb. Coll., George W.
Spicer. G. Jurors, Wm. L. Main, Robert E. Turner, Dudley R.
Thompson, Thomas Latham, James Norman, Jr. Assess., Wm.
J. Brown, Lyman A. Richards, Calvin W. Hewitt, George W.
Hurlbutt, Jonathan B. Beckwith. Board of R., Elisha S.
Allyn, Isaac E. Avery, Nehemiah M. Gallup, Calvin H. Roach.
Board of Ed , Isaac G. Geer, Russel Gallup, Albert Z. Brown,
1882; Christopher M. Gallup, Timothy A. Avery, George Fan-
ning, 1883; Wm. Brown, John S. Spicer, Wm. T. Cook, 1884.
Reg. of Voters, Isaac E. Avery, Nehemiah N. Gallup.

LISBON. Clerk and Treas., Henry Lyon. Reg., Russel W.
Fitch. Selectmen, Edward C. Hyde, Russel W. Fitch, James
H Kennedy. Const., George G. Bromley. Coll., Benjamin G.
Hull. G. Jurors, Elijah S. Barnes, Wm. A. Johnson. John F.
Hewitt. Assess., Cornelius Murphy, Jabez L. Benjamin.
Board of R., Edwin F. Appley, Charles J. Bromley, William A.
Johnson. Board of Ed , Edward C. Strong, *Albert A. Hills,
1882; Charles J. Bromley, John F. Hewitt, 1883; George A.
Ross, *Henry Lyon, 1884. Reg. of Voters, Augustus F. Reade,
James B. Palmer.

LITCHFIELD. Clerk and Reg., Willis J. Beach. Treas.,
George N. Woodruff. Selectmen, Jacob Norse, Wm. J. Hall,
Thomas C. Goslee, Malachi Tracy, Jerome D. Wheeler. Const.,
James Campbell, James H. Norse, Homer S. Noore, Wm.
Howard, Dexter E. Norse, John E. Sedgwick, Michael Keawin.
Coll , Wm. Norton. G. Jurors, George E. Jones, Frank E. Earle,
Wm. H. Palmer, Daniel G. Turney, G. B. Curtiss, John B.

Candee. Assess., Henry Clemons, Darius P. Griswold, Francis H. Hale, John L. Plumb, Norman B. Perkins. Board of R., Andrew J. Pierpont, Everett H. Wright. Holmes O. Morse, Henry G. Tyler, Jesse L. Judd. Board of Ed., S. O. Seymonr, D. C. Kilbourn, T. L. Jennings, F. S. Porter, E. H. Wright, George W. Mason. Reg. of Voters., John H. Morse, C. B. Bishop, Charles W. Talcott, A. M. Turner.

LYME. Clerk, Frederick Fosdick. Reg., Benjamin A. Rathbun. Treas., Henry B. Sisson. Selectmen, Charles Stark, H. B. L. Reynolds, Frederick W. Comstock. Const., R. M. Jewett, J. Ely Harding. Coll., Horace B. Royce. G. Jurors, Wm. C. Spencer, James Bingham, Wm. B. Fosdick. Assess., Charles A. Tiffany, Augustus D. Marvin, Helon Gates. Board of R., Reuben Lord, Wm. S. Hall, Calvin L. Ely. Board of Ed., Wm. C. Spencer. J. Griffin Ely, 1882; Benj. A. Hopkinson, J. R. Sterling, 1883; Henry B. Sisson, E. F. Burr, 1884. Reg. of Voters, John W. Bill, Hewlitt K. Anderson.

MADISON. Clerk and Reg., Henry B. Wilcox. Treas., C. Henry Whedon. Selectmen, John H. Meigs, Henry S. Hill, Joseph H. Hill. Const., Frederick T. Dowd, J. Samuel Scranton, Myron H. Munger. Coll., J. Sherman Buell, Myron H. Munger. G. Jurors, J. Willis Tucker, Wm. C. Miner, George W. Bunnell. Assess., Dwight S. Whedon, Noble S. Blatchley. Board of R., Timothy F. Wilcox, Heman C. Stone, Moses J. Stannard. Board of Ed., John H. Meigs, Wm. S. Hull, 1882; James A. Gallup, Nathan Howell, 1883; John P. Hopson, Ezra S. Smith. Reg. of Voters, Wm. B. Crampton, Wm. S. Hull.

MANCHESTER. Clerk, Reg., and Treas., Daniel Wadsworth. Selectmen, Charles D. Parsons, Elisha Williams, Giles M. Hills. Const , George A. Bidwell, Robert Rae, George W. Bidwell, Richard W. Pitkin. Coll., Charles S. Cheney. G. Jurors, Chauncey B. Knox, Robert N. Strong, John Loomis, George G. Griswold, Andrew H. Rockwell, Henry A. Griswold. Assess., John F. Williams, Wm. W. Hollister. Board of R., Henry H. White, George W. Cheney, Albert Taylor. Board of Ed., Oliver B. Taylor, J. B. Latham, 1882; John S. Cheney, C. W. Jaques, 1883; Silas W. Robbins, James F. Campbell, 1884. Reg. of Voters, Charles H. Arnold, Herbert J. Annis, Charles H. Owen.

MANSFIELD. Clerk, Reg., and Treas., R. W. Storrs. Selectmen, George L. Rosebrook, George F. Swift, George W Nore.

Const., Wm. Corbit, Frank Freeman.   G. Jurors, David Hooker, Jared Stearns, Edward P. Conant, Robert P. Barrows, George F. King, Andrew R. Brown.   Assess., A. W. Buchanan, Washington I. Swift.   Board of R., Robert P. Barrows, Darwin S. Read, Charles J. Mason.   Board of Ed., Henry Huntington, Samuel Hovey, A. J. Chapin, 1882; Edwin B. Sumner, Rich B. Glidden, Samuel S. Yeomans, 1883; Robert P. Barrows, Nathaniel Beach, Washington I. Swift, 1884.   Reg. of Voters, Joseph P. Barrows, Leroy G. Perkins.

MARLBOROUGH.   Clerk and Treas., Amos B. Latham.   Reg., Wm. F. Joyner.   Selectmen, John H. Fuller, Francis A. Dutton, Francis W. Coleman.   Const., John W. Day, Joel E. Hall, Addison L. West.   Coll., Charles Carter, Jr.   G. Jurors, John Lord, Francis A. Dutton, Adriel Huntley.   Assess., Henry D. Barrows, Theron B. Buell.   Board of R, Roland Buell, Charles Hall, Addison L. West.   Board of Ed., Horatio Bolles, Wm. F. Joyner, 1882; Amos B. Latham, John Lord, 1883; Jasper P. Harvey, James J. Bell, 1884.   Reg. of Voters, Henry D. Barrows, Theron B. Buell.

MERIDEN.   Clerk and Reg., Selah A. Hull.   Treas., W. W. Mosher.   Selectmen, D. S. Williams, E. J. Doolittle, Jr., Seth J. Hall.   Const., Franklin G. Bolles, Charles E. Goodrich, Geo. L. Hall, James E. Belden, John A. Leeds, Alvin Sweet.   Coll., Benjamin Page.   G. Jurors, George M. Howell, Charles H. Shaw, Charles H. Sawyer, Frank S. Fay, Charles Schraeder, C. H. Collins.   Assess., Hobart C. Hull, J. H. Converse, O. S. Williams.   Board of R., Joel I. Butler, A. C. Markham, George R. Wilmot, W. A. Miles, Nelson Hall.   Board of Ed., J. H. Chapin, Robert Cortiss, Ed. Miller, Jr., George R. Cortiss, F. D. Proudman, C. H. S. Davis, J. S. Wightman, J. T. Pettee, L. L. Sawyer.   Reg. of Voters, Linus Birdsey, J. C. Hinsdale.

MIDDLEBURY.   Clerk and Reg., Marcus DeForest, Jr.   Treas., William Tyler.   Selectmen, Levings Abbott, C. H. Lum, D. M. Fenn.   Const., G. B. Bristol, R. B. Wheaton, George S. Pope.   Coll., Silas Tuttle.   G. Jurors, James C. Scovill, George O. Ellis.   Assess., Charles H. Lum, John T. Basham.   Board of R., George B. Bristol, John T. Basham, Wm. R. Tucker.   Board of Ed., George B. Bristol, *H. W. Munson, 1882; James C. Scovill, C. H. Lum, 1883; Levings Abbott, George O. Ellis, 1884.   Reg. of Voters, G. B. Bristol, F. H. Wheeler.

MIDDLEFIELD Clerk, Reg., and Treas., Lyman A. Mills. Selectmen, Alva B. Coe, Valerius H. Coles, Isaac H. Cornwell. Const., Paschal A. Skinner, J. N. Coe, D. A. Burnham, H. E. Wilcox. Coll., J. C. Safford. G. Jurors, Albert R. Tucker, D. S. Coe. Assess., Enoch T. Birdsey, Waldo B. Miller. Board of R., Moses W. Terrill, Daniel H. Birdsey, Isaac W. Miller. Board of Ed., M. W. Terrill, Walter P. Hall, 1882; John O. Cone, A. C. Denison, 1883; Phineas M. Augur, Walter P. Hall, 1884. Reg. of Voters, Willis E. Terrill, Waldo B. Miller.

MIDDLETOWN. Clerk and Reg., Elihu W. N. Starr; Assistant Clerk, Frank F. Starr. Treas., James P. Stow. Selectmen, Charles R. Woodward, Charles H. Williams, Ichabod M. Roberts, Charles F. Browning, Martin Loveland. Const., Curtiss Bacon, Monroe Birdsey, John Hoar, Daniel Hurley, Nelson Nettleton, James Ross, John Wilcox. Coll., Sherman M. Bacon. G. Jurors, Elijah C. Birdsey, Frank B. Harris, James G. Hollister, Joseph R. Johnson, Charles W. Paddock, George L. Tuttle. Assess., Stephen B. Davis, George W. Lane, Henry S. Steele. Board of R., John Carroll, David Church, Charles A. Newell. Board of Ed., Alfred O. Smith, Josiah M. Hubbard, 1882; Horace H. Wilcox, Marius W. Wilcox, 1883; George W. Gray, Silas A. Robinson, 1884. Reg. of Voters, Thomas O'Connell, Fred'k Dickerson.

MILFORD. Clerk and Reg., John W. Fowler. Treas., Isaac T. Rogers. Selectmen, Charles W. Beardsley, Charles H. Peck, James T. Higley. Const., Lewis B. Beers, and Coll., Amos J. Brown, Charles W. Oviatt, Albert C. Platt, Frank R. Baldwin, Edward B. Smith, Patrick Burns. G. Jurors, James S. Tibbals, Thaddeus Smith, Alfred C. Oviatt, William Brotherton, Henry J. Bristol, George E. Platt. Assess., Wm. H. Augur, Edward G. Miles, Miles B. Merwin. Board of R., Nathan Royden, N. Truman Smith, James A. Smith. Board of Ed., *Nathan E. Smith, Wm. Brotherton, Henry N. Platt, C. A. Tomlinson, 1882; *Isaac T. Rogers, C. W. Baldwin, A. A. Baldwin, C. F. Bosworth, 1883; William G. Mitchell, Geo. M. Gunn, Geo. H. Griffin, Geo. E. Platt, 1884. Reg. of Voters, A. W. Burns, John W. Buckingham.

MONROE. Clerk, David A. Nichols. Reg., John D. Beach, Treas., William A. Clarke. Selectmen, Dunning J. Lake, Eli B. Seeley, Stephen French. Const., C. Edward Osborne, Charles S. French, John D. Beach. Coll., Oscar J. Sherwood. G. Jurors, Albert Wheeler, Samuel Hurd. Assess., Oscar J.

Sherwood, Orville H. Hull. Board of R., John T. Porter, Charles
Ν. Beardsley. Board of Ed., John G. Stevens, Daniel Osborne,
F. Ν. Cargill. Reg. of Voters, Geo. W. Lovejoy, L. Dwight Lane.

Νοντνιlle. Clerk, Henry A. Baker. Reg., Jonathan Rey-
nolds. Treas , Lewis Browning. Selectmen, H. R. Strickland,
C. Ν. Robertson, J. Ν. Beckwith. Const., D. Chester Comstock,
and Coll., Charles Perrin, J. L. Leffingwell. G. Jurors, David
Alexander, Aug. A. Parker, Alvin E. Goff. Assess., Calvin B.
Beebe, Charles H. Witter, George Latimer, Alvin G. Smith, Gur-
don R. Νiner. Board of R., M. V. B. Brainard, Chas. E. Church,
Albert A. Rogers. Board of Ed., Joseph S. Latimer, David
Alexander, Charles T. Ramage, 1882; Jedediah R. Gay, 2d,
Daniel D. Lyon, Silas H. Browning, 1883; Ν. V. B. Brainard,
John Davis, Alton E. Stephen, 1884. Reg. of Voters, George
N. Wood, Erastus D. Lyon.

Νorris. Clerk, Reg., and Treas., Darwin B. Randall. Select-
men, Wm. Griswold, Edwin H. Clark, Νonroe Throop. Const.,
E. H. Clark, J. Bradford Root, C. Wesley Cook. Coll., Hor-
ace Cowles. G. Jurors, Lucius E. Νunson, Samuel F. Burgess,
Leman H. Benton. Assess., Sidney Peck, Samuel W. Ensign.
Board of R., Phineas B. Randall, Homer Stoddard, Beebe S.
Hall. Board of Ed., Samuel Ν. Ensign, Dwight Griswold,
Charles H. Randall, Wm. H. Farnham, Clark L. Loveland, L.
W. S. Skilton. Reg. of Voters, Edgar Alvord, James Ν. Ben-
ton.

Naugatuck. Clerk, J. T. Garrison. Reg., Samuel J. An-
drews. Treas., David Smith. Selectmen, Homer Twitchell,
Thomas Conron, George Ν. Allerton. Const., Νichael Condon,
Samuel Platt, James Gilooley, Hooker Hotchkiss, Eldridge
Smith, Alfred French, Francis Νulvey. Coll., Oliver Evans.
G. Jurors, Owen Connell, Robert Baldwin, Samuel N. Andrew,
Patrick Riley, John Cawthorne, John V. Haslinger. Assess.,
William Kennedy, Harry S. Hotchkiss. Board of R., Eli C.
Barnum, Samuel N. Andrew, Eli Smith. Board of Ed., Burton
A. Peck, George Ν. Allerton, 1882; S. C. Leonard, James
Fagan, 1883; Dwight P. Νills, F. B. Tuttle, 1884. Reg. of
Voters, George D. Bissell, Geo. D. Squires.

New Britain. Clerk and Reg., Isaac Porter. Treas., A. P.
Collins. Selectmen, Levi S. Wells, Harvey G. Brown, James
P. Νoore. Const., Lester R. Bailey, Henry Gussman, Wm. H.

Gladden, Orville Jones, Jr., Augustus N. Bennett, Isaac T.
Norris, Wm. H. Allen. Coll., Wm. E. Latham. G. Jurors,
Job Dyson, Wm. N. Felt, Fred. C. Berg, Spencer H. Wood,
Cornelius Andrews. Assess., Lester A. Vibberts, Norris Bailey,
Charles S. Andrews. Board of R., Henry P. Strong, Stephen
R. Lawrence, Thomas Begley. Board of Ed., Justus A. Traut,
John B. Dyson, James H. Beach, G. H. Minor, 1882; Samuel
W. Hart, 1883; John N. Bartlett, *Henry E. Sawyer, Lawrence
Clean, Charles S. Andrews. Reg. of Voters, Charles O. Collins,
Michael O'Connell.

NEW CANAAN. Clerk and Reg., Theodore W. Benedict.
Treas., Andrew F. Jones. Selectmen, Benjamin P. Mead,
Joseph F. Silliman, William Wardwell. Const., Ezra S. Hall,
Edgar Bentley. Coll., Frank M. Bliss. G. Jurors, John E.
Whitney, William G. Webb. Assess., F. E. Chichester, James
Benedict, Lewis S. Olmsted. Board of R., Edwin Hoyt, F. E.
Weed, L. K. Hoyt. Board of Ed., B. D. Purdy, Wm. G. Brownson,
1882; Joseph Greenleaf, Wm. E. Husted, 1883; Edwin Hoyt,
L. M. Munroe, 1884. Reg. of Voters, Russell L. Hall, Samuel
N. Raymond.

NEW FAIRFIELD. Clerk and Reg., John J. Treadwell.
Treas., Charles D. H. Kellogg. Selectmen, Barzillai B. Kellogg,
James S. Whitehead, Alexander B. Brush. Const., Alexander
Turner, and Coll., Amos Hodge, Hendrick H. Wildman, Jr.
G. Jurors, Dimon Disbrow, Isaac H. Gerow, Norris B. Nichol-
son. Assess., David J. Sturges, David H. Disbrow, Henry O.
Leach. Board of R., Isaac H. Gerow, George N. Pearce, Joseph
C. Barnum. Board of Ed., *Hendrick H. Wildman, John J.
Treadwell, Alexander Turner, Edward Treadwell, H. O. Leach,
A. B. Brush. Reg. of Voters, H. H. Wildman, Edwin Hodge.

NEW HARTFORD. Clerk and Reg., J. C. Keach, Treas., E.
M. Chapin. Selectmen, H. M. Gates, S. N. Pettibone, Charles
F. Mayfield. Const., Henry C. Merrill, Henry Overton, H. H.
Stone, S. H. Henderson, F. A. Farley, J. R. Gillett, 2d, E. H.
Stone. Coll., S. H. Henderson. G. Jurors, J. C. Keach, Har-
vey Case, H. A. Kellogg, B. G. Loomis, George F. Douglas,
Orvis Griggs. Assess., Henry C. Merrill, John D. Betts. Board
of R., H. B. Kellogg, Trescott C. Barnes, Henry T. Smith.
Board of Ed., N. B. Merrill, F. H. Adams, 1882; Orrin Fitch,
L. C. Evarts, 1883; John Richards, Jared B. Foster, 1884.
Reg. of Voters, George W. Smith, Frank W. Fenn, Frank P.
Marble, Herman Clerk.

NEW HAVEN. Clerk, John Shuster. Reg., James J. S. Doherty. Treas., Harmanus M. Welch. Selectmen, James Reynolds, Frank S. Andrew, Philip Hugo, Edwin W. Cooper, Louis Feldman, William S. Beecher, Elizur H. Sperry. Const.. Joseph H. Keefe, Jacob Mailhouse, Michael R. Enscoe, Daniel Colwell, David K. Andrews, Philip Roller, John R. Gildea. Coll., Theodore A. Tuttle. G. Jurors, Timothy J. Fox, Joseph Scoville, Henry S. Cooper, James P. Hart, Adam Miller, Patrick McGuiness. Assess., Elias P. Merriman, Griswold Gilbert, Ezra B. Dibble. Board of R., Wm. W. Hotchkiss, Thomas O'Brien, Frank Chandler, Lucius B. Hinman, Oliver H. Bill. Board of Ed., Nathan T. Bushnell, Patrick Mahen, Joseph Gill. Reg. of Voters, Wm. O'Keefe, Edward F. Merrill.

NEWINGTON. Clerk and Reg., John S. Kirkham. Treas., David L Robbins. Selectmen, Jedediah Deming, Jacob Dix, Wm. M. Richards. Const., John S. Rowley, and Coll., James H. White, Walter B. Dorman. G. Jurors, Louis V. Durand, Jr., Lyman Wetherell, Charles E. Chapman, Calvin Whaples. Assess., Charles E. Chapman, Aholiab J. Corbin. Board of R., Samuel H. Kilbourne, Edward L. Wetherell, Pratt Francis. Board of Ed., Samuel A. Steele, E. Merwin Steele, 1882; Chas. K. Atwood, Roger Welles, 1883; John S. Kirkham, *John G. Stoddard, 1884. Reg. of Voters, Thomas R. Atwood, John R. Stoddard.

NEW LONDON. Clerk and Reg., Isaac W. Thompson. Treas., Thomas W. Williams. Selectmen, Charles J. Hewitt, C. Arnold Weaver, Charles L. Ockford. Const., Gideon Gray, John H. Rockwell, George H. Dart, George Pelton, William E. Goss, Coll., Eldridge P. Beckwith. G. Jurors, E. A. Denison, John H. Crocker, Daniel Fraser, Wm. H. Saxton. Assess., John C. Foster, Dudley B. Chapman, Charles Bishop. Board of R., Alfred Hempstead, Gurdon A Lester, Cortland S. Harris. Board of Ed, George E. Starr, William M. Tobey, William H. Chapman, 1882; Walter Learned, Benjamin Stark, F. N. Braman, 1883: Byron F. Woods, Ralph Wheeler, Alfred H. Chappell, 1884. Reg. of Voters, Ralph Wheeler, Charles F. Starr.

NEW MILFORD. Clerk and Reg., Russel B. Noble. Treas., H. LeRoy Randall. Selectmen, Albert S. Hill, Andrew J. McMahon, Frederic E. Starr. Const., Albert H. McMahon, and Coll., Lory Couch, John N. Meloney, Charles Planz, Lauren Evitts, John F. Murphy, John Talbot. G. Jurors, John R.

Bostwick, Frederick Raifstanger, James M. Hallock, James W. Orton, Marshall Marsh, John N. Squires. Assess., George Northrop, Edward P. Barton, C:arles H. Noble. Board of R., Lee Stone, Anson H. Squires, George W. Anthony. Board of Ed., *Cyrus A. Todd, Albert N. Baldwin, George Northrop, 1882; Charles N. Hall, Edward F. Morehouse, Starr Scott Buckingham, 1883; Amos H. Bowers, George W. Richmond, Ethiel S. Green, 1884. Reg. of Voters, Silas L. Erwin, Everett Sturges.

NEWTOWN. Clerk and Reg., C. H. Peck. Treas., L. B. Booth. Selectmen, William N. Northrop, William P. Sanford, John B. Wheeler. Const., William H. Glover, Dennis Quinlivin, Daniel Camp, John H. Blackman, George Winton, Patrick Campbell, Patrick Madigan. Coll., George H. Botsford. G. Jurors, John Stillson, Daniel Camp. Assess., Robert A. Clark, George W. Bradley, Daniel G. Beers. Board of R., Norman Northrop, Norman B. Glover, Nichols B. Hawley. Board of Ed., Silas B. Wheeler, Charles M. Parsons, 1882; Frederick Chambers, William C. Wile, 1883; James E. Madigan, James P. Hoyt, 1884. Reg. of Voters, Michael P. Bradley, Salmon S. Peck, John T. Carmody, John L. Sanford.

NORFOLK. Clerk, Reg., and Treas., Joseph N. Cowles, Selectmen, L. L. Whiting, Moses F. Grant, L. J. Butler. Const., W. B. Bigelow. Coll., O. J. Hallock. G. Jurors, S. S. Vail, Riley Stillman. Assess., Plumb Brown, Alva L. Cowles. Board of R , H. H. Riggs, Harvey Johnson. Board of Ed., J. F. Gleason, Riley Stillman, F. E. Porter, J. N. Cowles, R. J. Crissey. Reg. of Voters, George R. Bigelow, Henry J. Gaylord.

NORTH BRANFORD. Clerk, Reg., and Treas., Charles Page. Selectmen, Alden H. Hill, Willys Tucker, Edward R. Robinson. Const., George B. Stone, Edson S. Beardsley, Herbert O. Page, Sereno M. Foote, Charles E. Alling, Edmund M. Field, Russell M. Rose. Coll., John M. Foote. G. Jurors, George A. Gordon, Clark Russell, John M. Foote, Thomas Palmer, Henry B. Linsley. Assess., William D. Ford, Douglas Williams. Board of R., Martin C. Bishop, William Maltby, Newton M. Robinson. Board of Ed., Charles Foote, Henry N. Pardee, 1882; Dwight N. Prentice, *Charles Page, 1883; *William Maltby, William D. Ford, 1884. Reg. of Voters, 1st Dist., William D. Ford; Darwin Page; 2d Dist., Dwight M. Foote, John G. Phelan.

NORTH CANAAN, P. O. Canaan. Clerk, Reg., and Treas., J. B. Hardenbergh. Selectmen, Frederick Bronson, Patrick Fitzgerald, John B. Reed. Const., Charles H. Briggs, and Coll., Albert A. Hubbard, John C. Richmond, George E. Beebe, Thomas O'Neil, James M. Shultz, G. B. Gardner. G. Jurors, Jeremiah S. New, Horace Holt, Patrick Lynch. Assess., Wm. P. Pelton, Everardus Ives. Board of R., Henry J. Mead, Hiram Briggs, James L. Bragg. Board of Ed., Edward S. Roberts, Daniel L. Freeman, 1882; Charles H. Briggs, Charles Gillette, 1883; Miles B. Tobey, A. T. Roraback, 1884. Reg. of Voters, Henry J. Mead, Robert Van Deusen.

NORTH HAVEN. Clerk, Edward L. Linsley. Reg., Robert B. Goodyear. Treas., Francis H. Todd. Selectmen, Cyrus Cheney, Nelson J. Beach, Charles M. Tuttle. Const., Rufus Thorp, Payson B. Orcutt, George Gerwig, Olin H. Burnham, Merwin W. Tuttle, Zenas W. Mansfield, Edward L. Goodyear. Coll., Lewis J. Fowler. G. Jurors, Francis H. Todd, Robert W. Smith, Horace L. Hills, Julian W. Tuttle, Solomon T. Linsley, J. Boardman Smith. Assess., Lucius Brockett, George Munson. Board of R., Lyman Bassett, Jesse O. Eaton, James E. Smith, Edwin L. Mansfield, Bennett Todd. Board of Ed., Willis B. Hemingway, Oswin H. D. Fowler, Justus F. Brockett, 1882; Edward L. Linsley, Andrew F. Austin, O. Sherwood Todd, 1883; Sheldon B. Thorpe, *Robert B. Goodyear, Jesse B. Jacobs, 1884. Reg. of Voters, L. Peet Tuttle, Bennett Todd.

NORTH STONINGTON. Clerk, Reg., and Treas., William H. Hillard. Selectmen, Orrin Chapman, George W. Stewart, Horace F. York. Const., Gilbert Billings, LaFayette Park. Coll., Horace Greeley Lewis. G. Jurors, Joseph E. Lewis, Henry A. Tomlinson, Orrin T. Maine. Assess., Nelson A. Brown, Charles H. Maine, Amos P. Miner. Board of R., James F. Brown, Barnum C. Pierce, George W. Miner. Board of Ed., Francis W. Collins, Edwin H. Knowles, John L. York. Reg. of Voters, Allen Wheeler, Gilbert Billings.

NORWALK. Clerk, Frank W. Perry. Reg., James A. Brown. Treas., Wm. A. Curtis. Selectmen, Charles A. Burr, Nelson J. Craw, Wm. C. Sammis. Const., George B. St. John, and Coll., Edward Nelson, Aurelius J. Meeker, James C. Crowe, Joseph H. Richards, Wallace Dann, Franklin P. Crockett. G. Jurors, Clarence B. Coolidge, Spencer C. Horton, George W. Day, Francis V. Brush, Washington W. Sharrott. Assess., Thomas

Guyer, James Finney, Frederick W. Mitchell. Board of R., Bradley S. Keith, Jacob M. Layton, James M. Lane. Board of Ed., Wm. Randel Smith, Edwin Adams, Charles M. Selleck, Ira Cole, Moses B. Pardee, Thomas G. Osborn, William C. Burke, Jr., John S. Seymour, Robert T. B. Easton. Reg. of Voters, George N. Ells, Nathaniel Requa, Wm. S. Bouton, Theodore Wilcox, Wm. B. Hendrick, Winfield S. Hanford, 2d.

NORWICH. Clerk and Treas., Othniel Gager. Reg., David Young. Selectmen, Oliver P. Avery, Wm. R. Potter, Patrick McLaughlin. Const., Charles H. Dillaby, and Coll., Charles H. Miner, Jr., William W. Ives, Nathan C. Chapell, Joseph B. Corey, Wm. A. Baker, Henry R. Gardner. G. Jurors, Albert F. Park, Wm. H. Armstrong, Lyman W. Lee, Joseph Robinson, Daniel M. Dickinson, Robert F. Latour. Assess., Jonathan W. Hooker, Wm. C. Osgood, William Walsh. Board of R., Nathan Small, John P. Barstow, John Bowman. Board of Ed., G. G. Pitcher, George R. Hyde, P. J. O'Connor, 1882; *John W. Crary, Hiram P. Arms, Burrell W. Hyde, 1883; Palmer Bill, Robert P. Stanton, Timothy Kelly, 1884. Reg. of Voters, Joab B. Rogers, James Rigney.

OLD LYNE. Clerk, W. R. Champion. Reg., David Morley. Treas., G. W. DeWolf. Selectmen, N. S. Lee, R. W. Chadwick, F. W. Chapman. Const.. Henry Noyes, Richard W. Chadwick, N. H. Appleby, John Dickey, William Bates, A. H. Sanders, A. S. Bugbee. Coll., David Huntley. Henry H. Lay, Wm. H. Stannard. Assess., Herbert M. Caulkins, John Smith. Board of R., George H. Peckham, H. H. Lay, E. C. Peck. Board of Ed., William B. Cary, T. Swan, 1882; C. L. Morley, E. C. Smith, 1883; Charles G. Bartlett, John Swaney, 1884. Reg. of Voters, A. H. Sanders, John Smith.

OLD SAYBROOK. Clerk and Reg., Ozias H. Kirtland. Treas., John F. Bushnell. Selectmen, Edwin Ayer, Wm. H. Smith, William J. Clark. Const., William H. Smith, R. C. Shepard, John E. Ayer. Coll., John N. Clark. G. Jurors, William B. Tully, Henry Sizer, Robert B. Chalker. Assess., David W. Clark, George W. Denison. Board of R., William B. Tully, Joseph Kellogg, Henry Hart. Board of Ed., Edwin Ayer, John H. White, 1882; Joseph Kellogg, William J. Clark, 1883; Robert Chapman, George W. Denison, 1884. Reg. of Voters, John N. Clark, John H. Pratt.

ORANGE. (P. O. West Haven.) Clerk, Elias T. Main. Treas., Israel K. Ward. Selectmen, George R. Kelsey, Charles F. Smith, David Platt. Const., Zadoc R. Morse, Elizur B. Russell, George M. White, Seaman B. Smith, George I. Babcock, Jr., George S. Stratton. Coll., Walter A. Main. G. Jurors, Stiles D. Woodruff, Alonzo F. Wood, William C. Russell, Henry W. Painter, Isaac P. Treat, Henry A. Clark. Assess., Samuel L. Smith, 2d, Isaac P. Treat, Rollin W. Hine. Board of R., Donaldson S. Thompson, Albert F. Miles, Prosper Warner. Board of Ed., *Isaac P. Treat, John M. Aimes, 1882; Edward W. Worthington, Charles K. Bush, 1883; James Walker, John F. Barnett, 1884. Reg. of Voters, 1st Dist., Stephen E. Booth, John M. Aimes; 2d Dist., Frederick B. Perkins, Benjamin F. Somers.

OXFORD. Clerk and Reg., Lewis Barnes. Treas., Charles H. Butler. Selectmen, John B. Pope, James H. Bartlett, George R. Baldwin. Const., Anthony B. Hinman, and Coll., Legrand W. Lake, William N. Andrew, George Andrew. G. Jurors, Atwater Treat, Cornelius C. Rider, Henry E. Smith, William O. French, William M. Hubbell. Assess., Wooster B. McEwen, David. C. Riggs. Board of R., Clark E. Lum, William O. French, Wales Chatfield. Board of Ed, John Harger, Clark E. Lum, 1882; *Nathan J. Wilcoxson, Samuel Hawkins, 1883; Lewis Barnes, Orlando C. Osborn, 1884. Reg. of Voters, Benjamin Nichols, Egbert J. Thrall.

PLAINFIELD. Clerk and Treas., Reuben Weaver. Reg., George H. Hyde. Selectmen, John L. Chapman, Sessions L. Adams, William Dawley, Erastus L. Spalding, Albert C. Green. Const., Nathaniel P. Thompson, and Coll., Charles E. Barber, Augustus B. Shepardson. G. Jurors, Jeremiah M. Shepard, George Torrey, Joseph A. Dean, Edwin H. Kennedy, Augustus B. Shepardson. Assess., William B. Ames, Henry C. Starkweather. Board of R., George Loring, John S. French, Henry S. Newton, Fitch A. Casey, Walter Palmer. Board of Ed., Waldo Tillinghast, William I. Hyde, John A. Creadoh, 1882; Stephen Hall, Lucian Burleigh, *Asher H. Wilcox, 1883; Dwight Avery, *S. H. Fellows, *John N. Shipman, 1884. Reg. of Voters, Richard H. Ward, Henry C. Starkweather.

PLAINVILLE. Clerk and Reg., Robert C. Usher. Treas., Levi Hough. Selectmen, Burritt Hills, H. W. Higgins, R. F. Woodford. Const, Enos S. Belden, A. O. N. Bunnell, J. H.

Edmonds. Coll., F. L. Beach. G. Jurors, E. C. Chapman,
L. B. Warren, E. M. Baker. Assess., E. C. Chapman. D. B.
Hills, Isaac Alcott. Board of R., W. L. Cowles, Levi Hough,
A. J. Norton. Board of Ed., J. S. Corban, H. S. Potter, 1882;
A. E. Dennison, M. A. Nickerson, 1883; T. G. Wright, Peter
Brock, 1884. Reg. of Voters, I. P. Newell, F. B. Newton.

PLYMOUTH. Clerk and Reg., Edwin M. Talmadge. Treas.,
Horace Fenn. Selectmen, Abijah W. Welton, Byron Tuttle,
Walter H. Scott. Const., Homer E. Cooke, and Coll., Storey
A. Kelsey, James B. Baldwin, Edgar L. Pond, Albert I. Hotch-
kiss, Frank Blakeslee, Arthur S. Beardslee. G. Jurors, George
Langdon, Perry Cadwell, James Hunter, Elizur Fenn, Charles
Purrington, John W. Sullivan. Assess., James Woodruff,
Aaron P. Fenn, Henry L. Hinman. Board of R., Edward
Dailey, Enos Blakeslee, William B. Fenn. Board of Ed., R. D.
H. Allen, N. Taylor Baldwin, Abijah W. Welton, 1882: Aaron
P. Fenn. William W. Clemence, Timothy B. McNamara, 1883;
Leverett S. Griggs, Lyman D. Baldwin, Edwin M. Talmadge,
1884. Reg. of Voters, 1st Dist., Strong A. Kelsey, Adison Bun-
nell; 2d Dist., Edward S. Beach, Timothy B. McNamara.

POMFRET. (P. O. Pomfret Center.) Clerk, Reg., and Treas.,
E. P. Hayward. Selectmen, Thomas W. Williams, George W.
Taft, Edwin T. White. Const, Angell Wheaton, D. A. Col-
burn. Coll., Lafayette Wright. G. Jurors, Angell Wheaton,
Horace Clapp, Charles Osgood, I. P. Briggs, N. W. Chapman,
D. Matthewson. Assessors, Horace Clapp, Thomas O. Elliott,
R. J. Sabin. Board of R., Isaac P. Briggs, John W. Clapp,
Edwin T. White. Board of Ed., Albertus S. Bruce, Charles
W. Grosvenor, Frederick Hyde, 1882; Edward P. Matthewson,
*Isaac P. Briggs, Edward P. Hayward, 1883; John W. Clapp,
Charles P. Grosvenor, George Allen, 1884. Reg. of Voters, I.
P. Briggs, Philo T. Kingsbury.

PORTLAND. Clerk, William H. Bartlett. Reg., Stephen H.
Stocking. Treas., John I. Worthington. Selectmen, Joseph S.
Worthington, J. H. Pelton, Nelson Pelton. Const., Billings Neff,
and Col., Eben Hall, John Hall, George O. Mosher, Stephen
Hall, Amos A. Jones, Joseph Covell. G. Jurors, George B.
Cleveland, L. P. Stewart, Daniel Dunham, Daniel Crittenden,
W. S. Coe, C. G. Southmayd. Assessors, Henry Kilby, John
H. Hall. Board of R., Charles H. Sage, Andrew Cornwall, John
Bransfield. Board of Ed., C. A. Sears, J. S. Bayne, William S.

Strickland, 1882; George B. Cleveland, Charles H. White, Geo. H. Penfield, 1883; F. A. Parker, F. D. Harriman, Horace C. Markham, 1884. Reg. of Voters, Billings Neff, James A. Butler.

PRESTON. (P. O. Norwich.) Clerk and Treas., James F. Forsyth. Reg., James H. Fitch. Selectmen, Jonathan L. Hill, William Briggs, Henry H. Hopkins. Const., George L. Roath, Henry P. Jones. Col., Samuel Johnson. G. Jurors, Leander B. Hill, Stephen D. Moore, H. H. Roath. Assessors, P. McKiernan, John O. Peckham, W. E. Hiscox. Board of R., C. M. Barnes, Hiram Browning, Albert Wheeler. Board of Ed., Mason S. Hewitt, Thomas S. Phillips, W. E. Hiscox. Reg. of Voters, John Galligan, James H. Fitch, Nathan H. Ayer, Henry P. Jones.

PROSPECT. Clerk, Reg., and Treas., Watson C. Hitchcock. Selectmen, David R. Williams, George D. Fenn, Harris Platt, Const., Stephen Talmadge, Harry L. Payne. Coll., Frank L. Wilkinson. G. Jurors, George F. Tyler, David B. Hotchkiss, John F. Matthews. Assessors, William E. Kimball, Harris Platt. Board of R., William Berkley, Minor Blackman, Willis Ives. Board of Ed., Wm. H. Shipps, B. B. Brown, Minor Blackman, Merritt Clark, Frank L. Wilkinson, David B. Hotchkiss. Reg. of Voters, Watson C. Hitchcock, David M. Plumb.

PUTNAM. Clerk, Reg., and Treas., James W. Manning. Selectmen, Almanson Herendeen, John Carpenter, Edward Mullan. Const., George W. Carver, Arnold F. Leach, Edwin R. May, Asahel S. Davis, Wm. S. Perry. G. Jurors, Joseph W. Torrey, Charles Prentice, Jerome Tourtelotte, Sylvanus Alton. Assessors, Charles H. Chesebro, Edwin R. Wood, G. D. Post. Board of R., Richmond M. Bullock, Frederick Cutler, Reed Tourtelotte. Board of Ed., Jesse R. Davenport, Isaac N. Ross. Reg. of Voters, Samuel H. Seward, Otis Fisher.

REDDING. Clerk and Treas., Lemuel Sanford. Reg., Moses H. Wakeman. Selectmen, William H. Hill, William B. Hill, Stephen Sanford. Const., Wm. H. Burr, David S. Bartram, John H. Edmonds. Coll., William E. Duncomb, G. Jurors, George A. Sanford, George Albion, Charles H. Woodruff. Assessors, Samuel B. Osborn, Arthur B. Hill, Turney Sanford. Board of R., William E. Duncomb, John Todd, Jonathan B.

Sanford. Board of Ed., Wm. J. Jennings, Wm. E. Duncomb, K. Alanson Whiton. Reg. of Voters, 1st district, John N. Nickerson, Charles D. Meeker; 2d dist., Burr Bennett, Arthur B. Hill.

RIDGEFIELD. Clerk and Reg., Hiram K. Scott. Treas., Lewis C. Seymour. Selectmen, Aaron W. Lee, Edwin P. White, Edward H. Smith. Const., Benjamin K. Northrop, and Coll., Sereno S. Hurlbutt, George P. Gregory, John F. Holmes, Seth J. Benedict, Edward L. Smith, Samuel J. Barlow. G. Jurors, Philip L. Barhite, John W. Rockwell, George Boughton, John R. Sherwood, Aaron B. Gilbert, Aaron G. Hoyt. Assessors, Isaac Osborn, D. Smith Sholes. Board of R , Samuel Scott, John P. Keeler, Jared N. Olmsted. Board of Ed., L. W. Abbott, A. G. Paddock, Samuel J. Barlow, 1882; Lewis E. Smith, Francis A. Henry, D. Smith Sholes, 1883; Wm. W. Leete, John D. Nash, Edward H. Smith, 1884. Reg. of Voters, Benj. K. Northrop, D. Smith Sholes.

ROCKY HILL. Clerk and Reg., Samuel Dimrck. Treas., William G. Robbins. Selectmen, Moses W. Williams, James S. Stevens. Const., Ephraim Goodrich, and Coll., Charles D. Canfield, Robert H. Rhodes, Royal A. Porter, George W. Roe, William DeWolf. G. Jurors, Thomas D. Williams, Alden Hale, William Sessions, Horace R. Merriam, Lucius M. Beaumont, Allen A. Robbins. Assessors, Henry R. Taylor, Frederick Morton. Board of R., Benjamin Smith, Samuel Ashwell, James H. Warner. Board of Ed., *William G. Robbins, James H. Warner, Eugene S. Belden, Samuel Ashwell, Lucius M. Beaumont, *Albert D. Griswold. Reg. of Voters, William G. Robbins, James Warner.

ROXBURY. Clerk, George W. Hurlburt. Reg., Charles Sanford. Treas., Charles Beardsley. Selectmen, Albert L. Hodge, Orlando Lewis, Henry H. Warner. Const., Walter T. Buckingham, George H. Buckingham, Jos. G. Gorham, Edwin Leavenworth, Reuben S. Edwards, Jr., Charles W. Fowler, Charles B. Garlick. Coll., Aaron W. Fenn. G. Jurors, Henry W. Trowbridge, Isaac B. Prindle, Merrit P. Beers, George Hurlburt, Aaron W. Fenn. Assess., Aaron W. Fenn, John H. Leavenworth. Board of R., Cyrus E. Prindle, Minott L. Beardsley, Seth Warner. Board of Ed., Cyrus E. Prindle, *Charles Sanford, 1882; George W. P. Leavenworth, R. Randall Davidson, 1883; Charles W. Hodge, Levi Smith,

1884. Reg. of Voters, Herman B. Eastman, Sheldon B. Smith.

SALEM. Clerk and Treas., Charles A. Williams. Reg., Frank E. Williams. Selectmen, Austin O. Gallup, Samuel N. Morgan, Gurdon E. Allyn. Const., Henry E. Avery, and Coll., Edwin C. Treadway, David P. Chaples. G. Jurors, John C. Bushnell, David H. Seamon, Henry Fox. Assess., Edward De Wolf, David G. Gates, David Way. Board of R., Gurdon F. Allyn, John R. Treadway, Albert A. Witter. Board of Ed., Charles T. Williams, Austin O. Gallup, 1882; Nelson N. Williams, David H. Seamon, 1883; Henry N. Brown, James Bulkley, 1884; Reg. of Voters, John C. Bushnell, Charles F. Treadway.

SALISBURY. Clerk and Reg., John H. Blodgett. Treas., Silas B. Moore. Selectmen, Sidney P. Ensign, George H. Clark, Dwight Allyn. Const., William B. Perry, and Coll., James W. Spurr, John L. Owen, Henry Whitbeck, George Landon, Peter McArdle, Carlos W. Adams. G. Jurors, David W. Stone, Edward Ward, Aaron Mallory, Martin McCarty, Wm. A. Crowell, Patrick Lynch, Frank W. Holmes. Assessors, James H. Barnum, John P. Walton, William Kane. Board of R., Wm. Bundy, Harlon P. Harris, Martin Walsh, Wm. H. Raynsford, James Ensign. Board of Ed., Harlon P. Harris, Cornelius L. Kitchell, 1882; Henry J. Lynch, George B. Burrall, 1883; John H. Hurlburt, Dwight Allyn, 1884. Reg. of Voters, William B. Perry, William D. Reid.

SAYBROOK. Clerk and Reg., Samuel F. Snow. Treas., Henry R. Wooster. Selectmen, Dwight S. Spencer, Marshall Comstock. Const., Henry S. Ward, William D. Worthington, Henry O. Shailer. Coll., Horace G. Jones. G. Jurors, Horace P. Denison, Joseph B. Lord, Thomas L. Post, Horace G. Jones, William L. Jones. Assessors, Frederick W. Williams, Emory H. Peckham. Board of R., Felix A. Denison, Obadiah P. Pratt, Dwight S. Southworth. Board of Ed., Lozelle J. Platt, Davis M. Tyler, Joseph C. Fargo, J. Lockwood Lamb, 1882; Charles Jennings, Horace P. Denison, H. Christopher Kingsley, Dwight S. Southworth, 1883; George F. Spencer, Frederick L'Hommedieu, David R Post, Henry L. Denison, 1884. Reg. of Voters, Chas. R. Marvin, Henry C. Tyler.

SCOTLAND. Clerk, Reg., and Treas., William F. Palmer. Selectmen., S. B. Sprague, M. L. Barstow, Henry Lincoln.

Const., Arthur M. Clark, and Coll. G. Jurors, A. H. Maine,
Dwight Cary. Assess., J. W. Maine, John M. Palmer. Board
of R., Wm. G. Anthony, Samuel N. Ashley, Abner Robinson.
Board of Ed., Abner Robinson, William M. Burnham, 1882;
Caleb Anthony, Jr., Kendrick Douglass, 1883; A. Walker Maine,
Henry Lincoln, 1884. Reg. of Voters, A. Walker Maine, Abner
Robinson.

SEYMOUR. Clerk and Treas., S. H. Canfield. Reg., George
Smith. Selectmen, Robert Healey, Joseph Imson, John Davis.
Const., J. W. Tomlinson, George H. Washburn, M. McNerney,
A. B. Dunham, J. E. Buckley. Coll., George Leavenworth. G.
Jurors, Ashbel Storrs, M. Bunyan, W. N. Storrs, Eli Gillette,
A. W. Lounsbury. Assess., J. Kendall, Henry Bradley. Board
of R., James Swan, Ashbel Storrs, Frederick Beecher. Board
of Ed., L. A. Camp, W. R. Tomlinson, Nathan Holbrook, 1882;
J. Kendall, Carlos French, Henry Day, 1883; S. H. Canfield,
Robert Healey, H. N. Eggleston, 1884. Reg. of Voters, A. B.
Dunham, V. M. Beecher.

SHARON. Clerk and Reg., J. Wade Hughes. Treas., Elias B.
Reed. Selectmen, Baldwin Reed, 2d, Edwin W. Winchester,
Charles B. Everitt. Const., John C. Loucks, Michael McDon-
ald, Hiram Cooper. Coll., Edgar J. Reed. G. Juror, George
H. Smith. Assess., Charles E. B. Hatch, Clark N. Juckett,
Charles E. Benton. Board of R., John Boyd, Ozias Peck, Geo.
Gay. Board of Ed, Robert E. Goodwin, George A. Kelsey,
1882; Herman C. Rowley, Theodore L. Chase, 1883; John B.
Smith, William W. Knight, 1884. Reg. of Voters, William
Dakin, Frank B. Hamlin.

SHERMAN. Clerk and Reg., John N. Woodruff. Treas.,
William B. Hawley. Selectmen, George A. Barnes, J. M.
Pickett, Abram Briggs. Const., Oliver P. Woodruff. Coll.,
Isaac P. Hall. G. Juror, Rensellar Woodin. Assess, William
Caldwell, James Stuart. Board of R., George Hungerford,
Isaac B. Hall. Board of Ed., Theodore Rogers, John N. Wood-
ruff, Mills Hungerford. Reg. of Voters, Levi B. Hungerford.

SIMSBURY. Clerk, Reg., and Treas, James McKinney.
Selectmen, Jay Barnard, Charles Z. Case, Alonzo G. Case.
Const., Edward H. Bradley, and Coll., Porter White, William
R. Hall, Joseph L. Bartlett, Jeffery O. Phelps, Alonzo L. Lati-
mer. G. Jurors, Elizur H. Eno, Campbell P. Case, Orlando

Dean, Harvey Tucker, Henry W. Ensign, James Laughlin.
Assess., Henry J. Nobles, Frederick Pickett, Henry W. Ensign.
Board of R., Ebenezer G. Curtiss, John W. Alderman. Board
of Ed., Dudly B. McLean, Henry W. Ensign, 1882; Alonzo G.
Case, John B. McLean, 1883; Seymour Pettibone, George W.
Sanford, 1884. Reg. of Voters, Ebenezer G. Curtiss, Erwin
Chase.

SOMERS. Clerk, Reg., and Treas., Solomon Fuller. Select-
men, William H. Billings, William H. Burdick, John S. Field.
Const., George B. Pease. G. Jurors, John W. Little, John W.
Eaton, William H. Burdick, Lucius A. Kibbe, William L.
Brainard, Erwin D. Avery. Assess., Loren Griswold, William
L. Brainard, Leverett E. Pease. Board of R., Nathaniel A.
Patten, Joseph E. Dimock, James C. Pease. Board of Ed.,
Loren W. Percival, Myron F. Gowdy. Reg. of Voters, Amos
Pease, Charles Hibbard.

SOUTHBURY. Clerk and Reg., Granville S. Pierce. (P. O.
South Britain.) Treas., John Pierce. Selectmen, Henry S.
Wheeler, Reuben Pierce, Henry P. Hickox, George N. Platt.
Const., Stiles Bellfield, Isaac Wentsch, Theodore F. Wheeler,
Harley E. Warner, E. E. Burr, Charles K. Osborn, Charles H.
Stillson. Coll., Theodore F. Wheeler. G. Jurors, John M.
Wentsch, George H. Canfield, Harry N. Hicock, John L. Lee,
Oscar W. Ambler, Fred'k H. Gray. Assessors, Charles S.
Brown, Fred'k W. Fenn. Board of R., Philo J. Hawley, Chas
R. Oatman, Sanford Johnson. Board of Ed., Edgar Pierce,
Herman Perry, 1882; *Granville T. Pierce, Averill B. Canfield,
1883; *Charles S. Brown, Gedney A. Stiles, 1884. Reg. of
Voters, Henry M. Canfield, David M. Mitchell.

SOUTHINGTON. Clerk, Reg., and Treas., Charles D. Barnes.
Selectmen, Charles W. Hall, Charles Hitchcock, David M.
Monahan. Const., John C. Lewis, Charles H. Pond, Charles H.
Tolles, John H. Swift, Elbridge H. Bacon, Emory W. Doolittle,
Dennis P. Webster. Coll., Charles R. Bagley. G. Jurors,
Randolph W. Cowles, Ephraim H. Andrews, Lemuel Barber,
Wm. H. Cummings, David J. Phillips, Miles H. Upson. Assess.,
John J. Barnes, Wheaton S. Plumb, Joshua Bills. Board of R.,
Andrew F. Barnes, James F. Pratt, Levi C. Newell. Board of
Ed., *Andrew F. Barnes, Francis D. Whittlesey, 1882; *James
H. Osborn, Samuel W. Green, 1883; Stephen Walkley, Solomon
Finch, 1884. Reg. of Voters, John C. Lewis, Amon Bradley.

SOUTH WINDSOR. Clerk, Reg., and Treas., C. C. Vinton,
(P. O. Wapping.) Selectmen, George S. Bissell, Franklin A.
Sadd, Fred'k A. King. Const., Olin Wheeler, and Coll., Edgar
A. Farnham. G. Jurors, John A. Collins, Roswell Grant, Les-
ter Dewey, George Dart. Assessors, Henry W. Sadd, Nath-
aniel Jones. Board of R., Bradford H. Grant, Norman F.
Stoughton. Board of Ed., Charles N. Flanders, Cassius M.
Newberry, 1882; Bradford H. Grant, Nathaniel Jones, 1883;
George A. Bowman, William A. Taylor, 1884. Reg. of Voters,
Seth Vinton, Walter G. Newberry.

SPRAGUE. Clerk, Charles Wales. Reg., Mayden Hayes.
Treas., J. H. Woisard. Selectmen, Charles T. Hazen, R. A.
Batty, George Challenger. Const., C. L. Hazen, E. W. Bing-
ham, C. H. Ladd, Merrill Fitch, John McManus, Job Pickford.
Coll., Curtis Hazen. G. Jurors, H. C. Watson, Ebenezer Allen,
E. H. Hazen, William Nolan, C. A. Webb, Edward Fortier,
L. J. Branch. Assessors, J. E. Vickridge, Norman Smith,
Christopher Flynn. Board of R., Eli H. Hazen, R. A. Batty,
George Challenger. Board of Ed., Nathan Geer, William A.
Greene, 1882; M. K. Bunce, T. J. Stanton, 1883; N. Y. Bonney,
T. K. Peck, 1884. Reg. of Voters, H. C. Watson, Dennis
McCarty.

STAFFORD. Clerk, Reg., and Treas., M. C. Kinney. Select-
men, C. B. Newton, O. A. Richardson, E. C. Dennis. Const.,
G. S. Adams, and Coll., D. F. Mullin, Cyrus Banford, H. C.
Wheeler, Reuben Burley, Frederick Smith, C. N. Patten. G.
Jurors, H. W. Davis, W. E. Richardson, Lyman Cushman, J. V.
Squier, Lewis Chaffee, Henry Butterfield. Assess., Alvarado
Howard, John O. Booth, Wm. S. Shepard. Board of R., H. W.
Davis, Henry Butterfield, Wm. P. Amidon. Board of Ed.,
*G. V. Maxham, William R. Small, 1882; F. L. Batchelder.
John O. Booth, 1883, *Lina W. Ellis, David F. Whiton, 1884,
Reg. of Voters, Alba Perkins, J. C. Cross, J. W. Chandler,
Wm. P. Sweetser.

STAMFORD. Clerk and Reg., Clarles E. Holly. Treas.,
Robert Swartwout. Selectmen, William R. Lockwood, John W.
Harris, Samuel C. Waterbury. Const., Theodore Miller,
Richard Bolster, Charles S. Alphonse, George W. Anderson, Chas.
H. Daskam, Edward S. Downs. Coll, Charles H. Knapp,
Frank R. Leeds. G. Jurors, Charles W. Smith, George Gaylor,
John E. Keeler, A. C. Dixon, John W. Wardwell. Assessors,

Charles H. Knapp, Charles A. Weed, George E. Scofield, A. W. Williams, Hiram Curtis. Board of R., Charles Gaylor, Alvin Weed, John Unkles. Board of Ed., George H. Hoyt, Nathaniel B. Hart, Robert Swartwout, Radcliffe Hudson, Lewis R. Hurlburt, Samuel Roberts, Eleazer Porter, George B. Christison, F. A. Marden. Reg. of Voters, Charles A. Weed, James Mitchell.

STERLING. Clerk, James L. Young. Reg. Silas J. Matteson. Treas., Daniel T. Hart. Selectmen, Alfred Gallup, Silas A. Waite, Alven L. Cowry. Const, Allen Richmond, Luther Gallup, Benjamin Baton. G. Jurors, Daniel Matteson, Lewis K. Hammond, John B. Fenner. Assess., Russell Hill, Jeremiah L. B. Fenner, Josiah Slade. Board of R., Thomas D. Rhodes, Kinney S. Wilcox, Anos J. Gallup. Board of Ed., *Avery A. Stanton, Henry D. Dixon, Nehemiah J. Wood, John A. B. Douglass, Albert Frink, Ambrose H. Bates. Reg. of Voters, John M. Franklin, John A. B. Douglass.

STONINGTON. Clerk and Reg., Moses A. Pendleton. Treas., William J. H. Pollard. Selectmen, Elijah A. Morgan, George S. Brewster, Benjamin T. Stanton, 2d, Laughlin Hearty, Joseph S. Wilhams. Const., Samuel K. Tillinghast, W. H. Park, Elias G. Miner, Benjamin F. Crumb, Maurice O'Sullivan, Thomas H Hinckley, George F. Coats. Coll., Abel H. Hinckley. G. Jurors, George H. Greenman, John P. Williams, William R. Targee, Samuel L. Dickens, Warren C. Randall, Abel Hinckley, Assess., Charles Perrin, William C. Moss, George E. Tripp. Board of R., Nathan S. Noyes, Peleg S. Barber, Charles H. Hinckley. Board of Ed., James A. Dean, Charles H. Babcock, 1882; Charles H. Babcock, J. S. Anderson, 1883; Simeon Gallup, Charles H. Hinckley, 1884. Reg. of Voters, 1st Dist., James Pendleton, George C. Burtch; 2d Dist., Thomas D. Sheffield, Robert Woodburn; 3d Dist., Avery W. D. Noyes, Jas. A. Lord; 4th Dist., Elias Williams, Ira W. Jackson, 5th Dist., Charles E. Chipman, Stephen H. Wheeler.

STRATFORD. Clerk and Reg, Henry P. Stagg. Treas., Chas. P. Burritt. Selectmen, Alonzo J. Beardsley, Francis S. Avery, Leonard Wells. Const., J. Henry Blakeman, John J. Kugler, Joseph W. Dufour, Thomas W. Wood, Miles B. Beardsley, Wm. F. Thompson. Coll., Lemuel J. Beardsley. G. Jurors, Lucius B. Vail, William E. Wheeler, George Lewis, Peter P. Curtis, Allen Gregory, Charles E. Stagg. Assess., Peter P. Curtis, Alfred Beers, Albert Wilcoxson. Board of R., Anson H. Blake-

man, Joseph R. Lockwood, George H. Zink, Jr. Board of Ed.,
John R. Hull, Samuel O. Canfield, 1882; Peter P. Curtis,
Morton Beardsley, 1883; F. J. Beardsley, Albert Wilcoxson,
1884. Reg. of Voters, 1st Dist., Eugene Morehouse, Samuel
A. Patterson; 2d Dist., Thomas W. Wood, Charles E. Sherwood.

SUFFIELD. Clerk, Reg., and Treas., William L. Loomis.
Selectmen, Thaddeus H. Spencer, Charles J. Thrall, James H.
Haskins. Const., Wm. S. Graves, William F. Fuller, Edmund
Halladay, John L. Wilson, W. P. Frost. Coll., Webster E. Burbank. G. Jurors, Edwin A. Russell, James A. Hamilton, Oliver
C. Rose, Lewis C. Sheldon, Warren W. Cooper, Dwight S. Fuller. Assess., Webster E. Burbank, Cyrus H. King, A. F.
Austin. Board of R., B. F. Hastings, C. C. Warner, W. H.
Hastings. Board of Ed., James B. Rose, F. T. Latham, 1882;
S. C. Chandler, Edward Stone, 1883; George F. Kendall,
Charles Symington, 1884. Reg. of Voters, John L. Wilson,
Albert Austin.

THOMASTON. Clerk and Reg., Albert P. Bradstreet. Treas.
Arthur J. Hine. Selectmen, Aaron Thomas, Frederick E.
Warner, Daniel S. Carter. Const , Edwin A. Bradley, and Coll.,
William S. Judson, Joseph Wolf, William B. Atwood, Edgar
W. Bennett, Peter Duff, John R. Hoyt. G. Jurors, Thos. H.
Newton, Samuel S. Lamb, Gilbert I. Wooster, Joseph K. Judson,
Alfred B. Smith, Newell L. Webster. Assess., Israel B. Woodward, Joseph K. Judson, Daniel S. Carter. Board of R., Benjamin Platt, Edward P. Parker, Miles Morse. Board of Ed.,
Thos. S. Ockford, R. S. Goodwin, A. G. Heaney, 1882; George
A. Stoughton, Abel W. Smith, Eugene Gaffney, 1883; Samuel
M. Freeland, Albert P. Bradstreet, George B. Pierpont, 1884.
Reg. of Voters, Horton Pease, Edwin Alvord.

THOMPSON. Clerk, Reg., and Treas., James N. Kingsbury.
Selectmen, Marcus F. Town, Joseph N. Upham, John Elliott.
Const., William W. Cummings, George A. Putney, John W.
Gleason, Joseph Eagan, William N. Bates. G. Jurors, A. O.
Woodart, Joseph Bickford, John Wilkes, Josiah Dike, F. L.
Whittemore. Assessors, William W. Cummings, George T.
Murdock, Edwin T. White, Lemuel K. Blackmar, Asa Ross.
Board of R., George Flint, Japheth Costler, Simon A. Tingier.
Board of Ed., N. J. Pinkham, Stephen Ballard, Oscar Munyan.
Reg. of Voters, John D. Converse, James E. Bowen.

TOLLAND. Clerk, Reg., and Treas., Edwin S. Agard. Select-
men, Smith H. Brown, Henry Young, Spencer O. Grover.
Const., A. B. Clough, William J. Williams. Coll., John H.
Sparrow. G. Jurors, Charles Underwood, Charles Meacham,
Elisha Arnold, E. S. Agard, Henry Steele, Joseph Webster, Jo-
seph V. Lathrop. Assess., C. W. Bradley, Elisha Arnold,
Thomas G. Root. Board of R., A. L. Benton, A. P. Dickin-
son, A. B. Crandall. Board of Ed., C. Young, A. P. Dickin-
son, 1882; S. H. Brown, A. L. Benton, 1883; William C. Ladd,
*C. N. Seymour, 1884. Reg. of Voters, J. B. Fuller, William
D. Holman.

TORRINGTON. Clerk and Reg., Gideon H. Welch, Treas.,
Isaac W. Brooks. Selectmen, Nelson W. Coe, Squire Scoville,
Elijah Woodward. Const., Henry J. Allen, Frank L. Stocking,
Edward S. Miner, Lucien N. Whiting. Coll., Dexter W. Clark.
G. Jurors, Samuel J. Stocking, George W. Cole, Avery F. Mi-
ner, Roger C. Barber. Assess., Henry S. Patterson, Edward
B. Birge. Michael Batters. Board of R., Edward J. Hopkins,
Wilbur W. Birge, George W. Vaille. Board of Ed., *Clarence
H. Barber, Wait B. Wilson, Andrew Weigold, 1882; Burr Lyon,
L. Perrin, Avery F. Miner, 1883; G. H. Welch, J. W. Gam-
well, H. M. Sherman, 1884. Reg. of Voters, Henry J. Allen,
Charles F. Brooker.

TRUMBULL. Clerk, Samuel G. Beardsley. (P. O. Long Hill.)
Reg., Marcus O. Wheeler. Treas., Edward B. Burroughs.
Selectmen, Stephen H. Burroughs, David J. Botsford, Elbert E.
Edwards. Const., George S. Jennings, John S. Joyce, Horace
P. Nichols, W. F. Beach, A. S. Beach, Charles F. Osborne.
Coll., Joseph A. Treadwell. G. Jurors, George A. Hall, Eras-
tus Ryan, Charles N. Fairchild, George D. Mallett, Isaac E.
Booth, Henry V. Hallock. Assess., Erwin S. Fairchild, John
M. Beardsley, Sidney W. Nichols. Board of R., Theodore A.
Mallett, William C. Beach, Walter S. Hawley. Board of Ed.,
Clarence B. Sherwood, Charles J. Thorpe, 1882; John M.
Hough, Frank N. Burr, 1883; Frederick L. Beers, *Ormel
Hall, 1884.

UNION. Clerk, Reg., and Treas., D. L. Newell. Selectmen,
M. P. J. Walker, H. B. Booth, H. F. Corbin. Const., J. W.
Winch, and Coll., D. M. Newell. G. Jurors, L. M. Reed.
Assess., A. J. Wales, L. A. Corbin. Board of R., French
Crawford, Roscius Back, J. R. James. Board of Ed., E. C.

Booth, M. P. J. Walker, 1882; C. L. Orsmbee, A. E. Weld, 1883; Silas W. Newell, E. N. Lawson, 1884. Reg. of Voters, M. A. Marcy, A. E. Weld.

VERNON. Clerk, Reg., and Treas., Charles P. Thompson. (P. O. Rockville.) Selectmen, George Talcott, Nathaniel R. Grant, James Fitzgerald. Const., Henry G. Ransom and Coll., Benjamin Hirst, A. Palmer Dickinson, Henry J. Marshman, Lewis W. Hunt, Frederick Linker, Charles W. Pitkin. G. Jurors, Charles E. Harris, Nathaniel R. Grant, August Bever, Henry McCray, Gideon G. Tillinghast, W. Frank Fay. Assess., Henry McCray, Harry T. Miner, Abraham Laubscher. Board of R., E. Stevens Henry, Christian Cook, Cyrus Winchell. Board of Ed., George Sykes, Francis Keeney, 1882; Stephen G. Risley, Henry F. Parker, 1883; John S. Dobson, Gelon W. West, 1884. Reg. of Voters, George N. Brigham, James Carroll.

VOLUNTOWN. Clerk and Treas., Caleb P. Potter. Reg., George W. Rouse. Selectmen, James M. Cook, Seth Brown, Benj. S. Hall. Const., John A. Sweet, George R. Havens. Coll., Albert E. Bitgood. G. Jurors, Dwight Bromley, Henry C. Gardiner, E. Byron Gallup. Assessors, Robert H. Dixon, Joseph C. Tanner. Board of R., Benjamin Gallup, Thomas G. Congdon, John N. Gardiner. Board of Ed., Ezra Briggs, Wm. B. Ray, 1882; John E. Green, Frank A. Douglas, 1883; *John N. Lewis, A. E. Bitgood, 1884. Reg. of Voters, John E. Green, George W. Rouse.

WALLINGFORD. Clerk, Othniel I. Martin. Reg., James D. McGaughey. Treas., Friend A. Ives. Selectmen, B. Trumbull Jones, Henry Hall, Delano W. Ives. Const., Roger S. Austin, and Coll., Lewis A. Northrop, A. J. Goodrich, William H. McKenzie, J. C. Roach, J. F. Curzan, Silas J. Stow. G. Jurors, James J. Redmond, James A. F. Northrop, Mathew Harland, Homer R. Johnson, Seymour E. Hotchkiss, William E. Hall. Assessors, Henry S. Hall, 2d, Elizur R. Hall. Board of R., Bryant A. Treat, Elijah J. Hough, Street Williams, Walter J. Leavenworth, Michael O'Callaghan. Board of Ed., Henry L. Hall, J. G. Wildman, Henry S. Hall, George H. Smith. Reg. of Voters, Henry L. Hall, Harvey S. Hall.

WARREN. Clerk, Reg., and Treas., John B. Derrickson. Selectmen, N. B. Strong, G. S. Lyman, Buel Carter. Const., B. C. Norris, Miner A. Strong. Coll., E. P. Lyman. G. Ju-

8

rors, A. B. Camp, John H. Angevine. Assessors, A. T. Peck, Buel Carter. Board of R., A. R. Humphrey, L. G. Sheldon, C. W. Everett. Board of Ed., N. B. Strong, D. A. Youngs. Reg. of Voters, William F. Curtis, D. A. Youngs.

WASHINGTON. Clerk and Reg., Frederick N. Galpin. Treas., Simeon D. Platt. Selectmen, Charles L. Hickox, Stanley Williams, Joseph D. Barton. Const., A. H. Wyant, and Coll., H. O. Averill. G. Jurors, Truman H. Woodruff, James Aspinwall, Sherman Cogswell. Assess., Henry W. Seeley, Solomon T. Morehouse. Board of R., Eliada N. Moore, George K. Logan, George S. Cogswell. Board of Ed., George T. Sperry, Ralph I. Wheaton, 1882; Earle Buckingham, Charles N. Beach, 1883; Gould C. Whittlesey, George A. Tomlinson, 1884. Reg. of Voters, Sheldon J. Logan, William T. Odell.

WATERBURY. Clerk, James C. White. Reg., John J. Neville. Treas., Maier Kaiser, Selectmen, William Perkins, John Shanley, Orrin H. Bronson. Const., John W. McDonald, Patrick Higgins, John Burns, James J. McGrath, Daniel J. Rafferty, George H. Ford, Aretas W. Thomas. Coll., Eugene S. Wyman. G. Jurors, Charles Pritchard, Thomas Callahan, John L. Saxe, John Reed, Rudolph Berry, Samuel Nuttall. Assess., Chauncey B. Webster, Charles C. Commerford, Geo. A. Boughton. Board of R., Samuel Atwater, John Thompson, Albert Noether. Board of Ed., D. F. Webster, T. I. Driggs, Lawrence Walsh, 1882; J. W. Webster, Michael Donohue, D. G. Porter, 1883; Greene Kendrick, Michael A. Balfe, E. L. Griggs, 1884. Reg. of Voters, John J. Connor, John Blair.

WATERFORD. Clerk and Reg., Richard Tinker. Treas., Theodore F. Powers. Selectmen, James E. Beckwith, James E. Comstock, John B. Palmer. Const., William Littlefield, Edward A. Tinker, Ernest Smith, Andrew J. Hempsted, Albert Douglass, Elias F. Perkins. Coll., James A. Gallup. G. Jurors, Orlando Comstock, Ezra Miller, Sidney A. Smith, Anson Brown, P. G. Bindloss, Alonzo Beebe. Assessors, Griswold A. Chappell, Oliver Maxson, John Robertson. Board of R., Philip G. Bindloss, L. D. Howard, Alva A. Brown. Board of Ed., Fitch Comstock, C. Starr Chester, Ezekiah J. Hempsted. Reg. of Voters, John I. Chappell, Albert Lamphere.

WATERTOWN. Clerk and Reg., L. W. Cutler. Treas., Caleb T. Hickox. Selectmen, William G. French, George S. Atwood,

Frederick J. Partree. Const., Henry G. Scott, William J. Munson, Henry T. Dayton. G. Jurors, Joseph Wheeler, David M. Beardslee, William H. Smith, Albert T. Blakeslee, Albert J. Lounsbury. Assessors, George Woodward, Edward N. Woodruff. Board of R., Samuel T. Dayton, Jared Sperry, C. L. Dayton. Board of Ed., T. P. Baldwin, Charles W. Bidwell, 1882; James Stoddard, F. N. Woodruff, 1883; Walter S. Munger, Charles M. Noble, 1884. Reg. of Voters, Henry G. Scott, Daniel T. Hammon.

WESTBROOK. Clerk and Reg., George C. Moore. Treas., Horace T. Wilcox. Selectmen, William N. Kirtland, Edwin A. Hill. Const., Zadoc E. Morgan, William H. Cone, Alpheus H. Wright. Coll., Daniel S. Platt. G. Jurors, John A. Post, Samuel M. Pratt, Carlos H. Chapman, Wallace G. Spencer, David A. Wright. Assess., George C. Moore, Gilbert A. Post. Board of R., Samuel C. Holbrook, Oliver H. Morris, Carlos H. Chapman. Board of Ed., George C. Moore, Gilbert A. Post, 1882; Benjamin F. Bushnell, Edwin A. Hill, 1883; Julius H. DeWolf, David A. Wright, 1884. Reg. of Voters, James A. Pratt, Edwin C. Stevens.

WEST HARTFORD. Clerk and Reg., Leonard Buckland. Treas., Samuel Whitman. Selectmen, John E. Millard, Timothy Sedgwick, 2d, Edgar H. Seymour. Const., Jared A. Griswold and Coll., Edward A. Flagg, George T. Goodwin. G. Jurors, Edward Keney, Francis G. Butler, Charles E. Kellogg. Assess., Benjamin S. Bishop, Charles H. Flagg, Walter Cadwell. Board of R., James A. Griswold, Elmer G. Clark, Chas. M. Beach. Board of Ed., Franklin S. Hatch, Henry Talcott, 1882; Samuel Whitman, Samuel J. Bestor, 1883; Wm. H. Hall, Sidney E. Clark, 1884. Reg. of Voters, Benjamin S. Bishop, Leverett K. Seymour.

WESTON. Clerk and Reg., David L. Rowland. Treas., C. M. Parsons. Selectmen, Martin V. B. Rowland, Gregory T. Osborn, Wm. Cogswell. Const., Ebenezer Morehouse, Edward C. Ferguson, Lyman P. Smith. Coll.. Moses D. Treadwell. G. Jurors, Platt Keeler, Moses D. Treadwell, Oliver Perry. Assess., James Sturges, Dimon S. Fanton. Board of R., Oliver Perry, David S. Parsons, Ebenezer Fitch. Board of Ed., Ebenezer Fitch, D. L. Rowland, A. S. Jarvis, Lester Fanton, Edward Chauncey, D. S. Parsons. Reg. of Voters, Joseph S. Godfrey, Dimon S. Fanton.

WESTPORT. Clerk, Henry P. Burr. Reg., John S. Jones.
Treas., James L. G. Cannon. Selectmen, Silas B. Sherwood,
Henry B. Gilbert, John H. Jennings. Const., Henry I. Bennett,
Samuel E. Elwood, Charles H. Fairchild, Rufus D. Cable, Jas.
Hart, John Stuart, James S. Sherwood. Coll., Frederick
Kemper. G. Jurors, Philip G. Sanford, Abram Buckley, Wm.
Wood, Alfred N. Taylor, George J. Underwood, J. F. Murnan.
Assess., John W. Hurlburt, Charles H. Kemper, Henry B.
Wakeman. Board of R., William J. Finch, Moses Sherwood,
Wm. E. Dikeman. Board of Ed., T. D. Elwood, Wm. C. Hull,
1882; James S. Sherwood, William J. Jennings, 1883; John R.
Williams, A. N. Lewis, 1884. Reg. of Voters, John S. Jones,
Edward Wheeler.

WETHERSFIELD. Clerk and Treas., Albert Galpin. Reg.,
Abner S. Warner. Selectmen, Stephen Bulkley, Henry Gris-
wold, John Warner. Const., E. G. Woodhouse, and Coll., W.
W. Montague, George M. Richardson, E. N. Loveland, Lester
E. Adams, John Hanmer, Jr., Stephen T. Willard. G. Jurors,
Julius A. Deming, Samuel R. Welles, James T. Smith, Fred'k
A. Havens, C. Eugene Adams, Robert R. Wolcott. Assess, Jo-
siah G. Adams, Simeon Hale. Board of R., Francis H. Robbins,
Franklin W. Griswold, Stephen Morgan. Board of Ed., Mar-
tin S. Griswold, Luther W. Adams, 1882; John Welles, Henry
A. Deming, 1883; Howard S. Clapp, George D. Loveland, 1884.
Reg. of Voters, Albert H. Galpin, W. W. Adams.

WILLINGTON. Clerk and Treas., M. L. Dimock. Reg., W.
L. Kelsey. Selectmen, Seth C. Eaton, S. Taylor, L. D. Ide.
Const., Jason Bugbee, Jr., and Coll., Geo. A. Thomas. G. Ju-
rors, Philo Wright, Wm. Eldredge, N. S. Marcy, Wm. D. Ruby,
Daniel E. Benton, David K. Smith. Assess., Matthew Bur-
dick, Henry O. Sparks. Board of R., Charles F. Morrison, La-
throp Manning, Gilbert Ide. Board of Ed., C. W. Potter,
Arastus Cotton, L. W. Holt. Reg of Voters, James McFarland,
Henry O. Sparks.

WILTON. Clerk and Reg., Henry E. Chichester. Treas.,
Benjamin F. Brown. Selectmen, Samuel W. Ruscoe, Joseph O.
Dikeman, Elbert Olmstead. Const., Robert W. Keeler, and
Coll, Wm. B. Hurlbutt, Jr., Frederick Gregory, Josiah Gil-
bert. G. Jurors, Benajah Gilbert, Andrew Jackson, Charles
Sterling, Samuel B. Middlebrook, Albert Sturges. Assess.,
Frederick D. Benedict, Andrew Jackson, Eliphalet Morehouse,

William D. Gregory, Henry Finch. Board of R., Aaron M. Reed, Henry A. Barrett, John Lockwood. Board of Ed., *Harvey Bedient, Washington Post, 1882; Nathan M. Belden, Daniel G. Betts, 1883; Frederick D. Benedict, James T. Hubbell, 1884. Reg. of Voters, Samuel B. Fancher, John B. Sturges.

WINCHESTER. Clerk and Reg., Edward M. Platt. Treas., Henry C. Young. Selectmen, Orlow D. Hunt, Edward Finn, Elizur B. Parsons. Const., William A. Beardsley, Oscar F. Perkins, Alden H. Hubby, Clifford E. Bristol, Thomas Gloster, David York. Coll., Rollin L. Beecher. G. Jurors, John L. Tatro, Patrick Carroll, Leonard B. Hurlburt, John Keefe, LaFayette Granger. Assess., Samuel S. Newton, Charles A. Bristol, Rollin L. Beecher. Board of R., Hiram Perkins, Nelson D. Ford, Henry Gay. Board of Ed., Charles A. Bristol, Arthur Goodenough, 1882; H. Hungerford Drake, Midian N. Griswold, 1883; John F. Peck, Leo Da Saracena, 1884. Reg. of Voters, H. Hungerford Drake, George B. Cook.

WINDHAM. Clerk, Reg., and Treas., Henry N. Wales. Selectmen, M. Eugene Lincoln, J. Griffin Martin, W. B. Avery. Const., L. J. Hammond, E. H. Hall, Jr., George T. Spafford, George B. McCracken, E. W. Avery, Thomas F. Foran, A. G. Wickwire. Coll., E. H. Hall, Jr., L. J. Hammond. G. Jurors, John Bowman, Lloyd E. Baldwin, William Tracy, Martin Flint, Charles I. Barstow, Giles H. Alford. Assess., George Lincoln, E. H. Holmes, Jr., Albert Barrows. Board of R., Freeman D. Spencer, John Hickey, Frank S. Fowler. Board of Ed., Fl DeBruycker, William C. Jillson, John L. Hunter, 1882; John D. Wheeler, Henry W. Avery, George W. Melony, 1883; Marcus L. Tryon, E. H. Holmes, Jr., Albert Barrows, 1884. Reg. of Voters, Charles S. Bliven, John G. Kegwin.

WINDSOR. Clerk and Reg., John B. Woodford. Treas., Thomas W. Loomis. Selectmen, Henry E. Phelps, Robert Morrison, James C. Marshall. Const., Daniel W. Mack, Horace H. Thrall, James J. Holcomb. Coll., John Clark. G. Jurors, William Cornwall, James J. Merwin. Assess., Eli S. Hough, Morris B. Westcott, Elias B. Rhaum. Board of R., Joseph W. Baker, George W. Hodge, Edward F. Thrall. Board of Ed., William L. Bidwell, Thomas F. Tracy, 1882; E. S. Clapp, *R. H. Tuttle, 1883; G. C. Wilson, Eugene Brown, 1884. Reg. of Voters, George W. Barnes, Thomas W. Loomis.

WINDSOR LOCKS. Clerk, Reg., and Treas., Alfred W. Converse. Selectmen, Allen Pease, John W. Anderson, Joseph Reed. Const., Timothy F. McCarty, Patrick Noone, Thomas F. Gogarty. Coll., Patrick Gaynor. G. Jurors, M. J. Byrne, Elijah Ashley, Charles H. Easton. Assess., John B. Douglass, Elijah Ashley. Board of R., Charles E. Chaffee, John Abbe, William English. Board of Ed., John W. Coogan, J. R. Montgomery, 1882; John B. Douglass, James M. Tate, 1883; John Coats, William Conlan, 1884. Reg. of Voters, Michael J. King, William Mather.

WOLCOTT. Clerk and Reg., Henry Minor. Treas., Erastus W. Warner. Selectmen, Rufus Norton, Harmon Payne, Benj. L. Bronson. Const., John R. S. Todd, and Coll., Andrew J. Slater, William H. Brown. G. Jurors, Henry S. Parmelee, Lowrey S. Richardson, Levi Atkins. Assess., Rufus Norton, Albert N. Lane. Board of R., Erastus W. Warner, Henry Harrison, Mark Tuttle. Board of Ed., Elihu Moulthrop, Henry B. Carter, 1882; Rufus Norton, Albert N. Lane, 1883; *Frank G. Woodworth, John R. S. Todd, 1884. Reg. of Voters, Andrew J. Slater, Stiles S. Hotchkiss.

WOODBRIDGE. Clerk, Marcus E. Baldwin. Reg., James F. Nichols. Treas., Phineas E. Peck. Selectmen, Theron A. Todd, Rollin C. Newton, Theodore R. Baldwin. Const., Mark Tucker, Ellis N. Sperry, W. F. Tomlinson, Charles J. Peck, Frank Doolittle, James W. Rice. Coll., George P. Morgan. G. Jurors, William F. Morgan, William W. Peck, William Tomlinson, William A. Warner, Lauren Doolittle, E. L. Sperry. Assess., William F. Morgan, H. W. Chatfield. Board of R., Stephen P. Perkins, Frederick P. Newton, Daniel C. Augur. Board of Ed., *S. P. Marvin, Irvin P. Doolittle, 1882; Silas J. Baldwin, Elizur L. Sperry, 1883; William H. Warner, David C. Lines, 1884. Reg. of Voters, James F. Nichols, Warren F. Hotchkiss.

WOODBURY. Clerk, A. A. Root. Reg., Harmon W. Shove. Treas., F. A. Walker. Selectmen, George C. Bradley, Charles T. Terrill, Grandison Beardsly. Const., John W. Nichols, and Coll., George P. Crane, Willys Scoville, Thos. C. Galpin. G. Jurors, Thomas Bodycut, O. E. Norton, Daniel S. Lemmon. Assess., Charles D. Minor, Abernethy B. Stone. Board of R., Reuben B. Martin, Bennett A. Sherman, Henry Dawson, Walter E. Crofton, Wm. H. Allen. Board of

Ed., Harmon W. Shove, Nathan B. Burton, James Huntington, 1882; William J. Clark, George Brown, R. B. Judson, 1883; J. L. R. Wyckoff, F. F. Hitchcock, Harmon W. Judson, 1884. Reg. of Voters, Charles E. Strong, Michael F. Skelly.

WOODSTOCK. Clerk, Reg., and Treas., Herbert M. Gifford. Selectmen, Wm. B. Lester, Albert A. Paine, Henry K. Safford. Const., H. P. Hibbard, J. B. Tatem. Coll., George A. Penniman. G. Jurors, J. T. Morse, Martin Paine, William B. Chamberlin, Oliver A. Hiscox, Nelson Morse, John Paine. Assess., Amos M. Paine, Henry M. Bradford, David Aldrich. Board of R., John M. Paine, George Bugbee, Joseph F. Russell. Board of Ed., O. Fisher, P. S. Butler, Norton Randall, 1882; N. E. Morse, G. W. Child, J. M. Perrin, 1883; Lewis J. Wells, William W. Webber, Ebenezer Bishop, 1884. Reg. of Voters, William W. Webber, Charles M. Perrin, John F. Chandler, Albert Lippitt, J. M. Perrin, V. T. Wetherell.

HOSPITALS, &c.

RETREAT FOR THE INSANE, Hartford.—Pres., Wm. R. Cone; Vice-Pres., Calvin Day; Treas., Thomas Sisson; Auditor, William F. Tuttle; Sec., Jona. B. Bunce. Managers, Wm. R. Cone, Calvin Day, Gurdon W. Russell. Physician and Supt., Henry P. Stearns, M. D.; Assistant Phys., Charles W. Page; Steward, Rev. Geo. E. Sanborne; Matron, Mrs. Geo. E. Sanborne; Supervisor, Harriet E. Bacon.

CONNECTICUT HOSPITAL FOR THE INSANE, Middletown.— Trustees, Gov. Hobart B. Bigelow, New Haven; Robbins Battell, Norfolk; Ezra P. Bennett, M. D., Danbury; H. Sidney Hayden, Windsor; Lucius S. Fuller, Tolland; Samuel G. Willard, Colchester; R. M. Bullock, Putnam; Richard S. Fellowes, New Haven; Henry Woodward, Benjamin Douglas, Joseph W. Alsop, M. D., E. B. Nye, M. D., Middletown. Supt. and Physician, Abram M. Shew, M.D. Asst. Physicians, James Olmstead, Jr., William E. Fisher, C. E. Stanley. Treas., M. B. Copeland.

CONNECTICUT HUMANE SOCIETY.

Rodney Dennis, President; Henry E. Burton, Secretary; Ralph W. Cutler, Treasurer; all of Hartford.

STATISTICS OF TOWNS.

The first four columns designate the number of votes cast in the Presidential election, Nov. 1880. The second four give the number of votes for Governor, Nov. 1880. The other three give respectively the number of enrolled militia, the number of children between 4 and 16 years of age, and amount of the Grand List of the several towns of the State, Nov. 1881.

HARTFORD COUNTY.

Towns.	Garfield.	Hancock.	Weaver.	Dow.	Bigelow.	English.	Baldwin.	Rogers.	Militia.	Children.	Grand List.
Hartford,	4,502	4,727	84	2	4,527	4,707	85	5	5,714	9,590	$46,991,833
Avon,	133	110	7		133	110	7		132	238	479,782
Berlin,	282	264	2		281	265			256	557	1,066,020
Bloomfield,	140	210	2	1	141	210	2		169	273	798,465
Bristol,	607	625	2		603	625	4		756	1,094	2,194,569
Burlington,	104	159			112	151	1		158	318	381,501
Canton,	315	222			330	207			3?3	540	1,146,241
East Granby,	100	113			100	113			82	149	498,845
East Hartford,	390	410			391	408			463	786	1,792,402
East Windsor,	326	259		1	325	259		1	341	812	1,188,626
Enfield,	734	457	1	4	734	457	1	5	672	1,678	2,607,613
Farmington,	342	263	1		340	264	1		340	721	1,678,879
Glastonbury,	436	401	1	8	429	400	1	9	381	801	1,082,679

Town											Valuation
...ly,	208	161	3		208	161	3		216	284	500,209
Hartland,	90	85	1		90	85	1		97	146	263,834
...llr,	709	455		2	709	452		2	781	B59	2,563,626
Marlborough,	43	55			43	55			43	79	149,653
New Britain,	1,460	1,326	7	2	1,460	1,320	8	2	2,336	3,352	4,748,647
Newington,	98	101			98	101			79	228	382,340
Plainville,	256	178	1	1	250	181	1	5	288	429	1,083,949
Rocky Hill,	127	130	1	1	127	130		1	79	271	2,B7,011
...ury,	213	202	6	8	216	195	6	10	240	382	1,244,292
Southington,	631	611	16	1	628	612	16	1	638	1,363	1,865,244
South Windsor,	212	244	1	2	212	244	1	2	286	379	2,116,B04
Suffield,	465	374	1		463	375	1		358	721	1,239,457
West Hartford,	261	144			261	143			228	362	1,567,628
...field,	266	139	2		263	140	2	2	222	373	711,613
Windsor,	285	291	96	1	285	291	97	1	424	787	486,230
Windsor Locks,	184	272			184	272			278	720	622,852
	13,919	12,988	234	34	13,943	12,983	238	47	16,410	29,022	$83,582,044

NEW HAVEN COUNTY.

Town											Valuation
New ...en,	5,722	7,917	107	8	5,794	7,811	102	10	9,634	14,882	47,731,262
Beacon Falls,	44	23			43	24			36	129	304,868
Bethany,	35	118		2	35	118		2	70	115	296,154
Branford,	298	423	25	1	302	418	20	1	414	763	1,333,171
Cheshire,	281	232		4	279	234		5	276	B34	1,246,70
Derby,	1,124	1,218	7	2	1,122	1,274		2	1,160	3,104	3,775,313
East Haven,	412	330	7		415	329	6		504	B06	2,073,334
Guilford,	377	288	2	2	375	290	2	2	369	606	1,465,868

Towns.	Garfield.	Hancock.	Weaver.	Dow.	Bigelow.	English.	Baldwin.	Rogers.	Militia.	Children.	Grand List.
Hamden,	311	360	13	3	308	367	14	4	363	710	1,623,505
Madison,	254	172			257	170			212	351	35,717
Meriden,	2,014	1,689	47	10	2,024	1,677	47	13	2,294	4,393	8,938,214
ilbury,	104	47			D1	49			69	175	317,351
Milford,	374	467	1	2	375	468	1	2	510	651	1,339,897
Naugatuck,	354	491	8	3	345	487	24	2	649	989	1,614,457
North Branford,	154	117			155	116			150	188	489,636
Nth Hven,	217	150		5	217	148		7	239	338	783,259
Orange,	392	312	1		395	312	1		399	775	2,178,061
Oxford,	108	154			108	154			149	246	396,473
Prospect,	85	41			83	44			71	91	179,144
Seymour,	291	232	1		290	233	1		246	611	948,899
Southbury,	173	158			172	159			181	280	623,307
Wallingford,	427	614		3	426	615		3	755	1,080	2,362,356
Waterbury,	1,981	2,213		8	1,977	2,213	1	8	2,352	4,577	8,315,041
Wtt,	65	56			66	55			59	192	420,720
Woodbridge,	117	73			119	71			118	D7	220,964
	15,714	17,895	212	53	15,783	17,836	219	61	21,279	36,493	$89,513,761

NEW LONDON COUNTY.

Towns.	Garfield.	Hancock.	Weaver.	Dow.	Bigelow.	English.	Baldwin.	Rogers.	Militia.	Children.	Grand List.
New London,	1,003	1,103	13	52	978	1,103	12	78	1,480	2,090	6,640,313

Norwich,	2,260	1,633	64	25	2,245	1,641	21	26	2,551	5,073	18,169,572
Bozrah,	104	77	1		105	76	1		84	275	531,344
Colchester,	296	347	17		290	347	17		426	612	1,391,096
East Lyme,	224	128			224	126			193	384	95,845
Franklin,	104	52			103	53			68	133	324,657
Griswold,	323	195	3	8	323	196	3	8	347	664	1,293,652
Groton,	602	540	6	5	600	540	7	6	601	1,095	2,065,280
Lebanon,	280	149	9		280	148	10		236	398	1,102,289
Ledyard,	152	170			151	89	2	2	157	316	513,379
Lisbon,	68	81			69	81			79	83	283,519
Lyme,	136	121	1		136	121	1		148	239	291,942
Montville,	307	276	10	3	307	276	10		321	615	1,068,645
North Stonington,	294	154	2		295	154	2	3	247	387	731,047
Old Lyme,	121	181	2		121	180	3		181	337	474,817
Preston,	267	343	2		265	343	2		260	661	881,130
Salem,	75	74	3		75	74	3		71	137	255,549
Sprague,	95	123		77	96	123		76	260	1,066	1,197,883
Stonington,	743	612	16	11	744	611	16	12	846	1,640	5,390,80
Waterford,	312	283	4		312	283	4		308	634	1,254,181
	7,766	6,642	191	144	7,719	6,646	180	145	8,904	16,839	$39,456,270

FAIRFIELD COUNTY.

Bridgeport,	2,935	3,391		59	2,939	3,386	57		4,264	7,135	11,626,267
Danbury,	1,245	1,167	3	7	1,246	1,175	7	3	1,996	2,761	5,358,496
Bethel,	349	292			345	293		1	500	599	888,152
Brookfield,	113	164			113	163	2		113	242	600,824
Darien,	245	187			245	186			271	394	1,490,773

Towns.	Garfield.	Hancock.	Weaver.	Dow.	Bigelow.	English.	Baldwin.	Rogers.	Militia.	Children.	Grand List.
Easton,	165	153		6	95	153		6	125	88	438,478
Fairfield,	398	414	2		397	415	2		394	817	2,203,260
⋯h,	794	808			794	809			824	1,918	3,639,027
Huntington,	296	228			292	232			273	605	1,011,211
Monroe,	156	144			155	145			116	224	510,534
New Canaan,	319	300			317	302			260	614	1,250,113
New Fairfield,	60	135	1		59	135	1		76	159	417,050
⋯wn,	266	532	4	2	261	535	5		391	140	1,828,114
Norwalk,	1,338	1,271			1,564	1,269		3	1,716	3,136	5,399,730
Redding,	214	171			214	172			164	290	854,342
Ridgefield,	313	210			309	212			217	413	1,115,892
Sherman,	126	83			129	80			76	157	364,334
Stamford,	1,086	1,055	12	1	1,086	1,055	15	1	1,424	2,574	6,920,103
Stratford,	538	385		13	536	383	15		615	921	155,832
Trumbull,	172	174	3	1	176	170	3		168	260	624,260
Weston,	100	131			100	131			105	176	419,910
Westport,	287	459			289	452			451	829	2,079,108
Wilton,	238	210			237	210			155	412	711,613
	12,003	12,064	89	27	11,988	12,063	107	16	14,694	25,834	$51,357,423

WINDHAM COUNTY.

Towns.	Garf'd.	Hancock.	Weaver.	Dow.	Bigelow.	English.	Baldwin.	Rogers.	Militia.	Children.	Grand List.
Brooklyn,	225	140		5	226	138		6	160	510	1,462,979
Ashford,	148	160		1	147	160		1	157	222	327,987
Canterbury,	153	161	1		152	162		1	142	293	592,002
Chaplin,	98	47	1		97	47			75	137	233,616
Eastford,	124	98	9		126	96			98	204	232,120
Hampton,	123	71		2	124	71		7	116	180	368,457
Killingly,	723	434	2	3	721	434		3	758	1,666	2,185,568
Plainfield,	378	257			373	257	1		296	953	1,915,002
Pomfret,	196	95			96	97	9		161	292	770,622
Putnam,	515	251		1	513	251		4	634	1,446	1,802,210
Scotland,	90	68		1	91	67	2	1	67	108	335,375
Sterling,	96	102			96	101			104	227	301,762
Thompson,	399	151		2	396	152	3	4	385	1,286	127,350
*Voluntown,	170	70	3	16	170	70	1		91	343	224,672
Windham,	757	601	2	1	756	601		19	961	1971	3,800,810
Woodstock,	406	174			404	175		2	292	556	987,922
	4,596	2,880	18	32	4,588	2,879	16	48	4,497	10,394	$17,363,554

*Transferred to New London County, 1881.

LITCHFIELD COUNTY.

Town											
Litchfield,	341	381		1	333	386			494	773	2,019,480
Barkhamsted,	144	170	10		143	171	10		123	268	420,307
Bethlehem,	95	87			94	89			79	143	453,487
Bridgewater,	56	132			55	133			83	169	417,934
Canaan,	154	140			154	141		2	141	232	516,749
...k,	102	129	6		102	129	6		139	288	418,241
Cornwall,	202	188			201	188			205	408	612,585
Goshen,	117	109			116	110			118	259	762,846
Harwinton,	152	88		3	152	87		3	107	243	483,412
Kent,	180	195			180	196			173	380	472,825
Morris,	77	102			76	102			85	135	367,984
New Hartford,	313	238	5		311	238	5		399	793	1,052,217
New Milford,	407	587	2		407	583	2	1	498	844	1,945,854
North Canaan,	127	224	2		126	224	2		212	379	792,377
...k,	179	116			180	115		1	124	396	689,567
Plymouth,	296	223		3	295	222		5	333	563	1,016,872
Roxbury,	107	149			106	150			95	181	481,118
Salisbury,	311	485	11	6	311	483	11	5	393	882	194,862
Sharon,	254	319	7	3	254	319	8		336	638	1,369,915
...n,	399	253	1	1	397	251	1	3	342	842	1,434,549
Torrington,	451	342		1	449	341		2	472	146	2,129
Warren,	103	63			101	64		1	72	395	921,510
Washington,	188	186	1		186	188	1		194	1,105	1,578,000
Watertown,	282	197		2	282	198		2	206	455	2,749
Winchester,	597	555	59	3	598	555	57	3	761	309	1,058,216
...y,	310	228			308	228			329	723	1,441,377
	5,944	5,886	107	27	5,917	5,891	106	30	6,513	11,949	$25,720,672

MIDDLESEX COUNTY.

Town											
Middletown,	1,B9	1,280	45	27	1,139	1,271	45	33	1,521	2,651	$6,226,345
Haddam,	238	319	1	11	238	318	1		184	502	727,589
Chatham,	233	213	1	1	233	209	1	15	211	488	617,316
Chester,	187	100		8	185	101		1	155	226	433,218
Clin.,	200	166			200	166	4	4	164	292	656,335
Cromwell,	199	182	4	4	198	183		1	201	393	735, 54
Durham,	142	129		5	141	130			132	180	470,218
East Haddam,	432	263	6		430	263	6	5	337	666	1,316,779
Essex,	291	216		5	292	217		5	275	328	1,023, 34
Killingworth,	76	121		6	76	119	1		D1	123	231,504
Middlefield,	126	71		1	125	70		6	121	199	717,089
Old Saybrook,	152	137	1	1	168	136	1	1	110	278	1,938,116
Portland,	376	322		1	375	323		1	385	953	643,649
Saybrook,	236	106		3	235	107		3	173	244	482,988
Westbrook,	144	94		6	144	94		6	107	144	563,237
	4,171	3,719	58	68	4,164	3,707	59	81	4,167	7,667	$16,782,571

TOLLAND COUNTY.

Town											
Tolland,	165	134		2	170	123		2	95	284	353,972
Abr.,	65	61			65	61			58	67	234,542
Bolton,	69	73			68	73			58	115	188,198
Columbia,	83	89		2	83	89		2	72	189	726,215
Ely,	236	242		4	233	244		5	246	400	254,516
Ellington,	169	190		2	169	190		2	124	307	724,906
Hebron,	161	119			162	118			120	264	475,271
Mfield,	287	181		4	288	181		4	179	428	669,262

Towns.	Garfield.	Hancock.	Weaver.	Dow.	Bigelow.	English.	Baldwin.	Rogers.	Militia.	Children.	Grand List.
Somers,	183	136			181	136			173	261	596,747
Stafford,	472	476			472	477		1	526	1,038	1,100,211
Union,	70	92		1	70	92		1	71	144	157,933
Vernon,	835	472	6	1	834	475	6	7	895	1,773	2,670,395
Willington,	173	79	1	6	173	79		1	128	261	242,393
	2,968	2,344	7	23	2,968	2,338	7	25	2,745	5,531	$8,394,561

COUNTIES.	Garfield.	Hancock.	Weaver.	Dow.	Bigelow.	English.	Baldwin.	Rogers.	Militia.	Children.	Grand List.
Hartford,	13,919	12,988	234	34	13,943	12,933	238	47	16,410	29,022	$83,582,044
New Haven,	15,714	17,895	212	53	15,783	17,836	219	61	21,279	36,493	89,513,761
New London,	7,766	6,642	144	192	7,719	6,646	145	180	8,904	16,839	39,456,270
Fairfield,	12,003	12,064	89	27	11,988	12,063	107	16	14,694	25,864	51,357,423
Windham,	4,596	2,880	18	32	4,588	2,879	16	48	4,497	10,394	17,363,554
Litchfield,	5,944	5,886	107	27	5,917	5,891	106	30	6,513	11,949	25,720,672
Middlesex,	4,171	3,719	58	68	4,164	3,707	59	81	4,167	7,667	16,782,571
Tolland,	2,968	2,344	7	23	2,968	2,338	7	25	2,745	5,531	8,394,561
	67,081	64,418	869	456	67,070	64,293	897	488	79,209	143,759	$332,170,856

Total vote for President, November, 1880, 132,863; 39 votes returned as scattering. Garfield's majority, 1,299. Total vote for Governor, November, 1880, 132,763; 15 votes returned as scattering. Bigelow's majority, 1,377.

CITIES.

BRIDGEPORT. Mayor, John L. Wessels. Aldermen, 1, Edward W. Atwood; 2, Charles Sherwood; 3, Hobart W. Watson; 4, Martin Sykes; 5, Ashbel E. Bartram; 6, Henry Gowd. Councilmen, 1, Herman Gauss, Bradley H. Hull, Albert D. Laws; 2, William H. Rockwell, Ira De Ver Warner, Daniel W. Kissam; 3, Daniel O. Donnell, Lucien H. Copeland, Theodore W. Dowd; 4, Christopher A. Mooney, Charles A. Blakeman, Patrick McGrath; 5, Philo M. Beers, Lorenzo Follett, Wilbur A. Gleason; 6, John Walsh, Thomas Kelley, John J. Phelan. City Clerk, Bernard Keating. Treasurer, Isaac B. Prindle. Auditor, Rowland B. Lacey. Coll. of Taxes, Benjamin K. Mills. Coll. of Assessments, Henry H. Bostwick. City Att'y, Curtis Thompson. Judge of City Court, Alfred B. Beers. Assistant Judge, Charles A. Doten. Clerk of City Court, Ebenezer Burr, Jr. Prosecuting Att'y, J. C. Chamberlain. City Sheriffs, Thomas W. Stone. City Surveyor, Horace G. Scofield. Road and Bridge Com., George Mallory, Patrick Kennelly. William R. Hinckley, Jarratt Morford. Street Com., William Kirk. Fire Com., William R. Higby, Fred. S. Stevens, Samuel W. Baldwin, Eli Dewhurst. Fire Marshal, George N. Morgan. Chief Engineer, Charles A. Gerdenier. Police Com., William B. Spencer, Frank C. Bennett, Samuel Larkin, Charles K. Averill. Chief of Police, William E. Marsh. Health Officer, William H. Lacey.

HARTFORD. Mayor, Morgan G. Bulkeley. Aldermen, 1, Wm. Berry, Frank L. Howard; 2, DeWitt C. Pond, Henry E. Taintor; 3, William B. Clark, John N. B. Stevens; 4, George Best, Samuel Walker; 5, William C. Smith, Peter Chute; 6, George W. Fowler, Richard McCloud; 7, Samuel N. Benedict, Edgar F. Burnham; 8, George S. Merritt, Charles H. Hawley. Common Council, 1, Frank S. Kellogg, Edward C. Frisbie, Edward S. Sykes, Robert A. Griffing; 2, Nelson G. Hinckley, Lemuel T. Frisbie, Wallace T. Fenn, Charles H. Prentice; 3, Henry L. Bunce, George E. Taintor, Emery Downing, Edward R. Faxon; 4, James D. Johnson, John A. Crilly, Edward P. Whitney, William W. Winship; 5, James Morgan, Charles W. Scott, Henry E. Howe, Patrick Clifford; 6, Steph. G. Sluyter, Louis Levy, Moritz Wieder, George Giszewsky; 7, Albert S. Hotchkiss, Stephen Goodrich, Ralph Foster, J. Henry Martin; 8, John

9   -

H. Brocklesby, Charles H. Barber, George H. Brown, Thomas Farrell. City Clerk, John E. Higgins. Treasurer, Charles C. Strong. Auditor, John T. Peters. Collector, Frederick S. Brown. City Marshal, Thomas Longdon. Recorder, Edward B. Bennett. Judge of Police Court, Arthur F. Eggleston; Assistant Judge, Sherman W. Adams. Clerk of Police Court, William F. Henney. Prosecuting Attorney, Joseph L. Barbour. Surveyor, Charles H. Bunce. Coroner, Horace S. Fuller; Assistant Coroner, Eli Warner. Street Com., Joseph H. Sprague, Ebenezer K. Hunt, James Burns, Henry Kennedy, William E. Cone, Henry C. Dwight. Supt. of Streets, Richard S. Lawrence. Park Com., Samuel R. McNary, Charles D. Warner, Richard D. Hubbard, Gurdon W. Russell, Francis Goodwin. Fire Com., John R. Hills, Thomas J. Blake, Edwin J. Smith, Leander Hall, Gideon D. Winslow, Justin N. Mansuy. Chief Engineer, Henry J. Eaton. Fire Marshal, Edwin J. Smith. Police Com., Mayor Morgan G. Bulkeley, David A. Rood, George G. Sill, Lewis E. Stanton, G. Wells Root, George Ellis, Thomas Galvin. Chief of Police, ——— ———. Water Com., Rodney Dennis, Joseph Hall, James Bolter, Ezra Clark, Charles E. Perkins, William M. Charter.

MERIDEN. Mayor, E. J. Doolittle, Jr. Aldermen, 1, W. W. Mosher, William Homan; 2, Bela Carter, N. L. Bradley; 3, Charles A. King, Julius Andrews; 4, A. C. Markham, James R. Sutliff; 5, W. W. Lee, Robert H. Curtis. Councilmen, 1, W. R. Mackev, J. H. Converse, E. B. Cowles, A. H. Jones; 2, John Nagal, Lewis A. Lipsette, H. C Hull, Willis I. Fenn; 3, Edwin Cady, Charles J. Klein, William G. Gallagher, William R. Derby; 4, Oscar Parker, George C. Merriam, T. F. Breese, J. F. Green; 5. L. C. Brown, C. J. Heinneman, A. W. Harvey, Watson W. Clark. City Clerk, Selah A. Hull. Treasurer, David S. Williams. Collector, Benjamin Page. Auditor, Frederick B Derby. Sheriffs, James E. Belden, Jared P. Parker. Judge of City and Police Court, Levi E. Coe. Ass't Judge, John Q. Thayer. Surveyor, S. C. Pierson. Coroner, Charles H. Shaw.

MIDDLETOWN. Mayor, Edward Payne. Aldermen, 1, Chas. G. R. Vinal; 2, I. M. Bacon; 3, Leonard Bailey; 4, John Rodgers. Councilmen, George T. Meech, Rohert C. Youngs, John V. Adams, W. H. Palmer, Jr., Joseph J. Noxon, David R. Brownlow, Joseph T. Elliott, C. M. Newton, J. Peters Pelton, Frank B. Weeks, Charles Schondorf, Frederick W. Hubbard. Clerk and Treas., James P. Stow. City Attorney, William T. Elmer. Recorder, Charles A. Boardman. Collector, Horace Leonard. Assessor, Charles A. Newell. City Sheriff and Chief of Police, William C. Fielding. Chief Engineer, Frederick W. Wiley. Fire Marshal, Augustus Putnam. Water Com., Charles W. Harris, Thomas H. Linahen, Timothy O'Brien, Frederick W. Wiley, R. K. Pitkin, Charles R. Lewis.

NEW BRITAIN. Mayor, John B. Talcott. Aldermen, 1, Frank L. Hungerford; 2, William S. Judd; 3, Peter McAvoy; 4, Charles H. Parsons. Councilmen, 1, Ralph C. Dunham, Reuben L. Hubbard, Ferdinand Becker, Alonzo Aston; 2, Frederick N. Steele, John W. Carleton, James H. Eddy, Henry C. Bowers; 3, Thomas Fagan, Oliver Fenton, John E. Dunlav; 4, Frederick Kentschler, Francis Hart, 2d, Daniel Flynn, John T. Dwyer. City Clerk, Robert J. Vance. Treas., Augustus P. Collins. Auditor, William F. Walker. Collector, Wm. E. Latham. Sheriff, Isaac Porter. City Attorney, Julius H. Pease. Judge of Police Court, V. B. Chamberlain. Street Com., Ira B. Smith, William H. Hart, James Thompson, Henry P. Strong, Charles Peck, Lawrence Crean. Water Com., Thomas H. Brady, Philip Corbin, Wm. H. Relyea. Sewer Com, J. A. Pickett, E. H. Davison, George M. Landers.

NEW HAVEN. Mayor, John B. Robertson. Aldermen, 1, Wm. K. Townsend, William H. Law; 2, Richmond W. Armstrong, Eli Mix; 3, George J. Faulhaber; 4, James N. States, Jno. Clancey; 5, George A. Stevens, Simon J. Shoninger; 6, Ernst Klenke, Patrick Willis; 7, Charles Doty, James F. O'Keefe 8, Frank W. Tiesing, Frederick B. Farnsworth; 9, Joseph Sheldon, Lyman R. Griffin; 10, John P. Studley, Herbert E. Benton; 11, David C. Burwell, William T. Porter; 12, Seth W. Langley, William Kelley. Councilmen, 1, Frank A. Munson, William A. Cushing; Lyman E. Munson; 2, Dennis A. Blakeslee, Samuel H. Kirby, Michael C. Sullivan; 3, Mathew Kehoe, Patrick Bohan, Richard H. Coffee; 4, Charles E. Gerard, Samuel H. Barns, Michael McQueeney; 5, Patrick McKiernan, George S. Thomas, Frank I. Thompson; 6, Charles H. Hilton, Lawrence O'Brien. William Kaehrle; 7, Frank D. Welch, John F. Defrees, Wm. J. Bradley; 8, T. Atwater Barnes, James J. Bradnack, Benjamin E. Brown; 9, Alonzo A. Townsend, Henry R. Hill, Major G. La Forge; 10, Julius Twiss, Frank S. Platt, A. Wilson Holmes; 11, Alfred N. Wheeler, Herbert Jones, Edgar A. Johnson; 12, Michael Eagan, 2d, Michael Scally, Thomas G. W. Jefferson. City Clerk,

James P. Piggott. Treasurer, Harmanus M. Welch. Auditor, Charles Kimberly. Sheriff, Thos. C. Hollis. Judge of City Court, Joseph Sheldon; Asst. Judge, John P. Studley. Fire Marshal, Andrew J. Kennedy. Chief Engineer, A. C. Hendrick. Inspector of Streets, Patrick Doyle. Chief of Police, Charles Webster.

NEW LONDON. Mayor, Robert Coit. Aldermen, George F. Tinker, William A. Holt, Abner N. Sterry, Horace Coit, John E. Darrow, James Fitch, Frank H. Chappell, Wm. H. Bently, L. D. Clark. Councilmen, W. Astheimer, George Haven. T. M. Allyn, Noel B Gardner, Charles B. Ware, John Meade, Stephen Bolles, Frederic H. Harris, J. D. Cronin, M. R. Moran, Robert S. Hayes, Wm. E. Greene, W. H. Carroll, P. C. Dunford, F. H. Parmelee. Judge of City and Police Court, Charles W. Butler. Assistant Judge, William Belcher. Clerk of City and Police Court, Reuben Lord, Jr. City Att'y, Augustus Brandegee. Assist. Attorney, Ralph Wheeler. Coll., E. P. Beckwith. City Sheriffs, Allen Penhallow, James E. Metcalf, Timothy Lagrue. Street Com., John H. Brown. Engineer, E. B. Jennings. Inspector of Buildings, Lyman Baker. Captain of Police, Andrew J. Quinn.

NORWICH. Mayor, Hugh H. Osgood. Aldermen, Myron Sears, John P. Barstow, Robert Brown, Robert A. France. Councilmen, Stephen F. Whaley, David S. Gilmour, James A. Brown, Wm. H. Armstrong, Jas. H. Arnold, Alvah Francis, John Steiner, John Willard. City Clerk, Charles W. Gale. City Collector, Charles H. Dillaby. City Treasurer, Charles Webb. ' City Sheriffs, Joseph B. Corey, Joab B. Rogers, Judge of City Court, John C. Kellogg; Deputy, Lucius Brown. City Attorney, E. C. Cooke. Corporation Counsel, Allen Tenny. Clerk of City Court, Wm. S. Congdon. Chief of Police, Z. C. Crowell. Captain of Police, Wm. E. Whaley. Street Com., Mowry B. Cole. Chief Engineer, Joseph B. Carrier. Water Com., Sidney Turner, Wm. M. Williams, Henry L. Parker, Robert A. France, Albertus Peckham. Supt. Water Works, H. B. Winship.

SOUTH NORWALK. Mayor, Christian Swartz. Councilmen, Clarence Nash, John W. Bogardus, John W. Powell, James M. Lane, Wm. A. Raymond, Wm. W. Comstock. Coll., James M. Lane. Treas., Nelson Taylor, Jr. Auditor, W. S. Hanford.

Marshall, R. E. Kinney. Attorney, Nelson Taylor. Chief of Police, Marcus Pelham. Water Com., Alden Solmans, Jacob M. Laytin, R. H. Rowan. Treas. Water Fund, Nelson Taylor.

WATERBURY. Mayor, Greene Kendrick. Clerk, Edward G. Kilduff. Treas., Michael A. Balfe. Auditor, James E. Bissell. Sheriff, John W. McDonald. Water Com., Chas. C. Commerford, David B. Hamilton, Orville H. Stevens, Charles R. Bannon. Aldermen, Alfred J. Shipley, Augustus I. Goodrich, Earl A. Smith, Edward L. Bronson, Martin Hellmann, Chauncey B. Webster, John J. Connor, James Coughlan. Councilmen, G. W. Roberts, A. Oviatt, Thomas Fitzsimons, Jr., W. S. Frost, H. Nelson, C. R. Smith, J. H. Hart, T. R. Martin, S. F. Curtis, H. C. Seeley, F. L. Curtis, G. P. Chapman, P. R. Halm, W. Farrell, S. W. Chapman, A. Cunningham, W. C. Bannon, John Thompson, J. Healey, A. Wendeback. Chief of Police, William Laird. Chief Engineer Fire Dept., A. W. Goldsmith. Street Inspector, James M. Colley. City Attorney, S. W. Kellogg. Judge of Police Court, George H. Cowell; Deputy Judge of Police Court, A. P. Bradstreet. Clerk of Courts, Daniel F. Webster. Assistant City Attorney, Edward F. Cole.

BOROUGHS.

ANSONIA. Warden, Henry A. Shipman. Burgesses, Morris Drew, Patrick B. Fraher, Henry C. Spencer, Samuel B. Bronson, Henry C. Cook. Clerk, Egbert S. Bronson. Treasurer, Charles H. Pine. Bailiff, Daniel J. Hayes. Assessors, Chester A. Hawley, Charles Reed, W. B. Bristol. Auditors, Wm. Powe, J. G. Redshaw.

BETHEL. Warden, George M. Cole. Clerk, G. B. Andrews. Burgesses, Henry Gilbert, E. Starr Judd, Edward B. Richmond, E. N. Filleon. Treasurer, George H. Hickok. Bailiff, John M. Signor. Chief Engineer, Samuel Kyle.

BIRMINGHAM. Warden, Royal M. Bassett. Burgesses, Wm. C. Atwater, A. W. Phillips, Wm. E. Downes Patrick McManus, Henry Whipple, Henry Somers, John H. Barrow. Clerk, John C. Reilly. Treasurer, Theodore S. Bassett. Bailiff, Fred'k Baldwin. Fire Wardens, Peter McGovern, Orrin F. Lathrop, John Abbott.

COLCHESTER. Warden, Leander Chapman. Burgesses, E. S. Day, W. H. Hayward, W. A. Williams, H. P. Buell, C. H. Bailey, Wm. Foote. Clerk and Treas., P. R. Strong. Bailiff and Collector, N. P. Palmer.

DANBURY. Warden, Levi P. Treadwell. Burgesses, Edward S. Davis, Julius Meyers, Samuel C. Holley, Hendrick Barnum, Andrew J. Elwell. Clerk, Aaron C. Seeley. Treasurer, Harvey Williams. Bailiff, Franklin C. Hoyt. Auditors, Alfred A. Heath, Alson J. Smith. Water Com., James Fry, Turner Stevens, David Pearce.

DANIELSONVILLE. Warden, Wm. H. Chollar. Clerk and Treas., Edwin L. Palmer. Burgesses, Loren Bates, Samuel Hutchins, Henry C. Chamberlin, Ebenezer Scarborough, Wm. H. Chapman, Daniel H. Johnson. Bailiff and Coll., Edward S. Carpenter. Assess., Caleb W. Knight, Chauncey C. Young, Frank G. Bailey.

FAIR HAVEN EAST. Warden, Horace B. Strong. Burgesses, Jared Wedmore, Wm. A. Wright, Albert Rowe, John F. Hemingway, C. S. Brown, Henry R. Smith. Clerk, Charles E. Bray. Treasurer, A. L. Chamberlain. Assessors, C. W. Hemingway. A. C. Chamberlain, Martin Allen. [Collector, Samuel B. Hill. Bailiff, Joseph R. Bradley.

GREENWICH. Warden, John Voorhis. Burgesses, Joseph G. Mead, Matthew Merritt, L. P. Jones, A. Foster Higgins, J. H. Ray, Zophar Mead. Clerk and Treas., Frederick A. Hubbard. Collector, Benjamin A. Russell. Bailiff, Charles E. Merritt. Attorney, H. W. R. Hoyt.

GUILFORD. Warden, John S. Starr. Burgesses, H. W. Leete, A. B. Palmer, Beverly Monroe, J. Seymour Benton, George B. Spencer, William T. Dowd. Clerk, Harvey W. Spencer. Treasurer, Henry S. Wedmore. Assessors, L. R. Elliott, George L. Griswold.

NORWALK. Warden, William H. Smith. Burgesses, Clarence B. Coolidge, James G. Gregory, Charles P. Turney, Addison A. Betts, Gerardus P. Adams, George B. St. John. Clerk, Charles P. Woodbury. Assistant Clerk, William E. Montgomery. Treasurer, Robert S. Crauford. Collector, Elbert Curtis. Bailiff, Legrand C. Betts. Water Commissioners, Winfield S. Moody, A. C. Golding, Charles E. St. John. Assessors, Joseph B. Ells, D. Warren Fitch. Burr Smith. Board of Relief, Isaac Demmon, James Finney, William E. Dann. Fire Inspector, William B. Newcomb. Health Inspector, Joseph Tammany. Surveyor, C. G. Wood. Chief Engineer, J. Thornton Prowitt.

STAFFORD SPRINGS. Warden, G. C. Parkess. Burgesses, James McLaughlin, Alvarado Howard, A. Adams, John Brosnan, C. J. Holmes, Wm. A. Comins. Clerk and Treas., Wm R. Small. Collector, J. J. Gallivan. Bailiff, Louis Helm. Registrars, W. P. Sweetser, J. W. Chandler. Assessors, A. Howard, Lyman Cushman, M. P. Shahan. Board of R., A. Holt, J. A. Medbury, Florence McCarthy.

STAMFORD. Warden, Chas. A. Hawley. Burgesses, Edwin S. Holly, Warren H. Taylor, Erastus E. Scofield, George H. Hoyt, William D. Smith, Dwight Waugh, George W. Dean. Clerk, Edward W. Riker. Collector, Francis R. Leeds. Treasurer, George W. Glendinning. Bailiff, Charles H. Daskham.

STONINGTON. Warden, Albigence Hyde. Burgesses, Joshua Haley, A. B. Miller, N. H. Gates, George D. Brown, F. B. Noyes, O. D. Chesebro. Clerk and Treas., J. S. Anderson. Bailiff and Coll., Horace H. Lewis. Assessor, John R. Chesebro. Street Com., N. G. Smith, W. F. Reynolds, N. H. Gates.

WALLINGFORD. Warden, B. A. Treat. Burgesses, R. H. Cowles, J. C. Mansfield, W. J. Leavenworth, P. McKenna, Albert D. Judd, Martin P. O'Connell. Clerk, C. H. Brown. Coll., R. S. Austin. Treas., T. Pickford. Assessor, Henry Martin. Auditor, Henry L. Hall, 1st. Bailiff, L. A. Northrop.

WEST HAVEN. Warden, Israel K. Ward. Burgesses, Geo. R. Kelsey, James Graham, Rollin W. Hine, Charles K. Bush, Edward L. Kimberley, Clarence E. Thompson. Clerk, Edward W. Wilmot. Collector, Walter A. Main. Treasurer, Alonzo F. Wood. Auditor, Harry I. Thompson. Assessors, Samuel L. Smith, Stephen E. Booth, Leman G. Atwood. Bailiff, Squire S. Hyde.

WEST STRATFORD. Warden, E. E. Price. Burgesses, John Umstratter, Wheeler Hawley, Charles L. Price, Milo Loomis, Joseph Johnson. Clerk, Charles H. Hinman. Treasurer, H. B. Drew. Collector, Farrel O'Reilly. Bailiff, George Baker. Attorney, V. R. C. Giddings.

WILLIMANTIC. Warden, Roderick Davison. Burgesses, Chas. S. Billings, George M. Harrington, John M. Alpaugh, Henry L. Hall, Andrew J. Kimball, John G. Keigwin. Clerk and Treas., Charles A. Capen. Collector, Lucius M. Sessions. Bailiff, Giles R. Young.

WINSTED. Warden, Wilbur F. Coe. Burgesses, Elizur B. Parsons, Charles B. Andrews, William V. Barclay, Lawrence McDermott, Chas. B. Andrews, William V. Bartley, Alfred E. Moore, George W. Phelps. Clerk and Treas., Henry H. Drake. Bailiff, Joseph H. C. Batchelder. Street Com., Edward Finn. Water Com., Edward E. Culver, John E. Pine, Henry H. Drake.

CLERGY AND ECCLESIASTICAL STATISTICS.

CONGREGATIONAL.

GENERAL ASSOCIATION OF CONNECTICUT.

Founded 1709. Composed of ministers, delegates from fifteen Associations. Meets at Middletown, June 20, 1882; Rev. W. H. Moore, Hartford, Registrar and Treasurer.

GENERAL CONFERENCE OF THE CONGREGATIONAL CHURCHES OF CONNECTICUT.

Formed 1867; composed of ministers and laymen, delegates from four Consociations and twelve Conferences; office at Memorial Hall, Hartford. Rev. W. H. Moore, Hartford, Registrar and Statistical Secretary; Rev. Lavalette Perrin, Hartford, Annalist; Charles A. Sheldon, New Haven, Treasurer; E. B. Bowditch, New Haven, Auditor; Standing Committee, Rev. Messrs. Charles R. Palmer, George W. Banks, Myron S. Dudley, William H. Moore, Dea. Charles Northend, Dea. Richard E. Ried.

MISSIONARY SOCIETY OF CONNECTICUT. Directors, Rev. Messrs. Willard, Burton, Gallup, Hazen, Hawes, Hillard, Hallock, Scoville, Williams, and Messrs. Crump, Stickney, Northrop, Eldridge, Camp. Secretary, Rev. Wm. H. Moore, Hartford. Treasurer, Ward W. Jacobs, Hartford. Auditor, John W. Stickney, Rockville. Agent for Memorial Hall estate, Rev. Lavalette Perrin, Hartford.

FUND FOR MINISTERS. Trustees, Sec., Treas., and Auditor same as the Directors of the Miss. Soc. Conn.

Number of Churches, 297; pastors, 130; acting pastors, 124; communicants, 55,202.

CLERGY.

Those marked * have no pastoral care. Those marked † belong to the Presbytery.

Adams, A. C.	Thompson	Avery, Fred. D.	Columbia
Adams, F. H.	New Hartford	Avery, Jared R.*	Groton
Anderson, Jos.	Waterbury	Avery, John	Ledyard
Arms, H. P.	Norwich Town	Ayer, Chas. L.	Somersville
Armstrong, E. P.	Killingworth	Ayres, Milan C.	Southington
Atwater, E. E.*	New Haven	Bacheler, F. E. M.	Woodstock
Atwood, E. F.	Bridgewater	Backus, Jabez	Chester

Backus, J. W.	Rockville	Burroughs, G. S.	Fairfield
Bacon, E. W.	New London	Burton, Nathan'l J.	Hartford
Bacon, L. W.	Norwich	Carter, S. B.	Westminster
Bacon, Thomas R.	New Haven	Cary, W. B.	Old Lyme
Baird, John G.*	Hartford	Chamberlain, L. T.	Norwich
Baldwin, Elijah C.	New Haven	Chase, Austin S.*	Windsor
Banks, Geo. W.	Guilford	Chesebrough, A. S.	Durham
Barber, C. H.	Torringford	Clark, Daniel J.	East Haven
Barber, Luther H.	Bolton	Clark, Henry*	Avon
Barbour, W. M.	Yale College	Clarke, W. B.	Griswold
Barclay, Thos. D.*	Kent	Cleaveland, J. B.	Granby
Barnum, S. W.*	New Haven	Clift, Wm.	Hadlyme
Bartlett, H. M.	Pomfret	Colton, Erastus	Willington
Bayne, J. S.	Portland	Colver, Andrew W.	Woodbury
Beach, John W.*	Wind'r Locks	Colton, Willis S.	Warren
Beach, Nath.	Mansfield	Conkling, B. D.	Watertown
Beard, E. S.	Brooklyn	Cooper, James W.	New Britain
Beard, Wm. H.	So. Killingly	Couch, Paul	Mystic Bridge
Beardsley, B. B.*	Bridgeport	Countryman, F.	Georgetown
Bell, R. C	Broad Brook	Curtiss, George	Hartford
Berry, L. F.	Plantsville	Curtis, Lucius*	Hartford
Billings, R. S.	North Stamford	Curtiss, W. B.*	No. Branford
Billman, Howard	Southbury	Cutting, Chas.	Montville
Bingham, E. B.*	Rockville	Davenport, J. G.	Waterbury
Bissell, Oscar	Westford	Davies, T. E.	Unionville
Bissell, E. C., Prof.	Hartford	Day, Geo. E.	Yale College
Bissell, S. B. S. (Sec.)	Norwalk	Day, Guy B.*	Bridgeport
Bliss, J. H.	Clinton	Day, Henry N.*	New Haven
Bonar, J. B.	New Milford	Day, Theo. L.	Talcottville
Bond, Alvan*	Norwich	Denison, A. C.	Middlefield
Bonney, N. G.	Hanover	Denison, Daniel	Cobalt
Bosworth, Q. M.	Lebanon	Dennen, S. R.	New Haven
Bourne, J. R.	Sharon	Dingwell, Jas.	Danielsonville
Bowman, Geo. A.*	So. Windsor	Doolittle, E. J.*	Wallingford
Bradley, C. F.	Derby	Douglass, Sol. J.*	New Haven
Brandt, C. E.*	Farmington	Douglas, Thomas	Harwinton
Breed, David*	Lebanon	Drake, C. W.*	North Guilford
Brooks, C. S.	Putnam	Dudley, Martin*	Easton
Bryan, Geo. A.	Preston	Dudley, M. S.	Cromwell
Bryant, S. J.	South Britain	Dunning, H. N.	So. Norwalk
Bryant, Sidney*	South Britain	Dwight, Timothy	Yale College
Bullard, C. H. (Sec.)	Hartford	Edwards, G. L.*	Hartford
Burr, Enoch F.	Lyme	Elderkin. John	Ekonk
Burr, Zalmon B.*	Southport	Elliot, H. B.*	New Haven

Elliott, J. E.	Newington	Hartshorne, J. W.	Colebrook
Emerson, E. B.*	Stratford	Hatch, F. S.	West Hartford
Fellows, S. H.*	Wauregan	Hawes, Edward	New Haven
Fellows, F. E.	Bozrah	Hawley, Jno. P.	Westerley, R.I.
Fessenden, T. K.*	Farmington	Hazen, Azel W.	Middletown
Fisher, Geo. P.	Yale College	Hazen, Timothy A.	Goshen
Flanders, Chas. N.	So. Windsor	Headley, T. B. H.	So. Coventry
Forbes, S. B.	Rockville	Herrick, Henry*	N. Woodstock
Free, S. R.	Willimantic	Herrick, E. P.	Sherman
Freeland, S. M.	Thomaston	Hicks, L. W.	Wethersfield
Frost, D. C.*	Killingly	Higgins, L. H.	Mt. Carmel
Frost, D. D.*	Danbury	Hill, Charles J.	Middletown
Gage, W. L.	Hartford	Hillard, Elias B.	Plymouth
Gallup, James A.	Madison	Hine, Orlo D.	Lebanon
Gardner, Austin	Buckingham	Hine, Sylvester*	Hartford
Gaylord, S. D.	West Avon	Hoisington, H. R.	Coventry
Gidman, R. H.	North Madison	Holley, Platt T.*	Bridgeport
Gilbert, W. H. (Agt.)	So. No'wk	Holman, W. H.	Southport
Gleason, Charles H.	Somers	Hopkinson, B. B.	Lyme
Gleason, J. F.	Norfolk	Hoppin, J. M.*	Yale College
Glidden, Kiah B.	Mansfield C.	Hovey, H. C.	New Haven
Goldsmith, Alfred*	Hampton	Howard, W.	Poquonock
Goodell, J. H.	Windsor Locks	Hoyt, James P.	Newtown
Goodenough, Arthur,	Winchst'r	Hubbard, D. B.	Canton C.
Gordon, G. A.	Greenwich	Hubbell, J. W.	Danbury
Gregg, J. B.	Hartford	Hubbell, Stephen*	New Haven
Greenleaf, Jos.†	New Canaan	Hull, E. C.†	Ellsworth
Griffin, George H.	Milford	Hunt, Nathan S.*	Bozrah
Griggs, Leverett*	Bristol	Huntress, E. S.	Killingly
Griggs, L. S.	Terryville	Hurd, A. C.	Taftville
Griswold, J. B.*	East Haddam	Isham, Austin	New Preston
Grosvenor, C. P.*	Pomfret	Isham, Joseph H.	Cheshire
Hall, Alexander	Plainville	Ives, Joel S.	E. Hampton
Hall, E. E.*	New Haven	Jennings, Wm. J.	Redding
Hallock, L. H.	W. Winsted	Jewett, S. D *	Middlefield
Hallock, Wm. A.	Bloomfield	Jones, C. M.	Eastford
Hamilton, John A.	Norwalk	Jones, David E.	Roxbury
Harris, Samuel	Yale College	Jorden, F.F.	Torrington Hol'w
Harrison, George J.	Milton	Karr, Wm. S.	Hartford
Hart, Burdett	New Haven	Keeler, S. M.	Milford
Hart, Henry E.	Franklin	Keep, John R.*	Hartford
Hart, Wm.	Westport	Kellogg, George N.	Jewett City
Harvey, J. P.	Marlboro	Kelsey, H. S.	New Haven
Hartranft, C. D. Prof.	Hartford	Kendall, S. C.	Ellington

Kitchel, C. L.	Salisbury	Palmer, Chas. R.	Bridgeport
Knight, Merrick	E. Hartland	Palmer, Elliot*	Portland
Knouse, Wm. H.	Deep River	Palmer, Wm. S.	Norwich
Kopf, J. H.	Canterbury	Parker, Edwin P.	Hartford
Lamb, E. E.	Collinsville	Parmelee, E. H.	Lebanon
Lee, Timothy J.	Winsted	Parsons, John	Woodstock
Leete, T. A.	Northford	Payson, E. P.	Ansonia
Leonard, Edwin	Morris	Peck, Whitman*	New Haven
Leonard, S. C.	Naugatuck	Perrin, Lavalette	Torrington
Lewis, E. E.	Haddam	Pettibone, Ira	Winchester
Livermore, A. R.*	New Haven	Phipps, Wm. H.	Prospect
Loper, Stephen A.*	Hadlyme	Pierce, Asa C.	Brookfield C.
Lum, Samuel Y.	New Fairfield	Pope, H. W.	No. Manchester
Mack, J. A.	Gilead	Porter, N.	Pres. Yale College
Mallory, W. W.	Hartford	Potter, Frank C.	Stanwich
Mann, Joel*	New Haven	Potwin, Thos. S.*	Hartford
Marshall, H. G.	Middlebury	Pratt, D. M.	Higganum
Marvin, S. P.	Woodbridge	Pratt, Llewellyn Prof.	Hartford
McCall, Salmon	E. Haddam	Putnam, Austin	New Haven
McIntyre, A.	Long Ridge	Pyke, Chas.*	Waterbury
McLean, Allan	Litchfield	Rankin, S. G. W.	Glastonbury
McLeod, A. J.	Groton	Raymond, A. C.*	New Haven
McLaughlin, D. D. T.*	Litch'd	Relyea, Benj. J.	Greens Farms
McNeille, R. G. S.	Bridgeport	Reynolds, W. T.	North Haven
Mead, H. B	Stonington	Richardson, E. H.	New Britain
Meredith, Richard	E. Hartford	Riddle, Matthew B.	Hartford
Meserve, I. C.	New Haven	Robbins, S. W.	Manchester
Merwin, Nathan T.	Trumbull	Root, F. S.	Seymour
Merwin, S. J. M.*	Wilton	Russell, Charles H.*	Bridgep't
Miller, Wm.*	Rocky Hill	Sanborne, Geo. E.*	Hartford
Miner, Nathaniel*	Salem	Sanford, E. B. (Ed.)	Thomaston
Moore, Daniel M.	Falls Village	Savage, J. W.	No. Stonington
Moore, Wm. E. B.	West Staff'd	Scoles, R.	Nepaug
Moore, W. H. (St. Miss.)	H'tf'd	Scoville, Samuel	Stamford
Morris, M. N.*	West Hartford	Scudder, Wm. W.	Glastonbury
Morris, C. S.	Ashford	Seeley, Nicholas J.	Avon
Moses, Dighton	Westchester	Sessions, J. W.*	Westminster
Munson, Fred'k,	Haddam Neck	Sexton, W. D.	Old Saybrook
Murphy, Thomas D.	Centreb'k	Seymour, Bela N.	Vernon
Noyes, G. W.	New Haven	Seymour, Chas. N.	Tolland
Oakley, E. C.	Essex	Sharpe, Andrew*	Hebron
Oliphant, Chas. H.	Mystic Bdge	Shipman, T. L.*	Jewett City
Ordway, Jairus	Salem	Smith, Asa B.*	Rocky Hill
Osborne, C. P.	Branford	Smith, Burritt A.*	Middletown

Smith, Ed. A. Farmington
Smith, James A.* Unionville
Snow, F. E. Oxford
Southworth, Alden*Woodstock
Squires, N. J. West Haven
Staats, Henry T. Bristol
Stanton, Robert P.* Norwich
Starr, E. C. Northfield
Steele, C. E.* New Britain
St. John, S. N.* Georgetown
Stoddard, J. B.* Cheshire
Stone, E. G. West Suffield
Stowe, Calvin E.* Hartford
Sturges, T. B.* Greenfield Hill
Sullivan, Andrew J. Greenev'le
Swan, B. L.† Monroe
Symington, Charles† Suffield
Taylor, John P. New London
Taylor, F. H. Guilford
Taylor, Graham Hartford
Teller, Daniel W. New Haven
Tenney, H. M. Wallingford
Thompson, Frank Wilton
Thompson, Wm.(Prof.) Hartf'd
Thomson, W. J. So. Glastonb'y
Thrall, G. S. Bridgeport
Thrall, J. B. Derby
Tillotson, Geo. J.* Weth'rs'fld
Todd, John E. New Haven
Tomblen, C. L. Simsbury
Tomlinson J. A. Westbrook
Tomlinson, J. L.* Cromwell
Tuck, J. W.* Middletown

Turner, W. W.* Hartford
Twichell, Joseph H. Hartford
Upson, Henry* New Preston
Vaill, H. M. Staffordville
Vorce, J. H. Kent
Walker, G. L. Hartford
Waters, Geo. F. Bethel
Weitzel, C. T. Norwich Town
Welch, Moses C.* Hartford
White, O. H. New Haven
White, S. J. Cornwall
Whittlesey, Joseph* Berlin
Whittlesey, Wm.* New Haven
Wilcox, A. H. Plainfield
Willard, S. G. Colchester
Willard, James L. Westville
Williams, Francis Chaplin
Willis, J. G. Lisbon
Wilson, John S.* Bridgeport
Wilson, G. C. Windsor
Winch, G. W. Enfield
Winslow, Horace* Simsbury
Winter, Alpheus Hartford
Wood, George I.* Ellington
Wood, M. C. Burlington
Wood, Wm.* No. Branford
Woodruff, H. C.† Black Rock
Woodworth F. G. Wolcott
Woodworth, W. W. Berlin
Woolsey, T. D.* New Haven
Wright, Wm. S.* Glastonbury
Wyckoff, J. L. R. Woodbury

BAPTIST.
CONNECTICUT BAPTIST CONVENTION.

Annual Meeting, 3d Tuesday in October.

PRESIDENT, Rev. A. J. Sage, D.D., Hartford; VICE-PRESI-
DENT, Rev. G.H. Minor, New Britain; SECRETARY, Rev. Thos. A.
T. Hanna, Plantsville; STATISTICAL SECRETARY, Rev. F. B.
Dickinson, Ansonia; ASSISTANT STATISTICAL SECRETARY,
Elizur Cook, Hartford; TREASURER, James Lockwood, Hart-
ford; AUDITOR, G. F. Davis, Hartford.

TRUSTEES, Rev. Messrs. Lathrop, Palmer, Woods, Stifler, Hubbard, Folwell, Stubbert, Taylor, Pogson, Brown, Frost, Potter, Phelps, Samson, and J. B. Hoyt, J. L. Howard, J. W. Dimock, Taylor, Herr, Gaston, Piddock, Everts, Randall, Rowe, E. Morgan, J. W. Manning, Edward Miller, James Newcomb, W. H. Potter, George Alling, Isaac Anderson, C. F. Setchel, W. S. Bronson, M. E. Morris.

ASSOCIATIONS consist of pastors and delegates from each Church.

ASSOCIATIONS AND CLERKS.

Hartford, Rev. D. Dewolf, Bristol.
New Haven, Charles P. Ives, Meriden.
New London, Rev. W. E. Bates, Waterford.
Fairfield County, H. M. Prowitt, Norwalk.
Ashford, Rev. W. H. Randall, Thompson.
Stonington Union, Rev. E. Dewhurst, Mystic.

ASSOCIATIONS AND ANNUAL MEETINGS.

Hartford, 2d Wed. Oct.	Stonington Union, 3d Wed. June.
New Haven, 1st Wed. Oct.	Ashford, 1st Wed. Sept.
New London, 3d Wed. Sept.	Fairfield, 4th Wed. Sept.

Number of Churches, 119; Pastors, 97; other ordained Ministers, 41; Licentiates, 6; Baptisms, 588; Communicants, 20,830.

BAPTIST EDUCATION SOCIETY.—Pres., Edward Miller, Vice-Presidents, Rev. Messrs. J. K. Wilson, M. H. Pogson, Sec., Rev. G. H. Minor, New Britain; Treas., G. F. Davis, Hartford; Executive Committee, Rev. Messrs. Stone, Piddock, Everts, Folwell, and John W. Lamb.

CLERGY.

Allen, N. T.	Groton	Bestor, F.*	Hartford
Ambler, E. C.*	Danbury	Bond, E. P.	Wethersfield
Atkins, Irenus*	Bristol	Bowles, R. H.	New Hartford
Ball, A. H.	Fair Haven	Braithwaite, C.	Voluntown
Bailey, Simon B.	Mystic	Bronson, A. C.	Lebanon
Ballard, Joseph*	Norwalk	Bronson, J. J.	Warrenville
Batchelder, F. L.	Stafford	Brown, A. B.	Hartford
Bates, W. E.	Waterford	Brown, Joseph P.	N. London
Beardsley, E. N.	Northville	Brown, L. S.	Tolland
Benedict, N. D.	Easton	Brown, Wm. L.	Voluntown
Benedict, T.*	No. Colebrook	Burleigh, Lucian*	Plainfield
Bentley, E. D.	Norwalk	Butterworth, J.	Colchester

Carr, W. C.	Danielsonville	Lamb, J. C.	Haddam
Carter, S. S.*	Clinton	Latham, T. T.	Suffield
Chandler, A. J.	Clinton	Lathrop, Edw.	Stamford
Chaplin, A. J.	Mansfield	Lester, Geo. H.	Chesterfield
Chapman, B. F.*	Andover	Lord, W. K.	Plantsville
Chapman, D. F.	Pendleton Hill	Lovell, Andrew S.	Andover
Christie, W. W.	Hartford	Lyon, D. D.	Chesterfield
Crocker, W.	Haddam	Marten, Z.	New Haven
Denison, A. E.	North Lyme	Martin, R. M.	Deep River
Dewhurst, E.	Mystic	Mason, W.	South Windsor
Dewolf, D.	Bristol	Mathewson, E.P.	No.Stoningt'n
Dickinson, F. B.	Ansonia	Mathewson, P.	No. Ashford
Dickinson, T. N.*	Essex	Mattison, N. H.*	Norwich
Dowling, Thos.	Tolland	Maynard, M. P.*	New London
Everts, W. W. Jr.,	Hartford	Miller, E. C.	Poquonock Bridge
Fitch, L.	New London	Minor, G. H.	New Britain
Folwell, G. W.	Waterbury	Moehlman, J. H.	Meriden
Foster, J. C.*	New London	Morgan, H. A.	Middletown
Frost, C. C.	Norwich	Nichols, C. N.	Warrenville
Gage, L.*	North Woodstock	Nichols, G. E.	Southington
Gale, S.*	Mystic River	Noble, James G.	Chester
Ga Nun, G. J.	New Haven	Ogden, E. M.	Rowayton
Garton, J. V.	Meriden	Palmer, A. G.	Stonington
Goodwin, Wm.	No. Colebrook	Palmer, T. R.	Suffield
Gregory, Alva*	Easton	Phelps, S. D. (Ed.)	Hartford
Hanna, T. A. T.	Plantsville	Perkins, Stephen	Chesterfield
Harris, Wm.*	Old Lyme	Phillips, J. M.	Willimantic
Hart, L. B.	Bristol	Piddock, C. A.	Middletown
Hepburn, J.*	Gaylordsville	Pinkham, N. J.	Thompson
Herr, J. D.	Norwich	Pogson, M. H.	Bridgeport
Hill, E. S.	Preston	Potter, C. W.	Willington
Hinckley, G. W.	Rainbow	Randall, Wm. H.	Thompson
Holman, G. W.	Willimantic	Robinson, A. A.	Winthrop
Holman, J. W.	East Lyme	Ross, James G.	New Haven
Howard, Amasa*	Wethersfield	Rowe, C. C.	Mystic River
Howell, S.	Noank	Sage, A. J.	Hartford
Hubbard, A. C.	Danbury	Samson, T. S.	New Haven
Ingersoll, W. M.	Bridgeport	Sargent, O. C.	Jewett City
R. Jennings,	Deep River	Shailer, Davis T.*	Haddam
Jerome, E. M.	New Haven	Sherwood, D. W.	Stepney
Judd, T. O.*	Montowese	Shipman, J. N.	Moosup
Keeney, Curtis*	Groton	Silliman, S. G.*	Bridgeport
Knapp, S. J.	Essex	Smith, H. G.*	Bantam Falls
Kratz, Fred.	Danbury	Smith, H. P.	Wallingford

Smith, C. C.	Branford	Wakeman, L. H.*	Stamford
Smith, Wm. A.*	Groton	Walden, W. N.	Montville
Smith, W. B.	Woodstock	Walker, Wm. C.*	Andover
Stevens, H. S.	Cromwell	Warren, John*	Black Rock
Stifler, J. M.	New Haven	Watrous, A. D.*	Deep River
Stone, George M.	Hartford	Weaver, S. J.	Norwich
Stubbert, J. R.	Suffield	Whittemore, R. F.*	Clinton
Swan, J. S.*	New London	Wilcox, A. J.	Greeneville
Taylor, J. M.	South Norwalk	Willett, C.	Suffield
Tefft, Albert B.	New London	Wilson, James E.	Southington
Temple, J. F.	Packersville	Wilson, J. K.	New London
Terry, Thomas	Brooklyn	Woolsey, J. J.*	Stamford
Towne, E. S.	Plainville	Woods, B. A.	New London
Viets, A. P.*	Waterbury	Wynne, R. D.	Norwich

PROTESTANT EPISCOPAL.

DIOCESE OF CONNECTICUT.

Annual Convention, 2d Tuesday in June, place to be appoint-ed by the Bishop.

RT. REV. JOHN WILLIAMS, D.D., LL.D., Middletown, Bishop.

STANDING COMMITTEE.—Rev. Drs. Beardsley, Pynchon, Deshon, Tatlock, and Rev. Mr. Seymour. SECRETARY OF CONVENTION, Rev. Charles H. B. Tremaine, New Haven; ASSISTANT SECRETARY, Rev. Edwin S. Lines, West Haven. TREASURER, F. J. Kingsbury, Waterbury. REGISTRAR, Rev. Samuel Hart, Hartford.

MISSIONARY SOCIETY OF THE DIOCESE OF CONNECTICUT. Directors, Rt. Rev. John Williams, Rev. Dr. Tatlock, Rev. Dr. Giesy, Rev. Dr. Olmstead, Rev. Messrs. Goodwin, McConnell, Seymour, and J. C. Hollister, Benj. Stark (Sec. and Treas.), E s a Johnson, Walton Ferguson, Charles A. Warren, Robert Gli Ihike.

CHURCH SCHOLARSHIP SOCIETY.—Board of Education, Rt. Rev. John Williams, Rev. Dr. Pynchon, Rev. Messrs. E. E. Johnson, Francis Goodwin, W. F. Nichols (Sec. and Treas.), S. F. Giesy, C. M. Selleck, and Chas. H. Northam, Samuel Taylor, L. J. Hendee, A. C. Goodman, F. J. Kingsbury, G. W. Russell.

AGED AND INFIRM CLERGY, AND WIDOWS' FUND.—Trustees, Rt. Rev. John Williams, Rev. Dr. Vibbert, Rev. E. Harwood, Rev. Dr. Olmstead, J. W. Fowler, J. C. Hollister (Treas.), F. J. Kingsbury.

CLERGY.

Adams, Chas. G.	Southport	Darby, Henry	Bridgeport
Andrews, Wm. G.	New Haven	Davis, Sheldon	Ansonia
Ashley, Richard K.	Windham	Denslow, H. M.	New Haven
Babcock, E. W.	New Haven	Deshon, Giles H.	Meriden
Barbour, J. H.	Hartford	Duffield, S. B.	Monroe
Barnett, F. W.	Wilton	Eddy, Clayton*	Northford
Bartlett, Josiah M.	Essex	Ellsworth, J. W.	Hebron
Bates, John M.	West Hartford	Elwood, David M.	Southport
Breman, A. E.	Unionville	Fitch, Henry*	New Haven
Beardsley, E. E.	New Haven	Fitzgerald, J. H.	Milford
Beckwith, I.T. (Prof.)	Trin. Col.	Fogg, T. B.*	Brooklyn
Bennett, L. T.	Guilford	French, Louis	Darien
Betts, John H.	So. Manchester	Fuller, S. (Prof.)	Middletown
Bielby, Wm. F.	Putnam	Gardiner, E. C.	Hartford
Bingham, J. F.	Hartford	Gardiner, F. (Prof.)	Middlet'n
Binney, John (Prof.)	Middlet'n	Garfield, N. L.	New Haven
Bishop, David	Tariffville	George, J. F.	Woodbury
Bishop, E. F.*	Bridgeport	Giesy, Sam'l H.	Norwich
Bodley, H. I.	Canaan	Gilliland, J. D.	Plymouth
Bostwick, Wm. L.*	New Britain	Goldslordong, A.	Stonington
Brathwaite, F. W.	Stamford	Goodrich, J. B.	Windsor
Brewster, Joseph	New Haven	Goodridge, Ed.	Warehouse P'nt
Brown, E. R.	New Milford	Goodwin, Francis*	Hartford
Brush, Jesse	New Canaan	Gregory, Henry T.	Groton
Buck, Geo.	Hartford	Harriman, F. D.	Portland
Buckingham, W. B.	N. London	Harriman, F. W.	Portland
Bulkley, Wm. H.	Nashua	Hart, Samuel (Prof.)	Trin. Col.
Chapman, A. T.	Mid. Haddam	Harwood, Edwin	New Haven
Clapp, H. S.	Wethersfield	Henry, Francis A.	Ridgefield
Clark, Geo. H.*	Hartford	Horton, Sanford J.	Cheshire
Clarke, Sylvester	Bridgeport	Hoyt, R. B.	Norwalk
Coit, T. W. (Prof.)	Middletown	Huntington, J. T.	Hartford
Colburn, Wm. B.	Bridgewater	Hyde, Joseph W.	Stamford
Coleman, W. B., Jr.	Collinsville	Jacocks, J. G.	New Haven
Coley, James F.	Westport	Jarvis, S. F.	Brooklyn
Cooley, Wm. C.	Roxbury	Jewett, Edgar H.	Norwich

Johnson, E. E.	Hartford	Scott, James L.	Bristol
Johnson, W. A.	Salisbury	Selleck, Charles M.	Norwalk
Kelley, C. W.	Yantic	Seymour, S. O.	Litchfield
Knowles, W. C.	Killingworth	Shears, A. G.	New Haven
Lewis, A. N.	Westport	Shepard, P. L.	Old Saybrook
Lindsley, C. S.	Riverton	Sherman, H. M.	Wolcottville
Lines, E. S.	New Haven	Simonson, L.	Hartford
Lombard, J. K.	Fairfield	Sloan, Arthur	Stratford
Lounsbury, G. E.	Norwalk	Smith, Geo. H.	Yalesville
Lusk, Wm., Jr.	North Haven	Spencer, Wm. G., So. Norwalk	
Marble, N E.	Newtown	Spooner, C. A.*	Norwich
Marks, W. L.	North Guilford	Stanley, G. M.	Winsted
Mason, Arthur*	Hartford	Stoddard, James	Watertown
Mathison R. L.	Poquotannock	Stone, Hiram	Bantam
Maxcy, E. W.	Bridgeport	Sturgis, Isaac C.	Kent
McConnell, S. D.	Middletown	Sumner, Wm. G.(Prof.)Yale C.	
McCook, J. J.	East Hartford	Tarrant, H.	East Haven
McNulty, R.	Waterbury	Tatlock, William	Stamford
Meyrick, H. L.	Sandy Hook	Torrence, Geo. P.	Long Hill
Micou, R. W.	Waterbury	Thorne, R. T.	New Haven
Miller, A. Douglas	Middletown	Townsend, H.*	New Haven
Morris, L. F.	Bethany	Townsend, John	Middletown
Nichols, W. F.	Hartford	Tremaine, C. H. B.	New Haven
Ockford, T. S.	Thomaston	Tuttle, Ruel H.*	Windsor
Olmstead, Henry	Branford	Van Buren, Jas. H.	Seymour
Pardee, J. D. S.	Mystic Bridge	Vibbert, Wm. E.	Fair Haven
Pattison, E. C.	Bethel	Vinton, A. H.	Pomfret
Peck, William L.	Marbledale	Walker, Millidge	Lime Rock
Pine, G. S.	Bridgeport	Warner, Beverly E.	Manchester
Porter, T. A.	Pine Meadow	Warner, G. R.	Huntington
Potter, Collis I.	Clinton	Watson, John H.	Hartford
Powers, H. N.	Bridgeport	Welton, X. A.	Redding Ridge
Purves, John	New Haven	Whaley, P. H.	Sharon
Pynchon, T. R.	Pres. Trin.Col.	Whitcome, E. L.	Brookfield
Raftery, Oliver H.	Cheshire	White, J. H.	Saybrook
Randall, H. C.	Pomfret	Whitlock, H. R.	Rockville
Randall, A. T.	Meriden	Whittlesey, Elisha	Hartford
Richardson, N. S., E. Bridgeport		Widdemer, Howard T. Ansonia	
Robinson, J. B.	Bethlehem	Wildman, J. E.	Wallingford
Rogers, J. H.	New Britain	Williams, John R.	Westport
Rumney, Geo.	East Haddam	Witherspoon, O.	Birmingham
Russell, Francis T.	Waterbury	Woodward, F. B.*	Westville
Sanford, Elihu T.	Westville	Worthington, E. W.	West Haven
Sanford, D. L.	Thompsonville	Yardley, H.A.(Prof.)Middleto'n	
Sanford, D. P.	Thompsonville	Yarrington, B. M.	Greenwich

10

METHODIST EPISCOPAL.

CONFERENCES.—The churches on the east side of the Connecticut River belong to the New England Southern Conference, which meets at Fall River, Mass., April 14, 1882, and are about equally divided between the Providence and the Providence North Districts. The churches on the west side of the river nearly all belong to the New York East Conference, and are embraced in the New Haven and New York East Districts; this Conference meets April 6, 1882, at Brooklyn, N. Y. A few churches in the northwest corner of the State are attached to the Poughkeepsie district of the New York Conference.

PRESIDING ELDERS OF DISTRICTS.—NEW HAVEN, Rev. G. A. Hubbell, New Haven; NEW YORK EAST, Rev. Wm. T. Hill, New Haven; PROVIDENCE, Rev. D. A. Whedon, D. D , Providence, R. I.; PROVIDENCE NORTH, Rev. M. J. Talbot, D. D., Providence, R. I.

CLERGY.

Abbott, A. V. R.	Durham	Buck, C. H.	New Haven
Abbott, Ira*	Middlebury	Burnes, H. E.	Birmingham
Abbott, L. W.*,	Ridgefield	Cady, W. O.	Portland
Adams, B. M.	Meriden	Carroll, J. M.	Forestville
Adams, J. Q. N.	Grosvenordale	Causey, L. P.	Putnam
Amidon, Sandf'd E.	Woodstock	Church, A. J.	Greeneville
Anthony, E. M.	East Hampton	Clark, R.	Danielsonville
Arnold, H. H.	Tolland Depot	Coburn, G. L.	Wethersfield
Aston, H.	Greenwich	Codling, Robert*	Winsted
Ayers, E. J.	Moosup	Crawford, M.B	Tutor Middlet'n ·
Ayres, J. R.	West Haven	Cromlish, John	So. Norwalk
Barton, W. H.	Thomaston	Crook, Robert	Middletown
Belcher, F. J.	Falls Village	Cross, S. V. B.	East Thompson
Benton, Erastus*	Staff'dSpr'gs-	Davenport, Z.*	Saugatuck
Benton, J ..T*	Niantic	Davis, C. S.	South Glastonbury
Benton, S. O.	Burnside	Davis, J. W.*	Waterbury
Bentley, G. R.	Wapping	Dean, J. A.	Mystic
Bentley, L. D.	· Norwich	Dikeman, C. S.	Newtown
Blake, W.	New Fairfield	Dodge, J. O.	South Coventry
Blood, L. W.	West Thompson	Douglass, T. W.	Mashapaug
Booth, Albert	Kensington	Douglass, W. L.	Copper Hill
Bray, E. L.	Essex	Downey, D. G.	Rocky Hill
Brewster, G. W.	Danielsonv'le	Dusenberre, G. B.	Simsbury
Brown, D. L.	Mystic	Dyson, R. D.	Voluntown
Brown, Wm.	Bethel	Edwards, N.	Naugatuck

Eggleston, A. C.	Bristol	Livingston, H. W.	Madison
Ellis, W. W.	Vernon Depot	Loomis, R. H.	Ansonia
Eldridge, R. S.	Yalesville	Lovejoy, J.	Baltic
Emerson, Warren W.*	Thomps'n	Luce, W. A.	Ottawaugan
Ewer, C. H.	Niantic	Lyon, C. W.	Seymour
Farnsworth,R.W.C.	Dan'l'nville	McBurney, S.	Willimantic
Fernald, O. H.	Portland	McNichol, W.	West Stratford
Field, Julius*	Durham	Mackey, W. A.	Canaan
Fletcher, E. S.	Warehouse Pt.	Mallory, C. T.	Stepney
Ford, C. B.	Waterbury	Martin. W. W.	Mianus
Fuller, G. L.*	Norwalk	Mead, A. H.	Watertown
Gilman, B. A.	Pound Ridge	Mead, Nathaniel*	Stamford
Glenk, Frederick	New Haven	Millett, J.	Norfolk
Goodenough, A. H.	High Ridge	Mitchell,H.G.(Tutor)	Middlet'n
Goodrich, N.	Gale's Ferry	Moffitt, J. J.	Pleasant Valley
Gowan, J. C.	S. Manchester	Montgomery, H.	Norwich
Graves, G. A.	New Canaan	Munson, J. O.	Redding
Griffin, D. F.	Burlington	Munson, W. A.*	New Haven
Hammond, Chas.	Quarryville	Nash, David	Windsor
Harrington, C. S. (Prof.)	Midt'n	Newell, F. C.	N. Grosvenordale
Harris, C. E.	New Haven	North, C. J.	Torrington
Haulenbeck, G.	Norwalk	Northrop, A. M.	West Granby
Haugh, J. S.	North Canton	Oldham, J.	No. Manchester
Hill, A.	So. Norwalk	Osborn, David	Saugatuck
Hill, A. S.*	New Haven	Osborne, T. G.*	Norwalk
Hill, Morris*	New Haven	Parker, John*	Meriden
Hill, Moses*	Norwalk	Pease, H. F.	Berlin
HILL, W. T.	New Haven	Pegg, C. M.	Georgetown
Holden, C. W.	Colchester	Perry, L. P.	New Milford
Horne, J. W.	Clinton	Pilkington. J.	Milford
Hoyt, J. C.	Sharon	Pilsbury, Benjamin	Woodbury
Hoyt, W. C.*	Stamford	Phelps, B. C.*	Vernon Depot
Howson, John	Thompsonville	Porter, N. L.	Hamden
HUBBELL, GEO. A.	New Haven	Povey, Richard	Rockville
Hurd, W. W.	Bakerville	Prentice, Geo.(Prof.)	Middlet'n
James, J. H.	Norwich	Pullman, Joseph	West Winsted
Judd, H. Q.	Bridgeport	Reynolds, R. K.*	New Britain
Kay, R.	Gaylordsville	Rice, W. N. (Prof.)	Middleto'n
Kidder, B. F.	Cromwell	Richardson, L.	Darien
King, G. C.	Mystic Bridge	Robinson, H. D.	New London
Kristeller, S. ·	Bethlehem	Robinson, J.	West Goshen
Lansing, I. J.	Stamford	Robinson, James	Stamford
Latham, H. D.*	Madison	Robinson, W. J.	So. Britain
Lippitt, N. G.	Norwich	Roden, Robert	Bloomfield

Rogers, W. R.	Beacon Falls	Taylor, G. L.	Ridgefield
Sanford, Isaac *	Middlefield	Taylor, W. A.	Wapping
Saunders, F. W.	West Suffield	Taylor, James	Monroe
Saxton, Otis,	Rockland	Thomas, J. S.	Gurleyville
Scofield, Henry	Easton	Thomas, W. A.	Guilford
Scofield, S. W.*	Stamford	Thompson, G. L.	Hartford
Seaman, S. A.	Stratford	Tinker, E.	Norwich
Searles, J. E.	Bridgeport	Toles, S. W.	Middlefield
Sherman, J. H.	Versailles	Townsend, F. S.	Marlborough
Silliman, Cyrus*	Southport	Tregaskis, Jas.	Staffordville
Smith, E. F.	Moodus	Turkington, Wm.	Windsorville
Smith, Joseph	Southport	Turkington, W.H.	Tolland Cen.
Smith, Sylvester	Roxbury	Vinton, Joseph	Windsor Locks
Smith, S. K.	Westville	Wake, Wm.	Cornwall Bridge
Smith, W. F.*	Middletown	Wardell, W. H.	New Britain
Spencer, G. C.	Rowayton	Watt, T. J.	Litchfield
Stebbins, W. H.	Southington	Webster, W. R.	New Haven
Steele, W. C.	Danbury	Westgate,G.L. (Prof.)	Middlet'n
Stoddard, W. P.	Hockanum	White, M. C.(Prof.)	New Haven
Sumner, C. B.	Lyme	Wing, C. S.	Norwalk
Taylor, E. M.	Norwich	Woerz, G. J.	Hartford

AFRICAN METHODIST.

Morris, R. R.	Hartford	Houghton, F. M.	Middletown

PRESBYTERIAN.

PRESBYTERY OF WEST CHESTER.

Meets the 2d Tuesday of April and 1st Tuesday of October.

CLERGY.

Those marked * have no pastoral charge. Those marked †
are pastors of Congregational churches.

Anderson, Matthew†	N. Haven	Hammond,Ed.Payson*	Vernon
Barnum, F. S.	Thompsonville	Hodge, J. Aspinwall	Hartford
Bridgeman,Chester†	Torringt'n	Huntting, William*	Stamford
Child, T. S.*	Hartford	Karr, Wm. S.*	Hartford
Davenport, H. A.	Bridgeport	Lubkert, Ernest H.†	Weston
Elliott, Samuel E.*	N. Haven	McGiffert, Wm. H.†	Orange
Ely, James*	Thompsonville	McKelvey, H. A.*	Bridgeport
Gibbs, Daniel*	Hartford	Mosman, W. D.*	New Haven
Greenleaf,Joseph†	New Canaan	Northrop, H. D.†	New Haven
Griggs, C. E.*	Chaplin	Payson, Edward P.†	Ansonia

Read, Hollis*	Sharon	Uhlfelder, Sigmund*	N. Haven
Reid, Lewis H.†	Canaan	Upson. C. E.*	New Haven
Riggs, C. H.*	Bristol	Vail, Richard P. H.	Stamford
Sawyer, Rollin A.*	N. Haven	Wyckoff, J. L. R.†	Woodbury
Terrett, Wm. R.*	Sharon		

UNIVERSALIST.

State Convention meets on the third Wednesday and Thursday in September. Rev. J. H. Chapin, Ph. D., Meriden, Pres't; Emory Stockwell, Stamford, Vice-Pres't; Jas. E. Bidwell, Middletown, Treas.; Rev. D. M. Hodge, Danbury, Sec'y; J. E. Buss, S. Bissell, Augustus W. Merwin, Directors; Rev. D. M. Hodge, Rev. H. P. Osgood, J. L. Lockwood, Committee on Fellowship, Ordination, and Discipline.

The Convention has a Missionary Fund of $18,000.

ASSOCIATIONS. 1. Quinebaug, meets the 3d Wed. and Th. in June.

2. Southern, meets 2d Wed. and Th. in June.

CLERGY.

Amies, J. H.	New Haven	Houghton, F. M.	Middletown
Blackford, L. P.	Norwich	Lyon, John	Bridgeport
Chapin, J. H.	Meriden	Maxham, G. V.	Stafford
Davis, S. A.	Hartford	Nash, C. Elwood	Stamford
Dearborn, W. H.	Hartford	Stickney, W. A.	Cromwell
Dodge, J. S., Jr.	Stamford	Taber, M. W.	Thompsonville
Hodge, D. M.	Danbury	Waldo, J. C.	New London
Houghton, M. H.	New Haven	Weeks, J. J.	Long Ridge

ROMAN CATHOLIC.

Diocese of Hartford embraces Connecticut.

Rt. Rev. Laurence McMahon, Bishop.

Vicar-General, Thomas Walsh, Meriden.

CLERGY.

Brady, Hugh J.	Ansonia	Cooney, John	New Haven
Bray, Bernard	New Milford	Creedon, John	Moosup
Brodrick, Thos.	New London	Creighton, P. J.	Southington
Briscoe, Ambrose	New Haven	Cremmons, Denis	Fairfield
Byrne, Michael J.	Danbury	Desmond, Denis	Portland
Campbell, Jas. F.	Manchester	Donahoe, Michael	Waterbury
Carmody, Hugh	New Britain	Donahue, John C.	New Britain
Coleman, Thos.	New Haven	Donahoe, P.	Stafford Springs

Dougherty, J. B.	New Haven	Mulholland, Pat'k	Fair Haven
DuBruycker, F. L.	Willimantic	Murphy, John F.	Hampton
Duggan, John	Waterbury	O'Brien, E. J.	Hartford
Duggan, P.	Wolcottville	O'Brien, James C.	Hartford
Fagan, James	Naugatuck	O'Connell, Patrick E.	Bridgep't
Fitzpatrick, J. S.	New Haven	O'Farrell, J. J.	Norwich
Fitzsimons, Luke	Collinsville	Prerton, Thos.	Meriden
Fleming, John	Mystic	Princen, H.	Danielsonville
Fombrowe, Edw'd	Winchester	Quinn, John F.	Hartford
Furlong, John	Rockville	Roddan, M. C.	Bristol
Gaffney, Eugene	Thomaston	Rogers, John	E. Bridgeport
Galligan, Michael J.	Ansonia	Rogers, Wm.	Stamford
Gleason, J. J.	New Milford	Ryan, John	Cromwell
Gleason, Joseph M.	Thomp'ville	Russell, John	Norwalk
Harty, W. A.	Hartford	Saracena, Loda	Winchester
Hughes, James	Hartford	Schaele, Jos.	New Haven
Joynt, T. P.	Jewett City	Schatlers, J. L.	Jewett City
Keating, P.	Westport	Shahan, P. P.	Norwich
Keeffe, F.	Middletown	Sheffry, S. P.	New Haven
Kelly, M. J.	Windsor Locks	Shelly, Thomas	Birmingham
Kennedy, P.	Birmingham	Sheridan, B. O'R.	Collinsville
Larkin, James	New Haven	Sheridan, Philip	Chester
Lawler, Patrick	New Haven	Sheridan, Wm.	Lakeville
Lawlor, Martin	Danbury	Skelley, Peter	Manchester
Lenehan, John P.	New London	Slocum, John	New Haven
Lynch, Henry	Lakeville	Smith, Thos.	Greenwich
Lynch, Michael J.	Hartford	Sweeney, F.	Moosup
Lynch, Thomas	Westerly, R. I.	Synnott, Thos.	Bridgeport
Mallon, Hugh	Wallingford	Synnott, Joseph	Middletown
Marschall, M.	Grosvenordale	Tierney, M.	Hartford
Martin, Edward	Branford	Thompson, J.	Danielsonville
McAlenny, Paul	Hartford	Trainor, Hugh	Norwalk
McCabe, Bernard	Winchester	Van den Noort, J.	Baltic
McCabe, Philip	Hartford	Van Opysen, Alphonse	Putnam
McCartin, Jas.	Newtown	Vygen, Eugene J.	Putnam
McGivney, M. J.	New Haven	Walsh, Thaddeus	Danbury
McMahon, J. H. T.	E. Hartford	Walsh, Thomas	Meriden
Mulcahy, John	Thompsonville	Walsh, Laurence	Waterbury

CATHOLIC APOSTOLIC: S. J. Andrews, Hartford; C. A. G. Brigham, E. B. Smith, Middletown; Wm. W. Andrews, Wethersfield.

JEWISH: Victor Rundbacken, D.D., Hartford; Judah Wechsler, Samuel Kohn, New Haven; Casper Bruner, Bridgeport.

LUTHERAN GERMAN: C. H. Siebke, New Haven; Nicholas Soergel, Rockville; Chas. F. W. Rechenberg, Greenwich; C. A. Graeber, Meriden; T. A. Tilly.

MEDICAL.

CONNECTICUT MEDICAL SOCIETY.

Next Annual Meeting, 4th Wednesday of May, 1882.

PRESIDENT, Wm. Deming, Litchfield.

VICE-PRES., Wm. G. Brownson, New Canaan.

SECRETARY, C. W. Chamberlain, Hartford.

TREASURER, F. D. Edgerton, Middletown.

COMMITTEE OF EXAMINATION, D. A. Cleaveland, G. H. Preston, John Witter, J. G. Stanton, H. S. Fuller, C. E. Hammond, Elijah Baldwin, Orlando Brown.

To NOMINATE PHYSICIANS TO THE RETREAT FOR INSANE, Ashbel Woodward, G. L. Platt, L. Holbrook, C. H. Bill, S. G. Risley.

To NOMINATE PROFESSORS IN THE MEDICAL INSTITUTION OF YALE COLLEGE, G. W. Russell, C. H. Pinney, Isaac G. Porter, R. S. Goodwin, M. B. Bennett.

DISSERTATOR TO THE NEXT CONVENTION, N. Nickerson. Alternate, G. F. Fox.

STATE BOARD OF HEALTH.

Members appointed by the Governor and Senate.

PRESIDENT, Dr. J. S. Butler, Hartford.

SECRETARY, Dr. C. W. Chamberlain, Hartford.

Prof. C. A. Lindsley, M. D.,† New Haven.

Prof. Wm. H. Brewer, New Haven.

Hon. A. E. Burr, Hartford.

Dr. R. Hubbard, Bridgeport.

Hon. A. C. Lippitt, New London.

CONNECTICUT ECLECTIC MEDICAL ASSOCIATION.

Annual Meeting, 2d Tuesday of May.

PRESIDENT, E. M. Ripley, Unionville.

VICE-PRES., B. W. Pease, ———.

COR. SEC., H. I. Fisk, Guilford.

REC. SEC., N. D. Hodgkins, Rocky Hill.

TREAS., LeRoy A. Smith, Higganum.

CENSORS, Drs. Adams, Linquist, and Munn.

CONNECTICUT HOMEOPATHIC MEDICAL SOCIETY.

Annual Meeting, 3d Tuesday of May.

PRESIDENT, H. M. Bishop, Norwich.

VICE-PRES., W. B. Dunning, Hartford.

SEC. and TREAS., E. B. Hooker, Hartford.

LIBRARIAN, Grove H. Wilson, Meriden.

EXECUTIVE COMMITTEE, Drs. Bishop, Hooker, and Anderson.

CENSORS, Drs. Peltier, Case, Mansfield, Osborne, and Tabor.

- PHYSICIANS AND SURGEONS.

Members of the Connecticut Medical Society are designated thus †.

HARTFORD COUNTY.

G. W. Sanford, Simsbury, President; James Campbell, Hartford, Clerk.

HARTFORD, G. W. Avery,† J. F. Axtelle, W. T. Bacon,† A. W. Barrows,† D. T. Bromley,† John S. Butler,† Joseph A. Coogan,† David Crary,† David Crary, Jr.,† James Campbell,† C. W. Chamberlain,† Noah Cressey, F. S. Crossfield,† T. D. Crothers,† G. P. Davis,† John Dwyer,† P. W. Ellsworth,† H. S. Fuller,† C. E. Froelich,† Ellen F. Gladwin, P. M. Hastings,† Geo. B. Hawley,† Harmon G. Howe,† E. K. Hunt,† Wm. M. Hudson,† J. C. Jackson,† G. C. Jarvis,† M. M. Johnson,† W. W. Knight,† J. B. Lewis,† I. W. Lyon,† Nathan Mayer,† M. D. Mann,† William D. Morgan,† John O'Flaherty,† C. W. Page,† George B. Packard,† George L. Parmele,† G. W. Russell,† George R. Shepard,† H. P. Stearns,† J. A. Steven,† S. B. St John,† M. Storrs,†R. B. Talbot,† R. H. Tiffany,† W. H. Tremaine,† W. A. M. Wainwright,† Eli Warner,† F. F. Axtelle, August Berger, J. S. Curtis,

Ellen F. Hammond, Aretus Rising. *Hom.*, E. E. Case, James D. Johnson, W. B. Dunning, E. B. Hooker, I. S. Miller, P. D. Peltier, L. E. Richardson, P. S. Starr, C. A. Taft, G. Swan. *Ec.*, Henry Bickford, Thos. Simmons, LeRoy A. Smith.

AVON, William Howard,† *Ec.*, R. W. Alcott.

BERLIN, Elishama Brandegee,† E. H. Meade.†

BLOOMFIELD, Henry Gray.†

BRISTOL, Henry E. Way,† Joseph W. Camp. *Hom.*, Edward P. Woodward, George S. Hull. *Ec.*, F.H. Williams, H. B. Cutler.

BURLINGTON, Wm. Elton.

CANTON. COLLINSVILLE, Geo. R. Roberts,† Geo. F. Lewis,† B. Kasson. *Hom.*, J. M. Tabor.

EAST GRANBY, Herbert C. Belden.

EAST HARTFORD, Seth L. Childs,† Lucius W. Mackintosh,† S. C. Newton,† E. J. McKnight,† W. R. Tinker.†

EAST WINDSOR. BROAD BROOK, H. O. Allen.† WAREHOUSE POINT, Marcus L. Fisk.†

ENFIELD, Rial L. Strickland,† G. T. Finch,† Wm. L. Adams. *Hom.*, J. H. Darling. THOMPSONVILLE, Edward F. Parsons.†

FARMINGTON, Franklin Wheeler,† Chas. Carrington.† UNIONVILLE, Everett A. Towne. W. W. Horton. *Hom.*, E. C. King. *Ec.*, E. M. Ripley.

GLASTONBURY, H. C. Bunce,† J. W. Griswold.† *Eclectic*, Daniel T. Kingsbury. So. GLASTONBURY, Henry M. Rising.† E. GLASTONBURY, Sabin Stocking. BUCKINGHAM, George A. Hurlburt.†

GRANBY, Francis T. Allen,† G. W. Edwards.† W. A. Stratton.

HARTLAND, (East,) H. S. Bell.

MANCHESTER. *Hom.*, Oliver B. Taylor. No. MANCHESTER, R. M. Griswold,† F. H. Whiton C. H. Weaver.† So. MANCHESTER, J. N. Parker.† W. R. Tinker.† BUCKLAND, *Ec.*, C. W. Jaques, Rufus K. Mills, E. J. Vail.

NEW BRITAIN, George Clary,† B. N. Comings,† S. Waldo Hart,† E. B. Lyon,† J. S. Stone,† E. P. Swasey,† M. J. Coholan,† E. D. Babcock, Benjamin Way, L. M. Smith. *Hom.*, Geo. P. Cooley, George Welch.† *Ec.*, John Koplitz, L. S. Ludington. *Bot.*, L. M. Smith.

NEWINGTON, *Ec.*, Louis V. Durand.

PLAINVILLE, T. G. Wright,† Virgil Buell,† J. N Bull.†

ROCKY HILL, Rufus W. Griswold.† *Ec.*, N. D. Hodgkins.

SIMSBURY, WEATOGUE, R. A. White,† John M. French. *Hom.*, N. W. Holcomb. TARIFFVILLE, G. W. Sanford,† C. W. Wooster.

SOUTHINGTON, I. P. Fiske,† F. A. Hart, W. G. Stedman † *Hom.*, James H. Osborn, C. H. Pierson. PLANTSVILLE, A. J. Weed, S. J. Allen, Jr., Elmer Horton. *Hom.*, J. D. Quill.

SOUTH WINDSOR, E. WINDSOR HILL, Sidney W. Rockwell,† Wm. Wood.†

SUFFIELD, J. K. Mason,† Wm. H. Mather,† O. W. Kellogg, Matthew T. Newton, O. W. Kellogg. *Eclectic*, I. P. Leete.

WETHERSFIELD, Abner S. Warner,† Roswell Fox. *Ec.*, Samuel A. Castle.

WINDSOR, N. S. Bell,† Samuel A. Wilson,† J. P. Safford. POQUONNOCK, Robert E. Ensign.†

WINDSOR LOCKS, S. R. Burnap.† *Hom.*, Frank D. Main.

NEW HAVEN COUNTY.

Asa H. Churchill, Meriden, President; N. Nickerson, Meriden, Vice-President; C. W. Gaylord, Branford, Clerk.

NEW HAVEN, Willis G. Alling,† G. J. Augn,† W. O. Ayres,† Francis Bacon,† James C. Barker,† W. R. Bartlett,† Fred'k Bellosa,† E. H. Bishop,† Timothy H. Bishop,† Evelyn L. Bissell,† W. L. Bradley,† Henry Bronson,† W. H. Carmalt,† H. A. Carrington,† S. H. Chapman,† M. A. Cremin,† D. L. Daggett,† H. A. Du Bois,† Wm. B. DeForest,† F. L. Dibble,† James J. S. Doherty,† Edward Dwight,† Geo. B. Farnam,† H. Fleischner,† J. F. C. Foster,† T. P. Gibbons,† R. J. Gibson,† L. M. Gilbert,† William B. Graves,† Wm. H. Hotchkiss,† Stephen G. Hubbard,† Levi Ives,† Robert S. Ives,† P. A. Jewett,† Walter Judson,† D. C. Leavenworth,† A. W. Leighton, B. S. Lewis,† C. P. Lindsley,† Charles A. Lindsley,† J. F. Lines,† Max Mailhouse,† John Nicoll,† H. A. Oakes† M. C. O'Connor,† Henry Pierpont,† Arthur Ruickoldt,† Thomas H. Russell,† Wm. S. Russell,† L. J. Sanford,† Ira S. Smith,† James K. Thacher,† E. L. Thomson,† T. Beers Townsend,† David A. Tyler,† Moses C. White,† F. O. White,† F. H. Whittemore,† F. J. Whittemore,† A. E. Winchell,† C.

A. Bartholomew, J. J. Barry, Robert Crane, C. V. R. Creed, V. M. Dow, Rollin McNeil, L. C. Vinal, E. L. Washburne. *Hom.*, C. B. Adams, William D. Anderson, C.A. Dorman, B. H. Cheney, W. W. Rodman, Wm. H. Sage, Paul C. Skiff, Charles Vishno, E. J. Walker. *Ec.*, M. F. Linquist. FAIR HAVEN, S. D. Gilbert,† C. S. Thomson,† W. H. Thomson.† *Hom.*, H. E. Stone. WESTVILLE, J. W. Barker.†

BETHANY, B. E. Case. *Hom.*, Andrew Johnson.

BRANFORD, Walter Zink.† C. W. Gaylord,† E. W. Brainard, W. C. Holmes. STONY CREEK, Justin W. Smith.†

CHESHIRE, M. N. Chamberlin.† *Hom.*, W. C. Williams, George C. F. Williams.

DERBY, BIRMINGHAM, Ambrose Beardsley,† Geo. L. Beardsley,† Charles H. Pinney,† J. B. Jewett,† F. Hall. *Hom.*, A. W. Phillips. ANSONIA, F. P. Blodgett, S. R. Baker,† Wm. Welch, William Terry. Thomas J. O'Sullivan,† *Ec.*, F. C. Wangeroth.

GUILFORD, Alvan Talcott,† G. P. Reynolds,† F. P. Griswold. *Ec.*, Hiram I. Fisk.

HAMDEN, Edwin D. Swift,† E. E. Swift, O. F. Treadwell,† F. W. Wright.† *Bot.*, Henry I. Bradley.

MADISON, Daniel M. Webb,† Joseph J. Meigs.

MERIDEN, John Tait. WEST MERIDEN, E. T. Bradstreet,† A. H. Churchill,† E. M. Child,† C. H. S. Davis,† G. D. Ferguson,† Anna J. Ferris,† Frederick J. Fitch,† N. Nickerson,† J. D. Eggleston, A. W. Tracy.† *Hom.*, Grove H. Wilson, C. J. Mansfield. *Ec.*, E. C. Newport, S. D. Otis, SOUTH MERIDEN, *Ec.*, Charles E. Scott.

MIDDLEBURY, Marcus DeForest, Jr.

MILFORD, Hull Allen,† William H. Andrews,† Lucius N. Beardsley,† J. B. Heady,† Thomas A. Dutton.† *Hom.*, C. F. Sterling. W. E. Reed.

NAUGATUCK, E. S. Mears, Franklin B. Tuttle, A. E. May,† W. F. Hinckley.

NORTH BRANFORD, Edward A. Wood,† Wellington Campbell.

NORTH HAVEN, R. B. Goodyear,† Austin Lord.

ORANGE, WEST HAVEN, John M. Aimes,† John F. Barnett,† Durell Shepard.

OXFORD, Lewis Barnes,† John Lounsbury. *Bot.*, J. H. Pardee.

SEYMOUR, S. C. Johnson,† Joshua Kendall,† Thomas Stoddard.† *Hom.*, E. R. Warner, F. W. Palford.

SOUTHBURY, Anthony B. Burritt.† SOUTH BRITAIN, Nathan C. Baldwin,† W. S. Miller.†

WALLINGFORD, Hunt Atwater, Nehemiah Banks,† Henry Davis, Benjamin F. Harrison,† J. D. McGaughey.† *Bot.*, Vincent L. Baldwin, Hezekiah Hall.

WATERBURY, H. E. Castle,† Edw. L. Griggs,† E. W. McDonald,† J. J. M. Neville,† Alfred North,† Gideon L. Platt,† C. W. S. Frost,† Walter L. Holmes,† W. L. Barber,† J. R. Roberts. C. S. Rodman.† *Hom.*, G. P. Swift, E. A. Towne, *Ec.*, John J. Jaques, Stephen B. Munn.

WOODBRIDGE, Silas C. Hubbell, J. W. Barker.

NEW LONDON COUNTY.

E. C. Kinney, Norwich, President; A. Peck, Norwich, Clerk.

NEW LONDON, Isaac G. Porter,† F. N. Braman,† Thomas S. Steadman, George L. Andrews, R. A. Manwaring,† A. W. Nelson,† J. G. Stanton,† F. W. Caulkins, H. S. Cornwell, Albert Hobson. *Hom.*, A. H. Allen, D. P. Francis, G. S. Morgan, F. W. Smith, Oscar Sites. *Ec.*, O. W. Jewell.

NORWICH, L. B. Almy,† Chas. M. Carleton,† Patrick Casdy,† Elijah Dyer,† A. B. Haile,† E. C. Kinney,† W. H. Mason,† A. Peck,† Elisha Phinney,† Lewis S. Paddock,† Wm. S. C. Perkins,† S. L. Sprague,† C. B. Farnsworth, J. B. F. Fuller, O. F. Harris, S. E. Maynard, F. A. Tillinghast. *Hom.*, H. M. Bishop, J. E. Linnell, E. H. Linnell, C. E. Stark. *Ec.*, O. G. Bailey, A. F. Gallup, G. V. Wilson. *Bot.*, L. L. Button. GREENEVILLE, Wm. Witter.†

BOZRAH, Samuel G. Johnson,† Nathan Johnson, E. M. Leffingwell.

COLCHESTER, Seth L. Chase, R. R. Carrington, M. W. Robinson. *Hom.*, Soloman E. Swift, C. N. Gallup.

EAST LYME, Elisha Munger,† Daniel Caulkins.

FRANKLIN, Ashbel Woodward.†

GRISWOLD, George H. Jennings.† JEWETT CITY, *Hom.*, J. R. Rockwell, Wm. Soule.

GROTON, John L. Dodge. MYSTIC RIVER, Alfred W. Coates,† John Gray,† Edward Coates. NOANK, E. Barber, Orrin E. Miner.

LEBANON, W. P. Barber.† *Hom.*, C. B. Hobart. *Bone Setter*, Charles Sweet.

LEDYARD, J. A. Brewster.

LYME, HAMBURG, J. Griffin Ely, Edward B. Morgan.

MONTVILLE, John C. Bolles, Earl Mathewson. *Ec.*, J. R. Gay. UNCASVILLE, Wm. M. Burchard.†

NORTH STONINGTON, J. D. Nelson,† Edwin H. Knowles.

OLD LYME, P. O., LYME, Geo. W. Harris,† E. D. Griffin.

PRESTON, O. F. Harris.

SALEM, Francis H. Drew.

SPRAGUE, BALTIC, J. E. Gendron, L. J. Platt, Thos. A. Keables, T. J. Stanton.

STONINGTON, George D. Stanton,† Chas. E. Brayton.† MYSTIC, Mason Manning,† A. T. Chapman,† Frank A. Coates.† MYSTIC BRIDGE, E. Frank Coates.† *Hom.*, O. M. Barber, S. E. Peck.

VOLUNTOWN, Ransom C. Young.

FAIRFIELD COUNTY.

Wm. C. Wile, Sandy Hook, President; F. M. Wilson, Bridgeport, Clerk.

FAIRFIELD. *Hom.*, Jeremiah T. Denison. Sam'l Garlick, Joseph Dobson. SOUTHPORT, Justus Sherwood,† Curtis H. Osborn.† GREENFIELD HILL, M. V. B. Dunham.† Henry N. Pettit.

BRIDGEPORT, A. H. Abernethy,† J. D. Bragg,† W. H. Bunnell†, Curtis H. Bill,† William C. Blood, W. C. Bowers,† J. R. Cummins.† F. B. Downs,† Robert Hubbard,† Geo. F. Lewis,† Robert Lauder,† T. F. Martin,† B. W. Munson,† David H. Nash,† Gustave Ohnesorg,† G. L. Porter,† F. A. Rice,† Mary J. Rising,† Charles W. Sheffrey,† J. S. Silliman, Andrew J. Smith,† George M. Teeple,† W. J. Wakeman,† S. P. Warren,† F. M. Wilson,† N. E. Wordin,† J. W. Wright,† F. J. Young,† H. L. W. Burritt, Jas. D. Bragg, Joseph Maddox, T. F. Martin, Charles Kaemmerer, A. A. Holmes. *Hom.*, Wm. B. Beebe, B. F. Bronson, L. H. Norton, Charles E. Sanford. *Ec.*, J. W. King, L. A.

Shattuck, J. D. S. Smith, Joseph Fanyon. *Bot.*, H. M. Richardson.

DANBURY, A E. Adams,† Jas. Baldwin,† Ezra P. Bennett,†
R. H. Lynch, Wm. C. Bennett,† F. P. Clark,† John H. Benedict,
A. T. Clason,† Wm. F. Lacey,† Wm. F. Lacey, Jr., H. G.
Wildman.† *Hom.*, W. E. Bulkley,† Samuel M. Griffin, S.
Penfield. *Ec.*, E. A. Brown. *Indian*, G. C. Richards.

BETHEL, Alvin E. Barber,† Geo. Benedict, C. R. Hart.

BROOKFIELD, Amos L. Williams,† Anson P. Smith.

DARIEN, Samuel Sands,† R. L. Bowhanaran, Charles T.
Darby.

EASTON, C. B. Hart.

GREENWICH, Sylvester Mead, F. M. Holly. *Hom.*, James
H. Brush, L. P. Jones. ROUND HILL, J. C. White, Geo. H. Fisher.
MIANUS, James L. Marshall.

HUNTINGTON, Gould A. Shelton,† Thomas B. Jewett.

MONROE, E. M. Beardsley,† A. W. Lyon.

NEW CANAAN, W. G. Brownson,† M. F. Osborn, Wm.
C. Brownson. *Hom.*, Theodore Roberts, *Ec.*, Ellery Clark.

NEWTOWN, F. N. Bennett, Monroe Judson. SANDY HOOK,
Wm. C. Wile,† A. P. Smith, G. W. Benedict.

NORWALK, F. V. Brush,† James G. Gregory,† G. W.
Benedict, Jno. C. Kendall,† H. Hungerford,† W. A. Lockwood,†
Robert G. Nolan,† John A. McLean. *Hom.*, G. S. Comstock,
N. A. Mosman, Dexter Hitchcock. SOUTH NORWALK, W. C.
Burke, Jr.,† R. L. Higgins,† Moses B. Pardee,† John Hill.†

REDDING, Moses H. Wakeman.†

RIDGEFIELD, O. Starr Hicock,† Wm. S. Todd,† Nehemiah
Perry.

SHERMAN, John N. Woodruff. *Ec.*, Henry L. Mallory.

STAMFORD, George W. Birch, William H. Trowbridge,†
C. K. Daily, H. P. Geib,† R. G. Griswold, L. R. Hurlbut,
J. F. Phillips, Edward E. Rowell, Chas. E. Rowell, Thomas
Skelding. NORTH STAMFORD, Israel Prior, Francis J. Rogers.
Hom., Chauncey M. Ayers, Geo. F. Foote, J. F. Griffin, E. E.
Rowell.

STRATFORD, Edwin D. Nooney,† Almon S. Allen.† *Hom.*,
G. W. A. Collard.

TRUMBULL, Thomas Reid.† STEPNEY, Seth Hill.

WESTON, Frank Gorham.†

WESTPORT, Geo B. Bouton,† Fred'k Powers.† *Ec.*, Geo. W. Rubey.

WILTON, Alfred F. Emery,† Samuel H. Huntington, Andrew B. Gorham.

WINDHAM COUNTY.

H. W. Hough, Putnam, President; R. Robinson, Danielsonville, Clerk.

WINDHAM, Eliphalet Huntington,† S. H. Huntington†, F. O. Bennett.† WILLIMANTIC, L. F. Bugbee,† O. B. Griggs,† T. Morton Hills,† F. H. Houghton, C. H. David, Samuel David, Fred'k Rogers,† Chas. J. Fox, Casper Barstow,† D. D. Jacobs, F. H. McNally, Daniel McGinness. *Hom.*, D. C. Card, C. H. Colgrove. *Ec.*, Isaac B. Gallup.

BROOKLYN. James B. Whitcomb,† William Woodbridge, Alfred H. Tanner. *Hom.*, J. M. Coburn.

ASHFORD, John H. Simmons.† WESTFORD, George F. Shove. WESTBORO, Remus Robinson.

CANTERBURY, Charles B. Hicks, G. I. Ross. SOUTH CANTERBURY, Elijah Baldwin.†

CHAPLIN, Orrin Witter.

EASTFORD. *Ec.*, Elisha K. Robbins.

HAMPTON, Dyer Hughes,† Charles Gardiner.

KILLINGLY, A. E. Darling.† (EAST,) Edwin A. Hill.† (SOUTH,) Daniel A. Hovey,† E. P. Morse. (WEST,) Thos. Graves,† Samuel Hutchins,† Rienzi Robinson,† O. L. Jenkins.

PLAINFIELD, E. H. Davis.† CENTRAL VILLAGE, Charles H. Rogers.† MOOSUP, Wm. A. Lewis,† Frank S. Burgess. WAUREGAN, W. H. Judson.†

POMFRET, Frederick Sawtelle.

PUTNAM, F. X. Barolet,† Henry W. Hough,† John B. Kent,† Omer La Rue,† John Witter,† J. L. Bradley. *Hom.*, G. L. Miller, A. D. Crabtree.

THOMPSON, Lowell Holbrook.† E. T. Morse. NORTH GROSVENORDALE, James C. Lathrop,† C. C. Sargent. *Ec.*, G. W. H. Williams.

SOUTH WINDHAM, Casper Barstow.†

WOODSTOCK. (SOUTH,) *Hom.*, Geo. A. Bowen. (EAST,) John Cotton.† (WEST,) Milton Bradford.† WOODSTOCK VALLEY, A. S. Leonard.†

LITCHFIELD COUNTY.

Walter S. Munger, Watertown, President; Willis J. Beach, Litchfield, Vice-President; J. J. Newcomb, Litchfield, Clerk.

LITCHFIELD, Henry W. Buel,† Willis J. Beach,† William Deming,† H. E. Gates,† J. J. Newcomb.† *Northfield*, J. K. Wallace, E. L. Blake.

BARKHAMSTED, Bramwell Gidman.

BETHLEHEM, W. F. Follansbee.

CANAAN, FALLS VILLAGE, C. W. Camp,† C. B. Maltbie, James J. Averill.

CORNWALL, WEST CORNWALL, Edward Sanford,† Isaac R. Sanford.† CORNWALL BRIDGE, Thomas S. Hodge.

GOSHEN, Joseph H. North.†

HARWINTON, Virgil Buell,† R. G. Hassard.

KENT, John W. King.

MORRIS, Garry H. Miner,† C. H. Vibbert.

NEW HARTFORD, Jerry Burwell.† *Ec.*, Erskine D. Curtiss. PINE MEADOW, *Ec.*, Theo. T. Brockway, F. Brockway.

NEW MILFORD, J. K. Bacon,† James Hine, J. C. Barker. *Hom.*, Charles Taylor. GAYLORDSVILLE, Chas. F. Couch,† M. C. Northrop.

NORFOLK, William W. Welch,† J. H. P. Stevens.†

NORTH CANAAN, P. O., CANAAN, Chas. W. Camp.†

PLYMOUTH, J. B. Heath. TERRYVILLE, William P. Swett,† L. T. Platt, J. H. Trent.†

ROXBURY, Myron Downs.†

SALISBURY, B. S. Thompson,† John H. Blodgett. LAKEVILLE, Wm. Bissell,† R. P. Knight,† John J. Orton.

SHARON, Wm. W. Knight,† Charles H. Shears, Charles S. Browne.

THOMASTON, R. S. Goodwin,† A. G. Heaney,† William Woodruff,† Byron W. Pease, Theo. St. John, F. M. Cannon.

TORRINGTON, WOLCOTTVILLE, T. S. Hanchett,† L. H. Wood.† *Hom.*, Bela St. John.

WARREN, John B. Derrickson.†

WASHINGTON, Orlando Brown,† W. L. Platt, Remus M. Fowler.† NEW PRESTON, Ed. P. Lyman.†

WATERTOWN, Walter S. Munger,† Frank P. Easterly,† Allyn M. Hungerford, F. B. Woodward.

WINCHESTER, WEST WINSTED. John W. Bidwell,† James Welch,† F. E. Barrows,† Frank Gallagher, Edward H. Welch. *Hom.*, D. Warren. *Ec.*, Harvey B. Steele.

WOODBURY, Harmon W. Shove,† Francis W. Brown,† G. H. Atwood, Henry S. Kaasman, L. U. Ketcham, H. G. Richards.

MIDDLESEX COUNTY.

Rufus Baker, Middletown, President; W. S. Miller, Clinton, Clerk.

MIDDLETOWN, Joseph W. Alsop, Jr.,† Rufus Baker,† Geo. W. Burke,† F. Frank Calef,† Daniel A. Cleaveland,† Francis D. Edgerton,† W. E. Fisher,† E. P. H. Griswold,† John Morgan.† Elisha B. Nye,† James B. Olmsted,† A. M. Shew,† C. E. Stanley,† Joseph Barratt, P. Burnett,† J. F. Calef. *Hom.*, W. C. Bell, A. S. Osborne. *Ec.*, Leonard Bailey, Frank L. Burr. *Bone Setter*, Gideon H. Sweet.

HADDAM, Miner C. Hazen,† Selden W. Noyes.† HIGGANUM, *Ec.*, S. B. Bailey, L. A. Smith.

CHATHAM, EAST HAMPTON, Albert Field,† Wm. Notting. *Hom.*, L. F. Wood. MIDDLE HADDAM, A. B. Worthington.†

CHESTER, Sylvester W. Turner,† Ambrose Pratt.

CLINTON, G. O. Johnson,† David A. Fox. *Hom.*, Silas E. Peck.

CROMWELL, W. B. Hallock,† John Conland.† Charles F. Calef, D. L. Rood.

DURHAM, R. W. Mathewson,† E. A. Markham.

EAST HADDAM. N. O. Harris. MOODUS, A. W. Bell.† *Bot.*, H. C. Cook.

ESSEX, Alanson H. Hough,† Charles H. Hubbard.†

KILLINGWORTH, Edward P. Nichols.

OLD SAYBROOK, John H. Granniss.†

PORTLAND, C. A. Sears.† C. E. Hammond,† Samuel P. Ladd,† H. S. Day.

SAYBROOK, DEEP RIVER, Edwin Bidwell.†

WESTBROOK, G. C. H. Gilbert,† Thomas B. Bloomfield.†

11

TOLLAND COUNTY.

Stephen G. Risley, Rockville, President; Gilbert H. Preston, Tolland, Clerk.

TOLLAND, Gilbert H. Preston.†

BOLTON, Charles F. Sumner.†

COLUMBIA, Julian La Pierre, Theodore R. Parker.

COVENTRY, M. B. Bennett.† SOUTH COVENTRY, Henry S. Dean,† Eli P. Flint,† R. H. Goodrich.†

ELLINGTON, Joel A. Warren.†

HEBRON, Cyrus H. Pendleton.

MANSFIELD, O. G. Kittridge, Frederick Johnson.† MANSFIELD CENTER,̄ Edwin G. Sumner.

SOMERS, Erasmus E. Hamilton, Wm. B. Woods. Simon P. Houghton.

STAFFORD, Wm. N. Clark.† STAFFORD SPRINGS, C. B. Newton.† F. L. Smith, J. S. Clark. *Hom.*, L. B. Richards, H. D. Gould, J. C. Eaton.

VERNON, VERNON DEPOT, A. R. Goodrich.† ROCKVILLE, Francis L. Dickinson,† Stephen G. Risley,† Frederick Gilnack, E. K. Leonard, Thomas L. Rockwell. *Hom.*, Giles Pease, Elmer L. Styles, Charles L. Beach.

WILLINGTON, Wm. L. Kelsey.†

CONNECTICUT NATIONAL GUARD.

COMMANDER-IN-CHIEF.

His Excellency Hobart B. Bigelow, New Haven.

AIDS-DE-CAMP, Colonels William E. Barrows, William B. Rudd, Charles A. Russell, Frank L. Bigelow.

ADJUTANT-GENERAL, Brig.-Gen. George M. Harmon.

ASSISTANT, Colonel Simeon J. Fox.

QUARTERMASTER-GENERAL, Brig.-Gen. Alexander Harbison. Assistant, Lieut. Col. Henry C. Morgan.

PAYMASTER-GENERAL, Brig.-Gen. Frederick E. Camp.

COMMISSARY-GENERAL, Brig.-Gen. George H. Ford.

SURGEON-GENERAL, Brig.-Gen. James G. Gregory.

GOVERNOR'S GUARDS.

1st Horse, Hartford (chartered, 1788). Major, Chauncey B. Boardman; 1st Lieut., H. C. Hanmer; 2d Lieut., H. W. Rowley; Quartermaster, T. N. Griswold; Cornet, E. F. Griswold.

1st Foot, Hartford (chartered 1771). Major, Andrew H. Embler; Capt. and 1st Lieut., ——— ———; 2d Lieut., James C. Pratt; 3d Lieut., Theo. C. Naedle; 4th Lieut., J. Robert Dwyer; Ensign, Fayette C. Clark.

2d Horse, New Haven. Major, C. W. Blakeslee, Jr.; Capt., R. C. Newton; 1st Lieuts , V. A. Bartholomew, W. H. Farnham, Jr.; 2d Lieuts., W. B. Hall, H. B. Rowe; Cornet, Frank L. Newton: Quartermaster, I. W. Hine.

2d Foot, New Haven, (chartered 1775). Capt., Edward J. Morse; 1st Lieut., Albert M. Johnson; 2d Lieut., Frank D. Brett.

FIRST BRIGADE.

BRIGADIER-GENERAL, Stephen R. Smith, New Haven.

BRIGADE ADJUTANT, Lieut.-Colonel Lewis L. Morgan, New Haven.

BRIGADE INSPECTOR, Major John B. Clapp, Hartford.

BRIGADE QUARTERMASTER, Major Thomas L. Watson, Bridgeport.

BRIGADE COMMISSARY, Major Samuel C. Waldron, Stonington.

BRIGADE INSPECTOR OF TARGET PRACTICE, Major James E. Stetson, New Haven.

AIDS-DE-CAMP, Capts. Edwin McNeil, Litchfield; William H. Stevenson, Bridgeport.

FIRST REGIMENT.

Colonel, Lucius A. Barbour, Hartford; Lieut.-Col., William E. Cone, Hartford; Major, A. L. Goodrich, Hartford; Adjutant, John K. Williams, Hartford; Quartermaster, Richard O. Cheney, So. Manchester; Paymaster, Wm. B. McCray, Hartford; Surgeon, Geo. W. Avery, Hartford; Assistant Surgeon, Harmon G. Howe, Hartford; Inspector of Target Practice, J. L. Woodbridge, No. Manchester; Chaplain, James W. Cooper, New Britain.

Company Commissioned Officers.

A. Hartford. Capt., Wm. Westphal; 1st Lieut., Edward Schulze; 2d Lieut., Henry F. Smith.

B. Hartford. Capt., Patrick J. Moran; 1st Lieut., Thomas Flanigan; 2d Lieut., Patrick H. Smith.

D. New Britain. Capt., Aug. N. Bennett; 1st Lieut., John C. Bingham; 2d Lieut., Wm. E. Allen.

E. New Britain. Capt., C. B. Erichson; 1st Lieut., F. M. Hemenway; 2d Lieut., George O. McLean.

F. Hartford. Capt., Levi H. Hotchkiss; 1st Lieut., Thomas T. Welles; 2d Lieut., Alexander Allen.

G. Manchester. Capt., Arthur B. Keeney; 1st Lieut., Arthur J. Wetherell; 2d Lieut., Thos. H. Montgomery.

H. Hartford. Capt Geo. A. Cornell; 1st Lieut., Henry Simon, Jr. 2d Lieut., John W. Crane.

K. Hartford. Capt., Thomas M. Smith; 1st Lieut., Chas. E. Thompson; 2d Lieut., Samuel O. Prentice.

SECOND REGIMENT.

Col., Charles P. Graham, Middletown; Lieut.-Col., Josiah N. Bacon, New Haven; Maj., Chas. R. Bannon, Waterbury; Adjutant, Joseph T. Elliott, Middletown; Qr. Master, Clayton H. Redfield, New Haven; Paymaster, Edward S. Hayden, Waterbury; Surgeon, Evelyn L. Bissell, New Haven; Asst. Surgeon, Geo. L. Beardsley, Birmingham; Inspector of Target Practice, Andrew Allen, New Haven; Chaplain, Samuel D. McConnell, Middletown.

Company Commissioned Officers.

A. Waterbury. Capt., Fred. A. Spencer; 1st Lieut., Francis H. Smith; 2d Lieut., John B. Doherty.

B. New Haven. Capt., Frank W. Tiesing; 1st Lieut., Wiliam Kaehole; 2d Lieut., John Gutt.

C. New Haven. Capt., ―― ― ―― ; 1st Lieut., ―― ―― ; 2d Lieut., Edward Lynn.

D. New Haven. Capt., Luzerne I. Thomas; 1st Lieut., Geo. Laurence; 2d Lieut., Richard W. Waite.

E. New Haven. Capt., Henry R. Loomis; 1st Lieut., Samuel A. Downes; 2d Lieut., Charles W. Bogue.

F. New Haven. Capt., George S. Arnold; 1st Lieut., Arthur M. Howarth; 2d Lieut., Frank A. Bowman.

G. Waterbury. Capt., Patrick F. Bannon; 1st Lieut., James Horigan; 2d Lieut., John H. Reed.

H. Middletown. Capt., Henry J. Bacon; 1st Lieut., Everett O. Shaler; 2d Lieut., David A. Hutchings.

I. Meriden. Capt., Henry B. Wood; 1st Lieut., John N. Lane; 2d Lieut., Frederick T. Ward.

K. Wallingford. Capt., Walter J. Leavenworth, 1st Lieut., Geo. G. LaBarnes; 2d Lieut., Chas. O. Norton.

THIRD REGIMENT.

Colonel, Wm. H. Tubbs, New London; Lieut.-Col., ————
————, ————; Maj., William H. Bentley, New London; Adjutant, George Havens, New London; Quartermaster, George W. Phillips, Willimantic; Paymaster, Joseph W. Gilbert, Norwich; Surgeon, Charles M. Carleton, Norwich; Asst. Surgeon, Wm. B. Young, Norwich; Inspector of Target Practice, Alonzo W. Sholes, New London; Chaplain, Edward W. Bacon, New London.

Company Commissioned Officers.

A. Mystic Bridge. Capt., John H. Hoxie; 1st Lieut., Henry J. Hill; 2d Lieut., Wm. C. Jones.

B. Stonington. Capt., Michael Twomey; 1st Lieut., James O'Sullivan; 2d Lieut., Daniel Keleher.

C. Norwich. Capt., ———— ————; 1st Lieut., Charles S. Ebberts; 2d Lieut., Charles W. Gilbert.

D. New London. Capt., Fred'k E. St. Clare; 1st Lieut., Wm. M. Mason; 2d Lieut., Wm. W. Cronin.

E. Willimantic. Capt., Frank S. Fowler; 1st Lieut., James Haggerty; 2d Lieut., Alexander L. Fuller.

G. Putnam. Capt., ————· ————; 1st Lieut., ———— ————; 2d Lieut., Daniel G. Arnold.

I. New London. Capt., Abner N. Sterry; 1st Lieut., J. Emerson Harris; 2d Lieut., Chas. F. Chaney.

K. Willimantic. Capt., Myron P. Squires; 1st Lieut., Charles W. Harrington; 2d Lieut., Carlile P. Boynton.

FOURTH REGIMENT.

Colonel, George S. Crofut, Bethel; Lieut.-Col., Henry Skinner, Winsted; Maj.,Jas.C. Crowe, So. Norwalk; Adjutant, David T. Hubbell, Bethel; Quartermaster, Henry N. Fanton, Danbury; Paymaster, George S. Rowe, Winsted; Surgeon, George F. Lewis, Bridgeport; Asst. Surgeon, William C. Burke, Jr., Norwalk; Inspector of Target Practice, Samuel C. Kingman, Bridgeport; Chaplain, Samuel Scoville, Stamford.

Company Commissioned Officers.

A. Bethel. Capt., Frederick Cole; 1st Lieut., William F. Hoyt; 2d Lieut., George W. Wheeler.

B. Bridgeport. Capt., George W. Cornell; 1st Lieut., Francis A. King; 2d Lieut., Wilford T. Van Yorx.

C. Stamford. Capt., Wm. W. Studwell; 1st Lieut., Elias E. Palmer; 2d Lieut., Abraham M. Horton.

D. South Norwalk. Capt., Edward F. Jennings; 1st Lieut., Alvan A. Hauschildt; 2d Lieut., William F. Wardwell.

E. Bridgeport. Capt., Jas. Sheridan; 1st Lieut., James Donnelly; 2d Lieut., John J. Glennon.

F. Norwalk. Capt., Addison A. Betts; 1st Lieut., Ferdinand B. Smith; 2d Lieut., Harvey M. Kent.

G. Danbury. Capt., George C. Comes; 1st Lieut., George A. Vibbert; 2d Lieut., Cornelius Delury.

I. Winsted. Capt., Edward Finn; 1st Lieut., William B. Phillips; 2d Lieut., Alfred E. Moore.

K. Stratford. Capt., Henry M. Blakeslee; 1st Lieut., Chas. Wilcoxson; 2d Lieut., James Scofield.

FIFTH BATTALION. (Colored.)

Major, Frank M. Welch, Bridgeport; Adjutant, James O. Jones, New Haven; Quartermaster, Wm. P. H. Cross, Hartford; Assistant Surgeon, Courtlandt V. R. Creed, New Haven.

Company Commissioned Officers.

A. New Haven. Captain, George W. Ladieu; 1st Lieut., Wm. R. Keyes; 2d Lieut., Fleetwood C. Anthony.

B. Hartford. Captain, Lloyd G. Seymour; 1st Lieut., ——— ———; 2d Lieut., L. Eugene Seymour.

C. Bridgeport. Captain, William H. Latimer; 1st Lieut., Robert Butler; 2d Lieut., Charles H. Walker.

ARTILLERY.

Battery A. Captain, William H. Lee, Guilford.

First Platoon, Guilford. 1st Lieut., ——— ———; 2d Lieut., Wm. T. Foote.

Second Platoon, Clinton; 1st Lieut., Holcomb N. Jones; 2d Lieut., Reuben H. W. Kelsey.

BANKS.

COMMISSIONERS, JAMES W. HYATT, July 1, 1882, Norwalk; SAMUEL Q. PORTER, July 1, 1883, Farmington.

NATIONAL BANK EXAMINER, A. B. MYGATT, New Milford.

PRESIDENTS AND CASHIERS.

They reside where the bank is located, unless otherwise specified. The National Banks hold their elections on the 2d Tuesday of January, and therefore the officers given are those elected in 1881.

ÆTNA N. (Hartford.) Pres., Wm. R. Cone; Cash., A. R. Hillyer.

AMERICAN N. (Hartford.) Pres., Rowland Swift; Cash., John G. Root.

ANSONIA N. Pres., Thomas Wallace; Vice-Prest., George P. Cowles; Cash., Chas. H. Pine.

BIRMINGHAM N. Pres., Edward N. Shelton; Vice-President, David W. Plumb; Cash., Joseph Arnold.

BRIDGEPORT N. Pres., Monson Hawley; Cash., F. N. Benham.

1 N., BRIDGEPORT. Pres., E. S. Hawley; Cash., William E. Seeley.

CENTRAL N. (Middletown.) Pres., Jesse G. Baldwin; Cash., Henry B. Starr.

CHARTER OAK N. (Hartford.) Pres., J. F. Morris; Vice-Pres., Geo. Sexton; Cash., J. P. Taylor.

CITIZENS' N. (Waterbury.) Pres., F. J. Kingsbury; Cash., F. L. Curtiss.

CITY N. BANK OF BRIDGEPORT. Pres., D. N. Morgan; Cash., F. L. Bartholomew.

CITY N. BANK OF HARTFORD. Pres., G. F. Davis; Cash., P. S. Riley.

CITY BANK OF NEW HAVEN. Pres., George W. Curtis; Cash., Samuel Lloyd.

CLINTON N. Pres., John D. Leffingwell; Cash., E. E. Post.

N. B. OF COMMERCE, (New London.) Pres., William H. Barns; Cash., Charles W. Barns.

CONNECTICUT N. (Bridgeport.) Pres., Samuel W. Baldwin; Cash., Henry B. Drew.

CONNECTICUT RIVER BANKING Co. (Hartford.) Pres., Sam'l E. Elmore; Cash., M. W. Graves.

DANBURY N. Pres., Lucius P. Hoyt; Cash., Jabez Amsbury.

DEEP RIVER N. Pres., R. P. Spencer, Chester; Cash., Gideon Parker.

N. EXCHANGE. (Hartford.) Pres., Francis B. Cooley; Cash., John R. Redfield.

FAIRFIELD COUNTY N., (Norwalk.) Pres., F. St. John Lockwood; Vice-Pres., Joseph W. Hubbell; Cash., Chas. H. Street.

FARMERS AND MECHANICS N. (Hartford.) Pres., Alva Oatman; Vice-Pres., Henry Keney; Cash., William W. Smith.

HARTFORD N. Pres., Jas. Bolter; Cash., W. S. Bridgman; Asst. Cash., Joseph Breed.

1 N., HARTFORD. Pres., Erastus H. Crosby; Cash., C. S. Gillette; Asst. Cash., J. H. Knight.

HOME N. (West Meriden.) Pres., Eli Butler; Cash., A. Chamberlain, Jr.

HURLBUT N. (West Winsted.) Pres., Wm. L. Gilbert; Cash., Henry Gay.

N. IRON BANK OF FALLS VILLAGE. Pres., A. C. Randall, North Canaan; Cash., D. E. Dean.

1 N. BANK OF KILLINGLY. Pres., Henry Hammond; Cash., Henry N. Clamens.

1 N., LITCHFIELD. Pres., Henry R. Coit; Vice-Pres., Henry W. Buel; Cash., George E. Jones.

MECHANICS. (New Haven.) Pres., Chas. S. Leete; Vice-Pres., Jno. P. Tuttle: Cash., Chas. H. Trowbridge.

MERCANTILE N. (Hartford.) Pres., J. Watson Beach; Cash., J. B. Powell.

MERCHANTS N. (New Haven.) Pres., Nathan Peck; Cash., John C. Bradley.

MERCHANTS N. BANK OF NORWICH. Pres., John Brewster; Cash., Jas. M. Meech; Asst. Cash., Charles Webb.

MERIDEN N. Pres., Joel I. Butler; Cash., Owen B. Arnold.

MIDDLESEX COUNTY N. (Middletown.) Pres., Joel H. Guy; Cash., J. E. Bidwell.

MIDDLETOWN N. Pres., John H. Watkinson; Cash., Melvin B. Copeland; Asst. Cash., W. H. Barrows.

1 N., MIDDLETOWN. Pres., Benjamin Douglas; Cash., J. N. Camp.

MYSTIC N. Pres., John S. Schoonover; Cash., J. Watrous, Jr.

1 N., MYSTIC BRIDGE. Pres., Chas. Mallory; Vice-Pres., Geo. W. Mallory; Cash., Elias P. Randall.

MYSTIC RIVER N. Pres., Wm. Clift; Cash., Henry B. Noyes.

NEW BRITAIN N. Pres., C. B. Erwin; Cash., A. P. Collins; Asst. Cash., A. J. Sloper.

N., NEW ENGLAND. (Goodspeed's Landing, East Haddam.)
Pres., Thomas Gross, Jr.; Cash., —— Dayton.

N., NEW HAVEN. Pres., Wilbur F. Day; Vice-Pres., Henry
Trowbridge; Cash., Robert J. Couch.

1 N., NEW HAVEN. Pres., H. M. Welch; Cash., Wm. Moulthrop.

2 N., NEW HAVEN. Pres., Samuel Hemingway; Cash., Israel
K. Ward; Asst. Cash., Charles A. Sheldon.

NEW HAVEN COUNTY N. (New Haven.) Pres., James E. English; Cash., Leonard S. Hotchkiss.

NEW LONDON CITY N. Pres., J. N. Harris; Vice-Pres., E.
D. Avery; Cash., R. N. Belden.

1 N., NEW MILFORD. Pres., A. B. Mygatt. Vice-Pres., H. W.
Booth. Cash., Henry Ives; Asst. Cash., H. S. Mygatt.

N., NORWALK. Pres., Stiles Curtis; Vice-Pres., Edward P.
Weed; Cash., R. B. Craufurd.

1 N., NORWICH. Pres., Lucius W. Carroll; Cash., Lewis A.
Hyde.

2 N., NORWICH. Pres., E. R. Thompson; Vice-Pres., C. P.
Cogswell; Cash., E. A. Tracy.

NORWICH N. Pres., Frank Johnson; Cash., S. B. Meech.

N. PAHQUIOQUE, (Danbury.) Pres., B. B. Kellogg; Cash.,
Wm. P. Seeley.

PAWCATUCK N. (Stonington.) Pres., Peleg Clarke, Jr.; Cash.,
J. A. Morgan.

PEQUONNOCK N. (Bridgeport.) Pres., Charles B. Hotchkiss;
Cash., Isaac B. Prindle.

PHŒNIX N. (Hartford.) Pres., Henry A. Redfield; Cash.,
Edward M. Bunce; Asst. Cash., Niles P. Hough.

1 N., PORTLAND. Pres., F. Gildersleeve; Vice-Pres., William
W. Coe; Cash.. John H. Sage.

1 N., PUTNAM. Pres., Gilbert W. Phillips; Cash., J. A. Carpenter.

ROCKVILLE N. Pres., Chauncey Winchell; Vice-Pres., George
Maxwell; Cash., E. C. Chapman.

1 N., ROCKVILLE. Pres., George Talcott; Vice-Pres., C. D.
Talcott; Cash., John H. Kite.

SAYBROOK N., OF ESSEX. Pres., Jared E. Redfield, Essex;
Cash., Charles S. Hough.

SHETUCKET N. (Norwich.) ˉ Pres., Charles Osgood; Cash.,
Wm. Roath.

1 N., SOUTH NORWALK. Pres., Dudley P. Ely. Cash., J.
J. Millard.

SOUTHPORT N. Pres., Francis D. Perry; Cash., E. C. Sherwood.

STAFFORD N. (Stafford Springs.) Pres., R. S. Beebe; Cash., R. S. Hicks.

STAMFORD N. Pres., Charles A. Hawley; Cash., George W. Glendining.

1 N., STAMFORD. Pres., Charles W. Brown; Cash., A. R. Turkington.

STATE (Hartford.) Pres., Chas. H. Brainard; Cash., Geo. F. Hills.

1 N., STONINGTON. Pres., Stiles Stanton; Cash., Wm. J. H. Pollard.

1 N., SUFFIELD. Pres., I. Luther Spencer; Cash., A. Spencer, Jr.

THAMES N. (Norwich.) Pres., Franklin Nichols; Cash., Ed. N. Gibbs.

THOMPSON N. Pres., Jeremiah Olney; Vice-Pres., Stephen Crosby; Cash., Hiram Arnold.

TOLLAND COUNTY N. (Tolland.) Pres., Lucius S. Fuller; Cash., Arthur J. Morton.

N. TRADESMEN. (New Haven.) Pres., Matthew G. Elliott; Cash., George A. Butler.

UNCAS N. (Norwich.) Pres., Lyman Gould; Cash., Edw'd H. Learned.

N. UNION. (New London.) Pres., Wm. H. Chapman; Cash., L. C. Learned; Asst. Cash., J. L. Chew.

WATERBURY N. Pres., Augustus S. Chase; Cash., Aug. M. Blakesley.

1 N., WEST MERIDEN. Pres., Joel H. Guy; Cash., Charles L. Rockwell.

1 N., WESTPORT. Pres., Horace Staples; Cash., B.L. Woodworth.

N. WHALING, (New London.) Pres., Sebastian D. Lawrence; Cash., Joseph C. Douglass.

WINDHAM N. Pres., Thomas Ramsdell; Cash., Samuel Bingham.

WINDHAM COUNTY N. (Brooklyn.) Pres., John Palmer; Cash., John P. Wood.

1 N. WINSTED. Pres., Elias E. Gilman; Cash., Frank D. Hallet.

WINSTED N. (Winsted.) Pres., John G. Wetmore; Cash., Henry C. Young.

YALE N. (New Haven.) Pres., F. S. Bradley; Cash., John A. Richardson.

Statistics of Banks, December 1st, 1881.

The following Table contains the Capital, Par value of Shares, Discount Days, and Dividends paid during the past year, the amount and time when paid.

	Capital	Shs.	Dis. Days.	Dividends
Ætna N.	$525,000	100	M. W. F.	8 Jan July
American N.	600,000	50	M. W. F.	9 Jan. July
Ansonia N.	200,000	50	M. Th.	7½ Jan. July
Birmingham N.	300,000	100	Tu. F.	10 Jan. July
Bridgeport N.	215,850	50	Tu. F.	10 Jan. July
1st N. Bridgeport,	210,000	100	Tu. F.	11 May Nov.
Central N.	150,000	75	W. S.	10 Jan. July
Charter Oak N.	500,000	100	M. W. F.	8 Jan. July
Citizens N.	300,000	100	Tu.	10 Jan. July
City N. B. of Bridgeport,	250,000	100	Tu. F.	8 Jan. July
City N. B. of Hartford,	550,000	100	M. W. F	2 Aug
City B. of New Haven,	500,000	100	Tu. F.	3 Jan. July
Clinton N.	75,000	100	W.	10 Jan. July
N. B. of Commerce,	300,000	100	M. Th.	7 Jan. July
Conn. N. (Bridgeport),	332,100	100	Tu. F.	10 Jan. July
Conn. River B'k'g Co.	250,000	50	M. Th.	8 Jan. July
Danbury N.	327,000	100	W. S.	10 June Dec.
Deep River N.	150,000	100	M.	9 Jan. July
N. Exchange,	500,000	50	M. W. F.	9 Jan. July
Fairfield Co. N.	300,000	100	Tu. F.	8 Jan. July
Farmers & Mech's N.	750,000	100	M. W. F.	7 Jan. July
Hartford N.	1,132,800	100	M. W. F.	9 June Dec.
1st N. Hartford,	650,000	100	M. W. F.	6 Jan. July.
Home N.	600,000	100	Tu.	8 Jan. July
Hurlbut N.	205,000	100	daily	12 Jan. July
N. Iron,	200,000	100	M. Th.	8 Jan. July
1st N. Killingly,	110,000	100	M.	8 Jan. July
1st N. Litchfield,	200,000	100	daily.	8 Jan. July
Mechanics,	300,000	60	Tu. F	4 Jan. July
Mercantile N.	500,000	100	M. W. F.	7 Jan. July
Merchants N. (N. Haven),	500,000	50	Tu. F.	7 Jan. July
Merchants N. (Norwich),	300,000	40	M. Th.	3 Sept.
Meriden N.	300,000	100	W.	8 Jan. July
Middlesex Co. N.	$350,000	100	M. Th.	8 Jan. July
Middletown N.	369,300	75	Tu. F.	9 Jan. July
1st N. Middletown,	200,000	100	M. Th.	7 Jan. July
Mystic N.	52,450	50	Tu.	8 Jan. July
1st N. Mystic Bridge,	150,000	100	M.	6 May Nov.
Mystic River N.	100,000	50	Tu.	8 Jan. July
New Britain N	310,000	100	Tu F.	8 Jan July
N. New England,	130,000	100	M.	8 Jan. July
N. New Haven,	464,800	100	Tu. F	12 Jan. July

	Capital.	Shs.	Dis. Days.	Dividends.
1st N. New Haven,	500,000	100	M. Th.	
2d N. New Haven,	1,000,000	100	M. Th.	10 Jan. July
New Haven Co. N.	350,000	10	M. Th.	9 Apr. Oct.
New London City N.	100,000	100	Tu. F.	
1st N. New Milford,	125,000	100	daily.	5 Jan. July
N. Norwalk,	240,000	100	Tu. F.	6½ Jan. July
1st N. Norwich,	500,000	100	M. Th.	7 May Nov.
2d N. Norwich,	300,000	100	M. F.	7 May Nov.
Norwich N.	220,000	100	Tu. F.	7 June Dec.
N. Pahquioque,	250,000	100	W. S.	10 May Nov.
Pawcatuck N.	85,000	50	M.	7 Dec. June
Pequonnock N.	200,000	100	Tu. F.	8 Jan. July
Phœnix N.	1,000,000	100	M. W. F.	10 Jan. July
1st N. Portland,	150,000	100	M.	7½ Jan. July
1st N. Putnam,	150,000	100	aily.	8 Jan. July
Rockville N.	300,000	100	Tu. F.	6 Jan. July
1st N. Rockville,	200,000	100	Tb.	10 Jan. July
Saybrook N.	100,000	100	M.	8 Jan. July
Shetucket N.	100,000	100	M. Th.	8 June Dec.
1st N. South Norwalk,	200,000	100	Tu.	8 May Nov.
Southport N.	100,000	100	Tu. F.	12 Jan. July
Stafford N.	200,000	100	M.	6 Jan. July
Stamford N.	202,020	30	Tu. F.	12 Mar. Sept.
1st N. Stamford,	200,000	100	Tu. F.	10 May Nov.
State,	400,000	100	M. W. F.	6 Jan. July
1st N. Stonington,	200,000	100	M.	8 Feb. Aug.
1st N. Suffield,	200,000	100	M. Th.	7 May Nov.
Thames N.	1,000,000	100	Tu. F.	8 Mar. Sept.
Thompson N.	100,000	100	Tu.	7 Apr. Oct.
Tolland Co. N.	100,000	100	M.	5 Jan. July
N. Tradesmen,	300,000	100	Tu. F.	5 Jan. July
Uncas N.	300,000	50	M. Th.	6 May Nov.
N. Union,	300,000	100	Tu. F.	7 Jan. July
Waterbury N.	500,000	50	Tu. F.	6 Jan. July
1st N. West Meriden,	500,000	100	Sat.	8 Jan. July
1st N. Westport,	300,000	100	Tu.	7 Jan. July
N. Whaling,	150,000	25	M. Th.	9 Jan. July
Windham N.	100,000	100	W.	
Windham Co. N.	108,300	100	W.	7 Jan. July
1st N. Winsted,	50,000			
Winsted N.,	50,000			
Yale N.	750,000	100	Tu. F.	3 Apr. Oct.

SAVINGS BANKS.

The following Table contains the names of the Savings Banks in the State; the names of the Treasurers; the amount of deposits on the 1st of October, 1881; the dividends (per cent.) for the year ending October 1, 1881, and when paid:

Names and Treas.	Deposits.	Dividends.	
Ansonia, Egbert Bartlett,	$416,074.95	5	Ja. Jy.
Berlin, (Kensington) John Norton,	83,819.17	5	Ja. Jy.
Bridgeport, Chas. P. Porter,	3,056,422.85	4½	Ja. Jy.
Bristol, Miles L. Peck,	558,896.21	5	Ja. Jy.
Brooklyn, Clarence A. Potter,	419,316.43	4	Mh. Sep.
Canaan, Joseph W. Peet,	73,304.76	4	Ap. Oc.
Chelsea, (Norwich,) Geo. D. Coit,	3,301,336.08	4	Mh. Sep.
Chester, Edward C. Hungerford,	75,210.49	4⅓	Feb. Au.
Citizens, (Stamford,) Wm. C. Hoyt,	793,418.89	4½	Ja. Jy.
City, (Bridgep't,) S. M. Middlebrook,	1,852,982.38	4½	Ja. Jy.
City, (Meriden,) C. L. Rockwell,	423,985.70	5½	Ja. Jy.
Colchester, J. N. Adams,	164,038.92	4	Ap. Oc.
Collinsville, Samuel N. Codding,	268,879.90	4	Ja. Jy.
Connecticut, (N. H.,) Elliott H. Morse, Asst. Treas.,	2,776,547.22	4	Ja. Jy.
Cromwell, Dime, S. P. Polley,	96,130.68	4	Ja. Jy.
Danbury, Henry C. Ryder,	1,790,214.67	4	Ap. Oc.
Deep River, Henry R. Wooster,	531,700.85	5	May Nov.
Derby, T. S. Birdsey,	987,750.82	5	Ja. Jy.
Dime, (Hartford,) John W. Welch,	226,840.77	3	Oct.
Dime, (Middletown,) Abel C. Allison,	41,778.64	No Dividends.	
Dime, (Norwich,) J. Hunt Smith,	1,155,046.85	4	May Nov.
Dime, (Thompson,) Hiram Arnold,	376,756.51	4½	Feb. Au.
Dime, (Wallingford,) John Atwater,	89,389.16	5	Ja. Jy.
Dime, (Waterbury,) G. S. Parsons,	694,096.10	4	Ap. Oc.
Dime, (Willimantic,) J. L. Waldron,	511,350.47	4⅓	Ap. Oc.
Eastford, H. B. Burnham,	15,836.82	2	
Essex, Edward W. Redfield,	580,954.05	5	Ja. Jy.
Fairfield Co., (Norwalk) Lester S. Cole,	356,054.16	4	Ap. Oc.
Falls Village, U. H. Minor,	377,527.13	4	Ja. Jy.
Far's & Mech's, (Middletown,) G. N. Ward,	1,240,707.45	4	Feb. Au.
Farmington, Julius Gay,	1,758,866.01	4½	Ja. Jy.
Freestone, (Portland,) Jno. H. Sage,	207,770.68	6	Feb. Aug.
Greenwich, Mark Banks,	103,381.77	3½	Ja. Jy.

Names and Treas.	Deposits.		Dividends
Groton, Abel H. Simmons,	$571,894.93	4	Ap. Oc.
Guilford, Charles Griswold,	117,158.61	4	Ja. Jy.
Higganum, Edward D. Gilbert,	15,220.23	4	Ja. Jy.
Jewett City, H. T. Crosby,	325,794.20	5	Ap. Oc.
Litchfield, H. R. Coit,	744,288.63	5	Ja. Jy.
Mariners, (N. London,) J. E. Darrow,	1,260,728.87	4	Mh. Sep.
Mech's & Far's, (Br'p't,) L. S. Catlin,	232,331.29	4½	Ja. Jy.
Mechanics, (Hartford,) W. W. Jacobs,	1,245,644.78	4	Ja. Jy.
Mechanics, (Winsted,) E. E. Gilman,	304,039.87	5	Ja. Jy.
Meriden, S. H. W. Yale,	1,343,979.20	5	Ja. Jy.
Middletown, F. L. Gleason,	5,223,498.02	4	May Nov.
Milford, P. S. Bristol,	82,333.27	5	Ja. Jy.
Moodus, E. W. Chaffee,	138,141.03	4¼	Ja. Jy.
National, (New Haven,) H. B. Ives,	584,400.49	4	Ja. Jy.
Naugatuck, L. S. Platt,	116,386.35	5	Ja. Jy.
New Britain, W. F. Walker,	1,059,025.07	4	Ja. Jy.
New Canaan, Russell L. Hall,	181,098.99	4	Ja. Jy.
New Haven, J. P. Tuttle,	4,691,789.99	4	Ja. Jy.
New London, J. C. Learned,	3,166,294.47	4½	Ja. Jy.
New Milford, Charles Randall,	619,207.98	4	Ap. Oc.
Newtown, H. T. Nichols,	387,091.33	4½	Ap. Oc.
Norfolk, J. N. Cowles,	126,011.94	4	Ja. Jy.
Norwalk, G. E. Miller,	1,686,929.62	4	Ja. Jy.
Norwich, Costello Lippitt,	7,522,112.91	4	Ja. Jy.
Operatives, (N. Haven) —— ——	16.81	No Dividends.	
Peoples, (Bridgeport,) F. W.Marsh,	1,329,930.84	5	Ja. Jy.
Peoples, (Rockville,) E. S. Henry,	203,396.26	5	Ja. Jy.
Putnam, Jerome Tourtellotte,	728,264.27	4	Ap. Oc.
Ridgefield, D. Smith Gage,	65,764.64	4	Ja. Jy.
Rockville, Lebbeus Bissell,	682,628.84	5	Ap. Oc.
Salisbury, (Lakeville,) T. L. Norton,	464,879.59	4	Ap. Oc.
Society for Savings, (Hartford,) Z. A. Storrs,	8,540,832.11	4	Ju. Dec.
Southington, F. D. Whittlesey,	367,264.03	4½	Ja. Jy.
South Norwalk, John H. Knapp,	199,252.67	4	Ja. Jy.
Southport, O. H. Perry,	515,701.28	4	Ja. Jy.
Stafford, R. S. Hicks,	395,999.41	5	Ja. Jy.
Stafford Springs, Alvarado Howard,	293,891.03	4¼	Ja. Jy.
Stamford, A. A. Holley,	1,400,096.51	5	Ap. Oc.
State, (Hartford,) John W. Stedman,	1,789,905.04	4	Feb. Au.
Stonington, D. B. Spalding,	662,859.37	4	Ju. Dec.
Suffield, Samuel White,	125,553.61	6	Feb. Au.
Thomaston, G. A. Stoughton,	243,660.80	5	Ja. Jy.

Names and Treas.	Deposits.		Dividends.
Tolland, Arthur J. Morton,	118,323.60	2	July.
Union, (Danbury,) L. R. Treadwell,	530,239.49	4	Ap. Oc.
Waterbury, F. J. Kingsbury,	1,882,797.83	5	Feb. Au.
Westport, B. L. Woodward,	87,340.61	4½	Ja. Jy.
Willimantic, H. F. Royce,	620,594.28	4	Ap. Oc.
Windham Co. (Dan'lv'e,) Anth'y Ames,	814,424.41	4	Ap. Oc.
Windsor Locks, A. W. Converse,	57,454.54	4	Ap. Oc.
Winsted, George S. Rowe,	845,204.45	4½	Ja. Jy.
Woodbury, David S. Bull,	167,112.71	4	Ja. Jy.

TRUST COMPANIES.

HARTFORD TRUST CO. Pres., William Faxon; Vice-Pres., Chas. M. Joslyn; Sec. and Treas., R. W. Cutler. Capital, $250,-000.

CONN. TRUST AND SAFE DEPOSIT Co., Hartford. Capital, $300,000. Pres., Edward B. Watkinson; Vice-Pres., John B. Corning; Treas., M. H. Whaples.

SECURITY COMPANY, Hartford. Capital, $200,000; surplus, $10,000. Pres., Robert E. Day; Treas., William L. Matson; Sec., John C. Abbott.

UNITED STATES, Hartford. Capital, $100,000. Pres., Thos. O. Enders; Sec. and Treas., H. L. Bunce.

EQUITABLE, New London. Capital, $1,500,000. Pres., Jonathan Edwards; Vice-Pres., F. B. Elliott; Sec. and Treas., H. R. Bond; Asst. Sec. and Treas., Edwin S. Marston.

MERCHANTS LOAN AND TRUST, Willimantic. Capital, $100,-000. Pres., Wm. C. Jillson; Vice-Pres., Ansel Arnold; Treas., O. H. K. Risley.

MIDDLESEX BANKING Co., Middletown. Pres., Robert N. Jackson; Vice-Pres., M. E. Vinton; Sec., Chas. E. Jackson.

THAMES LOAN AND TRUST, Norwich. Capital, $100,000. Pres., Sec. and Treas., J. Hunt Smith.

THOMPSONVILLE. Capital, $25,000. Pres., R. B. Morrison; Vice-Pres., Lyman A. Upson; Sec. and Treas., Willis Gowdy.

UNION, New Haven. Capital, $100,000. Pres., Henry L. Hotchkiss. Sec. and Treas., William T. Bartlett.

INSURANCE.

INSURANCE.

COMMISSIONER, JOHN W. BROOKS, TORRINGTON, TO JULY 27, 1883; ACTUARY, E. A. STEDMAN; CLERK, LUTHER BRONSON.

FIRE INSURANCE COMPANIES.

HARTFORD. Capital, $1,250,000. Pres., George L. Chase; Sec., C. B. Whiting.

ÆTNA. (Hartford.) Capital, $3,000,000. Surplus, $4,000,000. Pres., Lucius J. Hendee; Sec., J. Goodnow; Asst. Sec., Wm. B. Clark; Gen. Agent, E. J. Bassett.

CONNECTICUT. (Hartford.) Capital, $1,000,000. (Large surplus.) Pres., J. D. Browne; Sec., Charles R. Burt; Asst. Sec., L. W. Clarke.

FAIRFIELD. (South Norwalk.) Capital, $200,000. Pres., Winfield S. Hanford; Vice-Pres., Tallmadge Baker; Sec. and Treas., Henry R. Turner; Asst. Sec., A. L. Frisby.

MERIDEN. Capital, $200,000. Pres., L. W. Clarke; V.-Pres., Eli Butler; Sec., E. B. Cowles; Treas., A. Chamberlain, Jr.

NATIONAL. (Hartford.) Capital, $600,000. Pres., Mark Howard; Sec., James Nichols.

NORWALK. Capital, $50,000. Pres., William C. Street; Sec., George R. Cowles; Treas., Samuel Lynes.

ORIENT. (Hartford.) Capital, $500,000. Pres., S. C. Preston; Vice-Pres., Newton Case; Sec. and Treas., Geo. W. Lester.

PHŒNIX. (Hartford.) Capital, $1,000,000. Pres., Henry Kellogg; V.-Pres., A. W. Jillson; Sec., D. W. C. Skilton; Asst. Sec., G. H. Burdick.

PEOPLE's. (Middletown.) Capital, $101,500. Pres., J. G. Baldwin; Sec. and Treas., S. H. Butler.

SECURITY, (New Haven.) Capital, $200,000. Pres., Charles Peterson; Vice-Pres., Charles S. Leete; Sec., Herbert Mason, Ass't Sec., G. E. Nettleton.

MUTUAL FIRE COMPANIES.

BRISTOL. Pres., Henry W. Gridley; Sec., S. R. Gridley.

CONNECTICUT. (West Meriden.) Pres., Joel H. Guy; Vice-

Pres., Chas. Parker; Sec., Jas. K. Guy; Treas., C. L. Rockwell.

DANBURY. Pres., Fred'k S. Wildman; Sec., Wm. S. Peck; Treas., Roger Averill.

FARMINGTON VALLEY. Pres., Augustus Ward; Sec. and Treas., Richard H. Gay.

FARMERS. (Suffield.) Pres., Samuel White; Sec. and Treas., W. E. Burbank.

FARMERS. (Woodbury.) Pres., Walter S. Curtiss; Sec. and Treas., David S. Hull.

GREENWICH. Pres., Thomas A. Mead; Sec., John Dayton; Treas., Odle C. Knapp.

HARTFORD COUNTY. Pres. and Treas., Wm E. Sugden; Sec. Wm. A. Erwing.

HARWINTON. Pres., Charles S. Barber; Sec. and Treas., Addison Webster.

LITCHFIELD. Pres., Abijah Catlin; Sec., Charles Adams; Treas., George C. Woodruff.

MADISON. Pres., George Dowd; Sec. and Treas., A. M. Dowd.

MIDDLESEX MUTUAL ASSURANCE CO. Pres., E. Ackley; Sec., H F. Boardman; Asst. Sec., C. W. Harris; Treas., Jno. N. Camp.

NEW LONDON COUNTY. (Norwich.) Pres., E. F. Parker; Sec., William Roath.

NORWICH MUTUAL ASSURANCE. Pres., —— ——; Sec. and Treas., Asa Backus.

ROCKVILLE. Pres., George Maxwell; Sec., A. T. Bissell; Treas., George Talcott.

STATE MUTUAL. (Hartford.) Pres., Ralph Gillett; Sec., Isaac Cross, Jr.

TOLLAND COUNTY. Cash Assets, $100,000. Pres., Lucius S. Fuller; Sec., John B. Fuller; Treas., E. S. Henry.

WASHINGTON MUTUAL. Pres., S. S. Logan; Sec., George K. Logan.

WINDHAM COUNTY. (Brooklyn.) Pres., David Greenslit; Sec. and Treas., John Palmer.

12

LIFE · COMPANIES.

ÆTNA. (Hartford.) Assets, $25,000,000. Pres., Morgan G. Bulkeley; V.-Pres., J. C. Webster; Actuary, H. W. St. John; Sec., J. L. English; Con. Phys., G. W. Russell.

CHARTER OAK. (Hartford.) Pres., George M. Bartholomew; Sec., Charles E. Willard; Con. Phys., J. C. Jackson; Med. Ex., W. A. M. Wainwright.

CONNECTICUT MUTUAL. (Hartford.) Assets, $49,000,000. Pres., Jacob L. Greene; V.-Pres., E. B. Watkinson; Sec., John M. Taylor; Asst. Sec., Daniel H. Wells.

CONNECTICUT GENERAL, (Hartford.) Assets, $1,400,000. Pres., T. W. Russell; Sec., Fred. V. Hudson.

CONTINENTAL. (Hartford.) Capital, $300,000. Pres., Jas. S. Parsons; Sec., Robt. E. Beecher; Supt. Agencies, H. P. Barton; Actuary, H. R. Morley; Med. Ex., W. M. Hudson.

HARTFORD LIFE AND ANNUITY. Capital, $250,000. Pres., E. H. Crosby; Sec., Stephen Ball; Med. Ex., Irving W. Lyon.

MUTUAL BENEFIT, (Hartford.) Pres, Alfred R. Goodrich; Sec., ——— ———.

PHŒNIX MUTUAL LIFE. (Hartford.) Assets, $10,500,000. Pres., Aaron C. Goodman; V.-Pres., Jonathan B. Bunce; Sec., John M. Holcombe; Con. Phys., A. W. Barrows.

ACCIDENT COMPANIES.

TRAVELERS INSURANCE CO. (Hartford.) (Life and Accident.) Capital, $600,000; Cash Assets, $5,500,000. Pres., J. G. Batterson; Sec., Rodney Dennis; Assist. Sec., John E. Morris; Actuary, George Ellis; Supt. of Agencies, E. V. Preston; Con. Surgeon, G. P. Davis; Surg. and Adjuster, J. B. Lewis.

HARTFORD STEAM BOILER INSPECTION AND INS. Co. Capital, $200,000. Pres., J. M. Allen; V.-Pres., Wm. B. Franklin; Sec., J. B. Pierce.

RAILROADS.

COMMISSIONERS.—George M. Woodruff, Litchfield, 1883; John W. Bacon, Danbury, July 1, 1884; William H. Hayward, July 1, 1885. Clerk, George T. Utley, Hartford.

NEW YORK, NEW HAVEN & HARTFORD.—Pres., George H. Watrous, New York; Vice-Pres'ts., C. P. Clark, E. M. Reed, New

York; Sec., E. I. Sanford, New Haven; Treas., Wm. L. Squire, New York; Supt., N.Y. & N. H. Division, John T. Moody; Supt., Hartford Division, C. S.Davidson; Supt., Shore Line Division, W. H. Stevenson. Directors, Augustus Schell, A. R. Van Nest, Wm. H. Vanderbilt, Wilson G. Hunt, New York; Geo. N. Miller, Southport; Wm. D. Bishop, Nath'l Wheeler, Bridgeport; E. H. Trowbridge, Geo. H. Watrous, E. M. Reed, New Haven; Charles M. Pond, Henry C. Robinson, Hartford; Chester W. Chapin, Springfield.

BOSTON AND NEW YORK AIR LINE.—Pres., H. B. Hammond, N. Y.; Sec., T. L. Watson, Bridgeport; Treas., D. B. Hatch, N. Y.; Supt., Jos. H. Franklin, New Haven. Directors, S. S. Sands, James D. Smith, E. H. Bonner, D. B. Hatch, N. Y.; T. L. Watson, Bridgeport; H. G. Lewis, Simeon E. Baldwin, New Haven; John N. Camp, Middletown; Silas F. Loomer, H. Walter Webb.

COLCHESTER RAILWAY, (Colchester to Turnerville.)—Pres., Erastus S. Day, Colchester; Sec., Ira A. Dinsmore, Colchester; Treas., Giles G. Wickwire, New London. Directors, E. S. Day, W. S. Curtis, Leander Chapman, Colchester; Giles G. Wickwire, New London; G.G. Standish, Willimantic.

CONNECTICUT CENTRAL, (Hartford to Springfield.)—Pres. and Treas., D. D. Warren, Springfield; Vice-Pres., Francis Gowdy, Melrose; Sec., T. M. Maltbie, Hartford; Directors, D. D. Warren, Wm. Birnie, James W. Perkins, Boston; Francis Gowdy, John M. Stiles, J. A. Thompson, Melrose; Simeon E. Baldwin, New Haven; N. S. Osborn, Lemuel Stoughton, East Windsor Hill; H. P. Stedman, East Hartford; E. Prickett, Hazardville; E. S. Henry, Rockville.

HARTFORD AND CONNECTICUT WESTERN, (Hartford to Millerton.)—Pres., Wm. L. Gilbert, West Winsted; Vice-Pres., C. T. Hillyer, Hartford; Sec. and Treas., E. R. Beardsley, Hartford. Supt., John F. Jones. Directors, A. H. Holley, Salisbury; Wm. H. Barnum, Lime Rock; Chas. T. Hillyer, L. B. Merriam, T. M. Allyn, H. S. Barbour, John F. Jones, Hartford; Wm. L. Gilbert, George Dudley, West Winsted; Lyman Dunning, East Canaan; Frederick Miles, Chapinville; E. T. Butler, Norfolk; Joseph Toy, Simsbury.

DANBURY AND NORWALK.—Pres., James W. Hyatt, Norwalk. Sec. and Treas., Harvey Williams; Supt., Lewis W. Sandiforth, Danbury. Directors, R. P. Flower, N. Y.: Wm. C.

Street, James W. Hyatt, Frederick St. John Lockwood, Norwalk; Edwin Sherwood, Southport; Orrin Benedict, Bethel; L. P. Hoyt, David P. Nichols, E. S. Tweedy, Nathan M. George, Danbury; Henry McHarg, Ridgfield.

HARTFORD AND CONNECTICUT VALLEY, (Hartford to Saybrook.)—Pres., and Supt., Samuel Babcock, Hartford; Vice-Pres., Gurdon Bill, Springfield, Mass.; Sec. and Treas., C. H. Smith, Jr., Hartford; Directors, Samuel Babcock, Henry Kellogg, Richard D. Hubbard, James J. Goodwin, Charles M. Beach, Franklin Chamberlin, Hartford; Chester W. Chapin, Gurdon Bill, Springfield; D. C. Spencer, Old Saybroook.

HOUSATONIC, (Bridgeport to Pittsfield, Mass.)—Pres., Wm. H. Barnum, Lime Rock; Vice-Pres., David S. Draper; Sec. and Treas., C. K. Averill; Supt., L. B. Stillson—all of Bridgeport; Directors, Edward Leavitt, Samuel Willetts, John B. Peck, New York; William H. Barnum, Lime Rock; George W. Peet, Falls Village; A. B. Mygatt, New Milford; Horace Nichols, David S. Draper, Wm. D. Bishop, New York.

NAUGATUCK, (Bridgeport to Winsted.)—Pres., E. F. Bishop; Sec. and Treas., Horace Nichols; Supt., George W. Beach—all of Bridgeport. Directors, E. F. Bishop, W. D. Bishop, Russell Tomlinson, Bridgeport; Royal M. Bassett, Birmingham; Henry Bronson, John B. Robertson, New Haven; J. G. Wetmore, Winsted, A. L. Dennis, Newark, N. J.; F. J. Kingsbury, Waterbury.

NEW CANAAN, (Stamford to New Canaan.)—Pres., S. Y. St. John, New Canaan; Vice-Pres., Joseph B. Hoyt, Stamford; Sec., A. F. Jones; Treas., George F. Lockwood; Supt., Wm. St. John—all of New Canaan. Directors, Selleck Y. St. John, Albert S. Comstock, William G. Webb, William E. Raymond, Edwin Hoyt, New Canaan; Joseph B. Hoyt, Stamford; Willard Parker, New York; S. B. St. John, Hartford.

NEW HAVEN AND DERBY, (New Haven to Ansonia.)—Pres., J. H. Bartholomew, Stony Creek; Vice-Pres., Charles L. English; Sec., F. E. Harrison; Treas., Charles Atwater; Supt., E. S. Quintard—all of New Haven. Directors, Henry S. Dawson, Charles L. English, N. D. Sperry, Joel A. Sperry, Charles Atwater, Isaac Anderson, New Haven; George W. Shelton, Edward N. Shelton, Thomas L. Cornell, George P. Cowles, Birmingham; J. H. Bartholomew, Stony Creek; Thomas Wallace, Franklin Farrell, Ansonia. City Directors, John B. Robertson, H. F. Holcomb.

NEW HAVEN AND NORTHAMPTON, (New Haven, Conn., to Conway Junction, Mass.)—Pres., Charles N. Yeamans, New Haven; Supt., Carl A. Goodnow, New Haven. Directors, Charles N. Yeamans, A. L. Kidston, M. G. Elliott, George J. Brush, Daniel Trowbridge, George H. Watrous, New Haven; William D. Bishop, Bridgeport; Charles M. Pond, Hartford; H. G. Knight, East Hampton, Mass.

NEW LONDON NORTHERN, (New London Conn., to Brattleboro, Vt.)—Pres. and Treas., Robert Coit, New London. Sec., J. A. Southard; New London; Supt., Geo. W. Bentley, New London. Directors, W.W. Billings, Wm. H. Barns, Benj. Stark, A. Brandegee, R. Coit, J. N. Harris, New London; C. H. Osgood, Norwich; Wm. H. Hill, Boston; Wm. Allen Butler, New York; Thomas Ramsdell, Windham; James A. Rumrill, Springfield, Mass.

NEW YORK AND NEW ENGLAND.—Pres., James H. Wilson; Sec., James W. Perkins; Treas., George B. Phippen; Supt. East Div., O. M. Shepard—all of Boston. West Div., J. C. Rawn, Hartford. Providence Div., L. W. Palmer, Providence. Woonsocket Div., O. M. Shepard, Boston. Directors, Jesse Metcalf, Legrand B. Cannon, Eustice C. Fitz, Cyrus W. Field, Jonas H. French, Jay Gould, R. Suydam Grant, William T. Hart, Henry L. Higginson, Hugh J. Jewett, Frederick J. Kingsbury, George B. Roberts, Russell Sage, James H. Wilson.

NEW YORK, PROVIDENCE AND BOSTON (New London to Providence, R. I.)—Pres., Samuel D. Babcock; Vice-Pres., David S. Babcock; Treas., Henry Morgan—all of New York; Sec., A. R. Longley Jr.; Engineer, A. S. Mathews, Stonington; Supt, J. B. Gardiner, Providence, R. I. Directors, Samuel D. Babcock, David S. Babcock, Wm. F. Cary, Jr., Henry Morgan, James B. Johnston, George M. Miller, New York; N. F. Dixon, Westerly, R. I.; John A. Burnham, Boston; Charles H. Salisbury, Providence; Henry Howard, Coventry, R. I.; A. S. Mathews, Stonington.

NORWICH AND WORCESTER.—Pres., F. H. Dewey, Worcester, Mass.; Treas., George L. Perkins; Sec., E. T. Clapp; Supt., P. St. M. Andrews—all of Norwich. Directors, J. F. Slater, Norwich; F. H. Dewey, Geo. W. Gill, Charles W. Smith, E. L. Davis, Worcester; W. F. Weld, Phila.; W. Bayard Cutting, N. Y.

RIDGEFIELD AND NEW YORK.—Pres., Ellwood Burdsall, Port Chester, N. Y.; Vice-Pres., Wm. J. Mead, Greenwich;

Sec., Epbraim Sours, Port Chester, N. Y.; Treas., Hiram K. Scott, Ridgefield.

ROCKVILLE (Vernon Depot to Rockville).—Pres., George Maxwell, Rockville; Sec'y and Treas., J.C.Hammond, Jr.; Supt., A. H. Putnam. Directors, George Maxwell, Crosley Fitton, H. L. James, J. C. Hammond, Jr., George Talcott, Rockville.

SHEPAUG (Litchfield to Hawleyville).—Pres., Henry W. Buel; Vice-Pres. and Treas., Henry R. Coit; Sec., Wm. Deming; Supt., Edwin McNeil—all of Litchfield. Directors, Henry W. Buel, H. R. Coit, Wm. Deming, L. W. Wessells, Dorsey Neville, H. O. Morse, Asahel H. Morse, Edwin McNeil, Litchfield.

SHORE LINE (New Haven to New London).—Leased to and operated by New York, New Haven & Hartford R. R. Co. Pres., S. B. Chittenden, New York; Vice-Pres., Samuel Hemingway, New Haven; Sec. and Treas., Wilbur F. Day, New Haven. Supt., W. H. Stevenson, New Haven. Directors, S. B. Chittenden, Chas. G. Landon, New York; William T. Bartlett, Samuel Hemingway, E. H. Trowbridge, H. L. Hotchkiss, New Haven.

SOUTH MANCHESTER (Manchester to South Manchester).— Pres., Frank W. Cheney; Sec. and Gen. Manager, Richard O. Cheney; Treas., Charles · S. Cheney. Directors, Ralph Cheney, Rush Cheney, Frank Cheney, Frank W. Cheney, Richard O. Cheney—all of South Manchester.

WATERTOWN AND WATERBURY.—Pres., Wm. D. Bishop, Bridgeport; Sec. and Treas., Leman W. Cutler, Watertown. Directors, Wm. D. Bishop, Russel Tomlinson, Horace Nichols, Bridgeport; Owen B. King, Leman W. Cutler, Merrit Heminway, Henry Merriman, Watertown; George W. Beach, Fred'k J. Kingsbury, Waterbury; Royal M. Basset, Derby.

Capital stock issued, $46,348,350. Total debt, $24,643,143. Gross earnings, $13,803,415. Net earnings, $5,228,127. Miles of road in the State, 1,269. Total cost of construction and equipments, $81,305,241. Passengers carried in 1881, 13,205,826. Dividends paid in 1881, $2,575,071. Operating Expenses, $8,-575,288.

GOVERNMENT OF THE UNITED STATES.

PRESIDENT, CHESTER A. ARTHUR, N. Y., Salary, $50,000
FRED'K T. FRELINGHUYSEN, N. J., Secretary of State, 8,000
CHARLES J. FOLGER, N. Y., Secretary of the Treasury, 8,000
ROBERT T. LINCOLN, Illinois, Secretary of War, 8,000
WILLIAM H. HUNT, La., Secretary of the Navy, 8,000
TIMOTHY O. HOWE, Wisconsin, Postmaster-General, 8,000
BENJAMIN H. BREWSTER, Penn., Attorney-General, 8,000
S. J. KIRKWOOD, Missouri, Secretary of the Interior, 8,000

THE JUDICIARY.

SUPREME COURT OF THE UNITED STATES.

Meets first Monday in December, at Washington.

CHIEF JUSTICE, Morrison R. Waite, Ohio; salary, $10,500.
JUDGES, Samuel F. Miller, of Iowa; Stephen J. Field, of
California; William B. Woods of Georgia; Joseph P. Bradley,
of New Jersey; Ward Hunt, of New York; John M. Harlan, of
Kentucky; Stanley Matthews, of Ohio; Horace Gray, of Mass.;
salary, $10,000.

Clerk, JAS. H. McKENNEY, Washington, D. C.
Marshal, J. G. NICOLAY, Washington, D. C.
Reporter, Wm. T. Otto.

XLVI. CONGRESS.

SENATE.

PRESIDENT *pro-tempore*, David Davis, Illinois.

SECRETARY,

The dates opposite the names of the Senators are those when
they entered the Senate, and when their present terms expire.

ALABAMA.		CONNECTICUT.	
John T. Morgan,	1877-83	Orville H. Platt,	1879-85
James L. Pugh,	1880-85	Joseph R. Hawley,	1881-87
ARKANSAS.		DELAWARE.	
Augustus H. Garland,	1877-83	Eli Saulsbury,	1871-83
James D. Walker,	1879-85	Thos. F. Bayard,	1869-87
CALIFORNIA.		FLORIDA.	
John F. Miller,	1887	Charles W. Jones,	1875-87
James T. Farley,	1879-85	Wilkinson Call,	1879-85
COLORADO.		GEORGIA.	
Henry M. Teller,	1876-83	Benjamin H. Hill,	1877-83
Nathaniel P. Hill,	1879-85	Jos. E. Brown,	1880-85

ILLINOIS.		NEW HAMPSHIRE.	
David Davis,	1877-83	Edward H. Rollins,	1877-83
John A. Logan,	1879-85	Henry W. Blair,	1879-85
INDIANA.		NEW JERSEY.	
Daniel W. Voorhees,	1879-85	John R. McPherson,	1877-83
Benjamin Harrison,	1881-87	Wm. J. Sewell,	1881-87
IOWA.		NEW YORK.	
James W. McDill,	1881-83	Elbridge G. Lapham,	1881-85
William B. Allison,	1879-85	Warner Miller,	1881-87
KANSAS.		NORTH CAROLINA.	
Preston B. Plumb,	1877-83	Matthew W. Ransom,	1872-83
John J. Ingalls,	1879-85	Zebulon B. Vance,	1879-85
KENTUCKY.		OHIO.	
James B. Beck,	1877-83	George H. Pendleton,	1879-85
John S. Williams,	1879-85	John Sherman,	1881-87
LOUISIANA.		OREGON.	
Wm. Pitt Kellogg,	1877-83	Lafayette Grover,	1877-83
Benjamin F. Jonas,	1879-85	James H. Slater,	1879-85
MAINE.		PENNSYLVANIA.	
Wm. P. Frye,	1881-83	J. Donald Cameron,	1879-85
Eugene Hale,	1881-87	John I. Mitchell,	1881-87
MARYLAND.		RHODE ISLAND.	
James B. Groome,	1879-85	Henry B. Anthony,	1859-83
Arthur P. Gorman,	1881-87	Nelson W. Aldrich,	1881-87
MASSACHUSETTS.		SOUTH CAROLINA.	
George F. Hoar,	1877-83	Matthew C. Butler,	1877-83
Henry L. Dawes,	1881-87	Wade Hampton,	1879-85
MICHIGAN.		TENNESSEE.	
Thomas W. Ferry,	1871-83	Isham G. Harris,	1877-83
Omar D. Conger,	1881-87	Howell E. Jackson,	1881-87
MINNESOTA.		TEXAS.	
William Windom,	1871-83	Samuel B. Maxey,	1875-87
S. J. R. McMillan,	1881-87	Richard Coke,	1877-83
MISSISSIPPI.		VERMONT.	
John Z. George,	1881-87	Geo. F. Edmunds,	1866-87
L. Q. C. Lamar,	1877-83	Justin S. Morrill, -	1879-85
MISSOURI.		VIRGINIA.	
George G. Vest,	1879-85	John W. Johnston,	1870-83
Francis M. Cockrell,	1881-87	William Mahone,	1881-87
NEBRASKA.		WEST VIRGINIA.	
Alvin Saunders,	1877-83	Henry G. Davis,	1871-83
Chas. H. Van Wyck,	1881-87	Johnson N. Camden,	1881-87
NEVADA.		WISCONSIN.	
John P. Jones,	1879-85	Angus Cameron,	1875-85
James G. Fair,	1881-87	Philetus Sawyer,	1881-87

HOUSE OF REPRESENTATIVES.

SPEAKER, J. Warren Keifer, Ohio. *

CLERK, Edward McPherson, Pennsylvania

THE HOUSE consists of 293 Members, and 8 Territorial Delegates who have no vote.

ALABAMA. 1, Thomas H. Herndon; 2, Hileary A. Herbert; 3, William C. Oates; 4, Charles M. Shelley; 5, Thomas Williams; 6, Goldsmith W. Hewitt, 7, William H. Forney; 8, Joseph Wheeler.

ARKANSAS. 1, Poindexter Dunn; 2, James K. Jones, 3, Jordan E. Cravens; 4, Thomas M. Gunter.

CALIFORNIA. 1, W. S. Rosecrans; 2, Horace F. Page; 3, Campbell P. Berry; 4, Romualdo Pacheco.

COLORADO. 1, James B. Belford.

CONNECTICUT. 1, John R. Buck; 2, James Phelps; 3, John T. Wait; 4, Frederick Miles.

DELAWARE. 1, Edward L. Martin.

FLORIDA. 1, R. H. M. Davidson; 2, Jesse J. Finley.

GEORGIA. 1, George R. Black; 2, Henry G. Turner; 3, Philip Cook; 4, Hugh Buchanan; 5, N. J. Hammond; 6, Jas. H. Blount; 7, Judson C. Clements; 8, Alexander H. Stephens; 9, Emory Speer.

ILLINOIS. 1, William Aldrich; 2, George R. Davis; 3, Chas. B. Farwell; 4, John C. Sherwin; 5, Robert M. A. Hawk; 6, Thomas J. Henderson; 7, William Cullen; 8, Lewis E. Payson; 9, John H. Lewis; 10, Benjamin F. Marsh; 11, James W. Singleton; 12, Wm. M. Springer; 13, Dietrich C. Smith; 14, Joseph G. Cannon; 15, S. W. Moulton; 16, William A. J. Sparks; 17, Wm. R. Morrison; 18, John R. Thomas; 19, R. W. Townshend.

INDIANA. 1, William Heilman; 2, Thomas R. Cobb; 3, S. M. Stockslager; 4, W. S. Holman; 5, Courtney C. Matson; 6, Thomas M. Browne; 7, Stanton J. Peelle; 8, Robert B. F. Pierce; 9, Godlove S. Orth; 10, Mark L. Demotte; 11, Geo. W. Steele; 12, Walpole G. Colerick; 13, Wm. H. Calkins.

IOWA. 1, Moses A. McCoid; 2, Sewall S. Farwell; 3, Thomas Updegraff; 4, Nathaniel C. Deering; 5, William G. Thompson; 6, Madison E. Cutts; 7, John A. Kasson; 8, Wm. P. Hepburn; 9, Cyrus C. Carpenter.

KANSAS. 1, John A. Anderson; 2, Dudley C. Haskell; 8, Thomas Ryan.

KENTUCKY. 1, Oscar Turner; 2, James A. McKenzie; 3, John W. Caldwell; 4, J. Proctor Knott; 5, Albert S. Willis; 6, John G. Carlisle; 7, J. C. S. Blackburn; 8, Philip B. Thompson, Jr.; 9, John D. White; 10, Elijah C. Phister.

LOUISIANA. 1, Randall L. Gibson; 2, E. John Ellis; 3, Chester B. Darrell; 4, Nathan C. Blanchard; 5, J. Floyd King; 6, Edward W. Robertson.

MAINE. 1, Thomas B. Reed; 2, Nelson Dingley; 3, S. D. Lindsey; 4, George W. Ladd; 5, Thompson H. Murch.

MARYLAND. 1, George W. Covington; 2, J. Fred. C. Talbott; 3, F. S. Hoblitzell; 4, Robert M. McLane; 5, Andrew G. Chapman; 6, Milton G. Urner.

MASSACHUSETTS. 1, William W. Crapo; 2, Benj. W. Harris; 3, A. A. Ranney; 4, Leopold Morse; 5, Zelwyn Z. Bowman; 6, Eben F. Stone; 7, William A. Russell; 8, John W. Candler; 9, William W. Rice; 10, Amasa Norcross; 11, George D. Robinson.

MICHIGAN. 1, Henry W. Lord; 2, Edwin Willits; 3, Edward S. Lacy; 4, Julius C. Burrows; 5, George W. Webber; 6, Oliver L. Spaulding; 7, John T. Rich; 8, Roswell G. Horr; 9, Jay A. Hubbell.

MINNESOTA. 1, Mark H. Dunnell; 2, Horace B. Stratt; 3, William D. Washburn.

MISSISSIPPI. 1, H. L. Muldrow; 2, Van H. Manning; 3, Hernando D. Money; 4, Otho R. Singleton; 5, Charles E. Hooker; 6, James R. Chalmers.

MISSOURI. 1, Martin L. Clardy; 2, Thomas Allen; 3, Richard G. Frost; 4, Lowndes H. Davis; 5, Richard P. Bland; 6, Ira S. Hazeltine; 7, Theron N. Rice; 8, Robert T. Van Horn; 9, Nicholas Ford; 10, J. H. Burrows; 11, John B. Clark, Jr.; 12, Wm. H. Hatch; 13, Aylett H. Buckner.

NEBRASKA. 1, Edward K. Valentine.

NEVADA. 1, George W. Cassidy.

NEW HAMPSHIRE. 1, Joshua G. Hall; 2, James F. Briggs; 3. Ossian Ray.

NEW JERSEY. 1, George M. Robeson; 2, John H. Brewer; 3, Miles Ross; 4, Henry S. Harris; 5, John Hill; 6, Phineas Jones; 7, Aug. A. Hardenbergh.

NEW YORK. 1, Perry Belmont; 2, Wm. E. Robinson; 3, J. Hyatt Smith; 4, Archibald M. Bliss; 5, Benjamin Wood; 6, Samuel S. Cox; 7, Philip H. Dugro; 8, Anson G. McCook; 9, R. P. Flower; 10, Abram S. Hewitt; 11, John Hardy; 12, Waldo Hutchins; 13, John H. Ketcham; 14, Lewis Beach; 15, Thomas Cornell; 16, Michael M. Nolan; 17, Walter A. Wood; 18, John Hammond; 19, Abraham X. Parker; 20, George West; 21, Ferris Jacobs, Jr.; 22, C. R. Skinner; 23, Cyrus D. Prescott; 24, Joseph Mason: 25, Frank Hiscock; 26, John H. Camp; 27, J. W. Wadsworth; 28, Jeremiah W. Dwight; 29, David P. Richardson; 30, John Van Voorhis; 31, Richard Crowley; 32, Jonathan L. Scoville; 33, Henry Van Aernam.

NORTH CAROLINA. 1, Louis C. Latham; 2, Orlando Hubbs; 3, J. W. Shackleford; 4, Walter R. Cox; 5, Alfred M. Scales: 6, Clement Dowd; 7, Robert F. Armfield; 8, Robert B. Vance.

OHIO. 1, Benjamin Butterworth; 2, Thomas L. Young; 3, Henry L. Morey; 4, Emanuel Shultz; 5, Benjamin Le Fevre; 6, James M. Ritchie; 7, John P. Leedom; 8, Joseph W. Keifer; 9, James S. Robinson; 10, John B. Rice; 11, Henry S. Neal; 12, George L. Converse; 13 Gibson Atherton; 14, George W. Geddes; 15, Rufus R. Dawes; 16, Jonathan T. Updegraff; 17, William McKinley Jr.; 18, Addison S. McClure; 19, Ezra B. Taylor; 20, Amos Townsend.

OREGON. 1, M. C. George.

PENNSYLVANIA. 1, Henry H. Bingham; 2, Chas. O'Neill; 3, Samuel J. Randall; 4, Wm. D. Kelley; 5, Alfred C. Harmer; 6, William Ward; 7, William Godshalk; 8, Daniel Ermentrout; 9, A. Herr Smith; 10, William Mutchler; 11, Robert Klotz; 12, Joseph A. Scranton; 13, Charles N. Barnum; 14, Samuel F. Barr; 15, Cornelius C. Jadwin; 16, Robert J. C. Walker; 17, Jacob M. Campbell; 18, Horatio G. Fisher; 19, Frank Beltzhoover; 20, Andrew G. Curtin; 21, Morgan R. Wise; 22, Russell Errett; 23, Thomas M. Bayne; 24, W. S. Shallenberger; 25, James Mosgrove; 26, Samuel H. Miller; 27, Lewis F. Watson.

RHODE ISLAND. 1, Henry J. Spooner; 2, Jonathan Chase.

SOUTH CAROLINA. 1, John S. Richardson; 2. S. Dibble; 3, D. Wyatt Aiken; 4, John H. Evins; 5, Geo. D. Tillman.

TENNESSEE. 1, A. H. Pettibone; 2, Leonidas C. Houk; 3, George G. Dibrell; 4, Benton McMillin; 5, Richard Warner; 6, John F. House; 7. W. C. Whitthorne; 8, John D. C. Atkins; 9, Charles B. Simonton; 10, Wm. R. Moore.

TEXAS. 1, John H. Reagan; 2, David R. Culberson; 3, Olin Wellborn; 4, Roger Q. Mills; 5, George W. Jones; 6, Columbus Upson.

VERMONT. 1, Charles H. Joyce; 2, James M. Tyler; 3, Wm. W. Grout.

VIRGINIA. 1, George T. Garrison; 2, John F. Dezendorf; 3, George D. Wise; 4, Joseph Jorgensen; 5, George C. Cabell; 6, John R. Tucker; 7, John Paul; 8, John S. Barbour; 9, Abram Fulkerson.

WEST VIRGINIA. 1, Benjamin Wilson; 2, John Blair Hoge; 3, John E. Kenna.

WISCONSIN. 1, Chas. G. Williams; 2, Lucien B. Caswell; 3, George C. Hazelton; 4, Peter V. Deuster; 5, Edward S. Bragg; 6, Richard Guenther; 7, H. L. Humphrey; 8, Thaddeus C. Pond.

TERRITORIAL DELEGATES.

ARIZONA. G. H. Ouray.
DAKOTA. R. F. Pettigrew.
IDAHO. George Ainslee.
MONTANA. Martin Maginnis.
NEW MEXICO. T. Luna.
UTAH.
WASHINGTON. Thomas H. Brents.
WYOMING. M. E. Post.

U. S. INTERNAL REVENUE.

1ST DIST., HARTFORD, TOLLAND, NEW LONDON, AND WINDHAM COUNTIES.

Collector, Joseph Selden, Norwich. Deputies, A. Irving Royce, Norwich; Wm. W. House, H. S. House, Hartford; Wm. H. Fuller, Suffield; George R. Case, Norwich. Gaugers, Alfred E. Sheldon, Hartford; Frederick A. King, Thompsonville; W. A. Stocking, Simsbury; David B. Hale, Collinsville; Samuel B. Knapp, Norwich. Store-keepers, E. T. Spooner, Joseph Dawson, Warehouse Point; Josiah F. Williston; H. D. Adams, Hartford. Clerk, F. E. Griffin, Norwich.

2D DIST., NEW HAVEN, MIDDLESEX, FAIRFIELD, AND LITCH-
FIELD COUNTIES.

Collector, David F. Hollister, Bridgeport. Deputies, F. E.
Barlow, Henry C. Lemmon; Clerk, William H. Kelsey, Bridge-
port; Henry L. Allen, West Winsted; John H. Rowland, H. J.
Kellogg, New Haven; John B. Wright, Clinton; W. R. Willi-
ams, Waterbury. Gaugers, John A. Boughton, Bridgeport; C.
G. G. Merrill, New Haven; Carlos P. Merwin, New Milford;
David B. Hale, Collinsville. Store-Keeper and Gauger, Bur-
ton G. Warner, New Haven.

CUSTOM HOUSE OFFICERS.

FAIRFIELD District, west of Housatonic River to State line.
—Collector, Julius S. Hanover, Bridgeport; Deputy Collector,
Inspector, etc., James H. Porter. Night Inspector, Samuel W.
Hodge, Bridgeport.

Inspector for Norwalk, Gould D. Jennings; for Stamford,
Geo. E. Scofield. Pilots, Bridgeport Harbor, S. A. McNeil,
John H. Plumb; Housatonic River, Rufus Buddington; Nor-
walk Harbor, Z. Rowland. Pilots of Tug-Boats, Bridgeport,
Wm. Hayes; Norwalk, Peter Decker.

MIDDLETOWN District, extending from Springfield, Mass.,
to Clinton, Conn.--Collector, Aug. Putnam, Middletown. Special
Deputy Collector and Inspector, Geo. W. Burke, Middletown.
Janitor, George S. Parmelee, Middletown. Storekeeper, Arthur
E. Howard, Hartford.

Hartford, Deputy Collector, Joseph F. Field; Inspector,
Samuel B. Dickinson, Saybrook Point.

NEW HAVEN District, extending from Madison to the Hou-
satonic River.—Collector, Cyrus Northrop. Deputy Collector,
Edmund Pendleton. Clerks, Jesse Peck, C. S. Bunnell, Edwin
Case. Weighers, Gaugers and Measurers, S. R. Crampton, John
W. Lane. Inspectors, E. D. S. Goodyear, H. O. Beach, W. R.
Lloyd, George S. Allen. Night Inspector, Edward Coe. Light-
house Keepers, Elizur Thompson, Gilbert A. W. Ford. Mes-
senger, Theodore Knipping. Janitor, George S. Loveland.
Boatsman, Tunis Bouns.

Inspector for Branford and Sachem's Head, Grant Smith.

Inspector for Derby and Milford, Lucius Gilbert.

NEW LONDON District.—Collector, John A. Tibbits. **Deputy** Collector and Inspector, C. G. Sistare. Inspectors, Wm. R. Austin, New London; Geo. W. Geer, John Bishop. Norwich; Boatman and Messenger, John W. Brown. Janitor, Anthony Jerome. Physician, Marine Hospital, John G. Stanton. Steamboat Inspectors, Elisha P. Beckwith, Philo B. Hovey, New London.

Pilots, Thames River, and Sound, Clark S. Rogers, B. W. Harris, Leonard Smith, Perkins Harris; Norwich, James M. Holt, Henry G. Roath, Edward Smith, Thomas Comstock; Lyme, John O. Miner.

STONINGTON District.—Collector, George Hubbard. Deputy Collectors and Inspectors, William Williams, Stonington; George D. Cross, Pawcatuck, Conn., and Westerly, R. I. Boat-Keeper, Stephen-D. Merret, Stonington.

. Deputy Collector for Mystic Bridge, Mystic River and Noank, Asa Fish.

POST-OFFICE DEPARTMENT.

Postage on Letters, prepaid by Stamps, 3 cents each ½ oz. or fraction thereof, to all parts of the country. Drop and Local letters, at offices of free delivery by carrier, 2 cents per ½ oz; at other offices 1 ct. Postal Cards, 1 cent each.

Registered letters, 10 cents each, in addition to the regular postage.

SECOND-CLASS MATTER.

Newspapers and periodicals, issued at stated intervals, as frequently as four times a year, including sample copies from an office of publication, or from a news agency to actual subscribers, 2 cents for each lb. or fraction thereof; one copy to each actual subscriber residing in the county where printed and published, free; but cannot be delivered at letter carrier offices, unless postage is paid at 2 cents a lb.

Newspapers (excepting weeklies), and periodicals not exceeding two ounces, 1 cent each; and periodicals, over two ounces, two cents each, when delivered from carrier office.

THIRD-CLASS MATTER.

Books (of any weight, if single), transient newspapers and periodicals, circulars, and other matter wholly in print, proof-sheets, corrected proof-sheets, and manuscript copy accompanying the same, date, and name of the addressed and of the sender of circulars, and correction of mere typographical errors. On matter of this class (and fourth class) name or address of sender on wrapper, or matter with word "from" preceding the same, and on books a simple manuscript dedication or inscription on cover or blank leaf, 1 cent for each two ounces or fraction thereof.

FOURTH-CLASS MATTER.

Metals, minerals, merchandise, samples of ores, blank cards, flexible patterns, seeds, cuttings, bulbs, roots, and all matter not in 1st, 2d, and 3d class, that will not injure the mails or the person, not over four pounds for each package, one cent for each ounce or fraction thereof.

Postage for each ½ oz.: to Europe, 5 cts.; to Canada, pre- . paid, 3 cents.

POST-OFFICES AND POSTMASTERS.

Abington,	R. L. Bullard	Bridgeport,	J. W. Knowlton
Andover,	E. Hall	Bridgewater,	George Lyon
Ansonia,	Charles E. Bristol	Bristol,	Silas M. Norton
Ashford,	W. M. Whitaker	Broad Brook,	F. M. Gowdy
Avon,	Oliver T. Bishop	Brookfield,	Andrew Northrop
Bakersville,	S. N. Pettibone	Brookfield Centre,	A. Somers
Ball's Pond,	Amzi H. Pearce	Brooklyn,	Lewis Searls
Banksville,	George Derby	Brooks' Vale,	Sam'l H. Brooks
Baltic,	Mayden Hayes	Buckingham,	C. J. Loomer
Bantam Falls,	S. E. Crossman	Buckland,	H. G. Parker
Barkhamsted,	Dwight S. Case	Burnside,	Moses Chandler
Beacon Falls,	John Wolfe	Burlington,	L. F. Turner
Berlin,	H. L. Porter	Burrville,	John M. Burr
Bethany,	Mary E. Hitchcock	Campbell's Mills,	G. P. Douglas
Bethel,	Amos Woodman	Campville,	Sarah M. Leonard
Bethlehem,	Herbert S. Jackson	Canaan,	A. T. Roraback
Birmingham,	Wm. J. Clark	Canaan Valley,	Miles Rockwell
Black Rock,	J. C. Smith	Cannon's Station,	A. M. Reed
Bloomfield,	Henry W. Rowley	Canterbury,	H. F. Williams
Bolton,	John A. Alvord	Canton,	C. M. Woodford
Bozrah,	George O. Stead	Canton Cnt'r,	Wm. H. Richards'n
Bozrahville,	Jas. M. Peckham	Central Vill.,	Jas. M. Wilcox
Branchville,	C. B. Morehouse, jr	Center Brook,	D. W. Spcucer
Branford,	Philo Hall	Center Groton,	Geo. L. Daboll

Center Hill, Mrs. Correl Tiffany
Chapinville,   John McElroy
Chaplin,   J. W. Lincoln
Chatham.   See East Hampton
Cheshire, -   Edwin R. Brown
Chester,   S. A. Wright
Chesterfield, Orrin H. Whiting
Clark's Crs., H.H. Starkweath'r
Clark Falls,   E. P. Chapman
Clinton,   Joseph C. Parker
Clintonville, G. W. Tallmadge
Cobalt,   Rufus D. Tibbals
Colchester,..   Chas. H. Rogers
Cold Spring,   O. S. Botsford
Colebrook,   Reuben Rockwell
Colebrook River,   Geo. S. Ives
Collinsville, Emerson A. Hough
Columbia,   Geo. B. Fuller
Comstock's Bridge, E. M.Brown
Copper Hill,   Wm. D. Viets
Cornwall,   J. W. Beers
Cornwall Bridge, Jas. A. Bierce
Cornwall Hollow, A. F. Palmer
Cos Cob,   A. Scofield
Coventry,   Sam'l T. Loomis
Cromwell,   John Stevens
Danbury,   John Tweedy
Danielsonville, F. A. Shumway
Darien,   George Clock
Dayville,   Marcus Wood
Deep River,   S. M. Shipman
Derby,   A. F. Sherwood
Durham,   Oscar Leach
Durham Center,   Henry Davis
Eagleville,   George Vinton
East Berlin,   Mrs. Jane Heald
East Canaan, George Dunning
East Cornwall,   Chas. S. Blake
Eastford,   Isaac Warren
East Glastonbury,   L. A. Weir
East Granby,   James R. Viets
East Haddam, W. C. Reynolds
East Hampton,   C. O. Sears
East Hartford, Chas. Merriman

East Hartland,   Benj. H. Selby
East Haven,   S. Hemingway
East Kent,   Elisha Fry
East Killingly,   Isaac Fogg
East Litchfield, Austin Weaver
East Lyme,   Gilbert P. Coats
East River,   Samuel D. Crut-
                              tenden
Easton,   Seleck N. Osborne
East Thompson, Isaac Sherman
E.Wallingf'd, Mrs. D. Williams
East Willington, ——— ———
East Windsor, Geo. B. Spencer
E. Windsor Hill, C. Z. Parmelee
EastWoodstock, G. O. Robbins
Ekonk,   Kinney S. Wilcox
Elliott,   Chas. F. Martin
Ellington,   Jas. W. Eaton
Ellsworth,   Geo. Peck
Elmwood,   W. S. Goodwin
Enfield,   F. J. Sheldon
Essex,   Charles S. Munger
Fairfield,   Charles B. Wakeley
Fair Haven, Sta. of New Haven
Falls Village,   Geo. W..Hall
Farmington,   Chauncey Rowe
Farms Village,   Phelps Tuller
Forestville,   J. F. Douglass
Franklin,   Andrew B. Smith
Gale's Ferry,   Isaac Bragaw
Gaylordsville,   A. H. Barlow
Georgetown,   James Corcoran
Gildersleeve's Landing, F. Gil-
                              dersleeve
Gilead,   Ralph T. Hutchinson
Glasgo,   Wm. P. Young
Glastonbury,   F. C. Covell
Glenville,   Webster Haight
Goshen,   Chas. J. Porter
Granby,   J. N. Loomis
Grantville,   M. F. Grant
Greenfield Hill,   B. B. Banks
Greeneville,   A. C. Greene
Greens Farms, G. E. Crossman

Greenwich,	Jos. E. Brush	Little River,	John W. Nichols
Greystone,	—— ——	Lockwood,	—— ——
Griswold,	Sarah E. Tillinghast	Long Hill,	Edward Platt
Grosvenordale,	Jas. Cranska	Long Ridge,	Geo. B. Christison
Groton,	John S. Morgan	Lyme,	Hiram Beckwith
Guilford,	Charles Griswold	Madison,	John Wilcox
Gurleyville,	Chas. A. Royce	Manchester,	Wm. B. Lincoln
Haddam.	L. H. Howard	Mansfield,	S. S. Fuller
Haddam Neck,	H. M. Selden	Mansfield Cent'r,	F. D. Fenton
Hadlyme,	John C. Comstock	Mansfield Dp't,	D. B. Denison
Hamburg,	B. A. Rathbun	Marbledale,	E. O. Sperry
Hamden.	Jesse Warner	Marion,	Catherine Zeilig
Hampton,	James S. Baldwin	Marlborough,	Mrs. H. R. Warner
Hanover,	Mrs. Maria Smith	Mashapaug,	J. W. Winch
Hartford.	L. A. Dickinson	Massapeag,	J. P. Turner
Hartland Center.	G. Miller	Mechanicsville,	J. Cunningham
Harwinton,	William Bryant	Melrose,	John M. Stiles
Hawleyville,	Robert Williams	Meriden,	E. D. Hall
Hazardville,	A. Landschultz	Merrow Station,	O. M. Merrow
Hebron,	Geo. S. Bestor	Merryall,	—— ——
Higganum,	E. D. Gilbert	Mianus,	Allen J. Finney
High Ridge,	James M. Ballard	Middlebury,	Fred'k G. Scott
Hockanum,	Edwin Brewer	Middlefield,	S. D. Jewett
Hop River,	W. C. Jillson	Middle Haddam,	Jno. A. Carrier
Hotchkissville,	H. H. Morris	Middletown,	Bartlett Bent
Huntington,	Frank W. Wooster	Milford.	Joseph R. Clark
Huntsville,	H. E. Wetherell	Millington,	F. W. Swan
Ivoryton,	Theodore F. Rose	Mill Brook,	Wm. P. Lawrence
Jewett City,	A. F. Brown	Mill Dale,	W. A. Hine
Johnsonville,	S. P. Clark	Mill Plain,	Henry M. Senior
Kensington,	R. R. Upson	Milton,	F. Barton
Kent,	Burrett Eaton	Minortown,	Bronson Atwood
Killingly,	Marcus Wood	Monroe,	Wm. A. Clarke
Killingworth,	O. E. Redfield	Montowese,	W. A. Robinson
Lakeville,	Thomas L. Norton	Montville,	Lewis Browning
Lanesville,	Mrs. Perry Chase	Moodus,	L. D. F. Gates
Lebanon,	N. C. Barker	Moose Meadow,	M. Burdick
Ledyard,	Edmund Spicer	Moosup,	Lucius Batty
Leesville.	Nelson Bowers	Morris,	Joseph W. Mason
Leetes Island,	C. Cranch	Mount Carmel,	James Ives
Liberty Hill,	Wm. A. Fuller	Mount Hope,	L. H. Hooker
Lime Rock,	Jas. H. Barnum	Mystic,	F. E. Crumb
Linville,	W. H. Pease	Mystic Bridge,	J. A. Rathbun
Litchfield,	H. E. Gates	Mystic River,	W. W. Packer

13

Naubuc,	Albert A. Bogue	Norwich Town,	John Manning
Naugatuck,	Luther S. Platt	Oakville,	Leslie E. Warner
Nepaug,	E. R. Merrill	Oneco,	Edwin A. Card
New Boston,	J. T. Murdock	Orange,	Sidney F. Oviatt
New Britain,	Walter Gladden	Ore Hill,	Charles Everts
New Canaan,	Cornelia Hoyt	Oxford,	Chas. H. Butler
New Fairfield,	A.Martin Couch	Packersville,	C. H. Truesdell
New Hartford,	H. L. Jones	Parkville,	Sherman Goodwin
New Haven,	Neh. D. Sperry	Pendleton Hill,	R. P. Palmer
Newington,	Erastus Kilbourn	Pequabuck,	Walter H. Scott
Newingt'n Junc.	J.C.Sternberg	Phœnixville,	C. A. Wheaton
New London,	Wm. H. Tubbs	Pine Meadow,	B. G. Loomis
New Milford,	David A. Baldwin	Plainfield,	Waldo Tillinghast
New Preston,	D. Burnham	Plainville,	E. F. Tomlinson
Newtown,	Z. S. Peck	Plantsville,	Heber S. Ives
Niantic,	Wm. Whaley	Plattsville,	George S. Platt
Noank,	Orrin E. Miner	Pleasant Valley,	Geo. Baker
Norfolk,	Mrs. Ann Wolcott	Plymouth,	Horace Fenn
Noroton,	J. S. Waterbury	Pomfret,	O. C. Spencer
No. Ashford,	Geo. W. Olds	Pomfret Centre,	Ethan Allen
No.Branford,	Jenny E.Wheaton	Pomfret Land'g,	C. G. Williams
North Canton,	George Adams	Poquetannock,	John H. Taylor
No. Colebrook,	Erastus Simons	Poquonnock,	C. B. Tourtelotte
North Cornwall,	Niles Scoville	Poquonoc Bridge,	H. J. Lacey
Northfield,	D. T. Wooster	Portland,	Chas. H. Edwards
Northford,	T. A. Smith	Preston,	Morrison Robbins
No. Franklin,	Mrs.A. Manning	Prospect,	David B. Hotchkiss
No. Granby,	Willis Phelps	Putnam,	Perry P. Wilson
N. Grosvenordale,	T. Wilbur	Putnam Heights,	S. Ames
No. Guilford,	B. C. Dudley	Quarryville,	Albert W. Cowles
North Haven,	Sarah J. Stiles	Quinebaug,	S. E. Amidon
North Lyme,	Charles Stark	Rainbow,	Wm. C. Hodge
North Madison,	Alvin A. Blake	Rawson,	H. H. Rollock
No. Manchester,	Moses Scott	Redding,	Mrs. Jane C. Johnson
North Stamford,	Alvin Weed	Redding Ridge,	H. Whitehead
No. Sterling,	—— ——	Reynolds Bridge,	Wm. Barbour
No. Stonington,	Wm. H. Hillard	Ridgebury,	George Boughton
Northville,	Merritt Hunt	Ridgefield,	Hiram K. Scott
No. Westchester,	Wm. E. Jones	Riverton,	Miron A. Hart
North Wilton,	Jas. Comstock	Riverside,	Edward B. Hewes
No. Windham,	Lester Hartson	Robertsville,	E. B. Brown
No. Woodstock,	N. D. Skinner	Rock Fall,	H. L. Parker
Norwalk,	Charles Olmstead	Rockville,	Geo. N. Brigham
Norwich,	E. G. Bidwell	Rocky Hill,	Henry R. Taylor

Romford Station,	S. S. Logan	So. Wilton,	Nelson Hanford
Round Hill,	Odle C. Knapp	So. Windham,	John B. Johnson
Rowayton,	Oliver Cook	So. Windsor,	H. Parmelee
Roxbury,	George Hurlburt	So. Woodstock,	N. H. Andrews
Roxbury Sta.,	Chas. W. Hodge	Springdale,	J. W. Waterbury
Salem,	Nelson N. Williams	Spring Hill,	N. Boynton
Salisbury,	D. T. Warner	Square Pond,	E. H. Dimock
Sandy Hook,	Ezra Patch	Stafford,	J. E. Pascoe
Sanford Station, ------ ------		Stafford Springs,	E. F. Whiton
Saugatuck,	Jas. E. Hubbell	Staffordville,	O. P. Eaton
Saybrook,	Thos. C. Acton, Jr.	Stamford,	Theodore J. Daskam
Saybrook Point,	Jos. Kellogg	Stanwich,	Geo. A. Lockwood
Scitico,	L. King	Stepney,	Burr Hawley
Scotland,	James Burnett	Stepney Dep't,	Chas. S. French
Seymour,	S. H. Canfield	Sterling,	Wm. Anderson
Shaker Sta.,	Albert J. Battles	Stony Creek,	Wm. T. Howd
Sharon,	Edward F. Gillette	Stonington,	Franklin Williams
Sharon Valley,	Geo. A. Kelsey	Stratford,	George H. Spall
Sherman,	Mrs. F. Hoag	Suffield,	Frank H. Reid
Silver Mine,	------ ------	Talcottville,	Sam'l A. Talcott
Simsbury,	Lucius G. Goodrich	Taftville,	Henry Hovey
Smith's R'ge,	Warner H. Keeler	Tariffville,	Philo B. Coe
Somers,	Leverett E. Pease	Terryville,	Newell M. Plumb
Somersville,	Wm. E. Dow	Thomaston,	E. T. Gates
Sound Beach,	H. F. Palmer	Thompson,	Jas. N. Kingsbury
South Britain,	H. P Downes	Thomps'nville,	Mrs. A. Houston
Southbury,	Andrew Perry	Tolland,	Joseph Root
S. Canaan,	Chas. J. Connelly	Torringford,	Stanley Griswold
So. Canterbury,	O. S. Francis	Torrington,	O. R. Tyler
So. Coventry,	Henry N. Moore	Torrington Hollow,	N. R. Pond
Southford,	H. Oatman	Trumbull,	Wm. S. Wheeler
S.Glastonbury,	Emily Dayton	Trumbull, Long Hill,	Edw. Platt
So. Haven,	Theod're Thompson	Turnerville,	P. W. Turner
Southington,	Jno. Hemingway	Tylerville,	A. W. Tyler
South Kent,	Edw'd Dakin	Tyler City,	C. H. Amesbury
South Killingly,	H. A. Tennant	Uncasville,	Wm. M. Burchard
South Lyme,	R. L. Chadwick	Union,	Geo. L. Baker
So. Manchester,	W. H. Cheney	Union City,	C. H. Smith
So. Meriden,	E. B. Clark	Unionville,	J. D. Cook
So. Norfolk,	Henry Pendleton	Vernon,	Hattie E. Ingraham
South Norwalk,	J. S. Dunning	Vernon Depot,	B. C. Phelps
Southport,	Levi F. Sherwood	Versailles,	W. P. Kelley
Southville,	S. F. Clark	Voluntown,	John N. Lewis
So. Wethersfield,	L. Hewitt	Wallingford,	L. M. Hubbard

Wapping,	J. C. Stoughton	West Stratford,	L. B. Vaill
Warehouse P't,	G.D.Woodward	West Suffield,	Miss E. D. Rose
Warren,	Orlando Swift	W. Thompson,	W. R. Case
Warrenville,	John A. Murphy	Westville,	Geo. T. Finney
Washington,	C. L. Hickox	West Willingt'n,	J. B.Carpenter
Washington Depot,	S. D. Platt	W. Winsted,	B. F. Marsh
Waterbury,	John W. Hill	West Woodstock,	Abiel Fox
Waterford,	F. P. Braman	Wethersfield,	Henry Lockwood
Watertown,	B. C. Atwood	Willimantic,	John Brown
Waterville,	Geo. H. Ford	Willington,	M. L. Dimock
Wauregan,	James Gough	Wilsonville,	S. H. Adams
Weatogue,	Seymour Pettibone	Wilton,	Chas. H. Betts
West Ashford,	N. L. Knowlton	Winchester,	W. M. Bronson
West Avon,	Martin Judd	Winchester Center, —— ——	
Westbrook,	Amos A. Wilcox	Windham,	William Swift
West Cheshire,	Ed. P. Dunham	Windsor,	Mrs. Mary J. Phelps
Westchester,	Mrs. Sam'l Brown	Windsor Locks,	A.W. Converse
West Cornwall,	C. E. Baldwin	Windsorville,	Sumner Shepard
Westford,	Henry H. Richmond	Winnipauk,	Jos. C. Randle
West Goshen,	Fred. A. Lucas	Winsted,	Harvey L. Roberts
West Granby,	Buel B. Alling	Winthrop,	Geo. G. Carr
W. Hartford,	Leonard Buckland	Wolcott,	Erastus W. Warner
West Hartland,	Amos. W. Dean	Woodbury,	F. A. Walker
West Haven,	Edw. W. Wilmot	Woodmont,	—— ——
Westminster,	Adolph Eimer	Woodstock,	John Morse
West Morris,	Sam'l F. Burgess	Woodstock Val.,	A.M. Bancroft
West Norfolk,	J. K. Shepard	Woodville,	—— ——
Weston,	John H. Gregory	Yalesville,	Daniel Chapman
Westport,	Wm. E. Nash	Yantic,	E. W. Williams
West Redding,	W. F. Mandev'le	Zoar Bridge,	Chas. E. Gilber
West Stafford,	D. E. Whiton		

EDUCATION.

YALE COLLEGE, New Haven.

Rev. Noah Porter, D. D., LL. D., President.

Rev. Elias Loomis, LL. D., Wm. A. Norton, M. A., S. Wells Williams, LL. D., James D. Dana, Ph. D., LL. D., Rev. Geo. E. Day, D. D., Rev. Samuel Harris, D. D., LL. D., Thos. A. Thacher, LL. D., Benjamin Silliman, M. D., Rev. Chester S Lyman, M. A., Rev. James M. Hoppin, D. D., M. D., Edward

J. Phelps, LL. D., William D. Whitney, Ph. D., LL. D., Moses C. White, M. D., Francis Wayland, LL. D., Rev. Geo. P. Fisher, D. D., Rev. Timothy Dwight, D. D., Chas. A. Lindsley, M. D., Hubert A. Newton, LL. D., Geo. J. Brush, M. A., Samuel W. Johnson, M. A., Wm. H. Brewer, Ph. D., Leonard J. Sanford, M. D.,Wm. C. Robinson, LL.D, Lewis R. Packard, Ph. D., Jno. F. Weir, N. A., M. A., John E. Clark, M. A., Cyrus Northrop, LL. B., Daniel C. Eaton, M. A., Arthur M. Wheeler, B. A., Addison Van Name, M. A., J. Willard Gibbs, Ph. D., Arthur W. Wright, Ph. D., Thos. R. Lounsbury, B. A., Rev. William M. Barbour, D. D., Othniel C. Marsh, M. A., Eugene L. Richards, B. A., John H. Niemeyer, M. A., Franklin B. Dexter, M. A., Simeon E. Baldwin, M. A., Oscar D. Allen, Ph. D., Tracy Peck, M. A., William I. Knapp, Ph. D., William H. Carmalt, M. D., Addison E. Verrill, M. A., Rev. Geo. E. Ladd, Wm. G. Sumner, B. A., Johnson T. Platt, M. A., Sidney I. Smith, Ph. B., Wm. G. Mixter, Ph. B., Henry P. Wright, Ph. D., James K. Thacher, M.D., Henry A. Beers, B. A., A. Jay DuBois, Ph. D., Edward S. Dana, Ph. D., Thomas D. Seymour, M. A., Frank E. Beckwith, M. D., William K. Townsend, D. C. L., Theodore S. Woolsey, LL. B., Henry W. Farnham, M. A., R. P. D., Leonard Waldo, S. D., Professors.

Oscar H. Cooper, Frank B. Tarbell, Ph. D., Wm. Beebe, B. A., Andrew W. Phillips, Ph. D., Arthur T. Hadley, B. A., Webster Merrifield, B. A., Charles C. Camp, B. A., Alfred L. Ripley, B. A.

SHEFFIELD SCIENTIFIC SCHOOL.

GOVERNING BOARD.—Rev. Noah Porter, D. D., LL. D., President; Geo. J. Brush, M. A., (Chairman,) Wm. A. Norton, M. A., Rev. Chester S. Lyman, M. A., Wm. D. Whitney, Ph. D., LL. D., Samuel W. Johnson, M. A., Wm. H. Brewer, Ph. D., John E. Clark, M. A., Daniel C. Eaton, M. A., Thomas R. Lounsbury. B. A., Oscar D. Allen, Ph. D., Addison E. Verrill, M. A., Sidney I. Smith, Ph. B., William G. Mixter, Ph. B., A. Jay DuBois, Ph. D., Henry W. Farnam, M. A., R. P. D.

TRINITY COLLEGE, Hartford.

Rev. Thomas R. Pynchon, D. D., LL. D., President.
John Brocklesby, LL. D., Rev. Edwin E. Johnson, M. A., Rev. Samuel Hart, M. A., George O. Holbrooke, M. A., Leonard Woods Richardson, M. A., H. Carrington Bolton, Ph. D.,

Rev. Isbon T. Beckwith, Ph. D., Professors. Rt. Rev. John Williams, D. D., LL. D., Geo. C. Shattuck, M. A., M.D., Wm. A. M. Wainwright, M. A., M. D., Wm. Hamersley, M. A., Professors and Lecturers. Rev. John Humphrey Barbour, M· A., Assistant Librarian.

WESLEYAN UNIVERSITY, Middletown.

Rev. John W. Beach, D. D., President.
John Johnston, LL. D., John M. Van Vleck, LL. D., Rev. Calvin S. Harrington, D. D., James C. Van Benschoten, LL. D., Rev. George Prentice, D. D., Rev. Wm. N. Rice, Ph. D., Wilbur O. Atwater, Ph. D., Rev. Geo. L. Westgate, D. D., Caleb T. Winchester, M. A., Professors. Ralph G. Hibbard, M. A., H. G. Mitchell, Ph. D., M. B. Crawford. M. A., Instructors. John C. Burke, M. A., Wm. L. Gooding, M. A., A. W. Harris, B. A., John P. Gordy, M. A., A. M. Wilcox, Ph. D., Tutors. C. T. Woods, B. S., Merrill Hitchcock, B. A., Wm. E. Mead, B. A., Assistants.

STATE NORMAL SCHOOL, New Britain.

Principal, Isaac N. Carleton, A. M. Associate Principal, Henry E. Sawyer, A. M.

AMERICAN ASYLUM FOR THE EDUCATION OF THE DEAF AND DUMB.—Pres., Calvin Day; Vice-Pres'ts, Roland Mather, Nathaniel Shipman, Geo. M. Bartholomew. John C. Parsons, Pinckney W. Ellsworth, Jona. B. Bunce, Rowland Swift, Sec., Atwood Collins. Treas., Roland Mather. Principal, Job Williams.

THEOLOGICAL INSTITUTE OF CONNECTICUT, Hartford.

Faculty.—Rev. William Thompson, D. D., Rev. Matthew B. Riddle, D. D., Rev. William S. Karr, D. D., Rev. Chester D. Hartranft, D. D., Rev. Lewellyn Pratt, D. D., Rev. Edwin C. Bissell, D. D.
Prof. Wm. Thompson, D. D., Dean of the Faculty; Rev. Jeremiah Taylor, D. D., President of Board of Trustees.

STATE BOARD OF EDUCATION.

Gov. Hobart B. Bigelow, New Haven; Lieut.-Gov. Wm. H. Bulkeley, Hartford; Storrs O. Seymour, Litchfield; Elisha Carpenter, Hartford. Sec., Birdsey G. Northrop, New Haven.

STATE BOARD OF AGRICULTURE.

Gov. Hobart B. Bigelow, New Haven, Pres.; E. H. Hyde, Stafford, Vice-Pres.; T. S. Gold, West Cornwall, Sec.; Nathan Hart, West Cornwall, Treas. Members appointed by the Gov. and Senate—E. H. Hyde, Stafford; Albert Day, Brooklyn; H. L. Stewart, Middle Haddam; J. P. Barstow, Norwich. Members appointed by Agricultural Societies—John S. Kirkham, Newington; J. J. Webb, New Haven; James A. Bill, Lyme; B. K. Northrop, Ridgefield; Alexander Warner, Pomfret; C. T. Hickox, Watertown; J. M. Hubbard, Middletown; A. R. Goodrich, Vernon.

STATE AGRICULTURAL EXPERIMENT STATION.

Prest., His Exc., Hobart B. Bigelow, New Haven; V. Prest., Hon. E. H. Hyde, Stafford; T. S. Gold, West Cornwall, W. O. Atwater, Middletown, Edwin Hoyt, New Canaan, James J. Webb, Hamden; Sec'y and Treas., W. H. Brewer, New Haven; Direc., S. W. Johnson, New Haven.

Chemists, E. H. Jenkins, Ph. Dr., H. P. Armsby, Ph. Dr., C. A. Hutchinson, B. R.; Direc., S. W. Johnson, New Haven.

STATE AGRICULTURAL SOCIETY.

OFFICERS.—Pres., James A. Bill, Lyme; Vice-Pres., J. P. Barstow, Norwich; Treas., Wm. H. Gross, Hartford; Cor. Sec., Levi E. Coe, Meriden; Rec. Sec., T. S. Gold, West Cornwall.

STATE PRISON, WETHERSFIELD.

Directors. Chairman, Francis Wayland, New Haven; Lewis Whitmore, Rocky Hill, Henry T. Sperry, Hartford, John H. Leeds, New Haven, Thomas McManus, Hartford, Nathan M. Belden, Wilton; Cyrus B. Newton, Stafford; Warden, Gustavus Sargent; Deputy Warden, Edward O Peck; Chaplain, Amasa Howard; Physician, A. S. Warner; Matron, Miss Addie L. Carpenter.

200 MISCELLANEOUS.

CONNECTICUT PRISON ASSOCIATION.

Prest., Francis Wayland, New Haven: Treas., John B. Corning, Hartford; Sec'y, John C. Taylor, Hartford.

STATE REFORM SCHOOL, MERIDEN.

Trustees, F. O. Bennett, Brooklyn; Charles Fitzgerald, Middletown; Vincent Colyer, Darien; John L. Houston, Thompsonville; Jabez S. Lathrop, Norwich; G. H. Preston, M. D., Tolland; Charles Fabrique, New Haven.

Resident Trustees, Isaac C. Lewis, Charles L. Upham, Owen B. Arnold.

Superintendent, George E. Howe.

GENERAL HOSPITAL SOCIETY OF CONN., New Haven.—Pres., Francis Waylannd; Vice-Pres., James E. English; Treas., L. S. Hotchkiss; Secretary, T. H. Bishop, M. D.; Supt., John H. Starkweather.

HARTFORD HOSPITAL.—Pres., Edson Fessenden; Vice-Pres., George B. Hawley; Sec'y and Treas., W. W. Jacobs; Executive Committee, Edson Fessenden, Geo. B. Hawley, M. D., Henry K. Morgan.

INDUSTRIAL SCHOOL FOR GIRLS, Middletown.—President, Frederic Gardiner, D. D., Middletown; Sec., Rev. Thomas K. Fessenden, Farmington; Treas., Chas. F. Browning, Middletown; Sup't, Charles H. Bond; Asst. Sup't, Mrs. Lydia M. Bond. Executive Committee, Samuel Russell, J. M. Van Vleck, Frederic Gardiner, C. F. Browning, Wm. W. Wilcox.

CROMWELL HALL, Cromwell, Conn.

An Institution for the treatment of Mental and Nervous Diseases.

W. B. Hallock, M. D., Supt.

Official Returns of the Census for 1870 and 1880.

Towns.	1870.	1880.	Towns.	1870.	1880.
Andover,	462	428	East Haven,	2,713	3,067
Ashford,	1,242	1,041	East Lyme,	1,506	1,731
Avon,	987	1,058	Easton,	1,289	1,145
Barkhamsted,	1,440	1,298	East Windsor,	2,882	3,010
Beacon Falls,		379	Ellington,	1,452	1,569
Berlin,	2,438	2,385	Enfield,	6,322	6,754
Bethany,	1,136	637	Essex,	1,664	1,855
Bethel,	2,312	2,726	Fairfield,	5,642	3,748
Bethlehem,	750	655	Farmington,	2,617	3,014
Bloomfield,	1,473	1,346	Franklin,	731	685
Bolton,	579	512	Glastonbury,	3,560	3,580
Bozrah,	987	1,155	Goshen,	1,224	1,093
Branford,	2,489	3,047	Granby,	1,516	1,340
Bridgeport,	19,876	29,148	Greenwich,	7,672	7,892
Bridgewater,	878	708	Griswold,	2,576	2,745
Bristol,	3,790	5,347	Groton,	5,119	5,127
Brookfield,	1,194	1,152	Guilford,	2,576	2,782
Brooklyn,	2,355	2,308	Haddam,	2,073	2,419
Burlington,	1,317	1,224	Hamden,	3,028	3,408
Canaan,	1,258	1,157	Hampton,	891	827
Canterbury,	1,552	1,272	Hartford,	37,825	42,553
Canton,	2,639	2,299	Hartland,	789	643
Chaplin,	704	627	Harwinton,	1,045	1,216
Chatham,	2,771	1,967	Hebron,	1,285	1,443
Cheshire,	2,344	2,284	Huntington,	1,527	2,699
Chester,	1,094	1,177	Kent,	1,744	1,922
Clinton,	1,404	1,402	Killingly,	5,712	6,721
Colchester,	3,383	2,974	Killingworth,	856	848
Colebrook,	1,132	1,148	Lebanon,	2,211	1,845
Columbia,	891	757	Ledyard,	1,392	1,073
Cornwall,	1,772	1,583	Lisbon,	503	630
Coventry,	2,057	2,043	Litchfield,	3,113	3,410
Cromwell,	1,857	1,640	Lyme,	1,179	1,025
Danbury,	8,754	11,669	Madison,	1,814	1,669
Darien,	1,810	1,948	Manchester,	4,236	6,462
Derby,	8,027	11,649	Mansfield,	2,402	2,154
Durham,	1,086	990	Marlborough,	473	391
Eastford,	984	855	Meriden,	10,521	18,340
East Granby,	853	754	Middlebury,	696	687
East Haddam,	2,952	3,032	Middlefield,	1,054	928
East Hartford,	3,013	3,500	Middletown,	11,143	11,731

Towns.	1870.	1880.	Towns.	1870.	1880.
Milford,	3,407	3,847	Sherman,	848	828
Monroe,	1,226	1,157	Simsbury,	2,051	1,830
Montville,	2,496	2,666	Somers,	1,248	1,242
Morris,	701	627	Southbury,	1,319	1,740
Naugatuck,	2,830	4,272	S8uthington,	4,316	5,411
New Britain,	9,480	13,978	South Windsor,	1,693	1,902
New Canaan,	2,496	2,673	Sprague,	3,462	3,207
New Fairfield,	871	791	Stafford,	3,405	4,455
New Hartford,	3,078	2,302	Stamford,	9,738	11,298
New Haven,	50,886	62,882	Sterling,	1,022	957
Newington,		934	Stonington,	6,320	7,353
New London,	9,580	10,529	Stratford,	3,032	4,251
New Milford,	3,586	3,907	Suffield,	3,277	3,225
Newtown,	3,683	4,013	Thompson,	3,804	5,051
Norfolk,	1,641	1,418	Thomaston,		3,225
North Branford,	1,035	1,025	Tolland,	1,218	1,169
North Canaan,	1,695	1,537	Torrington,	2,896	3,327
North Haven,	1,771	1,763	Trumbull,	1,335	1,323
No. Stonington,	1,759	1,769	Union,	627	539
Norwalk,	12,122	13,956	Vernon,	5,447	6,915
Norwich,	16,653	21,141	Voluntown,	1,052	1,186
Old Lyme,	1,362	1,387	Wallingford,	3,676	4,686
Old Saybrook,	1,215	1,302	Warren,	673	639
Orange,	2,633	3,341	Washington,	1,563	1,589
Oxford,	1,338	1,120	Waterbury,	13,148	20,269
Plainfield,	4,521	4,021	Waterford,	2,589	2,701
Plainville,	1,435	1,930	Watertown,	1,690	1,867
Plymouth,	4,149	2,350	Westbrook,	987	878
Pomfret,	1,488	1,470	West Hartford,	1,533	1,828
Portland,	4,694	4,156	Weston,	1,054	918
Preston,	2,162	2,519	Westport,	3,364	3,477
Prospect,	551	492	Wethersfield,	2,694	2,173
Putnam,	4,192	5,827	Willington,	942	1,086
Redding,	1,620	1,540	Wilton,	1,995	1,864
Ridgefield,	1,910	2,028	Winchester,	4,102	5,142
Rocky Hill,	1,012	1,109	W ndham,	5,413	8,265
Roxbury,	920	950	Windsor,	2,784	3,056
Salem,	718	574	Windsor Locks	2,154	2,332
Salisbury,	3,305	3.715	Wolcott,	491	493
Saybrook,	1,267	1,362	Woodbridge,	830	829
Scotland,	648	590	Woodbury,	1,931	2,148
Seymour,	2,123	2,318	Woodstock,	2,955	2,689
Sharon,	2,446	2,580			
Total, -	-	-	-	537,998	622,683

There are 167 Towns in the State—82 send two Representatives, and 85 one each, making 248 members of the House; these Towns are divided into 21 Senatorial Districts; and the eight Counties into 4 Congressional Districts.

Hartford County has 4 Senators and 45 Representatives.
New Haven County has 4 Senators and 33 Representatives.
New London County has 3 Senators and 30 Representatives.
Fairfield County has 4 Senators and 32 Representatives.
Windham County has 2 Senators and 24 Representatives.
Litchfield County has 3 Senators and 41 Representatives.
Middlesex County has 2 Senators and 22 Representatives.
Tolland County has 2 Senators and 22 Representatives.

A TABLE OF DISTANCES,

IN MILES, *from each Town in the State of Connecticut to* HARTFORD ; *being the established and legal distance as enacted by the General Assembly in* 1877. *Also the* NUMBER OF REPRESENTATIVES *to which each Town is entitled.*

Hartford County.

	To H'fd.	No. Rep.		To H'fd.	No. Rep.
HARTFORD,	—	2	Manchester,	9	1
Avon,	20	1	Marlborough,	30	1
Berlin,	13	1	New Britain,	9	2
Bloomfield,	6	1	Newington,	5	1
Bristol,	18	2	Plainville,	14	1
Burlington,	23	1	Rocky Hill,	8	1
Canton,	22	1	Simsbury,	15	2
East Granby,	20	1	Southington,	20	2
East Hartford,	2	2	South Windsor,	8	1
East Windsor,	14	2	Suffield,	17	2
Enfield,	18	2	West Hartford,	4	1
Farmington,	19	2	Wethersfield,	4	2
Glastonbury,	12	2	Windsor,	6	2
Granby,	18	2	Windsor Locks,	12	1
Hartland,	39	2			

New Haven County.

	To H'fd.	No. Rep.		To H'fd.	No. Rep.
NEW HAVEN,	36	2	Milford,	46	2
WATERBURY,	32	2	Naugatuck,	37	1
Beacon Falls,	41	1	North Branford,	45	1
Bethany,	45	1	North Haven,	29	1
Branford,	45	1	Orange,	42	1
Cheshire,	26	2	Oxford,	48	1
Derby,	48	2	Prospect,	29	1
East Haven,	40	1	Seymour,	44	1
Guilford,	52	2	Southbury,	55	1
Hamden,	34	1	Wallingford,	24	2
Madison,	56	1	Wolcott,	37	1
Meriden,	18	2	Woodbridge,	40	1
Middlebury,	38	1			

New London County.

	To H'fd.	No. Rep.		To H'fd.	No. Rep.
NEW LONDON,	61	2	Lisbon,	50	1
NORWICH,	50	2	Lyme,	43	2
Bozrah,	50	1	Montville,	58	1
Colchester,	40	2	North Stonington,	80	2
East Lyme,	56	1	Old Lyme,	45	1
Franklin,	42	1	Preston,	55	2
Griswold,	53	1	Salem,	58	1
Groton,	65	2	Sprague,	42	1
Lebanon,	42	2	Stonington,	75	2
Ledyard,	58	1	Waterford,	58	1

Fairfield County.

	To H'fd.	No. Rep.		To H'fd.	No. Rep.
BRIDGEPORT,	53	2	Newtown,	74	2
DANBURY,	92	2	Norwalk,	70	2
Bethel,	89	1	Redding,	87	2
Brookfield,	82	1	Ridgefield,	84	2
Darien,	74	1	Sherman,	96	1
Easton,	63	1	Stamford,	78	2
Fairfield,	58	2	Stratford,	50	1
Greenwich,	84	2	Trumbull,	57	1
Huntington,	62	1	Weston,	68	1
Monroe,	67	1	Westport,	65	1
New Canaan,	86	1	Wilton,	75	1
New Fairfield,	97	1			

Windham County.

	To Hf'd.	No. Rep.		To Hf'd.	No. Rep.
Brooklyn,	66	1	Pomfret,	50	2
Ashford,	46	2	Putnam,	56	2
Canterbury,	50	2	Scotland,	40	1
Chaplin,	44	1	Sterling,	61	1
Eastford,	50	1	Thompson,	61	2
Hampton,	44	1	Voluntown,	60	1
Killingly,	64	2	Windham,	35	2
Plainfield,	50	2	Woodstock,	60	2

Litchfield County.

	To Hf'd.	No. Rep.		To Hf'd.	No. Rep.
Litchfield,	58	2	Norfolk,	45	2
Barkhamsted,	34	2	North Canaan,	55	1
Bethlehem,	45	1	Plymouth,	26	1
Bridgewater,	96	1	Roxbury,	92	1
Canaan,	61	1	Salisbury,	62	2
Colebrook,	40	2	Sharon,	71	2
Cornwall,	71	2	Thomaston,	27	1
Goshen,	52	2	Torrington,	46	2
Harwinton,	53	2	Warren,	76	1
Kent,	80	1	Washington,	95	2
Morris,	62	1	Watertown,	39	1
New Hartford,	29	2	Winchester,	35	2
New Milford,	90	2	Woodbury,	45	2

Middlesex County.

	To Hf'd.	No. Rep.		To Hf'd.	No. Rep.
Middletown,	15	2	Essex,	39	1
Haddam,	27	2	Killingworth,	43	2
Chatham,	25	2	Middlefield,	21	1
Chester,	34	1	Old Saybrook,	43	1
Clinton,	51	1	Portland,	18	1
Cromwell,	13	1	Saybrook,	35	2
Durham,	24	2	Westbrook,	46	1
East Haddam,	33	2			

Tolland County.

	To Hf'd.	No. Rep.		To Hf'd.	No. Rep.
Tolland,	22	2	Mansfield,	36	2
Andover,	23	1	Somers,	24	2
Bolton,	20	1	Stafford,	52	2
Columbia,	28	1	Union,	60	2
Coventry,	28	2	Vernon,	17	2
Ellington,	20	1	Willington,	48	2
Hebron,	39	2			

States.	ELECTORAL VOTE, 1880.		Sessions of Legislature.
	Garfield.	Hancock.	
Alabama,		10	Biennial.
Arkansas,		6	Biennial.
California,	1	5	Biennial.
Colorado,	3		Biennial.
Connecticut,	6		Annual.
Delaware,		3	Biennial.
Florida,		4	Biennial.
Georgia,		11	Biennial.
Illinois,	21		Biennial.
Indiana,	15		Biennial.
Iowa,	11		Biennial.
Kansas,	5		Biennial.
Kentucky,		12	Biennial.
Louisiana,		8	Biennial.
Maine,	.		Biennial.
Maryland,		8	Biennial.
Massachusetts,	13		Annual.
Michigan,	11		Biennial.
Minnesota,	5		Biennial.
Mississippi,		8	Biennial.
Missouri,		15	Biennial.
Nebraska,	3		Biennial. '
Nevada,		3	Biennial.
New Hampshire,	5		Biennial.
New Jersey,		9	Annual.
New York,	35		Annual.
North Carolina,		10	Biennial.
Ohio,	22		Biennial.
Oregon,	3		Biennial.
Pennsylvania,	29		Biennial.
Rhode Island,	4		Annual.
South Carolina,		7	Annual.
Tennessee,		12	Biennial.
Texas,		8	Biennial.
Vermont,			Biennial.
Virginia,		11	Biennial.
West Virginia,		5	Biennial.
Wisconsin,	10		Annual.
Total,	214	155	

Vote for Congressmen, 1880.

First District.

Counties,	Buck, r.	Beach, d.	Hewitt, gr.	Johnson, p.
Hartford,	14,058	12,794	177	33
Tolland,	2,990	2,320	3	22
Total,	17,048	15,114	180	55

Buck's (Rep.) plurality, 1,934.

Second District.

Counties.	Phelps, d.	Wallace, r.	Harrington, p.
New Haven,	17,829	15,941	52
Middlesex,	3,803	4,127	72
Total,	21,632	20,068	124

Phelp's (Dem.) plurality, 1,564.

Third District.

Counties.	Wait, r.	Sanger, d.	Wolf, gr.	Palmer, p.
New London,	7,824	6,540	141	161
Windham,	4,587	2,868	10	43
Total,	12,411	9,408	151	204

Wait's (Rep.) plurality, 3,003.

Fourth District.

Counties.	Miles, r.	Peet, d.	Cleveland, gr.	Rogers, p.
Fairfield,	12,077	11,964	99	13
Litchfield,	6,091	5,670	104	24
Total	18,168	17,634	293	37

Miles' (Rep.) plurality, 534.

Vote on the Constitutional Amendments, Oct., 1880.

Judges of the Supreme Court of Errors, and of the Superior Court, to be appointed by the General Assembly upon nomination of the Governor.

Total vote, 26,953. In favor of, 18,668; against, 8,285. Majority, 10,383.

MANUAL AND ROLL

OF THE

General Assembly

OF

CONNECTICUT,

WITH

RULES AND ORDERS.

—

1882.

14

JOINT COMMITTEE ON MANUAL AND ROLL.

SENATE.

WILLIAM J. MILLS.

HOUSE.

DELOS D. BROWN,   JOHN W. ROGERS,

DANIEL O. REED.

THE
CONSTITUTION OF CONNECTICUT.

PREAMBLE.

The people of Connecticut, acknowledging with gratitude the good providence of God in having permitted them to enjoy a free government, do, in order more effectually to define, secure, and perpetuate the liberties, rights, and privileges which they have derived from their ancestors, hereby, after a careful consideration and revision, ordain and establish the following Constitution and form of civil government:

ARTICLE FIRST.

DECLARATION OF RIGHTS.

That the great and essential principles of liberty and free government may be recognized and established,

We Declare,

SECTION 1. That all men, when they form a social compact, are equal in rights; and that no man or set of men are entitled to exclusive public emoluments or privileges from the community.

SEC. 2. That all political power is inherent in the people, and all free governments are founded on their authority, and instituted for their benefit; and that they have at all times an undeniable and indefeasible right to alter their form of government in such a manner as they may think expedient.

SEC. 3. The exercise and enjoyment of religious profession and worship, without discrimination, shall forever be free to all persons in this State, provided that the right hereby declared and established shall not be so construed as to excuse acts of licentiousness, or to justify practices inconsistent with the peace and safety of the State.

SEC. 4. No preference shall be given by law to any Christian sect or mode of worship.

SEC. 5. Every citizen may freely speak, write, and publish his sentiments on all subjects, being responsible for the abuse of that liberty.

SEC. 6. No law shall ever be passed to curtail or restrain the liberty of speech or of the press.

SEC. 7. In all prosecutions or indictments for libels, the truth may be given in evidence, and the jury shall have the right to determine the law and the facts, under the direction of the court.

SEC. 8. The people shall be secure in their persons, houses, papers, and possessions from unreasonable searches or seizures, and no warrant to search any place, or to seize any person or things, shall issue without describing them as nearly as may be, nor without probable cause supported by oath or affirmation.

SEC. 9. In all criminal prosecutions, the accused shall have a right to be heard by himself and by counsel; to demand the nature and cause of the accusation; to be confronted by the witnesses against him; to have compulsory process to obtain witnesses in his favor: and in all prosecutions, by indictment or information, a speedy public trial by an impartial jury. He shall not be compelled to give evidence against himself, nor be deprived of life, liberty, or property, but by due course of law. And no person shall be holden to answer for any crime, the punishment of which may be death or imprisonment for life, unless on a presentment or indictment of a grand jury; except in the land or naval forces, or in the militia when in actual service in time of war or public danger.

SEC. 10. No person shall be arrested, detained, or punished, except in cases clearly warranted by law.

SEC. 11. The property of no person shall be taken for public use without just compensation therefor.

SEC. 12. All courts shall be open, and every person, for an injury done to him in his person, property, or reputation, shall have remedy by due course of law, and right and justice administered without sale, denial, or delay.

SEC. 13. Excessive bail shall not be required, nor excessive fines imposed.

SEC. 14. All prisoners shall, before conviction, be bailable by sufficient sureties, except for capital offenses, where the proof is evident, or the presumption great; and the privileges of the writ of *habeas corpus* shall not be suspended, unless when, in case of a rebellion or invasion, the public safety may require it; nor in any case, but by the legislature.

SEC. 15. No person shall be attainted of treason or felony by the legislature.

SEC. 16. The citizens have a right, in a peaceable manner, to assemble for their common good, and to apply to those invested with the powers of government, for redress of grievances, or other proper purposes, by petition, address, or remonstrance.

SEC. 17. Every citizen has a right to bear arms in defense of himself and the State.

SEC. 18. The militia shall, in all cases and at all times, be in strict subordination to the civil power.

SEC. 19. No soldier shall, in time of peace, be quartered in any house without the consent of the owner; nor in time of war put in a manner to be prescribed by law.

SEC. 20. No hereditary emoluments, privileges, or honors shall ever be granted or conferred in this State.

SEC. 21. The right of trial by jury shall remain inviolate.

ARTICLE SECOND.

OF THE DISTRIBUTION OF POWERS.

The powers of government shall be divided into three distinct departments, and each of them confided to a separate magistracy, to wit: those which are legislative, to one; those which are executive, to another; and those which are judicial, to another.

ARTICLE THIRD.

OF THE LEGISLATIVE DEPARTMENT.

SECTION 1. The legislative power of this State shall be vested in two distinct houses or branches; the one to be styled THE SENATE, the other THE HOUSE OF REPRESENTATIVES, and both together THE GENERAL ASSEMBLY. The style of their laws shall be, *Be it enacted by the Senate and House of Representatives in General Assembly convened.*

SEC. 2. There shall be one stated session of the General Assembly, to be holden in each year, alternately at Hartford and New Haven, on the first Wednesday of May,* and at such other times as the General Assembly shall judge necessary; the first session to be holden at Hartford; but the person administering the office of Governor may, on special emergencies, convene the General Assembly at either of said places, at any other time. And in case of danger from the prevalence of contagious diseases in either of said places, or other circumstances, the person admistering the office of Governor may by proclamation convene said Assembly at any other place in this State.

SEC. 3. The House of Representatives shall consist of electors residing in towns from which they are elected. The number of Representatives from each town shall be the same as at present practiced and allowed. In case a new town shall hereafter be incorporated, such new town shall be entitled to one representative only; † and if such

---

* Altered by amendments of 1872, 1875, and 1876.
† Altered by amendments of 1828, 1836, and 1875.

new town shall be made from one or more towns, the town or towns from which the same shall be made shall be entitled to the same number of Representatives as at present allowed, unless the number shall be reduced by consent of such town or towns.

SEC. 4. The Senate shall consist of twelve members, to be chosen annually by the electors.*

SEC. 5. At a meeting of the electors, held in the several towns in this State in April annually, after the election of Representatives, the electors present shall be called upon to bring in their written ballots for Senators.† The presiding officer shall receive the vote of the electors, and count and declare them in open meeting. The presiding officer shall also make duplicate lists of the persons voted for, and of the number of votes for each, which shall be certified by the presiding officer; one of which lists shall be delivered to the Town Clerk, and the other, within ten days after said meeting, shall be delivered, under seal, either to the Secretary or to the sheriff of the county in which said town is situated: which list shall be directed to the Secretary, with a superscription expressing the purport of the contents thereof; and each sheriff who shall receive such votes shall, within fifteen days after said meeting, deliver, or cause them to be delivered, to the Secretary.

SEC. 6. The Treasurer, Secretary, and Comptroller, for the time being, shall canvass the votes publicly. The twelve persons having the greatest number of votes for Senators shall be declared to be elected. But in cases where no choice is made by the electors in consequence of an equality of votes, the House of Representatives shall designate,‡ by ballot, which of the candidates having such equal number of votes shall be declared to be elected. The return of votes, and the result of the canvass, shall be submitted to the

* Altered by amendments of 1828, 1836, 1872.
† Altered by amendment of 1836.
‡ Altered by amendment of 1828.

House of Representatives, and also to the Senate, on
the first day of the session of the General Assembly;
and each House shall be the final judge of the election,
returns, and qualifications of its own members.

SEC. 7. The house of Representatives, when assembled shall choose a speaker, clerk, and other officers.
The Senate shall choose its clerk and other officers
except the President. A majority of each House shall
constitute a quorum to do business; but a smaller number may adjourn from day to day, and compel the
attendance of absent members in such manner, and
under such penalties, as each house may prescribe.

SEC. 8. Each House shall determine the rules of its
own proceedings, punish members for disorderly conduct, and, with the consent of two-thirds, expel a
member, but not a second time for the same cause;
and shall have all other powers necessary for a branch
of the legislature of a free and independent State.

SEC. 9. Each House shall keep a journal of its proceedings, and publish the same, when required by one-
fifth of its members, except such parts as, in the judg-
ment of a majority, require secrecy. The yeas and
nays of the members of either house shall, at the desire
of one-fifth of those present, be entered on the journals.

SEC. 10. The Senators and Representatives shall, in
all cases of civil process, be privileged from arrest
during the session of the General Assembly, and for
four days before the commencement and after the
termination of any session thereof. And for any
speech of debate in either House, they shall not be
questioned in any other place.

SEC. 11. The debates of each House shall be public,
except on such occasions as, in the opinion of the
House, may require secrecy.

ARTICLE FOURTH.

OF THE EXECUTIVE DEPARTMENT.

SECTION 1. The supreme executive power of the

State shall be vested in a Governor, who shall be chosen by the electors of the State, and shall hold his office for one year from the first Wednesday of May next succeeding his election, and until his successor be duly qualified. No person who is not an elector of this State, and who has not arrived at the age of thirty years, shall be eligible.

SEC. 2. At the meeting of the electors in the respective towns, in the month of April in each year,* immediately after the election of Senators, the presiding officers shall call upon the electors to bring in their ballots for him whom they would elect to be Governor, with his name fairly written. When such ballots shall have been received and counted in the presence of the electors, duplicate lists of the persons voted for, and of the number of votes given for each, shall be made and certified by the presiding officer, one of which lists shall be deposited in the office of the Town Clerk within three days, and the other, within ten days after said election, shall be transmitted to the Secretary, or to the sheriff of the county in which such election shall have been held. The sheriff receiving said votes shall deliver, or cause them to be delivered, to the Secretary within fifteen days next after said election. The votes so returned shall be counted by the Treasurer, Secretary, and Comptroller, within the month of April. A fair list of the persons and the number of votes given for each, together with the returns of the presiding officers, shall be, by the Treasurer, Secretary, and Comptroller, made and laid before the General Assembly, then next to be holden, on the first day of the session thereof; and said Assembly shall, after examination of the same, declare the person whom they shall find to be legally chosen, and give him notice accordingly. If no person shall have a majority of the whole number of said votes, or if two or more shall have an equal and the greatest number of said votes, then said Assembly, on the second day of their session, by joint

* Made to apply to biennial elections by amendment of 1876.

ballot of both Houses, shall proceed, without debate, to choose a Governor from a list of the names of the two persons having the greatest number of votes, or of the names of persons having an equal and highest number of votes so returned as aforesaid. The General Assembly shall by law prescribe the manner in which all questions concerning the election of a Governor, or Lieutenant-Governor, shall be determined.

SEC. 3. At the annual meetings of the electors, immediately after the election of Governor, there shall also be chosen, in the same manner as is hereinbefore provided for the election of Governor, a Lieutenant-Governor,* who shall continue in office for the same time, and possess the same qualifications.

SEC. 4. The compensations of the Governor, Lieutenant-Governor, Senators, and Representatives, shall be established by law, and shall not be varied so as to take effect until after an election, which shall next succeed the passage of the law establishing said compensations.

SEC. 5. The Governor shall be Captain-General of the militia of the State, except when called into the service of the United States.

SEC. 6. He may require information in writing from the officers in the executive department, on any subject relating to the duties of their respective offices.

SEC. 7. The Governor, in case of a disagreement, between the two Houses of the General Assembly, respecting the time of adjournment, may adjourn them to such time as he shall think proper, not beyond the day of the next stated session.

SEC. 8. He shall, from time to time, give to the General Assembly information of the state of the government, and recommend to their consideration such measures as he shall deem expedient.

SEC. 9. He shall take care that the laws be faithfully executed.

SEC. 10. The Governor shall have power to grant

---

* Altered by amendment of 1836.

reprieves after convicting, in all cases except those of impeachment, until the end of the next session of the General Assembly, and no longer.

SEC. 11. All commissions shall be in the name and by authority of the State of Connecticut; shall be sealed with the State seal, signed by the Governor, and attested by the Secretary.

SEC. 12. Every bill which shall have passed both Houses of the General Assembly shall be presented to the Governor. If he approves, he shall sign and transmit it to the Secretary, but if not he shall return it to the House in which it originated, with his objections, which shall be entered on the journals of the House; who shall proceed to reconsider the bill. If, after such reconsideration, the House shall again pass it, it shall be sent, with objections, to the other House which shall also reconsider it. If approved, it shall become a law. But in such cases the votes of both Houses shall be determined by yeas and nays; and the names of the members voting for and against the bill shall be entered on the journals of each house respectively. If the bill shall not be returned by the Governor within three days, Sundays excepted, after it shall have been presented to him, the same shall be a law, in like manner as if he had signed it; unless the General Assembly, by their adjournment, prevents its return; in which case it shall not be a law.

SEC. 13. The Lieutenant-Governor shall, by virtue of his office, be President of the Senate, and have, when in Committee of the Whole, a right to debate; and when the Senate is equally divided, to give the casting vote.

SEC. 14. In case of the death, resignation, refusal to serve, or removal from office of the Governor, or of his impeachment or absence from the State, the Lieutenant-Governor shall exercise the powers and authority appertaining to the office of Governor, until another be chosen at the next periodical election for Governor, and be duly qualified; or until the Governor, impeached or absent, shall be acquitted or return.

SEC. 15. When the government shall be administered by the Lieutenant-Governor, or he shall be unable to attend as President of the Senate, the Senate shall elect one of their members as President *pro tempore*. And if during the vacancy of the office of Governor the Lieutenant-Governor shall die, resign, refuse to serve, or be removed from office, or if he shall be impeached or absent from the State, the President of the Senate *pro tempore* shall, in like manner, administer the government, until he be superseded by a Governor, or Lieutenant-Governor.

SEC. 16. If the Lieutenant-Governor shall be required to administer the Government, and shall, while in such administration, die or resign during the recess of the General Assembly, it shall be the duty of the Secretary, for the time being, to convene the Senate for the purpose of choosing a President *pro tempore*.

SEC. 17. A Treasurer shall annually be chosen by the electors at their meeting in April; and the votes shall be returned, counted, canvassed, and declared in the same manner as is provided for the election of Governor and Lieutenant-Governor,* but the votes for Treasurer shall be canvassed by the Secretary and Comptroller only. He shall receive all moneys belonging to the State, and disburse the same only as he may be directed by law. He shall pay no warrant or order for the disbursement of public money, until the same has been registered in the office of the Comptroller.

SEC. 18. A Secretary shall be chosen next after the Treasurer, and in the same manner;* and the votes for Secretary shall be returned to, and counted, canvassed, and declared by the Treasurer and Comptroller. He shall have the safe keeping and custody of the public records and documents, and particularly of the Acts, Resolutions, and orders of the General Assembly, and

---

* Altered by amendment of 1836.

record the same; and perform all such duties as shall be prescribed by law. He shall be the keeper of the seal of the State, which shall not be altered.

SEC. 19. A Comptroller of the Public Accounts shall be annually appointed by the General Assembly.* He shall adjust and settle all public accounts and demands, except grants and orders of the General Assembly. He shall prescribe the mode of keeping and rendering all public accounts. He shall *ex officio* be one of the auditors of the accounts of the Treasurer. The General Assembly may assign to him other duties in relation to his office, and that of the Treasurer, and shall prescribe the manner in which his duties shall be performed.

SEC. 20. A sheriff shall be appointed in each county by the General Assembly,† who shall hold his office for three years, removable by said Assembly, and shall become bound, with sufficient sureties to the Treasurer of the State, for the faithful discharge of the duties of his office, in such manner as shall be prescribed by law. In case the sheriff of any county shall die or resign, the Governor may fill the vacancy occasioned thereby, until the same shall be filled by the General Assembly.

SEC. 21. A statement of all receipts, payments, funds, and debts of the State, shall be published from time to time, in such manner and at such periods as shall be prescribed by law.

ARTICLE FIFTH.

OF THE JUDICIAL DEPARTMENT.

SECTION 1. The judicial power of the State shall be vested in a Supreme Court of Errors, a Superior Court, and such inferior courts as the General Assembly shall, from time to time, ordain and establish; the powers and jurisdiction of which courts shall be defined by law.

---

* Altered by amendment of 1836.
† Altered by amendment of 1838.

SEC. 2. There shall be appointed in each county a sufficient number of justices of the peace, with such jurisdiction in civil and criminal cases as the General Assembly may provide.

SEC. 3. - The Judge of the Supreme Court of Errors, of the Superior and inferior courts, and all justices of the peace, shall be appointed by the General Assembly, in such manner as shall by law be prescribed.* The Judges of the Supreme Court and the Superior Court shall hold their offices during good behavior,* but may be removed by impeachment; and the Governor shall also remove them on the address of two-thirds of the members of each House of the General Assembly; all other judges and justices of the peace shall be appointed annually.* No judge or justice of the peace shall be capable of holding his office after he shall arrive at the age of seventy years.

ARTICLE SIXTH.

OF THE QUALIFICATIONS OF ELECTORS.

SECTION 1. All persons who have been, or shall hereafter, previous to the ratification of this Constitution, be admitted freemen, according to the existing law of this State, shall be electors.

SEC. 2. Every white* male citizen of the United States, who shall have gained a settlement in this State, attained the age of twenty-one years and resided in the town in which he may offer himself to be admitted to the privilege of an elector, at least six months preceding; and have a freehold estate of the yearly value of seven dollars in this State; or, having been enrolled in the militia, shall have performed military duty therein for the term of one year next preceding the time he shall offer himself for admission,* or being liable thereto shall have been, by authority of law, excused therefrom; or shall have paid a State tax within the year next preceding the time he shall present himself for

---

* Altered by amendments.

such admission; and shall sustain a good moral character, shall, on his taking such oath as may be prescribed
by law, be an elector.

SEC. 3.   The privileges of an elector shall be forfeited by a conviction of bribery, forgery, perjury, duel-
ling, fraudulent bankruptcy, theft, or other offense for
which an infamous punishment is inflicted.

SEC. 4.   Every elector shall be eligible to any office
in this State, except in cases provided for in this Constitution.

SEC. 5.   The selectmen and town clerk of the several towns shall decide on the qualifications of electors, at
such times and in such manner as may be prescribed by
law.

SEC. 6.   Laws shall be made to support the privilege
of free suffrage, prescribing the manner of regulating
and conducting meetings of the electors, and prohibit-
ing, under adequate penalties, all undue influence
therein, from power, bribery, tumult, and other im-
proper conduct.

SEC. 7.   In all elections of officers of the State, or
members of the General Assembly, the votes of the
electors shall be by ballot.

SEC. 8.   At all elections of officers of the State, or
members of the General Assembly, the electors shall
be privileged from arrest during their attendance upon,
and going to, and returning from the same, on any civil
process.

SEC. 9.   The meeting of the electors for the election
of the several State officers by law annually to be elected, and members of the General Assembly of this State,
shall be holden on the first Monday in April of each
year.*

ARTICLE SEVENTH.
OF RELIGION.

SECTION 1.   It being the duty of all men to worship

*Altered by amendment of 1875.

the Supreme Being, the Great Creator and Preserver of the Universe, and their right to render that worship in the mode most consistent with the dictates of their consciences, no person shall by law be compelled to join or support, nor be classed with, or associated to, any congregation, church, or religious association. But every person now belonging to such congregation, church, or religious association, shall remain a member thereof until he shall have separated himself therefrom in the manner hereinafter provided. And each and every society or denomination of Christians in this State shall have and enjoy the same and equal powers, rights, and privileges; and shall have power to support and maintain the ministers or teachers of their respective denominations, and .to build and repair houses for public worship, by a tax on the members of any such society only, to be laid by a major vote of the legal voters assembled at any society meeting, warned and held according to law, or in any other manner.

SEC. 2.   If any person shall choose to separate himself from the society or denomination of Christians to which he may belong, and shall leave a written notice thereof with the clerk of such society, he shall thereupon be no longer liable for any future expenses which may be incurred by said society.

ARTICLE EIGHTH.
OF EDUCATION.

SECTION 1.   The charter of Yale College, as modified by agreement with the corporation thereof, in pursuance of an Act of the General Assembly, passed in May, 1792, is hereby confirmed.

SEC. 2.   The fund called the SCHOOL FUND shall remain a perpetual fund, the interest of which shall be inviolably appropriated to the support and encouragement of the public or common schools throughout the State, and for the equal benefit of all the people thereof.   The value and amount of said fund shall, as soon as practicable, be ascertained in such manner as the General Assembly may prescribe, published, and recorded in the Comptroller's office, and no law shall ever be made authorizing said fund to be diverted to any other use than the encouragement and support of public or common schools, among the several school societies, as justice and equity shall require.

ARTICLE NINTH.

OF IMPEACHMENTS.

SECTION 1. The House of Representatives shall have the sole power of impeaching.

SEC. 2. All impeachments shall be tried by the Senate. When sitting for that purpose, they shall be on oath or affirmation. No person shall be convicted without the concurrence of two-thirds of the members present. When the Governor is impeached, the Chief Justice shall preside.

SEC. 3. The Governor and all other executive and judicial officers, shall be liable to impeachment; but judgments in such cases shall not extend further than to removal from office and disqualification to hold any office of honor, trust, or profit under this State. The party convicted shall, nevertheless, be liable and subject to indictment, trial, and punishment according to law.

SEC. 4. Treason against the State shall consist only in levying war against it, or adhering to its enemies, giving them aid and comfort. No person shall be convicted of treason unless on the testimony of two witnesses to the same overt act, or on confession in open court. No conviction of treason or attainder shall work corruption of blood or forfeiture.

ARTICLE TENTH.

GENERAL PROVISIONS.

SECTION 1. Members of the General Assembly, and all officers, executive and judicial, shall, before they

15 .

enter on the duties of their respective offices, take the
following oath or affirmation, to wit:

You do solemnly swear, or affirm (as the case may
be), that you will support the Constitution of the United
States, and the Constitution of the State of Connecticut, so long as you continue a citizen thereof; and that
you will faithfully discharge, according to law, the
duties of . . . . to the best of your abilities. So help
you God.

SEC. 2. Each town shall annually elect selectmen, and
such officers of local police as the laws may prescribe.

SEC. 3. The rights and duties of all corporations
shall remain as if this Constitution had not been adopted; with the exception of such regulations and restric-
tions as are contained in this Constitution. All judicial and civil officers now in office, who have been appointed by the General Assembly, and commissioned
according to law, and all such officers as shall be
appointed by the said Assembly, and commissioned as
aforesaid. before the first Wednesday of May next, shall
continue to hold their offices until the first day of June
next, unless they shall before that time resign, or be
removed from office according to law. The Treasurer
and Secretary shall continue in office until a Treasurer
and Secretary shall be appointed under this Constitution. All military officers shall continue to hold and
exercise their respective offices until they shall resign
or be removed according to law. All laws not contrary
to, or inconsistent with, the provisions of this Constitution shall remain in force until they shall expire by
their own limitation, or shall be altered or repealed by
the General Assembly, in pursuance of this Constitution. The validity of all bonds, debts, contracts, as
well of individuals as of bodies corporate, or the State,
of all suits, actions, or rights of action, both in law and
equity, shall continue as if no change had taken place.
The Governor, Lieutenant-Governor, and General Assembly, which is to be formed in October next, shall
have and possess all the powers and authorities not re-

pugnant to, or inconsistent with, this Constitution, which they now have and possess, until the first Wednesday of May next.

SEC. 4. No judge of the Superior Court, or of the Supreme Court of Errors; no member of Congress; no person holding any office under the authority of the United States; no person holding the office of Treasurer, Secretary, or Comptroller; no sheriff or sheriff's deputy, shall be a member of the General Assembly.

ARTICLE ELEVENTH.

OF AMENDMENTS TO THE CONSTITUTION.

Whenever a majority of the House of Representatives shall deem it necessary to alter or amend this Constitution, they may propose such alteration and amendments; which proposed amendments shall be continued to the next General Assembly, and be published with the laws which may have been passed at the same session; and if two-thirds of each House, at the next session of said Assembly, shall approve the amendments proposed, by yeas and nays, said amendment shall, by the Secretary, be transmitted to the town clerk in each town in the State, whose duty it shall be to present the same to the inhabitants thereof, for their consideration, at a town meeting, legally warned and held for that purpose; and if it shall appear, in a manner to be provided by law, that a majority of the electors present at such meetings shall have approved such amendments, the same shall be valid, to all intents and purposes, as a part of this Constitution.

Done in Convention, on the fifteenth day of September, in the year of our Lord one thousand eight hundred and eighteen, and of the Independence of the United States the forty-third.

By order of the Convention,

OLIV. WOLCOTT, *President.*

JAMES LYMAN,　}
ROBERT FAIRCHILD, }　*Clerks.*

AMENDMENTS TO THE CONSTITUTION.

ARTICLE I.
ADOPTED NOVEMBER, 1828.

From and after the first Wednesday of May, in the year of our Lord one thousand eight hundred and thirty, the Senate of this State shall consist of not less than eighteen nor more than twenty-four members, and be chosen by districts.

ARTICLE II
ADOPTED NOVEMBER, 1828.

The General Assembly, which shall be holden on the first Wednesday of May, in the year one thousand eight hundred and twenty-nine, shall divide the State into districts for the choice of Senators, and shall determine what number shall be elected in each; which districts shall not be less than eight nor more than twenty-four in number, and shall always be composed of contiguous territory, and in forming them no town shall be divided, nor shall the whole or part of one county be joined to the whole or part of another county to form a district; regard being had to the population in said apportionment, and in forming said districts, in such manner that no county shall have less than two senators. The districts, when established, shall continue the same until the session of the General Assembly next after the completion of the next census of the United States; which said Assembly shall have power to alter the same, if found necessary, to preserve a proper equality between said districts, in respect to the number of inhabitants therein, according to the principles above recited; after which said district shall not be altered, nor the number of Senators altered, except at any session of the General Assembly next after the completion of a census of the United States, and then only according to the principles above described.

ARTICLE III.
ADOPTED NOVEMBER, 1828.

At the meeting of the electors on the first Monday of April, in the year one thousand eight hundred and thirty, and annually thereafter, immediately after the choice of Representatives, the electors qualified by law to vote in the choice of such Representatives shall be called upon by the presiding officer in such meeting, in the several towns within their districts, respectively, to bring in their ballots for such person or number of persons to be Senator or Senators for such districts in the next General Assembly, as shall by law be allowed to such districts respectively;* which person or persons at the time of holding such meetings, shall belong to and reside in the respective districts in which they shall be so balloted for, as aforesaid: And each elector present at such meeting, qualified as aforesaid, may thereupon bring in his ballot or suffrage for such person or persons as he shall choose to be Senators for such district, not exceeding the number·by law allowed to the same, with the name or names of such person or persons fairly written on one piece of paper.* And the votes so given shall be received, counted, canvassed, and declared in the same manner now provided by the Constitution for the choice of Senators. The person or persons, not exceeding the number by law allowed to the districts in which such votes shall be given in, having the highest number of votes, shall be declared to be duly elected for such districts: But in the event of an equality of votes between two or more of the persons so voted for, the House of Representatives shall,

---

* Altered by amendment of 1836.

in the manner provided for by the Constitution, designate which of such person or persons shall be declared to be duly elected.

ARTICLE IV.
ADOPTED NOVEMBER, 1832.

There shall annually * be chosen and appointed a Lieutenant-Governor, a Treasurer, and Secretary, in the same manner as is provided in the second section of the fourth article of the Constitution of this State, for the choice and appointment of a Governor.

ARTICLE V.
ADOPTED NOVEMBER, 1836.

A Comptroller of Public Accounts shall be annually chosen by the electors, at their meeting in April, and in the same manner as the Treasurer and Secretary are chosen, and the votes for Comptroller shall be returned to, counted, canvassed, and declared by the Treasurer and Secretary.

ARTICLE VI.
ADOPTED NOVEMBER, 1836.

The electors in the respective towns, on the first Monday of April in each year, may vote for Governor, Lieutenant-Governor, Treasurer, Secretary, Senators, and Representatives in the General Assembly successively, or for any number of said officers at the same time, and the General Assembly shall have power to enact laws regulating and prescribing the order and manner of voting for said officers, and also providing for the election of Representatives at some time subsequent to the first Monday of April in all cases when it shall so happen that the electors in any town shall fail on that day to elect the Representative or Representatives to which such town shall be by law entitled: *provided,*

---

* Altered by amendments of 1875.

that in all elections of officers of the State, or members of the General Assembly, the votes of the electors shall be by ballot, either written or printed.

ARTICLE VII.
ADOPTED OCTOBER, 1838.

A sheriff shall be appointed in each county by the electors therein, in such manner as shall be prescribed by law, who shall hold his office for three years, removable by the General Assembly, and shall become bound with sufficient sureties to the Treasurer of the State for the faithful discharge of the duties of his office.

ARTICLE VIII.
ADOPTED OCTOBER, 1845.

Every white * male citizen of the United States, who shall have attained the age of twenty-one years, who shall have resided in this State for a term of one year next preceding, and in the town in which he may offer himself to be admitted to the privileges of an elector, at least six months next preceding the time he may so offer himself, † and shall sustain a good moral character, shall, on his taking such oaths as may be prescribed by law, be an elector.

ARTICLE IX.
ADOPTED OCTOBER, 1850.

The Judges of Probate shall be appointed by the electors residing in the several probate districts, and qualified to vote for Representatives therein, in such manner as shall be prescribed by law.

ARTICLE X.
ADOPTED OCTOBER, 1850.

The Justices of the Peace for the several towns in

* Altered by amendments of 1876.
† Altered by amendments of 1855.

this State shall be appointed by the electors in such towns; and the time and manner of their election, the number of each town, and the period for which they shall hold their offices, shall be prescribed by law.

ARTICLE XI.
ADOPTED OCTOBER, 1855.

Every person shall be able to read any article of the Constitution, or any section of the Statutes of this State, before being admitted an elector.   .

ARTICLE XII.
ADOPTED OCTOBER, 1856.

The Judges of the Supreme Court of Errors, and of the Superior Court, appointed in the year 1855, and thereafter, shall hold their offices for the term of eight years, but may be removed by impeachment; and the Governor shall also remove them on the address of two-thirds of each House of the General Assembly. No Judge of the Supreme Court of Errors, or of the Superior Court, shall be capable of holding office after he shall arrive at the age of seventy years.

ARTICLE XIII.
ADOPTED AUGUST, 1864.

[Every elector of this State who shall be in the military service of the United States, either as a drafted person or a volunteer, during the present rebellion, when absent from the State, because of such service, have the same right to vote in any election of State officers, Representatives in Congress, and electors of President and Vice-President of the United States, as he would have if present at the time appointed for such election, in the town in which he resided at the time of his enlistment into such service. This provision shall in no case extend to persons in the regular army of the United States, and shall cease and become inoperative and void upon the termination of the present war.

The General Assembly shall prescribe, by law, in what manner and at what time the votes of electors absent from this State, in the military service of the United States, shall be received, counted, returned, and canvassed.]*

ARTICLE XIV.
ADOPTED OCTOBER, 1873.

All annual and special sessions of the General Assembly shall, on and after the first Wednesday of May, A.D. 1875, be held at Hartford, but the person administering the office of Governor may, in case of special emergency, convene said Assembly at any other place in this State.

ARTICLE XV.
ADOPTED OCTOBER, 1874.

The House of Representatives shall consist of electors residing in towns from which they are elected. Every town which now contains, or hereafter shall contain, a population of five thousand, shall be entitled to send two representatives, and every other one shall be entitled to its present representation in the General Assembly. The population of each town shall be determined by the enumeration made under the authority of the census of the United States next before the election of Representatives is held.

ARTICLE XVI.
ADOPTED OCTOBER, 1875.

SECTION 1. A general election for Governor, Lieutenant-Governor, Secretary of State, Treasurer, Comptroller, and members of the General Assembly, shall be held on the Tuesday after the first Monday of November, 1876, and annually thereafter, for such officers as are herein and may be hereafter prescribed.

---

* Now inoperative.

SEC. 2. The State officers above named, and the Senators from those districts having even numbers, elected on the Tuesday after the first Monday of November, 1876, and those elected biennially thereafter on the Tuesday after the first Monday of November, shall respectively hold their offices for two years from and after the Wednesday following the first Monday of the next succeeding January. The Senators from those districts having odd numbers elected on the Tuesday after the first Monday of November, 1876, shall hold their offices for one year from and after the Wednesday following the first Monday of January, 1877; the electors residing in the senatorial districts having odd numbers shall, on the Tuesday after the first Monday of November, 1877, and biennially thereafter, elect Senators who shall hold their offices for two years from and after the Wednesday following the first Monday of the next succeeding January. The Representatives elected from the several towns on the Tuesday after the first Monday of November, 1876, and those elected annually thereafter, shall hold their offices for one year from and after the Wednesday following the first Monday of the next succeeding January.

SEC. 3. There shall be a stated session of the General Assembly in Hartford on the Wednesday after the first Monday of January, 1877, and annually thereafter on the Wednesday after the first Monday of January.

SEC. 4. The persons who shall be severally elected to the State offices and General Assembly on the first Monday of April, 1876, shall hold such offices only until the Wednesday after the first Monday of January, 1877.

SEC. 5. The General Assembly elected in April, 1876, shall have power to pass such laws as may be necessary to carry into effect the provisions of this amendment.

ARTICLE XVII.

ADOPTED OCTOBER, 1875.

The General Assembly shall have power, by a vote of two-thirds of the members of both branches, to restore the privileges of an elector to those who may have forfeited the same by a conviction of crime.

ARTICLE XVIII.

ADOPTED OCTOBER, 1876.

In case a new town shall hereafter be incorporated, such new town shall not be entitled to a Representative in the General Assembly unless it has at least twenty-five hundred inhabitants, and unless the town from which the major portion of its territory is taken has also at least twenty-five hundred inhabitants; but until such towns shall each have at least twenty-five hundred inhabitants, such new town shall, for the purpose of representation in the General Assembly, be attached to, and be deemed to be a part of, the town from which the major portion of its territory is taken, and it shall be an election district of such town for the purpose of representation in the House of Representatives.

ARTICLE XIX.

ADOPTED OCTOBER, 1876.

The provisions of Section 2, Article IV of the Constitution, and of the amendments thereto, shall apply, *mutatis mutandis*, to all elections held on the first Tuesday after the first Monday of November, 1876, and annually thereafter.

ARTICLE XX.

ADOPTED OCTOBER, 1876.

Judges of the Courts of Common Pleas, and of the District Courts, shall be appointed for terms of four years. Judges of the City Courts and Police Courts shall be appointed for terms of two years.

ARTICLE XXI.

ADOPTED OCTOBER, 1876.

Judges of Probate shall be elected by the electors re siding in their respective districts on the Tuesday after the first Monday of November, 1876, and biennially thereafter. Those persons elected Judges of Probate on the Tuesday after the first Monday of November, 1876, and those elected biennially thereafter, shall hold their offices for two years from and after the Wednesday after the first Monday of the next succeeding January. Those persons elected Judges of Probate on the first Monday of April, 1876, shall hold their offices only until the Wednesday after the first Monday of January, 1877.

ARTICLE XXII.

ADOPTED OCTOBER, 1876.

The compensation of members of the General Assembly shall not exceed three hundred dollars per annum, and one mileage each way for each session, at the rate of twenty-five cents per mile.

ARTICLE XXIII.

ADOPTED OCTOBER, 1876.

That Article VIII of the amendments to the Constitution be amended by erasing the word "white" from the first line.

ARTICLE XXIV.

ADOPTED OCTOBER, 1877.

Neither the General Assembly nor any County, City, Borough, Town, or School District shall have power to pay or grant any extra compensation to any public officer, employee, agent or servant, or increase the compensation of any public officer or employee, to take effect during the continuance in office of any person whose salary might be increased thereby, or increase the pay or compensation of any public contractor above the amount specified in the contract.

ARTICLE XXV.

ADOPTED OCTOBER, 1877.

No County, City, Town, Borough, or other municipality shall ever subscribe to the capital stock of any railroad corporation, or become a purchaser of the bonds, or make donations to, or loan its credit, directly or indirectly, in aid of any such corporation; but nothing herein contained shall affect the validity of any bonds or debts incurred under existing laws, nor be construed to probibit the General Assembly from authorizing any Town or City to protect, by additional appropriations of money or credit, any railroad debt contracted prior to the adoption of this amendment.

ARTICLE XXVI.

ADOPTED OCTOBER, 1880.

The Judges of the Supreme Court of Errors, and of the Superior Court, shall, upon nomination of the Governor, be appointed by the General Assembly, in such manner as shall by law be prescribed.

JOINT RULES OF PROCEEDINGS

FOR THE

SENATE AND HOUSE OF REPRESENTATIVES

OF CONNECTICUT.

I. Immediately after the organization of the Senate and House of Representatives, at the commencement of every stated session of the General Assembly, a Joint Committee, consisting of one Senator and eight Representatives, shall be appointed to examine the returns and canvass of votes given by the electors for Governor, Lieutenant-Governor, Treasurer, Secretary, and Comptroller of Public Accounts, and to report the names of the persons whom they shall find elected to those offices respectively. After this report shall have been accepted, a Joint Committee, consisting of one Senator and two Representatives, shall be appointed, to inform the Governor personally of his election and of the organization of the two houses, and their readiness to receive his communications.

II. On or before the third day of every stated session of the General Assembly there shall be appointed twenty Joint Standing Committees, each of which shall consist of one Senator and eight Representatives, except the Committee on Engrossed Bills, which shall consist of one Senator and three Representatives, viz.:

1st. A Committee on the Judiciary, who shall take into consideration all such matters touching public or private acts and judicial proceedings, as shall be referred to them, and to report their opinion thereon, together with such propositions relative thereto as to them shall seem expedient.

2d. A Committee on the School Fund, who shall

inquire into and report the actual state of the School Fund, the amount, value, and condition of its securities, and recommend such measures as they shall deem best adapted to secure its improvement and permanent safety.

3d. A Committee on Banks, who shall take into consideration all such matters relative to Banks, Savings Banks, and Savings and Building Associations, as may be referred to them, and report the facts, with their opinion thereon.

4th. A Committee on the State Prison, who shall examine the annual reports of the directors and officers in charge of the State Prison, the account of receipts and expenditures of the institution, together with such other matters as shall be referred to them by the two Houses of the General Assembly. And they may recommend such measures for the regulation and management of the Prison as they shall deem expedient.

5th. A Committee on New Towns and Probate Districts, who shall take into consideration all matters relating to the incorporation of new towns, the alteration of town lines, and the formation of probate districts, which shall be referred to them, and report their opinion thereon, together with the facts upon which such opinion is founded.

6th. A Committee on Roads and Bridges, who shall take into consideration all such matters relative to roads and bridges as shall be referred to them, and report the facts, with their opinion thereon.

7th. A Committee on Incorporations, who shall take into consideration all matters relative to private corporations, for which there may be no other appropriate committee, and report their opinion thereon, with the facts on which the same is founded.

8th. A Committee on Claims, which shall take into consideration all claims and demands upon the State which may be referred to them, and report their opinion thereon, with the facts on which the same is founded.

9th. A Committee on Education, who shall take into consideration all such matters relating to the subject of common school education as shall be referred to them, and recommend such measures touching the same as they shall deem expedient.

10th. A Committee on the Sale of Lands, who shall take into consideration all applications for the sale of lands which shall be referred to them, and report the facts, with their opinion thereon.

11th. A Committee on Finance, who shall take into consideration the financial concerns of the State, and inquire into the receipts and expenditures of the government, the investment of the public funds (the school fund excepted), the system of assessment and taxation provided by existing laws, and all other matters affecting the revenue of the State; and report such measures touching the same as they may deem expedient.

12th. A Committee on Railroads, who shall take into consideration all matters relating to railroads and railroad companies as may be referred to them, and report the facts, with their opinion thereon.

13th. A Committee on Military Affairs, who shall examine all military returns, and take into consideration all matters relating to the militia of this State which may be referred to them, and report thereon, with their opinion touching the same.

14th. A Committee on Agriculture, who shall take into consideration all such matters relating to Agriculture as may be referred to them, and report thereon, with their opinion touching the same.

15th. A Committee on Humane Institutions, who shall take into consideration all such matters relating to the Benevolent Institutions under the care or supervision of the State as may be referred to them, and report thereon, with their opinion touching the same.

16th. A Committee on Cities and Boroughs, who shall take into consideration all such matters relating to cities and boroughs as may be referred to them, and report the facts, and their opinion thereon.

17th. A Committee on Fisheries, who shall take into consideration all such matters relating to fisheries as may be referred to them, and report the facts, and their opinion thereon in the matter.

18th. A Committee on Insurance, who shall take into consideration all such matters relating to insurance that may be referred to them, and report the facts, and their opinion thereon.

19th. A Committee on Manufactures, who shall take into consideration all matters relating to manufactures that may be referred to them, and report their opinion thereon.

20th. A Committee on Engrossed Bills, whose duty it shall be to examine the engrossed copy of each bill for a public act, and of each joint resolution for a special act which has been passed by both houses, and to verify it, upon finding it to be a correct copy of the bill or joint resolution, and of the amendments, if any, as it was passed; and no engrossed copy of any bill for a public act, or of any joint resolution for a special act, shall be certified by the officers of either house as having been passed, until it has first been verified by the signature of at least two members of the committee.

III. In all meetings of Joint Committees, the Senators shall preside. All questions of order in their proceedings, and questions relative to the admission of evidence, shall be determined by a majority of votes; and in case the vote be equally divided, the Senators shall have a casting vote.

IV. All Committees of Conference, on disagreeing votes of the two Houses of Assembly, shall consist of one Senator and two Representatives, who were in the major vote of their respective Houses. The Committee of the House making the grant or appointment, or passing the bill, resolution, or amendment disagreed to, shall state their reasons, to be reported to the other House. And neither House shall request the other twice to confer on the same point of disagreement.

16

V. Whenever each House shall have adhered to its vote of disagreement, the bill or resolution shall be considered as lost.

VI. Every message sent from one House to the other shall be announced at the door, and shall be respectfully communicated to the Chair by the person by whom it may be sent.

VII. Whenever a bill shall have passed both Houses of the Assembly, and shall have been transmitted to the Governor for his approbation, if either House desires its return for further consideration, such desire shall be communicated by message to the other House, and a Joint Committee of one Senator and two Representatives shall then be sent to the Governor to request him to return the bill. If the Governor consents, the bill shall be returned first to that House in which the motion for its return originated, and the bill may then be altered or totally rejected by a concurrent vote of the two Houses; but if not altered or rejected by such concurrent vote, it shall be again transmitted to the Governor in the same form in which it was first presented to him.

VIII. Whenever the public business may require the Senate and House of Representatives to meet in Convention, either House may send its message to the other, requesting such Convention, and specifying the object. At the time designated, the Senate, with their President and Clerk, may proceed to the Hall of the House of Representatives, where suitable accommodations will be provided. The President of the Senate shall *ex-officio* preside in said Convention, and the proceedings thereof shall be entered upon the Journals of the two Houses.

When the Convention shall have been dissolved, the President of the Senate and the Speaker of the House of Representatives shall make report to their respective Houses of the proceedings of the Convention.

IX All bills for public acts which shall have been passed by both Houses of the General Assembly, engrossed, and signed by the Speaker of the House of Representatives and President of the Senate, and all bills for private acts and joint resolutions, which shall have been passed by the two Houses, shall, with the papers on which the same may be founded, be transmitted by the Committee on Engrossed Bills to the Secretary of State, for the purpose of being by him laid before the Governor. The presiding officers of the two Houses shall affix their signatures to all bills for public acts in the presence of one or more of the Engrossing Committee, or the Secretary.

X.   Every bill or resolution shall be written or printed without interlineation or erasure, on paper not smaller than a half sheet of foolscap, and any member offering such bill, resolution, or a petition shall endorse thereon his name in some conspicuous place. No bill or resolution shall, after it has been introduced, be altered either by addition or erasure. Any proposed changes in the text of such bill or resolution which may be deemed advisable by the Committee to which it has been referred, shall be reported in the form of amendments, or of a substitute bill.

XI.   The Clerk of the House to which any bill shall be first presented shall indorse thereon a statement of the contents, or objects of such bill or resolution, before transmitting the same to the other House.

XII.   All acts of incorporation by bill or resolution, and all acts in amendment or alteration thereof, and all private acts of whatever nature, shall, before the same shall be considered, be printed for the use of the General Assembly, at the expense of the party applying therefor.

XIII.   All bills for public acts reported favorably upon by the committee to which they have been or may be referred, with or without amendments, before being put upon their third reading, shall be laid upon the table, and three hundred copies of such bills, with their amendments, shall be printed for the use of the General Assembly; and no bill so reported shall be put upon its third reading until the day succeeding the distribution of such copies.

XIV. All bills for public acts, and all joint resolutions for special acts, which have been passed by both Houses, shall, without action, be referred to the Committee on Engrossed Bills, and (in addition, the duties prescribed in Rule No. 11) it shall be the duty of the committee, before any bill or joint resolution be engrossed, to immediately examine the same with a view to avoid repetitions, and to secure clearness, conciseness, and accuracy in the text, without changing the purport thereof. If the committee find that any correction should be made in the text or references, or in the title of any bill or joint resolution, they shall, within two session days after the passage thereof, report it back to the House which last took action upon it, with the proposed correction in the form of an amendment.

All reports from the Committee on Engrossed Bills shall be placed at the head of the calendar, and shall take precedence of all other business on the calendar; and the only question upon the report of the committee shall be, "Shall the proposed amendment be adopted?"

If the proposed amendment be adopted by both Houses, the bill or resolution shall be transmitted to the Secretary, who shall cause it to be engrossed as amended. If the proposed amendment be rejected by either House, the bill or resolution shall not be transmitted to the other House, but shall be sent to the Secretary, who shall have it engrossed as it was passed.

If, in consequence of the final adjournment of the General Assembly, or for any other reason, any bill or resolution which has passed both Houses fails to be amended, as recommended by the committee, the bill or resolution shall be engrossed as it was passed.

XV. All bills for public acts and joint resolutions for special acts adversely reported upon by any committee shall be first reported to the House in which they respectively originated; and any bill or joint reso-

lution so **reported** on adversely, **if** no objection is **made, may, on** motion of **the** member **who** introduced it, or at his request, be acted upon immediately. If the bill or resolution be not rejected, it shall then be entered upon the calendar to be acted upon in its regular order.

RULES TO REGULATE THE PROCEEDINGS

OF THE

SENATE OF CONNECTICUT.

Resolved, That the Rules and Orders following be, and they are hereby, adopted as the standing Rules and Orders of the Senate, and they shall be read at the commencement of each session of the General Assembly by the Clerk.

1st. The President shall take the chair every day, at the hour to which the Senate shall have adjourned, and after prayer shall immediately call the Senate to order, and if a quorum be present, proceed to business.

2d. The President shall preserve order, and shall decide questions of order without debate, subject to an appeal to the Senate. He shall rise to put a question, but may state it sitting. The question first moved and seconded shall be the first put, and in all cases the sense of the Senate shall be taken upon the largest number or sum, and the longest time proposed.

3d. No member shall in any way interrupt the business of the Senate while the journal or public papers are in reading, nor when any member is speaking in debate, nor while the President is putting a question.

4th. When any member is about to speak in debate, or deliver any matter to the Senate, he shall rise and respectfully address *"Mr. President"*; if two or more arise at once, the President shall name the member who is first to speak.

5th. No member shall speak more than twice upon the same question, without leave of the Senate, unless to explain.

6th. When a question is before the Senate, no motion shall be received but to adjourn, to lay upon the table, to postpone indefinitely, to postpone to a certain day, to commit, or to amend; which several motions shall have precedence in the order in which they stand arranged, and a motion for adjournment shall always be in order, and be decided without debate.

7th. If the question in debate contains several points, any member may have the same divided.

8th. When the yeas and nays shall be called for by one-fifth of the members present, each member called upon shall (unless for special reason he be excused by the Senate) declare openly his assent or dissent to the question.

9th. When a motion is made and seconded, it shall be stated to the Senate by the President, before any debate be had thereon; but every motion shall be reduced to writing, if the President so direct, or any member desire it.

10th. Every bill shall be introduced by a motion for leave, or by order of the Senate, or the report of a committee, and every bill for a public act shall receive three several readings in the Senate, previously to its being passed into an act. And no bill shall be read twice on the same day, without the order of the Senate. Nor may the President state the same to the Senate for debate, until the second reading.

11th. A committee of three shall, within the first two days of each session, be appointed by ballot to take into consideration all contested elections of members of the Senate, and to report the facts in issue, together with their opinion thereon.

12th. Committees of Conference shall be appointed by the Senate.

13th. All other committees shall be appointed by resolution by the Senate, unless the Senate shall otherwise order.

14th. When a motion has been stated by the President, or read by the clerk, it shall be considered to be in possession of the Senate, but may be withdrawn at any time before decision or amendment; but not after amendment, unless the Senate give leave.

15th.   No member who is interested in the decision of any question in such manner that he cannot vote may stay in the Senate when such question is discussed or decided: *provided*, however, that this rule shall not extend to the sitting members in contested elections.

16th.   When any member shall request a Committee of Conference on different votes of the two Houses of Assembly, a committee, consisting of one member, who was in the vote of the Senate, shall be appointed; and if any member who was not in such vote shall be nominated, he shall notify the Senate.

17th.   When the Senate has voted to appoint a committee to prepare a bill or resolve, upon any subject, no person shall be on such committee who was opposed to the vote of the Senate.

18th.   If any member, in speaking or otherwise, shall transgress the rules of the Senate, the President shall, and any member may, call to order, and if speaking, he shall sit down, unless permitted to explain; the Senate, if appealed to, shall decide the question without debate.

19th.   When a question shall have been once decided, it shall be in order for any member of the majority to move for a reconsideration thereof; but no such motion shall be made unless within three days of actual session of the Senate, after the day on which the decision to be reconsidered was made.

20th.   Before any petition or memorial address to the Senate shall be received and read at the table, whether the same shall be introduced by the President or a member, a brief statement of the contents or object of the petition or memorial shall be verbally made by the introducer.

21st.   All questions shall be put by the President of the Senate, and the Senators shall signify their assent or dissent by answering, *vivâ voce*, aye or no.   And whenever the vote shall be doubted or questioned, it shall be determined by the members rising, and in all cases the ayes shall be first * called.

22d. Every resolution or bill granting money from the Treasurer of the State shall, before its final passage, receive three several readings, only one of which will be on the same day.

23d. It shall be the duty of the Clerk to keep a calendar, on which he shall enter daily all bills and joint resolutions received from the House of Representatives for the action of the Senate, except the bills and joint resolutions which have not been referred by the Senate to any committee, and all bills and joint resolutions reported to the Senate from any committee; and these shall be entered on the calendar in the order in which they are reported; and no bill or joint resolution received from the House of Representatives or reported from a committee, shall be considered and acted upon until it is reached in its regular order on the calendar.

All bills and joint resolutions shall be entitled to be considered and acted upon when reached in their regular order on the calendar, and any bill or joint resolution not considered and acted upon in its regular order shall be placed at the foot of the calendar; unless the consideration of the same be by vote of two-thirds of the Senators present made the order of the day for some specified day named in the resolution.

24th. It shall be the duty of the Clerk of the Senate to keep a record of all petitions, resolutions, joint resolutions, and bills for public acts which are presented for the consideration of the Senate; and said record shall be so kept as to show by one and a single reference thereto, the action of the Senate on any specified petition, resolution, joint resolution, or bill for a public act, up to the time of such reference.

---

*As originally drawn, the 21st rule read as here printed. In 1864, apparently by accident, the word "first" was dropped out of the last clause. Its restoration is obviously necessary to give force to the provision.

RULES

OF THE

HOUSE OF REPRESENTATIVES

IN THE

GENERAL ASSEMBLY OF CONNECTICUT.

Resolved, That the Rules and Orders following be, and they are hereby, adopted as the Standing Rules and Orders of this House:

TOUCHING THE DUTY OF THE SPEAKER.

1. The Speaker shall take the chair every day, at the hour to which the House shall have adjourned; he shall immediately call the House to order, and after prayers and roll-call, if a quorum be present, proceed to business.

2. In the absence of a quorum, the Speaker may adjourn the House to the afternoon, or the next sitting day. At all other times during the session an adjournment shall be pronounced by the Speaker on motion.

3. The Speaker shall preserve order and decorum; and shall decide questions of order without debate (except at the request of the Chair), subject to an appeal to the House, on which appeal no member shall speak more than once.

4. In all cases when a vote is taken without a division, the Speaker shall determine whether it is or is not a vote; and in all doubtful cases he shall ask, "*Is it doubted?*" If the vote be disputed, it shall be tried again; but after the Speaker has declared the vote, it

shall not be recalled, unless by a regular motion for re-
consideration, made by a member in the vote of the
House.

5. If the Speaker still doubt a vote, or a division be
called for, the House shall divide; those in the affirma-
tive of the question shall first rise from their seats, and
stand until counted, and afterwards those in the nega-
tive.

6. In all cases of balloting the Speaker shall vote;
in other cases he shall not vote unless the House be
equally divided, or unless his vote, if given in the mi-
nority, will make the division equal; and in case of
such equal division, the question shall be lost.

7. In case of any disturbance or disorderly conduct
in the galleries; lobby, or aisles of the House, the Speaker shall have power to order the same to be cleared.

8. In case the Speaker wishes to leave the chair for
the purpose of taking part in the debate, or from indis-
position, or other cause, he may designate some member to preside, but not exceeding one day after the day
of such designation.

9. That in the case of the absence of the Speaker for
more than two daily sessions, the Clerk shall call the
House to order, at the hour to which the House stands
adjourned, and the first business in order shall be the
election of the Speaker *pro tempore*, which it shall immediately proceed to do without debate, by nomination
or ballot, as the House shall determine; these questions
shall also be decided without debate; and the Speaker
pro tempore thus elected shall preside in the House and
discharge all the duties of the Speaker until his return. ·

In case of the death or resignation of a Speaker, the
Clerk shall call the House to order, as provided in the
first clause of this rule, and the first business in order
shall be the election of a Speaker by ballot, which the
House shall immediately proceed to, without debate,
and the Speaker thus elected shall preside over the
House and discharge all the duties of the Speaker during the continuance of the General Assembly.

OF THE CLERK.

10. The Clerk shall not transmit any bill, resolution, or other paper, from the House to the Senate, on the same day upon which the action was had thereon, except the House otherwise orders.

11. The Clerk shall prepare the daily calendar as hereinafter provided.

12. The Clerk shall enter upon the Journal the language of any amendment that may be offered to any bill or resolution, provided the same is not withdrawn before action by the House.

OF THE MEMBERS.

13. When any member is about to speak in debate, or deliver any matter to the House, he shall rise and address "*Mr. Speaker;*" if two or more rise at once, the Speaker shall name the member who is first to speak.

14. No member shall speak more than twice to the same question, without leave of the House.

15. No member who is interested in the decision of any question in such a manner that he cannot vote, may stay in the House when such a question is discussed or decided.

16. Every member present, when a question is put by the Speaker, shall vote, unless excused by the House.

17. If any member, in speaking or otherwise, transgress the Rules and Orders of this House, the Speaker shall, or any member may, call to order; and if speaking, he shall sit down, unless permitted to explain. The House, if appealed to, shall decide the case, but without debate. If no such appeal be made, the Speaker shall decide the same.

18. For the purpose of more conveniently counting upon the division of the House, the floor thereof shall be divided by aisles in four divisions, to be numbered first, second, third, and fourth sections, commencing on the right of the chair; for each of which divisions

the Speaker shall appoint a member, whose seat is in said division, to be a teller to count and report to the chair.

OF MOTIONS, THEIR PRECEDENCE, ETC.

19.   When a motion is made and seconded, it shall be stated to the House by the Speaker, before any debate be had thereon; but every motion shall be reduced to writing, if the Speaker so direct, or any member desire it.

20.   When a motion is stated by the Speaker, or read by the Clerk, it shall be deemed to be in possession of the House; but may be withdrawn at any time before decision or amendment, but not after amendment, unless the House give leave.

21.   The question first moved and seconded shall be first put (except as modified by Rule 22); and in all cases the sense of the House shall be first taken upon the largest number or sum, and the longest time proposed, in any question.

22.   When a question is under debate, no motion shall be received but to adjourn, to lie on the table, for the previous question, to postpone indefinitely, to postpone to a certain day, to continue to next session of General Assembly, to commit, or to amend, which several motions shall have precedence in the order in which they stand arranged.

And no motion to lie on the table, to postpone indefinitely, or to commit, having been once decided, shall be again allowed at the same sitting, and at the same stage of the bill or subject-matter.

23.   A motion to adjourn shall always be in order, and said motion shall be decided without debate, as shall also a motion to lie on the table.

24.   No debate shall be allowed after a question is put and remains undecided.

25.   The yeas and nays shall be taken on any question, and entered upon the Journal, at the desire of

one-fifth of the members present, at any time before a declaration of the vote.

26. When a question shall have once been decided, it shall be in order for any member in the prevailing vote to move for a re-consideration thereof, if at the time the subject-matter be in possession of the House; but no such motion shall be made unless within two days of the actual session of the House, after the day on which decision was had thereon.

OF BILLS AND THE CALENDAR.

27. Every bill or joint resolution shall be introduced by motion for leave, or by order of the House, or by the report of a committee; and every public bill or joint resolution shall receive three several readings in the House previously to its being passed into an act, and no such bill or joint resolution shall be read twice on the same day; every member offering such bill or resolution shall indorse thereon its object, and the Speaker may not offer any bill or resolution to the House until after its first reading, and every bill or resolution may be referred on its first reading.

28. The first reading of a bill or resolution shall be for information, and, if opposition be made to it, the question shall be, "Shall this bill be rejected?" If no opposition be made, or if the question to reject be negatived, the bill or resolution shall go to its second reading without a question.

29. It shall be the duty of the Clerk to keep a calendar on which he shall enter daily (1) all bills and joint resolutions received from the Senate for the action of the House, except bills and joint resolutions which have not been referred by the House to any committee; and (2) all bills and resolutions reported to the House from any committee; and these shall be entered on the calendar in the order in which they are reported; and no bill or resolution received from the Senate, or reported from a committee, shall be considered and acted upon

until it is reached in its regular order upon the calendar.

Any bill or resolution not considered and acted upon in the regular order shall be placed at the foot of the calendar, unless the consideration of the same be, by a vote of two-thirds of the members present, made the order of the day for some specified time.

OF COMMITTEES.

30. At the opening of each session a Committee of Elections, consisting of three members, shall be appointed by the Speaker, to take into consideration all contested elections of the members of this House, and report facts, with their opinion thereon.

31. All committees, except committees of conference, shall be appointed by the Speaker, unless otherwise specially directed by the House.

32. When any member requests a committee of conference on different votes of the two Houses of Assembly, a committee, consisting of two members, shall be appointed on the part of the House; and in such case the committee shall consist only of such members as were in the vote of the House; and if any member be nominated on said committee who was not in the vote, he shall notify the House, and be excused.

33. It shall be the duty of the clerk to keep a record of all petitions, resolutions, joint-resolutions, and bills for public acts, which may be presented for the consideration of the House, and said record shall be so kept as to show by one and a single reference thereto the action of the House on any specific petition, resolution, joint resolution, or bill for a public act, up to the time of such reference.

34. Immediately after the appointment of the joint-standing committees, a committee of three shall be appointed to assign seats to the members of the House, and it shall be their duty: (1) To assign seats to be occupied by the Chairmen of all joint-standing commit-

tees, and of all Select Committees of the House. (2) To cause lots to be drawn for the assignment of seats to the other members of the House.

OF THE ORDER OF BUSINESS.

The order of business shall be as follows, viz.:
1. Reading and correction of the Journal.
2. Reception of Petitions.
3. Reception of Communications from the Governor, and Annual Reports.
4. Introduction of Resolutions.
5. Introduction and first reading of Bills.
6. Reports of Committees.
7. Reception of business from the Senate.
8. Business on the Calendar.
9. Motions, and miscellaneous business.

MISCELLANEOUS.

No standing rule or order of the House shall be-rescinded or changed without one day's notice being given of the motion therefor.

No rule shall be suspended, except by a vote of at least two-thirds of the members present.

THE CAPITOL BUILDING.

The capitol building located at Hartford, Connecticut, is a marble structure, that for beauty of design, grandeur of style, harmony of proportions, and adaptability may challenge comparison with any public building in the country. Its situation on the west side of Bushnell Park, on an eminence overlooking the city, and in the midst of beautiful surroundings, is peculiarly fortunate, not only for the transaction of legislative and judicial business, but for a display of the elegant proportions and the material of the building. The style of the structure may be called modern gothic, or an adaptation of gothic to civic purposes. The building has four fronts nearly corresponding with the four cardinal points of the compass. Its extreme length is 296 feet, extreme width 190 feet, and its height to the top of roof 93, and to top of crowning figure on the dome 257 feet. The foundation and cellar walls are of brown stone masonry, laid in cement mortar. The outer walls are faced with granite up to the plinth. The outer upper walls above the granite are of white marble facings, backed with brick-work. Over the main entrances the outer walls are supported by polished granite columns with capitals of carved marble, the columns supporting pointed arches with tympana richly ornamented with mouldings and carved crockets. These tympana, representing the upper portions of gothic arches, are intended to receive historical and symbolical carvings, as they may hereafter be ordered. One representing the famous Charter Oak tree has already been finished, and is situated over the door of the east entrance. It is very artistic in design, and was executed by Leopold Zaleski, of New Haven, Conn.

17

On each of the four fronts of the building are also carved corbels projecting from the walls, which support columns capped with pedestals for the reception of statues, a carved marble canopy over each pedestal completing the niche. Of these there are twenty-six in all. Two statues have been placed in position on the east front. One a statue of Governor Jonathan Trumbull, "Brother Jonathan" of revolutionary memory, the other Roger Sherman, a Connecticut signer of the Declaration of Independence. They are by Ives, the well-known sculptor, a native of Connecticut, and are cut from fine statuary marble. Between these statue niches are medallion stones intended for the reception of heads and profiles. Two are now finished, and occupy a place on the east side of the building. The one on the south side of the entrance is a head and bust of the late Rev. Horace Bushnell, D.D., LL.D., from whom Bushnell Park derives its name, the other on the north side, a head and bust of Noah Webster, LL.D. Both medallions were modeled by Mr. Carl Conrads, a noted Hartford sculptor.

The dormer windows on the roof, which make so marked a feature and so finely relieve the otherwise naked slopes, are of marble richly carved. The marble used in the building is from quarries in East Canaan, Connecticut, and is considered by the supervising architect and civil engineer as a strong, reliable building stone. The granite is from Westerly, R. I., Cape Ann, Mass., Jonesboro, Maine, and Stony Creek, Conn.

From the foundation to the roof, the piers and the tower for the support of the dome are rectangular, being corbeled out at the roof to receive the exterior tower, which is in cross section a dodecagon, making a twelve-sided tower supporting a cone 27 feet high from springing-point to apex, which is surmounted by a lantern 45 feet high, crowned with a colossal winged figure of bronze, 15 feet high, designed by Randolph Rogers, and denominated the "Genius of Connecticut." Around the base of the cone forming the dome arc twelve figures, symbolical or allegorical in character, representing Agriculture, Commerce, Science, Art, Force, Law, etc., and are by J. Q. A. Ward, the designer of the Putnam statue on Bushnell Park.

THE INTERIOR.

Inside the building there are two main stairways leading from the north and south entrances, but easily approachable from those on the east and west. These stairways are of marble, with steps and platforms of Westerly granite, and ornamented with 46 columns of the beautiful Stony Creek Granite. On the north and south walls, which are frescoed, are medallions, four in number, containing the coat of arms of Connecticut and of the United States, and the figures of Liberty and Justice.

THE SENATE CHAMBER

is situated on the mezzanine floor, and has a superficial area of 50 by 40 feet, with a height from floor to ceiling of 37 feet. It has three windows on the east front of the building admitting direct light, and the central panel in the ceiling is also a sky-light.

There are galleries on the north and south side, which will seat about 50 persons each.

THE REPRESENTATIVES HALL.

The hall of the representatives has a floor area 84 by 56 feet and a height of 49 feet. It is situated on the south projection of the building, on the same floor with the Senate, and is lighted by windows on the east and south, the gallery for spectators being on the north side, on which side is the Speaker's desk.

The length of the representatives hall is from east to west, and the floor is a series of platforms, four feet six inches wide, with risers or steps of seven inches. On these the members' desks and seats are arranged in amphitheatrical form, with raised aisles, leaving the space around the Speaker's desk for center.

THE GOVERNOR'S ROOMS.

The Governor's rooms consist of a private office and audience room in the southwest corner of the mezzanine floor, lighted by windows on the south and west. The oak wainscoating and oak mantels in these rooms are very substantial and elegant, and the decorations and furniture are of the most elaborate character.

LIEUT.-GOVERNOR'S ROOMS.

The corner rooms north and south of the Senate chamber, at the east end of the building, are for the Lieutenant-Governor and Speaker of the House of Representatives. They are similar in finish to the Governor's rooms.

THE SECRETARY.

The northwest corner rooms on the mezzanine floor are for the secretary. They are lighted by windows on the north and west, and correspond in size to the Governor's rooms.

STATE DEPARTMENT ROOMS.

On the ground floor are the rooms of the Comptroller, Treasurer, Insurance Commissioner, Adjutant-General, and Paymaster-General.

THE SUPREME COURT, STATE LIBRARY, ETC.

The Supreme Court room is on the second floor in the west portion of the building, and is lighted by six windows on the west side, arranged in two rows; is 50×31 feet on the floor, and has a height of 35 feet from floor to ceiling. The State Library room is on this floor, and has a superficial area of 85×55 feet, with a height same as that of the Supreme Court room—35 feet. It is situated on the north center, its north windows overlooking the northern entrance.

The Railroad and Capitol Commissioners, State Boards of Education and Health, also have rooms on this floor.

THE COST OF THE BUILDING.

The erection of the building commenced in 1872 and was finished in 1878. The formal transfer by the commissioners to the State authorities, took place January 1, 1879.

The following gives the total expense of building and grounds:

Appropriated by the State of Connecticut,	$2,000,000
Appropriated by the City of Hartford (for building), ...	500,000
Appropriated by the City of Hartford (for the site), ...	600,000
Total, ...	$3,100,000

STATE CAPITOL COMMISSIONERS.

ALFRED E. BURR, of Hartford, *President.*
JEREMIAH HALSEY, of Norwich.
NATHANIEL WHEELER, of Bridgeport.
WILLIAM P. TROWBRIDGE, of New Haven.
FRANKLIN CHAMBERLIN, of Hartford.
Architect, RICHARD M. UPJOHN, of New York.
Superintendent, WILLIAM B. FRANKLIN, of Hartford.
Civil Engineer, WILLIAM C. GUNNELL, of Hartford.
Contractor, JAMES G. BATTERSON, of Hartford.

THE GENERAL ASSEMBLY.
SENATE.

PRESIDENT.
Hon. WILLIAM H. BULKELEY, of Hartford.

PRESIDENT *pro tempore.*
Hon. ROBERT COIT, of New London.

[Senators from Districts having even numbers hold office for one year; from Districts having odd numbers for two years, from the Wednesday after the first Monday of January, 1882.]

1st District, John R. Hills, Hartford, r.
2d   "   John S. Cheney, Manchester, r.
3d   "   Rial Strickland, Enfield, d.
4th   "   Andrew S. Upson, Farmington, r.
5th   "   James S. Elton, Waterbury, r.
6th   "   Edward F. Jones, Branford, r.
7th   "   George M. Gunn, Milford, d.
8th   "   William J. Mills, New Haven, d.
9th   "   Robert Coit, New London, r.
10th   "   Charles P. White, North Stonington, r.
11th   "   Charles P. Sturtevant, East Lyme, r.
12th   "   Oliver Hoyt, Stamford, r.
13th   "   Tallmadge Baker, Norwalk, r.
14th   "   Morris W. Seymour, Bridgeport, d.
15th   "   William N. Northrop, Newtown, d.
16th   "   Henry Hammond, Killingly, r.
17th   "   Eugene S. Boss, Windham, r.
18th   "   Lorrin A. Cooke, Barkhamsted, r.
19th   "   Milo B. Richardson, Salisbury, d.

20th District, Albert P. Bradstreet, Thomaston, r.
21st   "   Richard P. Spencer, Saybrook, r.
22d   "   Joseph W. Alsop, Middletown, d.
23d   "   Ralph P. Gilbert, Hebron, r.
24th   "   Ebenezer C. Dennis, Stafford, r.

OFFICERS AND ATTACHES OF THE SENATE.

CHAPLAINS.

Rev. A. J. Sage, D.D., Hartford.
Rev. George L. Thompson, Hartford.

CLERK.

Charles Perrin, Stonington.

MESSENGERS.

Chauncey H. Eno, Simsbury.
L. W. Sessions, Windham.

DOORKEEPERS.

George S. Jeffrey, Meriden.
George W. Lovejoy, Monroe.
George A. Thompson, North Stonington.

REPORTERS.

John C. Kinney, Hartford Courant.
William O. Burr, Hartford Times.
E. Hart Fenn, Hartford Post.
Charles D. Page, New Haven Palladium.
Frank M. Lovejoy, New Haven Courier.
Amos A. Browning, Norwich Bulletin.

HOUSE OF REPRESENTATIVES.

SPEAKER.

Hon. JOHN M. HALL, R, of Windham.

HARTFORD COUNTY.

No. of Seat.

32—*Hartford*, George G. Sill, d.

11— Charles H. Cooley, r.

87—*Avon*, Frederick Ripley, r.

53—*Berlin*, Henry N. Galpin, r.

188—*Bloomfield*, Henry D. Barnard, d.

77—*Bristol*, Charles S. Treadway, r.

139— Elijah Manross, r.

46—*Burlington*, Charles C. McAleer, d.

108—*Canton*, George Mills, 2d, d.

8—*East Granby*, Jefferson R. Holcomb, d.

163—*East Hartford*, Arthur G. Olmsted, r.

244— Charles W. Roberts, d.

183—*East Windsor*, Orson S. Wood, r.

180— Charles E. Woodward, d.

51—*Enfield*, Loren H. Pease, r.

31— J. Warren Johnson, r.

79—*Farmington*, Thomas Cowles, r.

197— Lucius C. Humphrey, r.

145—*Glastonbury*, Charles H. Talcott, r.

120— Aaron W. Kinne, r.

175—*Granby*, Artemus G. Harger, r.

171— George R. Case, r.

201—*Hartland*, Henry J. Gates, r.

24— George H. Clark, r.

135—*Manchester*, Charles H. Owen, r.

 44—   Clinton W. Cowles, d.

194—*Marlborough*, John A. Haling, d.

 34—*New Britain*, Ambrose Beatty, d.

100—   James Thomson, d.

 78—*Newington*, David L. Robbins, d.

219—*Plainville*, Edward S. Towne, r.

 42—*Rocky Hill*, James H. Warner, d.

 26—*Simsbury*, Ebenezer G. Curtis, d.

212—   Daniel O. Reed, d.

208—*Southington*, J. Frank Pratt, r.

 27—   George F. Smith, r.

 28—*South Windsor*, John P. Jones, d.

 25—*Suffield*, Silas W. Clark, r.

245—   James Rising, r.

 35—*West Hartford*, E. Buel Root, r.

210—*Wethersfield*, Edwin F. Griswold, r.

 95—   Edward D. Robbins, r.

166—*Windsor*, Daniel W. Phelps, r.

181—   Lemuel R. Lord, r.

 96—*Windsor Locks*, John W. Coogan, d.

NEW HAVEN COUNTY.

 62—*New Haven*, A. Heaton Robertson, d.

176—   Timothy J. Fox, d.

143—*Beacon Falls*, Andrew W. Culver, r.

234—*Bethany*, Samuel R. Woodward, d.

114—*Branford*, William A. Wright, d.

136— *Cheshire*, Benjamin A. Jarvis, d.

 94—   Charles B. Terrell, d.

 47—*Derby*, William E. Downes, r.

 49—   Charles H. Pine, r.

248—*East Haven*, Orlando B. Thompson, d.

223—*Guilford*, Elisha C. Bishop, r.

147—   Edward Griswold, r.

232—*Hamden*, Bela A. Mann, d.

239—*Madison*, Horace O. Hill, r.

21—*Meriden*, William W. Lyman, r.

22—   Grove H. Wilson, r.

105—*Middlebury*, George O. Ellis, r.

20—*Milford*, Charles A. Tomlinson, d.

146—   Thomas W. Stow, d.

64—*Naugatuck*, Franklin B. Tuttle, d.

15—*North Branford*, William B. Curtis, r.

205—*North Haven*, Andrew F. Austin, r.

230—*Orange*, Edward E. Bradley, d.

217—*Oxford*, James H. Bartlett, r.

249—*Prospect*, George F. Tyler, r.

199—*Seymour*, John W. Rogers, r.

39—*Southbury*, Asahel F. Mitchell, r.

228—*Wallingford*, Phineas T. Ives, d.

128—   John W. Blakeslee, d.

2—*Waterbury*, Charles W. Gillette, r.

200—   Henry C. Griggs, r.

207—*Wolcott*, Samuel M. Bailey, r.

213—*Woodbridge*, Charles T. Walker, r.

NEW LONDON COUNTY.

72—*New London*, Henry B. Downer, d.

54—   Bryan F. Mahan, d.

97—*Norwich*, George C. Ripley, r.

59—   William S. Congdon, r.

159—*Bozrah*, Joshua C. Leffingwell, r.

214—*Colchester*, Uriah W. Carrier, d.

154—   John English, Jr., d.

235—*East Lyme*, John W. Luce, r.

43—*Franklin*, Oliver L. Johnson, r.

124—*Griswold*, Henry A. Lathrop, r.

116—*Groton*, Parmenas Avery, d.

117—   Sumner H. Gove, r.

123—*Lebanon*, Nathaniel B. Williams, r.

5—   Charles C. Loomis, r.

129—*Ledyard*, James A. Billings, r.

216—*Lisbon*, Augustus F. Read, d.

189—*Lyme*, Henry B. L. Reynolds, r.

198—   Benajah P. Bill, d.

153—*Montville*, Raymond N. Parish, r.

241—*North Stonington*, Orin Chapman, r.

238—   Charles H. Brown, r.

70—*Old Lyme*, Erastus E. Clark, d.

182—*Preston*, Chester W. Barnes, d.

68—   Charles P. Hewitt, d.

187—*Salem*, Gurdon F. Allyn, r.

12—*Sprague*, Dennis McCarty, g.

9—*Stonington*, Stiles T. Stanton, r.

138—   Alexander S. Palmer, Jr., d.

202—*Voluntown*, Timothy Parker, r.

10—*Waterford*, Nathaniel A. Chapman, d.

FAIRFIELD COUNTY.

110—*Bridgeport*, Augustus H. Abernethy, d.

18—   Peter W. Wren, d.

141—*Bethel*, Harry S. Glover, r.

144—*Brookfield*, Samuel Thornhill, d.

167—*Darien*, Charles Brown, r.

52—*Danbury*, Howard W. Taylor, d.

162—   Charles J. Deming, d.

169—*Easton*, Stephen D. Wheeler, r.

30—*Fairfield*, Henry F. Sherwood, d.

118—   Francis M. Pike, d.

4—*Greenwich*, Cornelius Mead, d.

226—   Charles E. Wilson, d.

191—*Huntington*, Daniel S. Brinsmade,

69—*Monroe*, Andrew B. Curtis, r.

179—*New Canaan*, Selleck Y. St. John, r.
 88—*New Fairfield*, Alexander Turner, d.
130—*Newtown*, William H. Glover, d.
211—   Edson W. Wilson, r.
 13—*Norwalk*, George R. Cowles, r.
204—   Charles W.'Bell, r.
 98—*Redding*, Thomas Sanford, d.
106—   Ebenezer F. Foster, d.
155—*Ridgefield*, Edward J. Couch, r.
 81—   Lewis E. Smith, r.
 23—*Sherman*, Allan W. Paige, r.
  1—*Stamford*, Edwin L. Scofield, r.
 83—   William W. Gillespie, r.
165—*Stratford*, Anson H. Blakeman, r.
 66—*Trumbull*, Elliott P. Nichols, d.
150—*Weston*, Gregory T. Osborne, d.
 90—*Westport*, John W. Hurlbutt, d.
186—*Wilton*, James T. Hubbell, d.

WINDHAM COUNTY.

 33—*Brooklyn*, Henry M. Cleveland, r.
 19—*Ashford*, Charles L. Dean, r.
131—   Danforth O. Lombard, r.
240—*Canterbury*, Marvin H. Sanger, d.
 92—   Francis S. Bennett, d.
 73—*Chaplin*, Erastus M. Loomis, r.
236—*Eastford*, Simeon A. Wheaton, d.
227—*Hampton*, Daniel M. Deming, r.
111—*Killingly*, Asahel J. Wright, r.
161—   James N. Tucker, r.
195—*Plainfield*, Henry F. Newton, r.
173—   Havilah M. Prior, r.
178—*Pomfret*, Frederick Hyde, d.
122—   Thomas O. Elliott, r.

61—*Putnam*, Lucius H. Fuller, r.
101— Thomas J. Thurber, r.
221—*Scotland*, M. Luther Barstow, r.
107—*Sterling*, Silas A. Waite, r.
125—*Thompson*, Edwin T. White, r.
65— William H. Arnold, r.
SPEAKER—*Windham*, JOHN M. HALL, r.
48— Samuel Bingham, r.
55— *Woodstock*, Henry M. Bradford, r.
185— Zenas Marcy, r.

LITCHFIELD COUNTY.

158—*Litchfield*, Willis J. Beach, d.
192— Garner B. Curtiss, d.
246—*Barkhamsted*, Hubert B. Case, d.
82— William H. Ward, r.
152—*Bethlehem*, Nehemiah L. Bloss, d.
142—*Bridgewater*, Peter Wooster, d.
190—*Canaan*, Samuel W. Bradley, d.
36—*Colebrook*, Andrew J. Terrell, d.
38— Solomon Sackett, r.
40—*Cornwall*, Charles H. Harrison, d.
132— Luman C. Wickwire, d.
50—*Goshen*, Hubert Scovill, r.
17— Franklin E. Wadhams, r.
170—*Harwinton*, Chester A. Hayes, r.
109— Horace W. Barber, r.
14—*Kent*, Charles Lee, d.
220—*Morris*, William Griswold, d.
168—*New Hartford*, Thaddeus L. Root, r.
148— Anson J. Allen, d.
74—*New Milford*, Frederick S. Richmond, d.
134— Amos H. Bowers, d.
160—*North Canaan*, Henry G. Williams, d.

215—*Norfolk*, Plumb Brown, r.

121—   Alva S. Cowles, r.

 57—*Plymouth*, Enos Blakeslee, r.

 58—*Roxbury*, Myron W. Odell, d.

112—*Salisbury*, John H. Hurlburt, d.

222—   Lewis P. Ashman, d.

104—*Sharon*, Edgar J. Reed, d.

242—   William Dakin, d.

113—*Thomaston*, Joseph K. Judson, r.

 75—*Torrington*, Frederick Devoe, r.

 89—   George A. Allen, r.

 67—*Warren*, Clark S. Swift, r.

196—*Washington*, Erastus J. Hurlbut, r.

 91—   Gould C. Whitlesey, r.

237—*Watertown*, Augustus N. Woolson, r.

 84—*Winchester*, Joseph H. Norton, r.

218—   John D. Yale, d.

243—*Woodbury*, William J. Clark, r.

137—   William Cothren, r.

MIDDLESEX COUNTY.

 60—*Middletown*, D. Ward Noithrop, d.

 74—   James Lawton, d.

164—*Haddam*, Henry H. Brainerd, r.

102—   Orrin Shailer, d.

127—*Chatham*, Delos D. Brown, r.

149—   Nathaniel C. Johnson, r.

 63—*Chester*, A. Hamilton Gilbert, r.

  3—*Clinton*, George A. Olcott, r.

119—*Cromwell*, Henry W. Stocking, r.

225—*Durham*, Talcott P. Strong, r.

  7—   Julius Davis, d.

 29—*East Haddam*, Richard H. Gladwin, r.

 85—   Joseph W. Hungerford, r.

56—*Essex*, William F. McCrery, d.

16—*Killingworth*, Augustus W. Stevens, d.

156—   Sidney T. Davis, d.

177—*Middlefield*, Alva B. Coe, r.

99—*Old Saybrook*, Ozias H. Kirtland, r.

224—*Portland*, John M. Penfield, d.

193—*Saybrook*, John Child, r.

206—   Ezra J. B. Southworth, r.

37—*Westbrook*, John A. Post, r.

TOLLAND COUNTY.

76—*Tolland*, Henry E. Steele, d.

184—   Charles Young, d.

80—*Andover*, Erastus D. Post, r.

233—*Bolton*, Joseph C. Alvord, r.

71—*Columbia*, Samuel B. West, r.

6—*Coventry*, William F. Sweet, d.

140—   Edgar Bass, d.

151—*Ellington*, J. Abbott Thompson, r.

103—*Hebron*, Alfred W. Hutchinson, r.

203—   Joel Jones, r.

231—*Mansfield*, George W. Merrow, r.

41—   Olon S. Chaffee, r.

133—*Somers*, Lorenzo Wood, r.

93—   Randolph Fuller, r.

86—*Stafford*, M. R. Griswold, d.

115—   William A. King, r.

172—*Union*, Hartley Walker, d.

126—   Thomas J. Youngs, d.

45—*Vernon*, Alvah N. Belding, r.

209—   Louis Phillipp, r.

157—*Willington*, William D. Irons, r.

229—   Matthew Burdick, r.

POLITICAL RECAPITULATION.

JANUARY SESSION, 1882.

SENATE,	Rep.	Dem.	Gr.	Ind.
	17	7		

HOUSE OF REPRESENTATIVES.

COUNTIES.

	Rep.	Dem.	Gr.	Ind.
Hartford,	28	17		
New Haven,	19	14		
New London,	17	12		
Fairfield,	15	17		
Windham,	20	4		
Litchfield,	20	21		
Middlesex,	14	8		
Tolland,	15	7		
	165	107	1	

Republican majority, 1882—Senate, 10; House, 48; Joint Ballot, 58.

OFFICERS AND ATTACHES OF THE HOUSE OF REPRESENTATIVES.

CHAPLAINS.

Rev. A. J. Sage, D.D., Hartford.
Rev. George L. Thompson, Hartford.

CLERKS.

Charles P. Woodbury, Easton.
Donald G. Perkins, Norwich.

TELLERS.

First Division, Tomlinson, of Milford.
Second Division, Northrop, of Middletown.

Third Division, Stanton, of Stonington.
Fourth Division, Cooley, of Hartford.

MESSENGERS.

John L. Wilson, Suffield.
Eugene Morehouse, Stratford.
Thomas J. Peck, Ashford.
Russell P. Foster, West Cornwall.

DOORKEEPERS.

James E. Smith, North Haven.
A. E. S. Bush, East Lyme.
Lloyd A. Wood, Haddam.
John A. Alvord, Bolton.
Edwin Killam, Enfield.

MESSENGER OF COMMITTEE ROOMS.

Stephen Sage, Winchester.

MESSENGER OF COAT ROOMS.

Nathan H. Newberry, Groton.
Edwin M. Thorne, Windham.

REPORTERS.

George D. Curtis, Hartford Courant.
E. Tracey Greaves, Hartford Times.
Ira E. Forbes, Hartford Post.
Alexander Troup, New Haven Union.
William Rodman, New Haven Register.
William F. Graham, Meriden Republican.

18

COMMITTEES.

JOINT STANDING COMMITTEES.

On the Judiciary.

       Supreme Court Room.

 Senator Bradstreet, *r*, 20th District.

 Messrs. Johnson of Enfield, *r*.
     Cothren of Woodbury, *r*.
     Sill of Hartford, *d*.
     Ripley of Norwich, *r*.
     Scofield of Stamford, *r*.
     Northrop of Middletown, *d*.
     Robertson of New Haven, *d*.
     King of Stafford, *r*.

On School Fund.

       School Fund Office.

 Senator Strickland, *d*, 3d District.

 Messrs. Wood of East Windsor, *r*.
     Jarvis of Cheshire, *d*.
     Reynolds of Lyme, *r*.
     Taylor of Danbury, *d*.
     Loomis of Chaplin, *r*.
     Reed of Sharon, *d*.
     Davis of Durham, *d*.
     Phillip of Vernon, *r*.

On Banks.

Room 35, Second Floor.

Senator Hammond, *r*, 16th District.

Messrs. Stanton of Stonington, *r*.

Treadway of Bristol, *r*.

Bradley of Orange, *d*.

St. John of New Canaan, *r*.

Deming of Hampton, *r*.

Norton of Winchester, *r*.

Lawton of Middletown, *d*.

Steele of Tolland, *d*.

On State Prison.

Room 45, 3d Floor.

Senator Upson, *r*, 4th District.

Messrs. Paige of Sherman, *r*.

Griswold of Wethersfield, *r*.

Bartlett of Oxford, *r*.

Mahan of New London, *d*.

Elliott of Pomfret, *r*.

Hurlbut of Washington, *r*.

Penfield of Portland, *d*.

Chaffee of Mansfield, *r*.

On New Towns and Probate Districts.

Room 55, Third Floor.

Senator White, *r*, 10th District.

Messrs. Chapman of Waterford, *d*.

Harger of Granby, *r*.

Tomlinson of Milford, *d*.

Foster of Redding, *d*.

Newton of Plainfield, *r*.

Messrs. Sackett of Colebrook, *r.*

Gladwin of East Haddam, *r.*

Fuller of Somers, *r.*

On Roads and Bridges.

Room 48, 3d Floor.

Senator Mills, *d,* 8th District.

Messrs. Post of Andover, *r.*

Galpin of Berlin, *r.*

Hill of Madison, *r.*

Chapman of North Stonington, *r.*

Glover of Newtown, *d.* •

Wheaton of Eastford, *d.*

Williams of North Canaan, *d.*

Hungerford of East Haddam, *r.*

On Incorporations.

Room 14, First Floor.

Senator Coit, *r,* 9th District.

Messrs. Cleveland of Brooklyn, *r.*

• Cowles of Manchester, *d.*

Fox of New Haven, *d.*

Lathrop of Griswold, *r.*

Gillespie of Stamford, *r.*

Yale of Winchester, *d.*

Gilbert of Chester, *r.*

Belding of Vernon, *r.*

On Claims.

Comptroller's Office, Room 6.

Senator Dennis, *r,* 24th District.

Messrs. Cowles of Norwalk, *r.*

Messrs. Clark of Suffield, *r*.
Austin of North Haven, *r*.
Barnes of Preston, *d*.
Hyde of Pomfret, *d*.
Allen of New Hartford, *d*.
Child of Saybrook, *r*.
Merrow of Mansfield, *r*.

On Education.
Room 42, 3d Floor.
Senator Cook, *r*, 18th District.
Messrs. Robbins of Wethersfield, *r*.
Mitchell of Southbury, *r*.
Palmer of Stonington, *d*.
Couch of Ridgefield, *r*.
Wright of Killingly, *r*.
Hurlburt of Salisbury, *d*.
Stevens of Killingworth, *d*.
Jones of Hebron, *r*.

On Sale of Lands.
Room 24, 2d Floor.
Senator Richardson, *d*, 19th District.
Messrs. Sanford of Redding, *d*.
Gates of Hartland, *r*.
Ives of Wallingford, *d*.
Loomis of Lebanon, *r*.
Barstow of Scotland, *r*.
Hayes of Harwinton, *r*.
Johnson of Chatham, *r*.
Walker of Union, *d*.

On Finance.
                                        Treasurer's Office.
    Senator Hoyt, *r*, 12th District.
    Messrs. Bingham of Windham, *r.*
         Pease of Enfield, *r.*
         Griggs of Waterbury, *r.*
         Parish of Montville, *r.*
         Wren of Bridgeport, *d.*
         Odell of Roxbury, *d.*
         McCrery of Essex, *d.*
         Thompson of Ellington, *r.*

On Railroads.
                                        Room 41, 3d Floor.
    Senator Baker, *r*, 13th District.
    Messrs. Gillette of Waterbury, *r.*
         Cooley of Hartford, *r.*
         Williams of Lebanon, *r.*
         Wilson of Greenwich, *d.*
         Lombard of Ashford, *r.*
         Richmond of New Milford, *d.*
         Southworth of Saybrook, *r.*
         Young of Tolland, *d.*

On Military Affairs.
                                        Room 15, 1st Floor.
    Senator Cheney, *r*, 2d District.
    Messrs. Pine of Derby, *r.*
         Phelps of Windsor, *r.*
         Parker of Voluntown, *r.*
         Deming of Danbury, *d.*
         Waite of Sterling, *r.*

Messrs. Devoe of Torrington, *r*.
Strong of Durham, *r*.
Youngs of Union, *d*.

On Agriculture.
Room 50, 3d Floor.

Senator Alsop, *d*, 22d District.
Messrs. Cowles of Farmington, *r*.
Curtiss of North Branford, *r*.
Bill of Lyme, *d*.
Nichols of Trumbull, *d*.
Bradford of Woodstock, *r*.
Bradley of Canaan, *d*.
Brainerd of Haddam, *r*. ·
Wood of Somers, *r*.

On Humane Institutions.
Room 37, 3d Floor.

Senator Sturtevant, *r*, 11th District.
Messrs. Wilson of Meriden, *r*.
Towne of Plainville, *r*.
Downer of New London, *d*.
Abernethy of Bridgeport, *d*.
Dean of Ashford, *r*.
Beach of Litchfield, *d*.
Coe of Middlefield, *r*.
West of Columbia, *r*.

On Cities and Boroughs.
Room 60, 3d Floor.

Senator Hills, *r*, 1st District.
Messrs. Condon of Norwich, *r*.
Coogan of Windsor Locks, *d*.

Messrs. Tyler of Prospect, *r.*
Bell of Norwalk, *r.*
Tucker of Killingly, *r.*
Bowers of New Milford, *d.*
Olcott of Clinton, *r.*
Sweet of Coventry, *d.*

On Fisheries.

Room 25, 2d Floor.

Senator Spencer, *r*, 21st District.
Messrs. Fuller of Putnam, *r.*
Woodward of East Windsor, *d.*
Griswold of Guilford, *r.*
Luce of East Lyme, *r.*
Mead of Greenwich, *d.*
Harrison of Cornwall, *d.*
Kirtland of Old Saybrook, *r.*
Alvord of Bolton, *r.*

On Insurance.

Room 16, 1st Floor.

Senator Boss, *r*, 17th District.
Messrs. Bishop of Guilford, *r.*
Lord of Windsor, *r.*
Johnson of Franklin, *r.*
Curtiss of Monroe, *r.*
Sanger of Canterbury, *d.*
Brown of Norfolk, *r.*
Stocking of Cromwell, *r.*
Bass of Coventry, *d.*

On Manufactures.

Room 76, 4th Floor.

Senator Jones, *r*, 6th District.

Messrs. Lyman of Meriden, *r*.

Smith of Southington, *r*.

Carrier of Colchester, *d*.

Brinsmade of Huntington, *r*.

Prier of Plainfield, *r*.

Ashman of Salisbury, *d*.

Shailer of Haddam, *d*.

Merrow of Mansfield, *r*.

On Engrossed Bills.

Secretary's Office, Room 40.

Senator Seymour, *d*, 14th district.

Messrs. Northrop of Middletown, *d*.

Downes of Derby, *r*.

Congdon of Norwich, *r*.

JOINT SELECT COMMITTEES.

On Temperance.

Room 46, 3d Floor.

Senator Hammond, *r*, 16th District.

Messrs. Downes of Derby, *r*.

Roberts of East Hartford, *d*.

Allyn of Salem, *r*.

Sanford of Redding, *d*.

Thurber of Putnam, *r*.

Wadhams of Goshen, *r*.

Post of Westbrook, *r*.

Griswold of Stafford, *d*.

On Federal Relations.

Room 14, 1st Floor.

Senator Elton, *r*, 5th District.

Messrs. Kirtland of Old Saybrook, *r*.

Talcott of Glastonbury, *r*.

Stow of Milford, *d*.

Read of Lisbon, *d*.

Pike of Fairfield, *d*.

Marcy of Woodstock, *r*.

Wickwire of Cornwall, *d*.

King of Stafford, *r*.

On Forfeited Rights.

Room 75, 4th Floor.

Senator Gilbert, *r*, 23d District.

Messrs. Owen of Manchester, *r*.

Wright of Branford, *d*.

Leffingwell of Bozrah, *r*.

Wheeler of Easton, *r*.

White of Thompson, *r*.

Bloss of Bethlehem, *d*.

Lawton of Middletown, *d*.

Jones of Hebron, *r*.

On Capitol Furniture and Grounds.

Comptroller's Office.

Senator Northrop, *d*, 15th District.

Messrs. Arnold of Thompson, *r*.

Manross of Bristol, *r*.

Walker of Woodbridge, *r*.

Avery of Groton, *d*.

Sherwood of Fairfield, *d*.

Messrs. Judson of Thomaston, *r.*
Case of Granby, *r.*
Hutchinson of Hebron, *r.*

On Revision of Joint Rules.

Room 25, 2d Floor.

Senator Gunn, *d,* 7th District.
Messrs. Beatty of New Britain, *d.*
Thompson of East Haven, *d.*
Gove of Groton, *r. .*
Thornhill of Brookfield, *d.*
Newton of Plainfield, *r.*
Swift of Warren, *r.*
McCrery of Essex, *d.*
Belding of Vernon, *r.*

On New Counties and County Seats.

Room 72, 4th Floor.

Senator Cheney, *r,* 2d District.
Messrs. Scofield of Stamford, *r.*
Olmsted of East Hartford, *r.*
Fox of New Haven, *d.*
Bishop of Guilford, *r.*
Billings of Ledyard, *r.*
Wilson of Greenwich, *d.*
Brown of Chatham, *r.*
Sweet of Coventry, *d.*

On Canvass of Votes.

Senator
Messrs. Barber of Harwinton, *r.*
Kinne of Glastonbury, *r.*
Culver of Beacon Falls, *r.*

Messrs. Hurlbutt of Westport, *d.*
Allen of Torrington, *r.*
Pratt of Southington, *r.*
McCarty of Sprague, *gr.*
English of Colchester, *d.*

Unfinished Business.

Senator Seymour, *d*, 14th District.
Messrs. Brown of Darien, *r.*
Curtiss of Litchfield, *d.*

On Manual and Roll.

Secretary's Office, Room 36.
Senator Mills, *d*, 8th District.
Messrs. Brown of Chatham, *r.*
Rogers of Seymour, *r.*
Reed of Simsbury, *d.*

On State Library.

Senator Coit, *r*, 9th District.
Messrs. Cothren of Woodbury, *r.*
Gillette of Waterbury, *r.*
Sill of Hartford, *d.*
Bingham of Windham, *r.*

House Committee on Constitutional Amendments.

Room 27, 2d Floor.
Messrs. Ripley of Norwich, *r.*
Clark of Hartland, *r.*
Bailey of Wolcott, *r.*
Wilson of Newtown, *r.*
Bennett of Canterbury, *d.*

Messrs. Blakeslee of Plymouth, *r.*
Davis of Killingworth, *d.*
Burdick of Willington, *r.*

House Committee on Contingent Expenses.

Messrs. Root of West Hartford, *r.*
Mead of Greenwich, *d.*
Wright of Killingly, *r.*

Senate Committee on Contingent Expenses.

Secretary's Office.

Senators Boss, *r,* 17th District.
Gunn, *d,* 7th District.

House Committee on Assignment of Seats.

Messrs. Stanton of Stonington, *r.*
Robertson of New Haven, *d.*
Fuller of Putnam, *r.*

Senate Committee on Contested Elections.

Senators Bradstreet, *r,* 20th District.
Seymour, *d,* 14th District.
Hoyt, *r,* 12th District.

House Committee on Contested Elections.

Room 33, 2d Floor.

Messrs. Owen of Manchester, *r.*
Dean of Ashford, *r.*
Wright of Branford, *d.*

THE EXECUTIVE DEPARTMENT.

EXECUTIVE OFFICE.

Governor.—HOBART B. BIGELOW, New Haven.
Executive Secretary.—Morris F. Tyler, New Haven.
Executive Clerk.—Frank D. Rood, Hartford.

GOVERNOR'S STAFF.

Adjutant-General—Brigadier-General George M. Harmon, New Haven.

Quartermaster-General—Brigadier-General Alexander Harbison, Hartford.

Surgeon-General—Brigadier-General James G. Gregory, Norwalk.

Commissary-General—Brigadier-General George H. Ford, New Haven.

Paymaster-General—Brigadier-General Frederick E. Camp, Middletown.

Aids-de-Camp—William E. Barrows, Hartford; William B. Rudd, Salisbury; Charles A. Russell, Killingly; Frank L. Bigelow, New Haven.

THE TREASURY.

Treasurer—*JAMES D. SMITH, Stamford.
Chief Clerk—George Williams, Hartford.
Assistant Clerk—E. B. L. Carter.

*Appointed by the Governor, January 1882, to fill vacancy, vice David P. Nichols, deceased.

SECRETARY'S OFFICE.

Secretary—CHARLES E. SEARLS, Thompson.
Chief Clerk—R. S. Hinman, Oxford.
Assistant Clerk—Horace Heath, Hartford.

COMPTROLLER OF PUBLIC ACCOUNTS.

Comptroller—WHEELOCK T. BATCHELLER, Winch'ter.
Chief Clerk—Emerson W. Moore, Talcottville.
Assistant Clerk—Louis B. Hubbard, Hartford.
State House Supt.—William Dibble, Hartford.
Asst. Supt.—Henry A. Cooley, Hartford.

STATE LIBRARY.

Committee—The Governor, the Secretary, and Hon.
Dwight W. Pardee, Hartford.
Librarian—CHARLES J. HOADLY.

SCHOOL FUND OFFICE.

School Fund Commissioner—JEREMIAH OLNEY, Thompson.
Chief Clerk—Carnot O. Spencer, Hartford.
Assistant—William H. Pond, Hartford.

AUDITORS OF PUBLIC ACCOUNTS.

R. W. Farmer, Hartford.
Thomas I. Raymond, Norwalk.

GOVERNORS OF CONNECTICUT.

		Length of term of office.
John Haynes,	1639-1640	1 year.
Edward Hopkins,	1640-1641	1 "
John Haynes,	1641-1642	1 "
George Wyllys,	1642-1643	1
John Haynes,	1643 1644	1
Edward Hopkins,	1644-1645	1
John Haynes,	1645-1646	1 ..
Edward Hopkins,	1646-1647	1 "
John Haynes,	1847-1648	1
Edward Hopkins,	1648-1649	1
John Haynes,	1649-1650	1
Edward Hopkins,	1650-1651	1
John Haynes,	1651-1652	1
Edward Hopkins,	1652-1653	1
John Haynes,	1653-1654	1
Edward Hopkins,	1654-1655	1
Thomas Wells,	1655-1656	1
John Webster,	1656-1657	1
John Winthrop,	1657-1658	1
Thomas Wells,	1658-1659	1 "
John Winthrop,	1659-1665	6 years.
John Winthrop,	1665-1676	11 "
William Leet,	1676-1680	, 4 "
Robert Treat,	1680-1687	7
Sir Edmund Andross,*	1687-1689	2
Robert Treat,	1689-1696	7
Fitz-John Winthrop,	1696-1707	11 ..
Gurdon Saltonstall,	1707-1724	17
Joseph Talcott,	1724-1741	17
Jonathan Law,	1741-1751	10
Roger Wolcott,	1751-1754	3
Thomas Fitch,	1754-1766	12 "

* Sir Edmund Andross was appointed by James II, Governor of *New England*. It was to him that the Charter was to be surrendered. All other Governors were elected.

		Length of term of office.
William Pitkin,	1766-1769	3 years.
Jonathan Trumbull,	1769-1784	15 "
Matthew Griswold,	1784-1785	1 year.
Samuel Huntington,	1785-1796	11 years.
Oliver Wolcott,	1706-1798	2 "
Jonathan Trumbull,	1798-1809	11 "
John Treadwell,	1809-1811	2
Roger Griswold,	1811-1813	2
John Cotton Smith,	1813-1817	4
Oliver Wolcott,	1817-1827	10
Gideon Tomlinson,	1827-1831	4
John S. Peters,	1831-1833	2 "
Henry W. Edwards,	1833-1834	1 year.
Samuel S. Foote,	1834-1835	1 "
Henry W. Edwards,	1835-1838	3 years.
William W. Ellsworth,	1838-1842	4 "
Chauncey F. Cleaveland,	1842-1844	2 "
Roger S. Baldwin,	1844-1846	2 "
Isaac Toucey,	1846-1847	1 year.
Clark Bissell,	1847-1849	2 years.
Joseph Trumbull,	1849-1850	1 year.
Thomas H. Seymour,	1850-June, 1853	3 yrs. 1 m.
Charles H. Pond,* June,	1853-1854	11 mos.
Henry Dutton,	1854-1855	1 year.
William T. Minor,	1855 1857	2 years.
Alexander H. Holley,	1857-1858	1 year.
William A. Buckingham,	1858-1866	9 years.
Joseph R. Hawley,	1866 1867	1 year.
James E. English,	1867-1869	2 years.
Marshall Jewell,	1869-1870	1 year.
James E. English,	1870-1871	1 "
Marshall Jewell,	1871-1873	2 years.
Charles R. Ingersoll,	1873-Jan., 1877	3 yrs. 9 m.
Richard D Hubbard,	1877-1879	2 years.
Charles B. Andrews,	1879-1881	2 "
Hobart B. Bigelow,	1881	

* Governor Pond was elected Lieutenant-Governor in April, 1853. and became Governor by the resignation of Governor Seymour in June, 1853, when he was appointed Minister to Russia.